# Shadow of the Racketeer

# Shadow of the Racketeer

## Scandal in Organized Labor

**DAVID WITWER**

UNIVERSITY OF ILLINOIS PRESS

Urbana and Chicago

Portions of this book appeared in a different form as "The Case of the
Two Percent Assessment and the Question of Union Susceptibility,"
*Trends in Organized Crime* 9, no. 4 (2006): 102–26; as "Westbrook
Pegler and the Anti-Union Movement," *Journal of American History*
92, no. 2 (2005): 527–52 (copyright © Organization of American
Historians http://www.oah.org. Reprinted with permission); portions
of chapter 5 appeared in a different form as "The Scandal of George
Scalise: A Case Study in the Rise of Labor Racketeering in the 1930s,"
*Journal of Social History* 36, no. 4 (2003): 917–40; and portions of the
conclusion appeared in a different form as "The Racketeer Menace
and Anti-unionism in the Mid-Twentieth-Century U.S.," *International
Labor and Working-Class History* 74 (Fall 2008).

Library of Congress Cataloging-in-Publication Data
Witwer, David Scott.
Shadow of the racketeer : scandal in organized labor / David Witwer.
p.   cm. — (The working class in American history)
Includes bibliographical references and index.
ISBN 978-0-252-03417-6 (cloth : alk. paper)
ISBN 978-0-252-07666-4 (pbk. : alk. paper)
1. Labor unions—Corrupt practices—United States. 2. Organized
crime—United States. 3. Labor movement—United States—History.
4. Labor leaders—United States—History. 5. Racketeering—United
States. 6. Pegler, J. Westbrook (James Westbrook), 1894–1969.
7. Journalists—United States—Biography.
I. Title.
HD6490.C642U589      2009
364.1'067—dc22      2008035616

# Contents

Acknowledgments    vi

Introduction: "Peglerized"    1

1. The Columnist: A Crusading Journalist    15

2. The Outfit: Organized Crime and Labor Racketeering    37

3. Browne, Bioff, and Scalise: The Dynamics of Union
   Corruption    59

4. The Hollywood Case: Racketeering in the 1930s from
   a Business Perspective    83

5. Union Members and Corruption: Exploitation and
   Disillusionment    103

6. Union Members and Corruption: The Potential for Reform    119

7. The Newsmen: "Molders of Public Opinion"    147

8. The Scandal's Political Impact: Pegler and Antiunionism    175

9. "Labor Must Clean House": The Challenge of Responding
   to Pegler    205

Conclusion: Opportunities Lost and Opportunities Taken    233

Notes    255

Index    319

# Acknowledgments

While writing this book, I received assistance from a range of sources and I am happy to have this opportunity to express my gratitude. Lycoming College provided financial support in the form of professional development grants and a semester's sabbatical leave. The Herbert Hoover Presidential Library gave me two research grants and a wonderful location in which to do a great deal of my research. Grants from the Bentley Historical Library at the University of Michigan and the Gilder Lehrman Institute of American History aided my research, as did a Summer Stipend from the National Endowment for the Humanities (NEH). A fellowship from the NEH allowed me to devote a year to completing the bulk of the writing and without that support this book might never have been written.

Archivists and librarians at the following locations went above and beyond the call of duty to provide materials to an obscure researcher contacting them from the wilds of north central Pennsylvania. In particular, I am grateful to the staffs of the Herbert Hoover Presidential Library, the National Archives Records Administration at College Park, the Center for Legislative Archives, the Franklin D. Roosevelt Presidential Library, the Labor Archives and Research Center at San Francisco State University, the Bentley Historical Library at the University of Michigan, the Kheel Center for Labor-Management Documentation & Archives at Cornell University, the New York City Municipal Archives, and the Screen Actors Guild Historian, Valerie Yaros. Boris Kostelanetz generously made his news clipping file from the Hollywood racketeering trial available to me and shared his personal memories of that time period as well. At Lycoming College, Janet Hurlbert, Sue Beidler, and especially Marlene Neece worked to facilitate all of my many research requests, supplying the kind of constant, dependable support over the years, which means everything for a project like this one.

A number of colleagues and friends provided emotional support and guidance over the years. I consider myself especially fortunate to have landed at Lycoming College right out of graduate school. The college administration, especially the Dean, John Piper, supported and encouraged my efforts unstintingly. My colleagues in the History Department are also my valued friends and I have looked to them over the years as professional models, especially Bob Larson and Dick Morris, who mentored me in the classroom and out. Other friends and colleagues at Lycoming College spent time either listening to too many Westbrook Pegler anecdotes or desperately finding ways to temporarily distract me from my monomania; I want in particular to mention: Phil Sprunger, Liz Yoder, Susan Ross, Rob Ross, Sandy Kingery, Bob Zurowski, Charles and Melissa Mahler. Kristin Conklin generously provided shelter and hospitality during my many research stays in New York and Lucy Barber provided similar assistance in Washington, D.C.

Over the years as this book came together, I benefited from the feedback of those who read drafts of the work-in-progress, responded to conference papers, or offered incisive comments on articles drawn from the larger manuscript. In particular, Gareth Davies, Joseph McCartin, Robert Zieger, Andrew Kersten, Dick Morris, William Leuchtenberg, David Nasaw, David Nord, Richard Pious, William Puette, Stephen Tuck, Joseph McCartin, Joanne Meyerowitz, and Elizabeth Fones-Wolf gave me the benefit of their wisdom and their encouragement. Nelson Lichtenstein read complete drafts of the entire manuscript twice and provided both much needed praise and constructive criticism. I also want to thank the anonymous reader at the University of Illinois Press who read the entire work and offered many useful comments. At the University of Illinois Press, Jennifer S. Clark oversaw the copyediting with a combination of professionalism and patience that I greatly appreciate. Laurie Matheson shepherded the project through the entire process, from proposal to the final edition and I am most grateful for her support.

I have saved the most important acknowledgments for last. Catherine Rios has always been there for me, with love and encouragement. Our daughter Mira provided great joy and a measure of much needed perspective. Finally, I am dedicating this book to two friends who have been my mentors over the years. They set a standard with their scholarship that I have aspired to emulate and they have been tireless supporters of my career. I think that because they chose to believe in me, I have been able to do many things that would not otherwise have been possible. Frankly, they are the kind of friends you can always count on. To Jim Patterson and Mel Dubofsky, I want to say thank you with all my heart.

**Before The Bar**

This cartoon appeared in the *Washington Post* on April 23, 1940, the day after George Scalise was arrested on extortion charges. The looming figure in the background labeled "A.F. of L." is William Green, president of the American Federation of Labor (AFL). The cartoon implies that Green and the AFL are on trial for complicity in Scalise's corruption, echoing a claim made by Westbrook Pegler. © 1940, *The Washington Post*. Reprinted with permission.

# Introduction
## *"Peglerized"*

Detectives from the New York district attorney's office came to George Scalise's expensive room at the Commodore Hotel at three o'clock in the morning on April 21, 1940, to arrest him for extortion. Scalise, the president of the Building Service Employees' International Union (BSEIU), answered the door wearing white silk pajamas. He was alone, the papers reported, except for two pieces of alligator-skin luggage that he planned to take with him the next day on a train trip to Chicago. At the arraignment later that morning, his attorney asked the judge to set a low bail in consideration of the fact that his client was a union official holding a responsible position and a respectable family man with ties to the community. Scalise listened in silence as the prosecutor mocked these claims, charging that he had used his union for extortion "as a burglar uses a jimmy." Scalise had victimized not only businessmen, the prosecutor charged, but also the members of his union, many of whom were poor scrubwomen. Having heard both sides, the judge set a high bail, and Scalise was taken to the courthouse jail, the Tombs, while his attorney tried to raise the bail money. As he was pulled from the courtroom, Scalise told the reporters present, "I have been Peglerized."[1]

He coined the expression to describe his dramatic reversal of fortune and also to identify the man he blamed for it. Three months earlier, Scalise had enjoyed success, power, and relative obscurity. He led a union that had grown significantly over the course of the 1930s, but that still remained comparatively small, with 70,000 members. Outside the union movement, few people would have recognized his name.[2] Then in January 1940, the newspaper columnist Westbrook Pegler exposed Scalise's criminal past, revealing that twenty-three years earlier the union leader had been convicted of violating the Mann Act; in everyday language, he had been charged with white slavery, compelling a woman to engage in prostitution and transporting her across state lines for that purpose. Pegler also alleged that Scalise had ties to organized crime and that these ties explained how he had risen so quickly to the office of union president only three years after having joined the organization.[3] Over the next three months, Pegler's columns maintained a steady drumbeat of revelations and denunciations on the subject of Scalise. A story on the criminal records of his associates was followed a week or so later by one on his luxurious lifestyle. Other columns asserted that the rank and file members of the union had no real control over the organization's officers and the members had never even voted for Scalise in a proper union election.[4] Pegler made Scalise into a notorious public figure, a symbol of the problem of union corruption.

Scalise's arrest on extortion charges appeared to be the culmination of this campaign, and Scalise blamed his fate both on District Attorney Thomas Dewey's desire for publicity and Pegler's "contemptible personal assaults."[5] Although it phrased the point differently, the *Washington Post* agreed. "The person who deserves chief credit for making Mr. Scalise a national figure is Westbrook Pegler," a *Post* editorial said.[6]

Scalise's story unfolded alongside that of another union official targeted by Pegler. In November 1939, two months before his exposé on Scalise, Pegler produced similar revelations regarding William Bioff, the West Coast representative of the International Alliance of Theatrical Stage Employes (IATSE). Pegler had uncovered the fact that Bioff had been convicted back in 1922 on a pandering charge in Chicago for managing a brothel. Although Bioff had been sentenced to serve a six-month jail sentence, Pegler discovered that he had served only seven days, and then, after getting out on bail, had never completed the rest of his term. As with Scalise, Pegler alleged that Bioff had ties to organized crime and that his powerful position in the Stage Hands Union stemmed from those ties. The columnist regularly returned to Bioff's story, pressuring law enforcement authorities in Illinois to make him finish his sentence and tracing the criminal links of his associates.[7]

Both of these exposés dramatically unmasked the long-hidden, disreputable pasts of men who had risen to positions of power and respectability in organized labor. As leaders in a movement that championed the cause of the oppressed, their crimes were especially unsavory, and Pegler highlighted the salacious details of their involvement in prostitution. Readers of Pegler's column learned, for instance, that on the day of Bioff's arrest in 1922, he had received $29 from a prostitute known as Rose, who had taken thirteen men up to the brothel's second-floor rooms that day. The column explained that typically Bioff "would obtain $2 or $3 from each woman after each visit to a room with a man." The exposé on Scalise was similar. The judge at Scalise's trial, Pegler wrote, had referred to the details of his crime as "nauseating." The woman involved had been "beaten, seduced and persuaded to live with your distinguished colleague in the labor movement [Scalise] on false promises of marriage." Both men were, Pegler asserted, nothing more than pimps. "They got their training for the post of bargaining agent [in unions] by serving as such for prostitutes," he wrote.[8]

Bioff and Scalise responded in similar ways. The two men denounced the columnist for dredging up misdeeds from their distant pasts, when they had been young and admittedly made mistakes. Both claimed to have led law-abiding lives in the intervening years, becoming involved in organized labor and devoting their careers to bettering the lives of working people. The current revelations, they asserted, were an attempt to sabotage their efforts, inspired—possibly paid for—by employers who resented the success of their labors on behalf of their membership.[9] "I would call my plight persecution," Bioff told reporters. "Maybe I have been doing too much for the working man. I think the big interests are after me." He asked rhetorically, "Who would be interested in going back all these years to dig up a skeleton and make an issue of it?"[10]

They received support from others within the labor movement. In the wake of the initial exposés, both men offered to resign from their official positions, and in both cases their fellow union officers rejected these resignations. The executive board of the Building Service Employees Union announced a vote of confidence in Scalise.[11] In Hollywood, where Bioff chaired the Conference of Studio Unions, his fellow union officers voted to keep him on as chairman even as he was being extradited to Illinois to complete his long-forgotten prison sentence. They claimed that, if necessary, Bioff could conduct negotiations with employers "by long distance telephone."[12] William Green, president of the American Federation of Labor, refused to condemn either man. In fact, Pegler revealed that Green had earlier supported a petition by Scalise to win a presidential pardon. The AFL president told reporters, "I don't think a man should be hounded to the end of his life for a crime committed as a youth and for which he has paid the penalty."[13]

In contrast, Pegler argued that the two men's stories revealed the existence of widespread corruption within organized labor, a subject of keen interest for him. Indeed the columnist had been motivated to publicize the stories of

Bioff and Scalise in an effort to draw attention to the issue of labor racketeering. He depicted both cases as indicative of a larger pattern of racketeering, marked by dictatorial union officials and the growing influence of gangsters within organized labor. These two men were, he claimed, merely the tip of the iceberg. "I have recently named two racketeers in control of two big A.F. of L. international unions, but I could name a hundred thieves and gangsters, embezzlers and terrorists who hold office in unions of the American Federation of Labor."[14]

For Pegler, labor racketeering stemmed from the growing size and power of unions, a development fostered, in turn, by the New Deal. The National Labor Relations Act of 1935, better known as the Wagner Act, had granted unions formal legal protections. Workers now had a right to organize, and employers were obligated both to recognize unions as legitimate bargaining agents and to negotiate with them. Though it had not taken the lead in pushing through this legislation, the New Deal administration of President Franklin D. Roosevelt (1933–1945) had supported its passage. In a host of other ways, the New Dealers worked to encourage the growth of union organization. While others celebrated these developments, Pegler had come to agree with conservative critics, who charged that union leaders had acquired too much power and were using their organizations to exploit both employers and their own membership. In August 1939, just a few months before breaking his story on Bioff, Pegler warned, "As it is organized labor is assuming the powers of government without the responsibility of government, and with business in shackles that is a lopsided arrangement which cannot continue indefinitely." Highlighting the criminal misdeeds of individual union leaders bolstered his campaign against the dangers presented by a growing labor movement. Such stories fed, Pegler declared, a growing public reaction to "extortion, mob violence, racketeering . . . and the establishment of an irresponsible invisible government in the hands of union leaders."[15]

Pegler argued that the failure of other union leaders to denounce Bioff and Scalise indicated just how irresponsible the union movement had become. With no legal safeguards to protect union democracy, Pegler charged that the rank and file membership were largely powerless within their own organizations. The federal government, under the New Deal, had formed a political alliance with the unions' leadership, and thus law enforcement, he claimed, rarely moved against corrupt officials. "It is not only the employers who have trouble with labor leaders," he wrote in one column. "There are many union members who are members against their will, but unprotected from terrorism, physical and economic, because no statesman will come to their aid for fear of being called an enemy of labor." The membership's only hope rested on the willingness of other responsible union officials, such as President Green of the AFL, to intervene.[16]

Green's refusal to move publicly against either Bioff or Scalise therefore became a recurring theme in Pegler's columns. It indicated that those union leaders who were not corrupt were complaisant, he asserted, and the result was that organized labor's power was being used to profit the likes of Bioff and Scalise and not the membership. Pegler claimed in one column, "The rottenness of the American Federation of Labor is demonstrated in one dramatic particular by the case of Willie Bioff." That case, and Scalise's, indicated the general corruption of the AFL. "If it [the AFL] were able," Pegler wrote, "it would kick out the criminals, and if it were honest it could not co-operate with them or even associate with them."[17]

The eventual downfall of both Scalise and Bioff vindicated Pegler's journalism and—for many people—his depiction of organized labor. Arrested in April 1940, Scalise was tried in September of that year on charges that he had fraudulently siphoned $60,000 out of his union's treasury. At the trial, several of his top aides pleaded guilty and testified for the prosecution, describing not only Scalise's embezzlement but also how he had used his ties to gangsters to become president of the union. A jury convicted him and the judge sentenced him to serve a ten- to twenty-year jail sentence.[18]

A year later, Bioff and the president of the Stage Hands Union, George Browne, went on trial in federal court on racketeering charges. A number of Hollywood film studio executives testified that Bioff and Browne had extorted over half a million dollars from them. Both men were convicted.[19] Bioff was sentenced to ten years in prison and Browne to eight. By 1943, they had decided to cooperate with authorities, and at another federal trial they testified about how Chicago gangsters had arranged to make Browne president of the Stage Hands Union. The money collected from the Hollywood studios, they explained, had mainly gone to Chicago organized crime figures. That trial led to the convictions of six top Chicago gangsters, the heirs to the Capone gang.[20]

These convictions did not stem directly from Pegler's initial revelations, but he nonetheless received a great deal of credit for the outcomes. Following Scalise's arrest in April 1940, the *Washington Post* editorial page highlighted the union leader's complaint that he had been "Peglerized." "That remark," the editorial asserted, "was an unwitting tribute to the success of Westbrook Pegler's efforts to focus public attention upon certain A.F. of L. labor leaders with criminal records."[21] Other commentators followed with similar praise.

The *Chicago Daily News* observed that the paper had often disagreed with Pegler. "At this time, however, we wish to pay tribute where it is due . . . To date Mr. Pegler has dangling from his belt the scalps of Willie Bioff and George Scalise, who had succeeded in muscling in on the labor movement."[22]

These exposés transformed Pegler, as the successful columnist now also became a respected authority on organized labor and honored investigative journalist. In 1941, Pegler became the first columnist ever to receive a Pulitzer Prize for reporting; the prize committee cited his "articles during the year 1940 on scandals in the ranks of organized labor."[23] In its story on the prize, the *New York Times* followed the trend of emphasizing the effects of his stories by reporting that Pegler won "in recognition of his articles on scandals in the ranks of organized labor that led to the exposure of and conviction of George Scalise."[24]

His fame as a crusading columnist made him a prominent public figure. In late December 1941, the editors of *Time* announced that "reader nominations for *Time*'s Man of the Year are now closed. Latest tabulations showed President Roosevelt in front, Comrade Stalin second and Columnist Westbrook Pegler third."[25] A year earlier, the *Saturday Evening Post* described him as "undoubtedly one of the leading individual editorial forces in the country." A survey of 500 editors of daily newspapers, conducted by the University of Wisconsin School of Journalism in 1942, ranked him the nation's "best adult columnist." In the early 1940s, his columns went out six days a week to 174 newspapers that reached an estimated 10 million subscribers.[26]

Pegler used this prominence to promote a conservative agenda, one that grew more extreme over time. His influence, his pugnacious style, and his ability to generate strong reactions from his readers all prefigured the later rise of the conservative radio shock jocks and cable news commentators. In the 1950s and 1960s, as his conservative views became more strident and his writing style increasingly shrill, he earned the tag of "the stuck whistle of journalism." He denounced the civil rights movement, embraced anti-Semitism, and ended up in the early 1960s writing for the John Birch Society—until he proved too cantankerous even for them.[27] Those who still remember Pegler today tend to view him as nothing more than an irresponsible extremist.

But in 1941, as *Time* magazine's readers made clear, Pegler's long slide into cranky irrelevance remained in the future. In the wake of his exposé on Bioff and Scalise, Pegler commanded respect and wielded great influence, a fact acknowledged by his friends and enemies alike. An article by George West in the liberal journal the *New Republic* referred to Pegler's widespread influence in 1942 by asserting sadly, "What we are up against is the Westbrook

Pegler mind." West blamed Pegler for "giving greater aid and comfort to our domestic fascists than any other one man in the United States." But in the same article, West also wrote that "in spite of the exasperation and disgust that his column often inspires when he either shows a perverse failure to see straight or hits below the belt in true guttersnipe fashion," he still considered Pegler "my favorite reactionary." He meant this as more than just faint praise. "Pegler is an artist, a man of great courage, a hater of tyranny," West explained, "and he calls the shots as he sees them."[28]

If the fate of Scalise and Bioff vindicated Pegler, it produced opposite results for organized labor, especially the American Federation of Labor. The labor movement had enjoyed unparalleled growth in the 1930s. While the successes of the Congress of Industrial Organizations (CIO) tend to receive greater attention, the AFL had in fact surged alongside its rival in the late 1930s, with the two federations matching each other in the size and scale of their membership gains. By 1940, over 7 million American workers belonged to unions—less than 3 million had belonged in 1932. About 2 million of them were in CIO-affiliated unions and over 4 million belonged to AFL organizations.[29] At the state and federal level, organized labor benefited from strong political alliances with the Democratic Party, exemplified by the Roosevelt administration's regard for union interests.[30] In the late 1930s, close to three-quarters of Americans, when polled, expressed support for labor unions.[31] Meanwhile, the Depression era marked the nadir of political fortunes for the business community. As historian Elizabeth Fones-Wolf has noted, "Business lost enormous prestige and power as it came under increasing public attack and governmental regulation." Business-sponsored antiunionism suffered accordingly.[32]

Pegler's exposés of Bioff and Scalise pulled together two separate cases of corruption, which in the press coverage became one big union corruption scandal, and as this scandal unfolded through the early 1940s, the political landscape for organized labor changed dramatically. Critics attacked the CIO for wartime strikes and the role of Communists in its affiliate organizations, but they also drew on this scandal to criticize the legitimacy of union leadership in even the most conservative of labor organizations. Green and the AFL became the target of bitter editorial comment. Numerous publications joined Pegler in depicting the Federation as racket-ridden and complaisant towards corruption.[33] At the same time, polls showed a decline in public support for organized labor in general. The pollster George Gallup warned in October 1941, "No student of social trends in the past decade can escape the conclusion that labor unions face a serious public relations problem today."[34] In early 1941, three-quarters of those polled said they agreed with Pegler that many union officials were racketeers.[35] In Congress, conservatives used this scandal and wartime strikes to justify efforts to amend the Wagner Act, and in 1941 and 1943 they scored legislative victories that marked the beginning of the turning of the tide against the New Deal. By 1944 the Republican Party had made the issue of union abuses and union power a central theme in its appeal to the electorate. Republicans gained control of both houses of Congress in 1946 by centering their campaign on the issue of union abuses.[36]

Realizing the damage that was being done, labor leaders scrambled to respond, but their efforts ended largely in frustration. The attempts by union leaders to voluntarily reform union governance in order to curtail corruption often received negative coverage, which depicted such efforts as halting or half-hearted. "The American Federation of Labor has fired the opening gun of its war on racketeers and gangsters in labor ranks, with the resounding crash of a popgun," the *Chicago Tribune* editorialized in 1940.[37] The paper dismissed AFL statements on the problem as "threadbare evasions" and "pallid precepts."[38] Labor leaders were forced to watch in frustration as the scandal eroded public support and conservatives capitalized on the opportunities they presented.

Over the course of the 1940s and 1950s, legislation, court rulings, and the administrative policies of key government agencies increasingly undercut the protections unions had won in the New Deal. Although organized labor still had a sizeable membership in these decades, unions had become vulnerable to the employer counteroffensive that followed that era.[39] Concern about union corruption provided a solid foundation for these antiunion efforts. In the sense that the labor movement too had suffered a reversal of fortune, it also could claim to have been "Peglerized."

The union corruption that Pegler exposed had grown out of connections that emerged in the 1930s between businessmen, organized crime, and unions. As employers warily reacted to a renascent union movement, organized crime was also evolving, developing a more effective organization and moving into new roles in society. The careers of Bioff and Scalise were the product of these disparate developments. Using their ties to organized crime, they brokered arrangements with employers, who sought to gain some control over the role unions would play in their workplace. This was a significant development in modern American history, one that set the U.S. apart from other countries. As one legal scholar wrote, "No other country has a history of significant organized crime infiltration of its labor movement, and no other country has an organized crime syndicate with a power base in labor unions."[40]

The intersection of powerful media interests and the conservative response to the New Deal also shaped this scandal. Although Pegler took center stage in uncovering the misdeeds of the three union officials, he received support from an important conservative publisher, Roy Howard, who had lined up alongside other prominent publishers in that era in an effort to mold public opinion and turn back the New Deal. Pegler consciously used his exposés to support a larger campaign against the Roosevelt administration and its liberal programs. This story demonstrated the potency of journalism as a political weapon, its ability to focus public attention on a particular issue and make that problem a matter of national concern.

The anti-New Deal efforts that the publisher Howard took part in were the genesis of a new generation of conservatism. According to historian David Kennedy, the late 1930s saw the emergence of "the first systematic expressions of antigovernment political philosophy [that] had deep roots in American political culture but only an inchoate existence before the New Deal." Kennedy argued this period marked a critical turning point in the history of twentieth-century conservatism. "The crystallization of this new conservative ideology, as much as the New Deal that precipitated its articulation, was among the enduring legacies of the 1930s."[41]

Pegler's campaign against union corruption was central to that process of crystallization. He argued that by giving power to the leaders of organized labor, New Deal regulations had robbed working people of basic rights and left them vulnerable to exploitation by crooked officials such as Scalise and Bioff. In this way, opposition to government expansion could be justified in the name of protecting working-class Americans. This issue offered New Deal opponents a way to avoid the appearance of opposing reform solely in the name of protecting the interests of the well-to-do.

The history of this scandal also helps to explain the long-term decline of organized labor in the United States. Labor historians have offered different explanations for this decline, including criticism of the movement for choosing cooperation and bureaucratization over more radical strategies. Others have focused on the efforts by antiunion groups to weaken the legal protections offered by the Wagner Act. The success of these efforts has been explained in different ways, with some citing the role of the judiciary, others the evolution of enforcement of the laws by the federal government. In general, scholarship assumes that the political fortunes of organized labor declined from a peak that occurred in the early years of the New Deal, a high point that was marked by the passage of the Wagner Act.[42] In all of this work, however, the role of corruption scandals and the man who promoted them has been largely overlooked.[43] This book seeks to correct that scholarship.

This was not the first union corruption scandal, nor would it be the last. Such scandals have reoccurred throughout the modern history of the United States, often punctuating periods of union growth and political power. They have made a lasting impression on public opinion regarding organized labor, with the result that while most Americans after 1935 continued to support the aims of unions, by the 1940s and 1950s they came to distrust union leaders and to be wary of union power.

Polls in the 1970s, for instance, found that 85 percent of Americans believed that "in many industries, unions are needed so the legitimate complaints and grievances of workers can be heard and action taken on them." In a similar vein, 59 percent said, "If there were no unions, most employers would quickly move to exploit their employees."[44] But most Americans also believed that union leaders were "generally immoral and unethical." Sixty-four percent agreed with the statement that "many union leaders have known ties with racketeers and organized crime." Not surprisingly given such views, a 1974 poll found that 63 percent of Americans felt unions had too much power in the country. Summing up these polling results, the social scientists William Schneider and Seymour Martin Lipset observed, "Unions are clearly seen as 'needed,' 'legitimate,' 'good forces,' protective of employees' interests, and socially progressive. But they are also seen as too powerful and their leaders as arrogant, abusive, self-serving, and corrupt." Throughout the 1970s, public support for organized labor steadily declined.[45]

This trend began in the 1940s. As one pollster explained in 1941, "The situation seems to be that there is an acknowledged respect for the rights of the laboring man . . . [but] there is a feeling that the present mechanism for gaining labor's rights and the present labor leadership involved are far from satisfactory."[46]

To put the matter simply, the image of unions as corrupt eroded public support for organized labor, even though most people still agreed with the basic goals of unions. This corrupt image made people reluctant to see unions wield the power that they needed to accomplish their larger economic goals. And it was a pattern of recurring scandals that fostered a widespread image of corruption. As William J. Puette noted in his 1992 study of the media's depiction of organized labor, "Because the average newspaper reader, who has only a peripheral awareness of unions, is not likely to distinguish the Teamsters from other national or local unions, media attention to any one union's or one local's corruption tends to tar the whole labor movement with the same brush."[47] Union corruption scandals are therefore important, if little-studied, phenomena that have played a central role in organized labor's decline.

This book profiles one of the most important union corruption scandals, but it does so from a distinct perspective. It covers the transgressions that occurred when the labor leaders Scalise, Bioff, and Browne betrayed the membership of their respective unions. But their transgressions were really only one of the ingredients in this scandal. Organized crime, political corruption, and businessmen following their own economic imperatives were all among the forces that played important roles in shaping what happened. So was the press, by the virtue of the way it reported the story. Including this broader range of forces creates a more complex history of the scandal and its impact, moving beyond a simple morality tale about the misdeeds of three union officials. This is the story of the story behind the scandal.

This broader perspective, however, should not be misunderstood as an effort to minimize the significance of what Pegler had uncovered. Corruption was real and a serious problem for the labor movement at the time. Pegler had uncovered a concerted campaign by organized crime groups to subvert elements of the labor movement. In this way, although he was a conservative, Pegler exemplified the muckraking tradition in U.S. history. He had uncovered an unsavory situation that cried out for correction. And like his muckraking forebears in the Progressive Era, Pegler demonstrated the power of the journalistic exposé. His dramatic reporting made labor racketeering a political issue and drew public attention to the plight of the workers being victimized by Bioff, Scalise, and other corrupt union leaders. This was a significant achievement, really a shining example of the impact that crusading journalism could have.

The problem was that the coverage of the scandal, and the reactions that it engendered, did little to constructively address the problem of abuses in union governance or organized crime's growing role in labor racketeering. An opportunity for reform slipped away. Pegler truly cared about the plight of union members trapped in corrupt labor organizations, but he sacrificed them in pursuit of political gains for the conservative movement. He canted the coverage of the scandal in ways that skewed the perspective it could offer to the reading public. Other news outlets followed Pegler's lead. The American public never received an accurate description of union corruption, the role of organized crime, and the underlying sources of union abuses. As a result, this union corruption scandal, like others before and since, did nothing but undercut the labor movement by tainting the public's opinion of organized labor. No constructive reforms resulted, and as the public wearied of news reports on this subject, its attention turned to other matters. The union members whom Pegler had championed were left facing the same types of problems he had exposed. By the 1950s, similar abuses in the Longshoremen's Union and the Teamsters triggered another period of scandal whose history echoed this one.[48]

This scandal thus marks a pivotal moment in twentieth-century U.S. history in a number of ways. The fortunes of a reborn labor movement were undercut, and conservatives mounted a powerful counteroffensive to the New Deal. The scandal highlighted organized crime's relatively new and significant involvement in labor racketeering, a problem that would bedevil certain unions throughout the post-World War II era. Pegler drew on the traditions of the Progressive Era muckrakers, but he also prefigured the later role of conservative radio and television news commentators in using the media to advance the conservative cause.

Finally, an opportunity to address serious problems facing the labor movement was lost. As the author of a recent study of union corruption has asked, "What might America look like today if at least part of the American labor movement had not been hijacked by labor racketeers?"[49] To that useful hypothetical question I would add two others: what might America look like today if in the early 1940s an effective system of legal protections for union members had been created and if organized labor had found an effective way to respond to the problem of union corruption? A skewed portrayal of this scandal made such developments unlikely, and an opportunity for positive reform was missed.

Pegler's part in all of this was central. He publicized compelling cases of union corruption and out of them constructed an alarming picture of widespread abuses and general complacency within the ranks of organized labor. His depiction in turn provided a rallying point for the ongoing conservative opposition to unions. Legislative victories for conservatives followed, first the Smith-Connally Act (1943) and later the Taft-Hartley Act (1947). Both laws levied new restrictions on organized labor in the name of protecting Americans from the depredations of labor racketeers.

At this crucial juncture in labor and political history, Pegler shaped the discourse with which people discussed "union power" and mobilized public opinion against unions. His ability to do so, abetted by the labor movement's ineffective response and by a broader antiunion movement, helped alter the course of U.S. labor history. While it would not be correct to attribute this turnabout to Pegler alone, any serious account of labor's reversals in these years must reckon with union corruption and the way Westbrook Pegler framed that issue to labor's maximum disadvantage.

One could call this negative perception of union power the shadow of the racketeer. The racketeer represents the historic reality of organized crime's influence in some unions, a phenomenon that emerged in the 1930s. The shadow is the common assumption that most union leaders, and thus most unions, are corrupt and therefore the power of organized labor is fundamentally illicit. That shadow first fell across the labor movement during the course of this scandal, a moment marked with the creation of the new word, "Peglerized."

Figure 1.1: This autographed studio photograph of Westbrook Pegler is inscribed, "To the head-man with love from his #1 head-ache." Pegler gave the photo to his publisher and longtime friend Roy W. Howard in 1937, signing it "Bud," the name his closest friends used. Describing himself as a headache, Pegler acknowledged his prickly personality and his tendency to spark controversy. Courtesy of Roy W. Howard Archive, School of Journalism, Indiana University–Bloomington.

# 1

# The Columnist
## *A Crusading Journalist*

Westbrook Pegler pioneered a type of journalism that has become familiar to Americans. He was a tough-talking, conservative commentator who depicted himself as the champion of the common citizen against the elite, liberal establishment. In an age before cable news outlets, before television, when Americans were devoted newspaper readers, Pegler broadcast his opinions through a daily column, or, as he described them, "these right-thinking, spade-calling, straight from the shoulder dispatches." His political attacks were strident, colorful in language, and often personal in nature. He tagged members of the New Deal administration and their supporters as "big-name bleeding hearts and double domes," the latter being his pet term for intellectuals. At other times he referred to the administration as "Mr. Roosevelt and some of his little friends and coat-holders." They were, the columnist charged, incompetent and distant from the world of the ordinary American; in his words, they were "a lot of wabble-wits stuck away in offices in Washington."[1]

Pegler wrote from the point of view, he claimed, of the common man, whose freedom was threatened by a new liberal establishment that had ensconced itself in the federal government. Frequently his columns reported the experiences and concerns of George Spelvin, a fictional character Pegler created. The columnist used Spelvin "to record the mixed ruminations, the prejudices and the bafflement of the Average American."[2] Spelvin's hapless befuddlement offered Pegler opportunities to skewer the New Deal's reform campaign from a populist perspective. And Pegler's critique of these reforms was direct and biting. The Roosevelt administration, he claimed, had used the suffering of the Great Depression to seize power and create a new category of privilege. "New Dealism is special privilege and the exploitation of the great national emergency of poverty and idleness for personal profit and political power and the use of public money to put the poor in a grateful mood at election time."[3]

In the face of this perceived threat to liberty, the columnist put himself forward as a fierce champion of resistance, too angry and too indignant to moderate his language. A classic example of his style appeared in November 1941, when he wrote to urge Congress to pass new restrictions on unions in the face of opposition from the Roosevelt administration. "What a miserable, fumbling, timid aggregation of political trimmers and panhandlers our Congress is these days when it is openly said and never denied because it is wretchedly true, that the lawmaking body of the greatest republic on earth is afraid to pass any law that would place decent restraints on an organized mob of racketeers and dictators because the president won't give the high-sign." Pegler maintained that same tone throughout the column. He asserted, for instance, that the Congressmen "whimper like a kennel of curs because the President won't give them his gracious permission to do their obvious duty."[4]

Reading him today, the language comes across as extreme and irresponsible. It would be easy therefore to dismiss Pegler's impact, but that would be a mistake. His style garnered him a devoted readership, and, especially after his exposés of William Bioff and George Scalise, Pegler was one of the most popular political columnists of the 1940s.[5] In later decades, his appeal faded as the stands he took became more extreme. However, as his biographer noted, in Pegler's heyday, "it was possible for many millions of Americans, not all of them dunderheads, reactionaries and bigots by any means, to open their newspapers with a little quickening of the pulse, wondering whom Westbrook Pegler would clobber that day."[6] The stridency of his tone was part of his appeal. In an editorial titled "Mr. Pegler Leads the Way Again!" the *Los Angeles Times* in 1941 referred to him as the "nation's master prodder."[7]

His supporters claimed that Pegler challenged complacency and generated much-needed debate. He took on issues, they asserted, that other commentators feared to raise.[8] When the editorial cartoonist Jay "Ding" Darling depicted Pegler in a November 1941 cartoon, he considered the columnist to be "the most stalwart commentator of the American Press today." Darling wrote Pegler about "the great mass of your ardent followers" and cited the prevalent "dinner-table discussions, lunch club quotations and Pullman smoking compartment bull sessions on your stuff."[9] Or as Robert R. McCormick, the conservative publisher of the *Chicago Tribune* wrote to one of his subordinates in 1940, "Everybody is talking about Pegler." The publisher declared that the *Tribune* needed to start carrying the columnist's pieces, either by hiring him or paying his syndication fees. "If we can't get him, let's put his price up."[10]

This was the journalist who pushed Scalise and Bioff into the limelight in the winter of 1939-1940. Pegler had come up through the ranks of his profession, an ambitious, talented, and hardworking newspaper reporter. His big break came as a sportswriter, and in the 1930s he parlayed the distinctive style he developed in that field into a syndicated opinion column. He was part of a significant journalistic phenomenon of the period, an era when syndicated columns proliferated and assumed a growing importance in presenting the news. Commenting on a range of subjects in his columns, Pegler took on the role of "professional dissenter," and controversy became a hallmark of his writing. But he was also a crusading journalist, one with a conservative agenda.[11]

By the late 1930s, he made the subject of union abuses a central part of that agenda, and this emphasis led eventually to his exposés of Bioff and Scalise. Pegler labeled the typical victim of union corruption "the Forgotten Man" and referred to "thousands of individual cases of persecution." This approach to the phenomenon of growing union power offered a potent trope for attacking the Roosevelt administration. Seizing on this tactic, Pegler cited these individual cases again and again in his columns as evidence that the New Deal threatened not just the privileges of the rich but the freedom of average working Americans.[12]

But if the issue of union abuses offered political leverage, it was also an issue to which the columnist connected on an emotional level. Pegler had achieved financial success by the 1930s, but he still saw himself as one of those average working Americans about whom he so often wrote. That perspective, in turn, guided his politics. Always ambitious, he had labored hard to achieve success, and he resented any perceived threats to it. Throughout his career, Pegler had used his reporting to take moral stands, often casting himself in the role of champion for individuals or groups he saw as the powerless victims of some hypocritical system. His response to the rise of organized labor reflected these patterns.

He was the son of a Chicago newspaper writer who had barely managed to support his family on the meager wages that typified the lower ranks of the journalist's profession.[13] At the age of sixteen, Pegler dropped out of a vocational high school to work as an office boy at the United Press's (UP) Chicago office. He manned what was called the pony wire, condensing news stories and sending them over the phone to small papers in the Midwest too poor to pay regular wire-service subscription rates. "I thought the job was wonderful," he later recalled. He viewed it as the first step to a career as a journalist, and his boss, Ed Conkle, encouraged him by occasionally letting Pegler cover minor assignments.[14]

In contrast to college-trained journalists (who became more common in later decades) Pegler's education as a writer came by working his way up through the newspaper industry. He had only a brief encounter with higher education, leaving the wire service for a year and a half at the age of eighteen to attend a prep school, the Loyola Academy. He soon came back to the UP and went to work as a cub reporter.[15] His later disdain for intellectuals may have reflected defensiveness about his own limited education.

For the next few years, he shifted around to various papers in the Midwest and West doing the yeoman work of a junior reporter and hoping to get noticed. The papers he worked at were part of the Scripps-McRae chain, a component of the same media conglomerate that operated the UP wire service.[16] By 1915 Pegler stood out enough to be transferred to the UP's New York bureau, a prestigious assignment. In a letter to a friend that December, Pegler wrote, "I did wince for a moment at the thought of diving so abruptly into what is alleged to be the fastest game in the newspaper world."[17]

He covered anything and everything for the UP, including sports and trials, and he kept his eyes firmly fixed on success. In another letter from this period, he wrote about his assignment to report on a murder trial in Providence, Rhode Island. "It is bound to be a great trial and it's my first experience as the correspondent in charge. My Dad won most of his reputation covering big trials and I hope to a cop a few laurels myself this time."[18] When the UP asked if he would be willing to manage their bureau in Denver, he leaped at the chance. As he described it, "At three-thirty Thursday, a week ago, I was beating yards of Jess Willard [a boxing story] out of my grumbling typewriter when the manager asked me if I wanted to go to Denver. I said, 'yes' and he said 'allrightgwanhomeanpackyerothershirt.' Which I did. At six I was on the Pennsylvania [railroad] bound west."[19]

After Denver, he was sent to Kansas City, and then as self-described "itinerant bureau manager extraordinary," he was assigned to Dallas in 1916. Border tensions with Mexico made this a hot spot for the news at the time. The Mexican insurgent Pancho Villa had raided north of the border, and General John "Black Jack" Pershing was in Texas massing American troops for a response. For Pegler, it amounted to a potential career opportunity. Writing from San Antonio that spring, he observed, "If the [Pershing] expedition becomes a war I may put on a boy scout suit and get into the game as a correspondent with the troops. That's one reason why I'm pulling for war."[20] Meantime, he did what he could to get ahead, pouring out as many as 3,200 words a day in stories on the Mexican conflict and other general news events in the Southwest for the UP.[21]

War with Mexico never broke out, but Pegler's ability and hard work did win him another plum assignment. In 1916, the UP sent him to their London Bureau where he covered the British war effort in World War I. On the eve of his departure, Pegler wrote to the woman he was courting at the time, "I expect the next couple of years will tell me whether I am to be a star or just a deckhand in this game—they'll probably be the most diligent years I have ever put in." Once in London, he "whaled into the work," as he put it, "with a determination to 'arrive' on this assignment." He covered Britain's Foreign Office, the Admiralty, and the Press Bureau and interviewed the famous and the powerful as part of a prestigious wartime posting. Most importantly, he had a chance to write the kind of feature stories that got him noticed and that eventually became the mainstay of his career.[22]

But seizing this opportunity also meant a lot of hard work for not very much pay. As Pegler described it in one of his less enthusiastic letters from that time, a reporter at UP's London Bureau "gets a shot at assignments and feature writing and then finds himself with his coat off and his sleeves rolled up swinging a pick in the same old news trenches; skeletonizing, condensing, disinfecting news for American and South American consumption."[23] The hours were long. Pegler and another junior UP reporter switched off, each one taking a two-week stint covering the night shift from nine o'clock at night to seven in the morning, seven days a week, while the other one covered days. "At the end of a trick," he later recalled, "we got a couple of days off to get plastered and adjust ourselves to daylight."[24] The UP was not a generous employer; it was understood that reporters worked not so much for the salary as the chance to build their reputation.[25] In the meantime, an ambitious young journalist like Pegler scrimped by and looked to the future. Pegler noted in 1916, "A fellow lives about the same [in London] as he would in any typical American village, only not so much."[26]

But his effort paid off in the summer of 1917. After the United States entered World War I, the UP sent him to cover the Allied Expeditionary Force (AEF) in France; at twenty-three he was the youngest accredited American reporter on the western front.[27] He was now a part of an elite group of journalists. The U.S. military had decided to allow only twelve accredited correspondents to report on the AEF from the front lines. The valuable spots went to the top reporters at the wire services and the major daily newspapers of the day.[28] In a letter from the front, Pegler wrote, "This assignment is the best in the American newspaper business. It's first-page stuff all the time." And it was also, for the junior member of this particular press corps, a new level of competition. "One needs must work out here," he observed, "or one will find one's self scooped to a pink and palpitating pulp. So I work."[29]

What he produced were usually stories intended to bolster America's war effort. Thus a report on a briefing from General Pershing in October 1917 included Pegler's claim that Pershing had delivered a "smashing rejoinder to-day to pacifists and pro-Germans at home who have been hammering away a proposition that military victory [is] impossible."[30] Like the other members of the AEF's press corps, Pegler had made a formal agreement with the military to accept restrictions on what he reported in return for the front-line access he was being given. The ideal of this kind of journalism was cooperative, not antagonistic. There were limits on what details he might include in his stories, for instance a prohibition on naming the location of particular U.S. military units lest it aid the enemy's intelligence. He and the other reporters also agreed to submit their stories to military censors before filing them.[31]

Since both Pegler and his employer, the UP, supported the war, there was not initially any conflict about accepting this censorship. Even in London, Pegler had noted that once the United States entered the war in April 1917 his stories were written to encourage America's military efforts. "While we aren't avowed propagandists in our shop, we are getting over some stuff that has a strong sentimental leaning toward the most active participation by the U.S. in the war."[32]

As the American military effort unfolded, however, Pegler and the other reporters started to bridle at the Army's restrictions. The first American units began to take up front-line positions in the late fall of 1917. Their numbers in the trenches were relatively small and their presence was meant mainly to make a symbolic statement about America's commitment to the cause. Most of the troops arriving in France that winter were stationed some distance from the front and engaged in training. The big American offensives would come in the spring of 1918. But in the meantime, the problems with logistics and supply that would dog the American effort throughout the war already had appeared. Soldiers arrived without the weaponry and the ammunition they needed. As the cold weather set in, they lacked proper clothing and appropriate lodging for the winter. Frostbite and serious illness were rampant. But when Pegler and the other reporters tried to write about the situation, the Army stopped them.[33]

In fact, censors blocked all kinds of stories that fall, and the reporters came to resent restrictions that they now believed had less to do with promoting the war effort than protecting military commanders from having their incompetence exposed. As one correspondent wrote in a private communication in November 1917, "Our [military] staff is viciously incompetent and is covering up the incompetence which it may suspect by huge pretense of desk-slamming and cursing."[34]

Pegler's reaction that winter presaged a pattern that marked the rest of his career. He mocked the stupidity and hypocrisy of these restrictions, using a biting humor to make his point. One such piece was entitled "The Day the Expedition Landed in France." It opened with a description of two American soldiers: "pink-cheeked, and with the typical innocence of the veteran top-sergeant, they sallied forth into the seaport city to visit the public library to read 'Pilgrim's Progress' for a quiet hour." In this way Pegler skewered the restrictions that barred reporters from describing American soldiers entering a drinking establishment; such reports were believed to be harmful to morale at home where they might offend Prohibitionist sentiment.[35]

In another step that he would follow again and again over the years, Pegler made himself the champion of the people he saw as the innocent victims of a hypocritical system. He took up the cause of the rank and file soldiers suffering from want of proper supplies and shelter in an Army that refused publicly to acknowledge their plight. He wrote feature stories that offered American readers a firsthand view of the conditions the troops faced. In one story, he toured a barn where fifty men were sleeping. "Come and take a peek into that barn and you'll laugh at a mere coal-shortage back there in your comfortable cities and towns." Pegler described a rickety building with floorboards that gave way and large gaps in the roof. "You discover an inch of snow on some of the cots, blown in through chinks in the walls and holes in the roof." There was no effective heat, so when the soldiers "take off their shoes at night . . . as a rule they find them frozen stiff in the morning."[36]

Other stories featured different targets of complaint. He wrote an article on the inferior footwear given to American soldiers and the way it led to cases of frostbite among the ranks. Pegler claimed that the top commanders ignored the problem, and the story included a jab at these elites. "The only man I ever heard defend them [the current-issue shoes] was a general officer. I looked down and saw he wasn't wearing field shoes but a pair of highly-polished russet-boots that must have cost about $40."[37]

In the file that the American Expeditionary Force maintained of Pegler's articles, these pieces—and others like them—do not bear the stamp of the military censor. Without that stamp, the story was not authorized to be published. Aware that the military's restrictions would block him from publicizing the plight of the soldiers, Pegler took one more step that indicated his emotional commitment on this issue.

In late 1917, Pegler wrote his publisher at the UP, Roy Howard, asking him to intervene against the censorship restrictions. He argued that these restrictions were hurting the war effort by keeping U.S. citizens unaware—and therefore unable to address—supply problems. "Under our present restrictions, with Headquarters holding to its present conceptions of what publicity can do and what censorship is for, we might have a repetition of the British shell shortage and be unable to write a word of warning." Also, he asserted, the stupidity of the restrictions hurt the reporters' ability to produce stories that could achieve the goal of both the UP and the AEF: to bolster support for the war. "The fact is," he wrote of the censors, "that they have repeatedly dulled the edge of splendid propaganda." Pegler was doing more than blowing off steam; he was asking his boss to use his political influence as head of an important wire service. "I suggest that you take steps in Washington to remedy the present state of affairs. Literary censorship should be prohibited and we should have the right to criticise. Also Headquarters must adopt a more open policy in dealing with the correspondents."[38]

For a junior reporter whose assignment to the AEF press corps had marked a turning point in his career, Pegler was taking a big risk, and he knew it. He was aware that the military could react to his complaint by canceling his accreditation and demanding his removal from France. Nor was there much hope of keeping his complaint to Howard a secret, although Pegler did what he could in this regard. All of the correspondents' mail in France was censored, as was the mail of the entire AEF, and so Pegler had the letter hand delivered by another correspondent to the UP's London bureau chief, Ed L. Keen. As Pegler later remembered, "Ed. L. Keen was to decide whether the allegations contained in the letter were sufficiently grave to justify the risk of dismissal which I knowingly assumed in asking him to forward the letter to Howard in New York."[39]

Apparently Keen agreed that Pegler's charges were worth sending on to Howard. Pegler soon encountered the repercussions. On December 8, 1917, British military intelligence intercepted Keen's mail, found Pegler's letter, and copied it. They forwarded a copy to Pershing's staff, and within two weeks Pershing personally requested that Howard have the UP replace Pegler.[40] By early February 1918, Pegler had been removed and the UP sent in his replacement. For Pegler it was a devastating outcome, and, according to one account in the military records, he broke down and cried when he learned his fate.[41]

The episode highlighted that combination of ambition and moral commitment that shaped Pegler's career as a journalist. He wanted desperately to be a success, "a star" and not "just a deckhand" as he put it in 1916. To achieve that goal, he would work tirelessly and seize every opportunity. But even as a twenty-three-year-old getting his big break, he wanted his articles to right wrongs and oppose what he saw as hypocrisy and injustice.

The rest of Pegler's wartime experience was anticlimactic. The UP sent him back to the London bureau, and within a few months Pegler enlisted in the Navy. He did this despite the dim view he had acquired of the war. Writing his mother about his enlistment, he admitted, "You know that I hate the war and I have seen enuff of it to like it if there was anything that anyone could possibly like about it."[42] But he also believed the United States had legitimate reasons to be in the conflict. And, as he wrote in another letter, if others had to fight he could not justify avoiding service himself. "Our family hasn't any patent right to peace that I ever heard of and besides, when it's all over, I'd like to be able to say I was in it."[43] He served in the Navy for a year, and when he got out in the spring of 1919, he went back to work for the UP in New York.[44]

## Sportswriting

In the postwar era, he was determined to make good, to achieve financial success as a journalist. "Hereafter—and hear me right now," he wrote to his father in 1918, "I'm going to cash in on all this experience which I have earned by doing the work of a competent all-round correspondent at the pay of a cub."[45] He decided to make himself a sportswriter because, as he later remembered, he wanted "to make the most possible money out of my ability in the newspaper market at that time."[46]

In the 1920s, Pegler became one of the nation's most prominent sportswriters. At the UP in the first years after the war, he began writing feature stories on sports events, making a particular specialty of covering the big boxing matches of the day. He gained a reputation for expertise and humor that boosted his career. In 1925, the *Chicago Tribune* hired him as the paper's eastern sports representative, giving him the job of covering sporting events throughout the East and the Midwest. His articles were syndicated through the *Chicago Tribune* Press Service, and in time the *Tribune* gave him his own column in the sports section.[47]

Along with this prominence came financial security and then prosperity. He and his wife settled down in a house in the suburbs north of New York City. At about the same time, Pegler took up golf, he recalled, "both as a sport and as a social gain." "I had never had more than a hundred dollars until I was about twenty-six years old and, looking back, I realize that I felt that I had begun to 'succeed' when I could join the little country club."[48]

His success was based upon hard work and a distinctive writing style that Pegler honed during these years. One of the sports editors at the *Tribune* recalled that Pegler was "one of the hardest working men I've ever had the opportunity to be associated with. He was an inspiration to us all."[49] He labored hard to create articles that seemed anything but labored; or, as one profile explained, his writing "reads as if it had been dashed off with ease."[50] Pegler's style combined lively, idiomatic prose with a skeptical but humorous perspective on the sports scene. He debunked and gently mocked the various pretensions of sport, from the nominally amateur status of professional tennis players to the alleged character-building qualities of college football.[51] Despite its idealistic claims, Pegler reminded his readers that sport, especially at the professional level, was nothing more than a business.

He pointed out, for instance, the logical absurdity of fan loyalty towards teams in professional leagues. In 1930, Pegler wrote a story about a group calling itself the Loyal Giants Rooters, who were asking more New Yorkers to come out to the Polo Grounds to cheer their team on. "Just why the people should stand by John McGraw's Giants any more devotedly than they should stand by John Wanamaker's department store, the appeal does not specify, and perhaps it would be stupid of me to ask," Pegler observed. "But I am stupid that way, at least, and considering that Wanamaker's employs several thousand local citizens whereas the Giants are all out-of-town boys who cut for home the minute baseball season is over, I should think the department store would have a prior claim on the loyalty of the people."[52]

He also wrote tongue-in-cheek humorous pieces on the colorful characters who inhabited the world of sports.[53] A piece on a rained-out game in the 1925 World Series included this profile of Pittsburgh's catcher Earl Smith, who had gained notoriety for his ability to discombobulate the opposing team's batters with his chatter. "Young Mr. Smith's a blond Arkansawer with a jaw that juts out like a cow-catcher. His low-voiced homilies are filtered through a large poultice of sucking tobacco and the Athletes call him 'Loose-Lip' for reasons that can't be explained if they aren't obvious."[54]

Pegler carved out a niche for himself as an iconoclastic humorist in the world of sports reporting. An advertisement in the *Los Angeles Times* from

1926 touted the paper's coverage of an upcoming boxing match that would include four "All-Star" reporters. In the ad, Pegler's profile followed that of the legendary Grantland Rice, labeled the "Dean of sports writers." The *Times* described Pegler as, "The scribbling comedian, who guarantees some real humor in every line pounded out of his laughing type writer. See the funny side of the big battle through Pegler's eyes."[55] It was humor with an edge. An in-house publication at the *Chicago Tribune* in 1927 captioned a photo of him with the label, "Westbrook Pegler: A crusty cuss, and very comical."[56]

If he was known as a humorist, Pegler was viewed as a crusader as well. In fact, despite the cynical tone of much of his sportswriting, Pegler continued to take moral stands with his journalism. He mocked the sporting world's elite, but Pegler also celebrated the lesser-known athletes who actually lived by the ideals of sport. He wrote, for instance, a glowing piece in 1932 on the young athletes training for the U.S. Winter Olympic team tryouts. They were true amateurs, Pegler claimed, spending a big part of the winter in rustic cabins in upstate New York for nothing more than the love of their sports.[57]

In another example of this moralistic theme, Pegler took up the problem of corruption in professional boxing. His treatment of the issue followed a pattern similar to his reporting as a frontline correspondent in World War I. He poked fun at the problems he saw. He derided the hypocrisy and blatant commercialism of staged grudge matches, where managers and boxers engaged in prefight theatrics aimed at generating more press coverage and bigger gate receipts. "It would be almost enough to arouse doubts in the minds of a skeptic but, fortunately for those interested, the customers are not skeptics," he wrote after one such episode. "If they were, they would not be customers."[58] An article on an obviously fixed fight in 1932 involving former featherweight champion Bat Battalino included this description of the fight's pivotal moment: "Battalino, who is one of the best prize fighters in the world, had gone down from a terrific jab to the shoulder and, when the referee made him get up, swooned again, quite helpless from a furious volley of lefts and rights to the elbows."[59]

Pegler wrote in a much more cutting tone in 1927 about Tiger Flowers, a recently deceased middleweight fighter. As depicted by Pegler, Flowers was an honest man in a crooked sport who deserved better than what he had received. Pegler used a feature article on Flowers's plight to skewer the hypocrisy of the system and to champion its rank and file victims; the reporter had used feature articles on the conditions of rank and file American troops in World War I in the same way. Commenting on the tributes being printed of Flowers, Pegler wrote, "I notice that in all their praises there is the most delicate avoidance of comparisons between the Tiger and the type of men he had to deal with in the racket which Gene Tunney calls the cleanest of all sports." "I suppose they avoided such comparisons out of a feeling that it would serve no worthy purpose to make others who enjoyed great social and cultural advantages look mean and low and cheap."[60]

An editorial in 1927 from a newspaper in Kokomo, Indiana, praised Pegler's campaign against corruption in the boxing industry. "Pegler is landing some hard blows on the brutal sport of prize fighting," the editorial claimed. It noted that the sportswriter made his most telling points through his cutting humor. "Pegler's satire is fine. It is the strongest weapon against error or wrong wherever found."[61]

Pegler himself later compared this campaign to his attacks on union abuses. In 1941, he claimed that at a certain point in the 1930s he had realized that the "rackets" in the fight business were comparable to "the union racket." In both cases, sharp operators traded on the public's idealistic assumptions to cover unsavory practices. News coverage influenced by those idealistic claims, he argued, had avoided tackling problems in either field. The victims were also similar. In the case of union abuses, "the workers and the whole public were victims," Pegler wrote, "just as the poor lopears [that is, boxers] and the public had been the victims of the chiseling piece-men, bootleggers and other vicious parasites of the ring."[62]

## Syndicated Opinion Columnist

He moved from the sports section to the editorial page in 1933. His old boss and friend at the United Press, Roy Howard, offered Pegler the chance to write a daily opinion column that would be syndicated through the Scripps-Howard Syndicate. The career shift culminated a steady evolution that had been occurring in his writing. As far back as 1924, Pegler had done occasional pieces on political events. His coverage of the Democratic and Republican Party presidential conventions had become a regular feature at the *Chicago Tribune*.[63] When the paper sent him to Washington, D.C., in 1932 to apply his writing style to politics in the nation's capital, it proved a popular experiment. As one reader put it, "The result is the best picture of the stuffed shirts in Washington and their picayune, idiot cunning, passed off as statesmanship, that you have in our memory printed. Please keep Pegler at a task worthy of his talent and give him free reign."[64]

Scripps-Howard advertised in December 1933 that Pegler, whom they labeled a "saturnine realist," would be free to write on "any subject under the sun" in his columns. The publishing company promised that Pegler would bring to these subjects his "pungent wit" and the writing skill that had led *Time* magazine to credit him with "some of the best critical sports reporting in the United States for the last eight years." The advertisement went on to position Pegler among a field of popular columnists of the day, claiming, "Critics attribute to him the drollery of Ring Lardner, the iconoclasm of Henry Mencken, the homely insight of Will Rogers."[65]

The advertisement highlighted the fact that Pegler was part of a larger journalistic phenomenon in this period: the rise of the syndicated political opinion columnists. Syndicated columnists had emerged at the turn of the century, and there had begun to appear within this field a class of specialized political commentators. A standard format spread from newspaper to newspaper that placed these political columnists on the page opposite the paper's editorials. When Pegler joined this group in the 1930s, syndicated columns had become a regular feature of newspapers across the country.[66]

The growing popularity of syndicated columnists stemmed from the need to give newspapers a human face as standards of objectivity and business priorities increasingly pushed local publishers to make their product inoffensive—and as a result a bit dull. Columnists supplied such interest while at the same time insulating the local publisher from possible repercussions. Should this more lively and opinionated writing happen to cause offense with the paper's readership, the publisher could disavow any connection with the ideas expressed.[67]

Given the role they played, columnists had little reason to exercise moderation, and indeed the most successful ones, like Pegler, were known both for the intensity of their views and the ferocity with which they expressed them. Neither informed insight nor a reputation for fairness guaranteed a columnist success or influence over the public mind. Thus Raymond Clapper enjoyed widespread respect among his fellow journalists for his judicious reporting on the Washington scene, but the popularity of his columns lagged behind Pegler's.[68] One commentator wrote of Clapper, "He was earnest, quietly honest, always painstaking and sometimes dull."[69] Pegler's columns might be less insightful than Clapper's, but his opinions—strongly expressed and sure to generate a reaction—brought him a wider readership. Profiling him in 1940, the *Saturday Evening Post* explained that Pegler appealed to readers who "get a vicarious satisfaction out of his persistent swats at the objects of his displeasure. Thousands of others who find that they usually disagree with him, read his column as a kind of tonic for their adrenal glands. He infuriates them and they enjoy it."[70]

Like any other form of media, the precise impact of these syndicated columnists is hard to pin down. A survey by *Fortune* in 1937 found that about 35 percent of newspaper readers regularly followed the syndicated columns, and therefore the magazine discounted their significance. But although that 35 percent constituted a minority of newspaper readers, they were also more likely to be a better informed and more politically active group. Thus, as some observers noted, the nature of the columnists' audience heightened their significance.[71]

Certainly their critics feared the influence that columnists wielded. In his critical survey of the dangers presented by the conservative press, Harold Ickes, the secretary of the interior during the New Deal, paid special attention to the role of the syndicated columnist. "Evidently these modern knights of the typewriter exert considerable influence on the public mind and therefore, they must be reckoned with as a major social-political force in the country."[72] President Roosevelt bitterly hated them as an institution, resenting the role they played in shaping the news that reached the general public.[73]

Part of the reason why columnists garnered the readership they did was the way they provided a mix of news and entertainment, which contrasted with the dry objectivity of most reporting. Thus as he sought to promote his new columnist, Pegler's publisher, Roy Howard, warned him against making his columns too serious. In a letter written in January 1934, Howard admonished Pegler, "If I might add a word of advice, it would be this: Don't try to reshape the government or save the nation. Don't get heavy or try to become an authority. Certainly that field is over-crowded. Keep your eye peeled for the things that will stand a little kidding and a little debunking. Try and get a little bit more of a smile into even those sentences and paragraphs which are going to carry a sting." And perhaps in response, Pegler's columns often demonstrated a wry sense of humor and occasionally there were even instances of whimsy.[74] On January 3, 1938, for example, his entire column consisted of the same sentence repeated fifty times, the hard lesson learned from a New Year's Day hangover: "I must not mix champagne, whisky and gin."[75]

But even in 1938, he faced critics who pointed to his columns' tendency towards denunciation.[76] A contemporary journalist called Pegler "one of the most consistently resentful men in the country." Friends allegedly labeled a pond on Pegler's rural property "Lake Malice" and claimed that his small boat should be titled "Rancors Away." One reviewer writing on a collection of Pegler's columns in 1936 asserted that Pegler had never developed much of a "whimsical chuckle in print." Instead, the reviewer said that Pegler "keeps his face hard almost all the time, and frequently scowls when he is merely talking to himself."[77]

Those comments raise a central issue regarding his opinion columns: to what extent did they represent the real Pegler? He had developed a distinctive voice as a writer, and the relationship between that voice and Pegler as an individual was complex. He was not simply the man that readers encountered in his pieces. Interviewers expecting to meet an abrasive curmudgeon were surprised to find Pegler quite different in person. He was a large, affable man, standing about six feet tall, with graying, sandy red hair and blue eyes framed by bushy eyebrows set amid a freckled face.[78]

His fellow columnist Ernie Pyle profiled Pegler in 1942 and began by correcting a series of common assumptions: "No. Westbrook Pegler is not a mean man or a sourpuss. He is pleasant to be with. . . . He is not on the wagon. He smokes, drinks and swears, as do almost all newspapermen. He does none of them to excess." Pegler in fact had an endearing domestic side to his personality. Pyle observed that "among all of my acquaintances I don't know of a man who absolutely dotes on his wife as Pegler does."[79] Other interviewers as well emphasized Pegler's pleasant personality and his devotion to the quiet life of his home in suburban Westchester County, New York.[80]

One way to explain the divergence between Pegler's columns and his actual personality was to assert that the writing voice was nothing more than an assumed character, a kind of flamboyant act, done to garner more attention and readership. Pyle put it this way: "It is hard for readers to reconcile Pegler the Professional Hater with Pegler a Human Being. If he isn't mean at heart, they figure, then his column hating must be just a pose by which he can make a lot of money." Pyle concluded, however, "That definitely is not true." He found Pegler completely sincere. "He is so serious and sincere about his work," Pyle wrote of Pegler, "that it occupies a large portion of his thoughts, even when he's on vacation."[81] The journalist James Cameron Swayze realized in his profile of the columnist in 1938 that, instead of an act, Pegler's writing voice was both an adaptation and a true reflection of his personality. "After several visits with him during his Kansas City stay," Swayze wrote, "I think the critical view for which he's famous is partly a writing style, a style he has found proves popular, and partly the result of a penetrating quality of his make up. He wants to get behind the malarkey and see things as they really are. It's the attitude of a good reporter."[82]

Responding to critics who complained about his tendency to rancor, Pegler defended himself as a reporter engaged in a serious endeavor. He was, he explained, a cautious conservative, bent on using his columns to protect freedom, tolerance, and decency in American public life. He worried about the tendency of Americans to look for easy solutions to the problems they faced. In so doing, he thought many were all too willing to sign away important freedoms that as American citizens they had come to take for granted. In 1938, he saw this tendency both on the right and the left, and it troubled him. "I don't know," he wrote, "whether this people can be terrified away from dictatorship of one label or another, both being alike, or not." But he clearly intended to try. Similarly, he declared, "I am for tolerance, and I think the best boost for tolerance is to emphasize the savagery of intolerance, which was one of the forces that drove out of the old countries and over to this one the parents or grandparents of some of the very people who now think tolerance shouldn't include those whom they dislike." In this period, his columns attacked, among other things, anti-Semitism and the ubiquitous discrimination against African Americans.[83]

And he opposed corruption. "I think the best way of opposing corruption in [public] office . . . is to nail it, specifically, not just prate of honesty and high principled restraint." He justified his tendency towards denunciation by writing, "You can't keep a clean face just by loving cleanliness. You have to use soap."[84] He aspired to be more than just a popular journalist; he was a crusader who hoped to use his writing to move the public in a particular direction.

## Opposition to New Deal and Organized Labor

With these aspirations and given his own background, Pegler had not begun the 1930s as antiunion or even as anti-New Deal. He voted for Roosevelt in 1932 and again in 1936, and in personal letters he offered the president encouragement and support. Pegler closed a note to FDR in 1934 by writing, "Would it be presumptuous of me to say that you are getting along very well in your work?"[85] The columnist was skeptical about some of the New Deal's proposed solutions, but he believed something had to be done for the victims of the Great Depression. His columns profiled the plight, for instance, of an Idaho farming couple in 1934, contrasting their straightened circumstances with the profligate wealthy. Another piece sympathetically depicted the plight of the long-term unemployed. Like the best of his writing, it sought to put the reader in the shoes of the rank and file victim of larger forces, in this case the out-of-work man who had lost all hope.[86]

Writing in 1934, he denounced the well-to-do who objected to an increased tax burden that New Deal relief programs would inevitably require. Citing the case of a wealthy heiress who had recently staged an extravagant wedding to a Russian prince, Pegler observed, "You would think that people with that much money would have the discretion to hold still and play poor in such a time as this instead of traveling in private [railroad] cars which run through the bitterest neighborhoods, where the people stand aside from their coal-picking, or gather at frosted windows of their shanties, to watch the private cars go by."[87]

The columnist asserted that "this revolution, or New Deal," would provide a much-needed correction for such members of the irresponsible upper class. "In various ways the government is going to lighten the task and solve the problem of people who think they are performing a public service in scattering money on frivolity and unimaginable luxury." "For one thing, if a poor little rich girl finds that she has an income of two million dollars a year, derived from a string of five-and-ten-cent stores, the government is going to make her kick back so much money in wages to the poor little poor girls who stand eight-hour tricks on their feet behind the counters of the five-and-ten-cent stores that the accumulation of money will not be any great problem at all in a few years from now."[88]

Similarly, Pegler initially mocked employers who expressed concerns about the New Deal's effort to protect the rights of workers to organize. In 1935, in an effort to forestall labor legislation, the National Association of Manufacturers and the Chamber of Commerce issued assurances that even without government intervention, employers could be counted on to offer workers fair treatment. Pegler's sarcastic response was that workers somehow had misinterpreted this so-called fair treatment in the past. "Always in the past the workman's best friend was the employer, although some of the working people, being ignorant and easily misled by self-seeking agitators, sometimes allowed themselves to doubt this and to try to befriend themselves. Some there were who hadn't the breadth of mind or intelligence to understand that when the employer cut a workman's wages or laid him off or put him out of his cabin and ran him down the road at the point of a bayonet it hurt the employer worse than it hurt him."[89]

But Pegler's attitudes changed by the late 1930s, and he became skeptical both of the New Deal and organized labor. His shifting view of the New Deal coincided with a trip to Europe in late 1935 and early 1936 that affected Pegler deeply and left him alarmed about the danger of fascism emerging in America.[90] He worried about the growing role of the federal government under the New Deal and a slow slide to fascism in America. In April 1936, for instance, Pegler wrote, "Roosevelt has been inching up very close to a dictatorship, whether he thinks so or not."[91] Still, as the 1936 election approached, it was

Roosevelt's opponents, particularly Father Charles Coughlin and Dr. Francis Townsend, who seemed to Pegler to present the surest route to fascism.[92]

Roosevelt's astounding reelection victory removed them as viable opponents and offered the New Deal an apparent mandate for further change that Pegler found alarming. In the months that followed the 1936 election, the columnist became a vocal opponent of the New Deal. When Roosevelt announced a plan to reorganize the Supreme Court that would give the president power to appoint up to six new additional justices, Pegler denounced it as the first step on the road to a dictatorship. "All dictators," he warned, "pack the courts by legal means as a preliminary to the promulgation of their dictatorial laws."[93]

During this same time period, Pegler took up the issue of union abuses. His changing attitude towards unions reflected his own experiences with organized labor and his wary view of any threats to his success. By the late 1930s, Pegler was one of the top-paid writers in America.[94] Like most self-made men, he considered his success hard won, and he bridled at any apparent infringements on it. He claimed to work long hours researching and writing his columns. Seeing himself as a hardworking reporter, Pegler joined the Newspaper Guild in 1934, when his fellow columnist Heywood Broun formed the union and first began organizing news writers and editorial staff. But in late 1936 and early 1937, Pegler stood against a proposed strike at the Scripps-Howard flagship paper, the *New York World-Telegram*.[95]

In so doing, he gained a new perspective on organized labor. He felt that he and other moderates were outmaneuvered at union meetings. "I didn't like the Guild tactics," he remembered, "and I watched them closely." His stand made him a target for recrimination within the union and he later recalled bitterly, "I began to see that Broun and the Guild were not opposed to kicking around in principle. It was okay with them if they could do the kicking around." In the event of a strike, if he did not go along with the Guild, he would be forced out of the union. Then, when the strike was settled, the Guild could demand his removal, along with other strike breakers, and bar him from working at any newspaper with a union shop contract. From Pegler's point of view, an unprincipled minority had gained the ability to threaten his hard-earned success, and the experience left him embittered and increasingly suspicious of unions.[96]

Given his financial circumstances, which differed dramatically from most of the editorial and reporting staff, and given his close ties to his employer, the publisher Howard, with whom Pegler had been friends for decades, the columnist's disaffection with the union was probably inevitable. This would have been true regardless of how the meetings had been run. But Pegler always referred to this episode as his moment of disillusionment, and he used it to explain his decision to investigate misconduct in other unions. Pegler later wrote, "That was when I decided that unions were as dirty in their ways as the corporations ever were and, finally, that the rank and file had no chance under the present laws and the New Deal hypocrisy which persecuted and oppressed them through union bosses while pretending to befriend them."[97]

His growing distrust of organized labor matched the experience of many Americans who viewed the CIO sit-down strikes in early 1937 with alarm. Roosevelt's efforts to reorganize the Supreme Court during this same period exacerbated a growing conservative reaction. As Nelson Lichtenstein has written, "To many, and not only the Republican old-guard, both actions seemed to be assaults on the social order and property rights." Pegler's columns, in other words, reflected both his own shifting views and changing public opinion. In 1937, he began criticizing both the lawlessness of the sit-down strikes and what he saw as the hypocrisy of liberals who failed to object to these job actions. Over the next two years, his critique gradually expanded. A column denouncing the aggressiveness of John L. Lewis, the head of the CIO, would appear and, later, another column would raise concerns about the rights of nonunion workers who wished to stay on the job during strikes.[98] Pegler's positions were never set out methodically but rather accumulated as he turned again and again in his daily columns to the issue of unions. The cumulative effect was an indictment of union power.

He depicted himself as the guardian of the rights of individual workers, often overlooked, he claimed, in the prounion environment of the day. He made their cause his own in a way that echoed his earlier advocacy for WWI doughboys and the pug-eared boxers of the 1920s. As early as January 1937, in the midst of the sit-down strikes, Pegler asserted, "American labor is a big term. It includes millions of unorganized working people and millions of others who belong to unions but aren't orators or parliamentarians and have little or nothing to say about the actions of the smart professionals who run their affairs."[99] His point, one that he would repeat frequently throughout his career, was that nonunion employees were workers too, whose rights should be considered, and that unions did not always represent the will of their members. Two years later, he portrayed himself as an advocate for "those who refuse to join unions, or [who] do join them under silent protest, [and] have lacked a means of presenting their case." Such workers were, he explained, the forgotten men of the new labor relations system. "The employer and the labor faker can make themselves heard, but the persecuted individual in the middle receives no hearing from the public and no respect from a government board [the National Labor Relations Board] which was established with the frank purpose of assisting organized labor."[100]

Individual workers and the public in general were left in the lurch, Pegler concluded, because of basic flaws in the Wagner Act. The law granted unions too much power and imposed no effective restrictions on their actions or responsibilities on their governing bodies. He claimed that unions had assumed the "powers of government," which their leaders now used, free from any meaningful legal restraints, in a "lopsided" contest they waged against a business community shackled by New Deal regulations. In administering the law, the National Labor Relations Board (NLRB) forced businesses to bargain and sign agreements with unions, but no legal authority existed to require unions to adhere to the contracts that they had signed. Individual workers were made to join unions, he asserted, but then no one protected their legal rights within those bodies. As members, they could be expelled from the organization for simply opposing the incumbent officers, and, once forced out of the union, individual workers could find themselves excluded from their occupation because of closed shop agreements.[101]

Additionally, unions engaged in a range of practices that Pegler found increasingly objectionable. He abhorred the violence that occurred on the picket line and denounced "all of those labor fakers and pub-crawling liberals" who refused to condemn it. "It is my rather juvenile belief," he wrote in the spring of 1937, "that a violation of law or denial of civil liberties is as bad on one side as on another, and therefore I see no choice between coercion by Henry Ford and coercion by someone from Union Square." He objected to jurisdictional strikes in which rival unions interfered with commerce to settle internal union disputes. Secondary boycotts, in which a union threatened a job action against one company in order to put pressure on another business, victimized innocent bystanders. Union finances were conducted without any effective government oversight, and abuses, Pegler claimed, were frequent. Some labor organizations set unreasonably high initiation fees and the dues check-off system (where dues were automatically deducted from an employee's paycheck) constituted extortion, he claimed, because a member who did not pay would be expelled and denied work. Union political contributions forced members, who might themselves favor one political group, to submit to a financial levy in support of a group or an ideal that they themselves found objectionable. That these contributions went to the Democratic Party was particularly galling to Pegler as his opposition to the Roosevelt administration increased.[102]

He carefully focused his criticisms, however, on the leadership of the unions, not the members, who he depicted as victims, either unwitting or unwilling. In August 1939, George Meany, secretary-treasurer of the AFL, warned of a growing hostility in the public arena to working Americans. Pegler charged back that Americans resented not workers but union leaders, or, as he called them, "unioneers." These unioneers, Pegler asserted, "have been dealing with working people in a manner comparable to that of the Chicago racketeers who sold 'protection' to businessmen." Continuing with his argument, Pegler wrote, "What he [Meany] should have said was that there had been a reaction against extortion, mob violence, racketeering . . . and the establishment of an irresponsible invisible government in the hands of union leaders."[103]

Three months after writing that column, Pegler's dramatic exposé on William Bioff demonstrated that the West Coast representative of the president of the International Alliance of Theatrical and Stage Employes was in fact a Chicago racketeer, whose unsavory past made his current position of power a cause for alarm. The columnist produced similar revelations regarding the president of the Building Service Employees' Union, George Scalise, two months later.

Pegler's exposés of union corruption in 1939–40 represented something different from the sudden discovery of the sordid background of two previously obscure labor leaders. Instead, these news stories stemmed from a campaign that Pegler had mounted against the growing power of unions. That campaign, in turn, reflected Pegler's background and aspirations, which led him to oppose both the New Deal and organized labor. He saw his own hard-earned success being threatened, and he perceived his situation as all too common. For the columnist, this was another example of an injustice that needed to be opposed. And as Pegler had done at earlier stages in his career as a journalist, he took on the role of a champion who would defend the rank and file victims of an unfair system. Despite his tendency towards bombastic language, despite its political usefulness as a tactic against the New Deal, he was sincere in this effort.

But in waging this campaign and joining it to a larger effort against the New Deal, Pegler eventually would shape his reports on union corruption and abuses in particular ways. The resulting slant in his coverage was echoed in other news reports, and it resulted in an incomplete and inaccurate description of the problem of union corruption. Nothing demonstrates this pattern better than the way that organized crime's role in the problem of union corruption was covered.

Figures 2.1 and 2.2: The official mug shots of Frank Nitti (1930) and Al Capone (1931) were taken at the time of their arrests on federal charges for tax evasion. Convicted in 1930, Nitti finished serving his sentence eighteen months later, just as Capone was leaving to begin his. *New York World-Telegram* and the *Sun* Newspaper Photograph Collection, Library of Congress.

# 2

## The Outfit

### *Organized Crime and Labor Racketeering*

Al Capone went to jail on tax charges in 1932, but the criminal organization he had built up and led for much of the 1920s survived his legal downfall. Capone's removal did, however, generate a leadership crisis, which was initially resolved by creating a kind of board of trustees to run things in his stead.[1] In this four-way "regency of underworld characters" as the FBI described it, Frank Nitti came to play the dominant role and, at least in the press, was sometimes referred to as "the chairman of the board."[2]

Born in Salerno, Italy, in 1886, Francesco Nitto, as he was known then, came to the United States in 1891, when his stepfather, a barber, immigrated to Brooklyn. Although Nitto remained his legal name, an early newspaper report repeated a misspelling in a court document and this became the convention in subsequent written accounts (a convention followed in this text in order to avoid confusion). Like Capone, who was reputed to be his cousin, Nitti belonged to a street gang in his youth. As a young man, again like Capone, he moved to Chicago. For a while he worked as a barber during the day and sold stolen jewelry at night, but by 1923 he was associated with Capone's group. Nitti eventually became the gang's collector, overseeing its myriad financial transactions. Convicted of tax evasion, he served eighteen months in Leavenworth prison. He got out in March 1932, just a couple months before Capone left to serve his eleven-year sentence and in time to assume a leadership role in this period of transition.[3]

Compared to the big and brash Capone, Nitti was more unassuming. Slight of stature, he stood about five and a half feet tall and weighed around 140 pounds. His dark eyes were set off by a Roman nose, and in pictures he wears a serious expression. The two men were more than just physical opposites. Nitti eschewed Capone's flamboyance for a more buttoned-down style. He parted his hair carefully just off-center and dressed expensively but conservatively. The *Chicago Tribune* reported that police referred to Nitti as a "classy little fellow." While Capone had seemed to revel in his power, the pressure of the position ate away at his successor. Nitti suffered from ulcers for years, and on at least one occasion during his leadership tenure, he was hospitalized for nervous exhaustion.[4]

Nitti took over Capone's gang and turned it into what became known as the Outfit, in the process leading it into other fields of endeavor that assumed more importance as Prohibition came to an end in 1933 and the profits from bootlegging declined. The group's distinctive characteristics—its power, ties to the local government, and nationwide contacts—aided its move into the field of labor racketeering. The term *labor racketeering* is open to a wide range of uses, but its most basic (and straightforward) meaning refers to the illicit use of unions by organized criminal groups. This was a particular specialty of the Chicago gang. In turn, the Outfit was an example of a new kind of criminal organization, one that became the face of organized crime in the decades after World War II. Understanding the context in which this racketeering scandal unfolded requires understanding the nature of the Outfit. It also requires understanding the limited options available to union officials who sought to resist the Outfit.

## Organizational Structure and Power

The Outfit was a hybrid. It drew on the traditions of southern Italian criminal societies, such as the Neapolitan Camorra and the Sicilian Mafia. But it also included aspects of the American organizations with which Capone and his associates had developed great familiarity: the political machine and American business enterprise. In some ways, it resembled other Mafia organizations—known as families—then emerging in the United States, but this similarity went only so far. Like those Mafia families, only men of Italian descent held the very top-level positions in the Outfit. Leaders in the Outfit also took on the role of mafiosi in their interactions with the heads of Mafia organizations in other U.S. cities. In 1931, the preeminent Mafia leader in the United States, Salvatore Maranzano, formally recognized Capone "as the head of the Chicago Family" at a national conclave. Yet despite that benediction, Capone and those who succeeded him had little commitment to the clannish, tradition-bound world of the Mafia. Joseph Bonanno, the long-time boss of the New York Bonanno family, considered the policies of Capone, a Neapolitan, to be a bastardization of the Sicilian traditions that underlay the authentic Mafia. Referring to corrosive effects wrought by assimilation to American values, Bonnano wrote, "An example of this trend was Al Capone, a non-Sicilian who was accepted into our world but who was never a representative of our Tradition."[5]

As a result, Bonanno explained, "Chicago enjoyed a quasi-independent status in the politics of our world."[6] Unlike the traditional Mafia, the Chicago group was definitely not ethnically exclusive; non-Italians held a range of positions within the Outfit, including significant roles as trusted advisors in the council that governed the organization. In Chicago there was no formal Mafia initiation ceremony, with the burning picture of the saint, the sacred oath—the type of ceremony that linked Mafia families in New York to the secret society traditions that had first emerged in nineteenth-century Sicily. Instead, when someone became a "made" member of the Outfit, it was essentially a promotion to a leadership position, perhaps marked with a formal dinner and nothing more. The terminology also was different. Outfit members did not refer to their organization as *Cosa Nostra* (literally "Our Thing"), which was the traditional Sicilian expression to describe the Mafia. Nor did they use other traditional terms such as godfather or *capomafioso* to denote organizational roles.[7]

Instead the Outfit was structured something like a cross between a business enterprise and a political machine. At the top, a group of senior partners managed the overall operation and received a large share of the profits. In 1930, Capone's attorney sent the Internal Revenue Service a letter explaining that Capone received as his own personal income one-sixth of the profits of his organization; his three other senior partners—Frank Nitti, Jake Guzik, and Ralph Capone—each received a similar one-sixth share. Their portion of the profits reflected their critical leadership roles. Nitti was the gang's collector and enforcer. Guzik oversaw gambling and prostitution, and Ralph Capone, Al's brother, managed the bootlegging operation. The remaining one-third of the profits was distributed to the rest of the organization's personnel. By the 1930s, after Capone's departure, Nitti apparently shared these partnership duties in a similar manner and disbursed the profits according to a similar formula.[8]

Below that top level of leadership were half a dozen street crews, each run by its own crew boss. These crews had jurisdiction over a particular area of Chicago and might also exercise jurisdiction over certain kinds of criminal activities. Crew members received regular payments from the crew boss as a kind of baseline salary, but they supplemented it with money earned from their own criminal activities, which in turn were overseen by the crew boss. The crews constituted simple networks of patron-client ties, resembling the links between a local political boss and his supporters. The personal nature of these ties differed radically from any kind of formal, bureaucratic structure, such as a military organization.[9]

While many other Prohibition Era gangs fell apart with the loss of their leaders, the Outfit's structure allowed it to survive Capone's removal, but the group's power stemmed from more than just its organizational durability. First and foremost, the Outfit's power reflected its violent capabilities. During Prohibition, a kind of Darwinian struggle had occurred in Chicago between rival bootlegging gangs, wherein the stronger gangs either absorbed or eliminated the weaker ones. Capone himself survived a series of assassination attempts by rival gangs; his most persistent opponent was the group based on Chicago's North Side, also known as the Bugs Moran Gang. In September 1926, for instance, North Side gang members in a convoy of six cars sought to kill Capone by firing over a thousand rounds from machine guns into his headquarters at the Hawthorne Inn.[10]

Capone survived the attack, and in general his gunmen proved more successful in this ongoing contest than their rivals. Over time, a succession of the North Side gang leaders were killed. The rival gang faded away entirely after the St. Valentine's Day Massacre in 1929, when four of Capone's men, posing as policemen, machine gunned to death six members of the North Side group. The victims had been lined up against a wall and their bodies were so riddled by bullets that, according to one account, "they were together in one piece only by shreds of flesh and bone." Shotguns had been fired at point-blank range into the faces of two of the victims, apparently to insure that they had been killed.[11]

This notorious attack exemplified the well-planned assassinations that were a hallmark of the Outfit. Capone's top associates had put together the initial plan for the hit months earlier. Lookouts tracked the rival gang's movements using a rented apartment across the street from the garage where the North Siders sometimes gathered. Meanwhile Capone's people assembled an assassination team made up of experienced gunmen who would not be familiar to the North Siders. These men were fitted out with specially purchased Thompson submachine guns, police badges, and a car rigged to look like the kind typically used by Chicago police detectives. On the appointed day, when the North Siders had gathered at the garage, the lookout called the assassination team who had assembled at a nearby location. Because the hit squad appeared to be policemen, they allayed the suspicions of the North Siders, who otherwise would have fought back.[12] The result was a brutally successful multiple homicide, a crime for which no one was ever prosecuted. Time and again over the years, the Outfit demonstrated that it could kill its chosen targets, be they rival gangsters, witnesses, politicians, or even policemen.

Strong ties to corrupt government officials played another part in the Outfit's powerful role in Chicago. In the mid-1920s, when a reform mayor took office in Chicago, Capone essentially co-opted the city governments in two suburbs adjacent to Chicago, Cicero and Burnham, giving his organization a safe base of operations.[13] In 1927, he reportedly contributed a quarter of a million dollars to William H. Thompson's successful bid to win election as Chicago's mayor. A close associate of Capone served in Mayor Thompson's cabinet and represented the gang's interests in areas such as police promotions and assignments. The ties between the Republican Thompson administration and Capone were notorious. Indeed, they were at least partly responsible for Thompson's defeat by the Democrats in the mayoral race in 1931.[14]

Thompson's downfall, however, failed to end the pervading climate of corruption. The Democratic Party's administration of Chicago in the 1930s was known as the Kelly-Nash machine, named for Mayor Edward Kelly and Democratic Party chairman Patrick Nash. This administration soon became notorious its own right. As one magazine writer in 1940 explained, liberals who had hoped for reform in 1931 instead saw the situation go from bad to worse. "For the relatively harmless complaisance of the Big Bill Thompson regime, they had substituted the Nash-Kelly-Arvey machine, which has given Chicago the most corrupt and ruthless government in America."[15] Jacob Arvey was a prominent city assemblyman who succeeded Nash as chairman of the Democratic Party organization in Cook County.

Not everyone would agree with such a blanket condemnation. Historian Roger Biles argues that the Kelly-Nash machine actually did an exemplary job of administering city finances and providing public services. But the machine's honesty in those matters, according to Biles, meant that it had to fund its organization through corruption in other areas, in particular by taking in millions of dollars from illegal gambling operations. Here the Kelly-Nash machine worked with the Outfit to tax illegal betting parlors, casinos, and bookies, taking a share of their profits in return for allowing such businesses to operate unmolested.[16]

Biles asserts that these arrangements constituted a "covert partnership" between the Democratic machine and "the Capone syndicate heirs," in other words, the Outfit.[17] As one informant explained to the Chicago Crime Commission, "In order to open a bookie [bookmaking shop] . . . protection is handled through the syndicate [that is, the Outfit]."[18] The Outfit kept track of the illegal gambling operations for the Kelly-Nash machine and oversaw the steady flow of protection payments, and in the process levied their own fee on these businesses.[19]

A similar covert partnership existed between the Outfit and those local law enforcement agencies that operated independently of the mayor's office. Cook County's sheriff was sometimes called "Blind Tom" O'Brien because of his tolerance for Outfit-sponsored gambling activities in his jurisdiction. A list of the Outfit payoffs acquired by the *Chicago Tribune* in 1941 showed significant amounts going to O'Brien and several of his key subordinates. Further confirmation of this relationship came when reporters photographed the sheriff department's chief patrol officer meeting with the Outfit bagman who handled protection payments for gamblers.[20]

Police connections offered Outfit members protection against being arrested; the group's ties with the prosecutor's office provided similar protection against conviction. The prosecutor's office in this period was held by Cook County state's attorney Thomas Courtney, who had been elected in 1932 on a reform platform. Here too, however, reform had proven illusory. Courtney's office did develop some cases against gangsters, but this state's attorney never successfully prosecuted a member of the Outfit. It was commonly believed that the lack of success in such cases was intentional; Courtney's ties to the Outfit had become an open secret by the early 1940s.[21]

The conduit for this relationship was police captain Daniel Gilbert. Later tagged the "The World's Richest Cop" by Chicago newspapers, he served as the chief investigator for the state's attorney's office. Known to friends and opponents as "Tubbo," Gilbert's role as the intermediary for payoff money surfaced publicly in 1941 when the same Outfit record sheet obtained by the *Tribune* that listed payments to various Sheriff's Department officials showed a $4,000 monthly payment to "Tub"; it was the largest amount on the sheet.[22] Insiders had known about his role long before the *Chicago Tribune* published that payoff record. William Drury, who was a sergeant of police under Gilbert from 1932 to 1937, later wrote that in cases involving the arrest of "top-flight members of the National Crime Syndicate, he [Gilbert] either speedily released them, or, if the newspapers played them up too big, fixed their court cases." Drury recalled, "When I arrested Frank Nitti in 1933, while he was the boss of the Chicago branch of the Crime Syndicate, he said 'Dan [Gilbert] will get me on the street in an hour,' and he did just that."[23]

Gilbert apparently profited greatly from his ties to the Outfit. Over the years he acquired significant personal wealth, with traceable assets that in 1950 amounted to $365,000. Little of that money came from Gilbert's official income. A U.S. Senate investigating committee in 1950 questioned Gilbert about income tax returns where he declared an annual income of $45,000 while his official salary at the state's attorney's office was only $9,000.[24]

This kind of corruption did more than give the Outfit members legal immunity: it also provided them with another weapon to use against potential rivals. The police often functioned as allies of the Outfit. One participant in the St. Valentine's Day Massacre later explained to the FBI that "Chief of Detectives Stege of the Chicago Police Department was on the payroll of the Capone Syndicate, receiving $5,000 per week, and kept the members of the syndicate informed as to the whereabouts of Bugs Moran," the North Side gang leader.[25]

Criminal groups who survived open warfare with the Outfit risked harassment, arrest, or worse at the hands of law enforcement officials in the pay of—and therefore allied to—Capone's group. In one case, an earlier leader of the North Side gang, Vincent Drucci, was shot and killed while in the custody of a Chicago police officer named Dan Healy. A boyhood friend of Capone's bodyguard Frank Rio, Healy claimed that while he and three other officers were driving Drucci to the courthouse, the gang leader had reached for Healy's shoulder holster. He had killed Drucci, Healy asserted, in self-defense. Not everyone believed this account, and while the police officially ruled Drucci's death accidental, his widow filed suit against the city challenging that ruling. As her attorney put it, "We never did find out how an unarmed man in a police squad car surrounded by armed policemen can be shot to death by one of them without the act being called murder." In the years that followed, Healy's career prospered and he moved up the ranks of the Chicago Police. A fellow officer told the FBI in 1941 that it was "rumored that Healy had obtained his position as lieutenant because of his influence with the syndicate."[26]

Another example of this kind of collaboration involved a famous prosecution. In 1934, one of the Outfit's last remaining rivals, Roger Touhy, who led a bootlegging gang in the Northwest suburbs, was convicted of kidnapping in a case that was spearheaded by Gilbert. Two decades later a federal judge ruled that Touhy had been framed and ordered his release from prison.[27]

The ability to harness the police to serve its own ends, as well as its power to murder chosen targets, distinguished the Outfit from other criminal organizations that had existed in earlier eras in American history. One criminologist has coined the term "power syndicates" to refer to groups like the Outfit. The term applies to organized crime groups that emerged in the 1930s, including the more traditional *Cosa Nostra*. Unlike earlier criminal groups whose main income came from providing illegal goods and services or from stealing, power syndicates used their superiority of force to extort money from other individuals and groups engaged in illegal activity.[28] Steadily through the 1930s and beyond, the Outfit moved to require individuals engaging in criminal activity in the Chicago area, from gamblers to thieves, to pay for protection, to avoid being killed by the gang or harassed by the police.[29] Criminologists refer to that activity as *licensing*, essentially charging a street tax, and it is one of hallmarks of the organized crime groups that emerged in the wake of Prohibition.[30]

Another hallmark of these groups was the level of cooperation that existed between criminal organizations based in different cities. Here too a transition had occurred over the course of Prohibition and in its wake. Moving alcohol across national borders and transporting it to cities around the country during Prohibition encouraged cooperation between criminal gangs operating in different locales. The gangs needed to make arrangements to protect shipments from hijackers and from police along routes that ran far outside their own territory. These arrangements fostered protocols for cooperation that apparently were formalized in a series of conferences in the late 1920s and early 1930s. In Atlantic City, for instance, newspaper articles referred to a gathering of prominent criminals from across the country, including Capone, during four days in May 1929. Reports described a meeting in which gang leaders discussed ways to limit the competition and violence that were undercutting bootlegging profits. Other conferences received less press, but we know they occurred. From time to time, police in various locales stumbled upon other smaller-scale gatherings of gang leaders from different regions.[31]

Two key meetings took place in 1934. In these conferences, the attendees created a national commission, a panel made up of prominent gang leaders from each of the major metropolitan areas. Members of the commission agreed to abide by a set of rules intended to foster cooperation between regions and to discourage violent gang wars that drew hostile public attention while sapping profits. The goal was cooperation, not consolidation. The arrangements embodied in this commission left each gang an autonomous organization, sovereign in its own territory. A member of an outside group coming into that territory had to get permission from the local gang leader before conducting any business. For his part, the local gang leader was expected to provide assistance to outside gang members if requested, for instance, by making available his local political or police connections. As one account describes this understanding, "every mob, the country over, had the right to call on any other for cooperation and assistance." The commission would arbitrate any disputes that might arise between different groups, in that way forestalling violence and costly gang wars. In another bid to control violence, the rules required that the killing of any prominent gang member first had to be approved by the commission.[32]

This relatively loose set of protocols worked; the commission did facilitate cooperation between gangs in different cities. Examples of this cooperation emerged during the government's investigation of the Outfit's control over the Stage Hands Union. Testifying at the trial of Outfit leaders in 1943, Bioff recalled that Paul Ricca, a prominent Outfit leader who succeeded Nitti, "told me and Browne many times to be free to call on Charlie Lucky [Luciano] or on Frank Costello [both prominent New York Mafia leaders] if we find any difficulties here [in New York City] in our work, and if we need anything to call on them, because that is their people."[33] These ties went both ways. FBI reports indicate that in New York City, the prominent Jewish gang leader Louis Buchalter told his associates in the 1930s that they could call on Bioff for assistance in matters that might arise in Los Angeles.[34] The Outfit had sent Bioff to Los Angeles in 1936, and his labor contacts constituted a valuable resource for members of another organized crime group.

The change in organized crime that occurred in the 1930s was limited but still significant. The commission did not create some kind of nationwide corporate structure for organized crime. Instead it functioned more like a Chamber of Commerce, facilitating criminal activity by fostering contacts between members and setting up a guidelines for mutual endeavors.[35] The resulting intergang contacts, however, proved quite useful. With the help of the commission and the cooperation that it encouraged, the Outfit was able to pursue ambitious criminal schemes. It could draw on the assistance of gangsters in other parts of the country to help it gain control over a national union's top officers. The ability to do this changed the scale, if not the nature, of labor racketeering in the 1930s.

## Union Leaders Under Assault

As the organization's power grew, Outfit leaders turned to labor racketeering at the end of the 1920s. The timing predated the end of Prohibition, reminding us that the shift into other activities reflected the growing power of these types of organized crime groups, the new power syndicates. Just as the Outfit moved to license criminal entrepreneurs involved in gambling, the group aimed to levy a kind of tax on labor organizations as well. The gangsters wanted access to the union funds, the money accumulated from the membership's dues payments. But the Outfit also sought a cut of the money that came from arrangements made between certain union leaders and employers, collusive agreements that long had been common in certain Chicago industries to control competition. These arrangements often constituted antitrust violations and therefore existed in the same kind of legal netherworld as other so-called victimless crimes such as prostitution and gambling. And like vice entrepreneurs such as bookmakers and brothel operators, the union officials involved in those collusive arrangements had limited recourse to the justice system for protection. Engaged in illegal activities themselves, they were reluctant to turn to the police for help.

But even where union leaders did not engage in collusive activities, they remained vulnerable to pressure from the Outfit. Union leaders had long occupied a marginal position in Chicago, their organizing efforts and strike activities often pitting them against employers and involving them in legal difficulties. As a result, the union officials targeted by the Outfit usually succumbed to the pressure to collaborate with the gang.

The Outfit made its initial move into this area sometime around 1929. The method of the approach was apparently simple and direct. Matt Taylor, who led a Chicago local of elevator operators, described being given a stark choice in early 1936: put one of the Outfit's people on the union payroll and agree to cooperate, or be killed.[36] There is little reason to think that the technique had differed six years earlier.

Among the unions first targeted by the Outfit was a group known as the Chicago Teamsters, a collection of locals that had broken away from the International Brotherhood of Teamsters (IBT) back in 1908. Here the similarity between labor racketeering and licensing is apparent. The Chicago Teamsters initially left the IBT in response to efforts by the national leadership to weed out notoriously corrupt local officials. Those local officials had built their power on collusive arrangements with groups of employers. Coal Teamsters Local 704, for instance, maintained an arrangement with coal dealers organized in the Coal Merchants Association to help them limit competition. Independent coal dealers who tried to compete with members of the association faced retribution—strikes and boycotts—by Local 704. In turn, the local and its officials received firm support from employers who in other circumstances might have been bitter opponents of organized labor.[37]

Into this network of legally problematic relationships that the Chicago

Teamsters maintained, there entered a group of gangsters associated with Capone's organization and led by George "Red" Barker and Murray Humphreys. Both men were violent criminals who had drifted into Capone's organization during the 1920s. Barker had an extensive arrest record, and according to his file at the Chicago Crime Commission, he was "a $2,000 a day [strong arm] specialist and . . . one of Chicago's highest paid pressure 'business' men." The crime commission also noted police reports in 1930 that labeled Barker "the most dangerous man at large in Chicago today."[38]

For his part, Humphreys enjoys almost legendary status in the works of people who have written about the Outfit. Born Llewellyn Morris Humphreys in Chicago in 1899, he was the son of Welsh immigrants. All accounts agree that he was one of the cagiest members of the Outfit and probably the moving force behind its turn towards labor racketeering. "He was the shadowy man-behind-the-scenes in the syndicate's high command," the *New York Times* explained in his obituary. Tall, ruggedly handsome, with sandy hair, Humphreys dressed well and usually was soft-spoken, even charming. When the occasion arose, however, he could be truly menacing. He allegedly participated in several murders over the course of his career. In 1932, when the Chicago Crime Commission adjusted its rankings in response to the prison sentence that removed Capone from the city, the group listed Humphreys as the new Public Enemy Number One.[39]

Barker and Humphreys led the Outfit's move to license the Chicago Teamsters, and local union leaders who resisted faced threats and violence. When the head of the Coal Teamsters refused to cede control of his organization, gunmen visited him at his summer cabin in Wisconsin and, in front of his wife and children, shot him twice at close range, once in each leg.[40] The attack served as punishment and as a warning to other union leaders considering resistance. Soon Barker and his associates appeared on the payroll of various Chicago Teamsters locals, drawing large amounts of money out of the union funds in the form of salary and expenses.[41]

The Outfit, however, aimed to do more than just raid local union funds; they also sought money from the employers. In the construction industry, the scheme went this way: after driving the leader of the Excavating, Grading, and Asphalt Teamsters out of town, the new official installed by Barker demanded that construction contractors drop their membership in the existing Chicago Contracting Team Owners' Association. Instead they were required to join two new employers' associations, organized by Barker's people. In this way, Barker gained access not only to union dues but to the dues paid by employers to these associations; the gangster thus taxed both workers and their bosses in these industries. Employers paid a $50 initiation fee and $10 per truck per month.[42]

There was one more aspect to this scheme. Those mob-controlled employers' associations also controlled competition through collusive price agreements and by assigning customers to particular contractors. This type of collusion was nothing new, but now the Outfit charged a fee for it. A bid-rigging scheme set up in the construction industry, for instance, allowed contractors to allocate work and inflate prices, but in return they were told to pay a fee, set on a sliding scale, to the association that Barker controlled. Those fees could be substantial, with sums of $5,000 to $7,500 per job mentioned. Employers were told to simply add these amounts to the contract bids that they were submitting.[43]

## Resistance Fails

Some labor leaders in Chicago did try to resist the Outfit. Mostly these efforts failed, and the failure of that resistance reveals the vulnerable position of labor leaders in American society. Though they exercised some power in urban America, union officials lacked the status of their counterparts in business and government. When gunmen killed the head of the Laundry Drivers Union, John Clay, in 1928 by firing shotguns through his office window, the Teamsters mourned the loss of "one of the best and most loyal men connected with our organization, always faithful and serving his people with loyalty." From the perspective of his fellow labor leaders, the Laundry Drivers' sizeable treasury indicated Clay's honesty and suggested the motive for his killing. But the *Chicago Tribune*'s article tagged him as nothing better than a "racketeer," and treated the murder as a routine, internecine gangland slaying.[44]

This example of relative indifference was repeated throughout the following decade. Ten years after Clay's death, in August 1938, gunmen murdered James Dungan, a business agent in the Painters Union, shooting him down as he walked out the front door of his house. According to the *Chicago Tribune*, police officials surmised that "gangsters were trying to take control of the union away from Dungan and that he resisted to the death." This particular outcome had been expected, apparently even by Dungan. The local Chicago police precinct captain told reporters, "Dungan came to see me less than a year ago. He told me he expected an attempt would be made to kill him as he would be leaving his home or returning to it." The story mentioned no measures taken by the police to protect Dungan, although the authorities had not been completely inactive. They had arrested Dungan several times for carrying a weapon.

He was the fourth Painters Union official killed that decade; three of them were murdered as they entered or exited their homes by gunmen lying in wait for them. The exception had been Elsie Henneman, the wife of another Painters Union official; she was killed in January 1936 by a man who fired a shotgun into the car in which she and her husband were sitting. He survived the assassination attempt, but she died from gunshot wounds suffered in the attack.[45]

Over the course of the 1930s at least thirteen prominent Chicago labor leaders were killed.[46] The murders were widely credited to organized crime's efforts to control labor unions, but they failed to generate editorial outrage or draw an effective police response. No one was ever convicted for any of these murders, a fact that given the links between the Outfit and local law enforcement was unsurprising. Indeed, in at least one case, the Chicago Crime Commission later concluded that a high-ranking member of the Chicago police actually was a coconspirator in one of the murders.[47] Faced with the threat of violence by the Outfit, union officials searched in vain for assistance and protection. The story of how the Outfit came to dominate officials in the Building Service Employees International Union (BSEIU) and the Chicago Bartenders Union demonstrates the labor leaders' vulnerability.

BSEIU had originally been organized in the 1910s in Chicago, first as a local of flat janitors (that is, janitors who worked in residential buildings). Led by William F. Quesse, the union conducted a fiercely fought organizing campaign marked by violent incidents committed by both sides. In 1921, the union's top leadership, ten officers including Quesse, were indicted in Chicago on a range of charges including extortion and conspiracy to blow up buildings. Historian John B. Jentz has traced how employers' organizations, promoting an antiunion campaign, played a pivotal role in this prosecution. Convicted on the broadest of the conspiracy charges, the leadership of BSEIU was sentenced to one to five years in state prison. It was only the union's strong political ties to Chicago's Mayor William Thompson that protected the organization from destruction at the hands of this employer offensive, and eventually, in 1924, won the union's leaders a pardon from the governor.[48]

A few years later, when the union faced attack from organized crime, it could not count on that kind of political assistance. The links that had developed between Mayor Thompson's administration and the Outfit meant that BSEIU leaders could expect little help from their political allies this time around.[49] At the same time, the union's experience with law enforcement gave them little hope for help from that quarter. Given the scale of corruption in the police force, this cynicism was justified.

Instead, in 1930 as the Outfit began its efforts to extort money from union leaders, BSEIU's president Jerry Horan joined a group of union leaders turning for assistance to Roger Touhy, whose gang was based in the Northwest suburbs of Chicago. Horan and the city's top Teamster official, Patrick Berrell, led a faction of union officials who moved up to the northwest suburbs seeking protection from Capone's people. According to Touhy, these unions raised a defense fund and hired bodyguards.[50]

But the scale of violence and the reality of living under siege eventually shook the resolve of these union leaders. In June 1932, someone with a machine gun (probably from Touhy's gang) ambushed Capone's lieutenant, "Red" Barker, putting thirty-six bullets into him as he got out of his car one morning. A month later, in apparent retaliation, gunmen cut down the Teamster official Berrell and his bodyguard.[51] In the wake of Berrell's death, the other union leaders who had fled to Touhy's territory abandoned their resistance and came to terms with Capone's organization.

Among them was Horan. Touhy claimed that the BSEIU president had been deeply affected not just by Berrell's murder but by the killing of his brother-in-law and fellow union official William J. Rooney, who was gunned down in front of his home in March 1931.[52] A union leader and not a gangster, Horan was not cut out for the kind of life that continued resistance would require. Touhy recalled, "He [Horan] was even afraid of the men who were supposed to be his bodyguards." In April 1933, according to Touhy, Horan and Art Wallace, a leader in the Painters Union, came to him and said they were going to give up the fight. Horan then went to a meeting that Gilbert, the chief investigator for the state's attorney's office who was on the Outfit payroll, had arranged with one of the leading figures in the Outfit. With Gilbert officiating, Horan agreed to turn over control of his union. After that, Touhy explained, the Building Service Union president took instructions from Murray Humphreys.[53]

A bootlegger, a rival of Capone, and himself the target of allegations that he strong-armed union officials, Touhy's account should be read with a healthy amount of skepticism.[54] But it generally squares with the accounts provided by other sources, and it helps explain how the Outfit came to wield influence over the Building Service Union.[55] In 1934, when Bioff met with Outfit leaders, they referred to Horan and the Building Service Employees as one of the leaders and one of unions that they controlled.[56]

In the meantime, in July 1933 Gilbert pursued kidnapping charges against Touhy and several of his associates.[57] The key figure in sustaining the charges, the alleged victim, was Jake Factor, a con artist and an associate of Humphreys, who later helped represent Outfit interests in Las Vegas.[58] FBI reports indicate that Bureau agents informed both their boss, J. Edgar Hoover, and State's Attorney Courtney that Factor was committing perjury.[59] Still, the dubious charges achieved Gilbert's apparent goal. Touhy's arrest that July was followed by a series of trials, eventually a conviction, and a lengthy jail sentence, an outcome that was not overturned for two decades. To all intents and purposes, Touhy's gang, the last major rival to the Outfit, ceased to exist.[60] With his incarceration, union officials had lost their only local ally in their struggle against the Outfit.

The lack of such an ally became painfully clear to George McLane, who led the Chicago Bartenders Union, Local 278, an affiliate of the Hotel and Restaurant Employees International Union (HREIU). McLane had started out as a bartender and became an official in Local 278 in 1916. Over time he moved up the ranks, from assistant business agent to business representative, to general business agent, effectively the top position in the local.[61] A "heavy-set, hearty-looking man" with graying hair and a florid face that was framed by a line of bushy black eyebrows, McLane's long career in the union gave him a vested stake in the organization, one he was loathe to abandon.[62]

Trouble came with the repeal of Prohibition. Bartenders Local 278 had limped through the dry era by expanding its jurisdiction to include soda clerks, but with repeal the union was poised to grow dramatically. At the same time, union officials began to face problems with the Outfit. According to the FBI's summary of his statement, McLane recalled that "business became quite strong and the first inkling of any intimidation by underworld characters was in 1934 and that in 1935 it became quite evident." Many nightclubs and taverns had organized crime connections, and here especially the union encountered trouble. Pickets were roughed up and union officials threatened.[63]

In 1935, McLane received instructions to go to the LaSalle Hotel and see Frank Nitti, who maintained his headquarters at that location. "The proposition was presented," McLane explained, that the union would "have to put one of their fellows to work and that there would be [in return] no molesting of business agents and pickets." Nitti warned him that failure to do this would be fatal. "You'll put our man in or you will get shot in the head." Called to a subsequent meeting, McLane this time found Nitti accompanied by three other men, one of whom he thought was Humphreys. Gesturing towards the individual who McLane would be asked to put on the union's payroll, Nitti told him, "Here is your man," and introduced him to Louis Romano, one of the Outfit's people. McLane was instructed to put Romano on union salary for $75 a week, which he did; promptly the violence against Local 278 officials and pickets came to an end.[64]

Over time the Outfit raised the stakes. In 1937, Local 278's president died of natural causes, and Nitti and Humphreys instructed McLane to make Romano the new president of the local. The next year they urged McLane to run for the presidency of the national union, HREIU, promising to rally support for him from other local officials around the country. At a meeting with Nitti, the Outfit leader "pointed out the different [union] Presidents that they had made and that they were friendly with particularly the building service employees, the laundry workers, the moving picture operators and the common laborers."[65] McLane testified during a civil proceeding in 1940, "They said they only needed me in that job for two years. Nitti said the Syndicate would make enough in two years to give the union back to us."[66]

Previous studies of union corruption have emphasized the issue of temptation, blaming the proliferation of labor racketeering in this era on labor leaders whose greed shaped their responses to organized crime. John Hutchinson, in his comprehensive book on the subject, *The Imperfect Union* (1970), argued that although other factors played a role, corrupt unions became corrupt because of the weak morals of their leaders. Those leaders succumbed to temptation, in turn, because the philosophy of business unionism (the emphasis on simple bread and butter goals) provided little incentive to take the moral high road. As Hutchinson saw it, "in the presence of temptation or error the so-called business unionists could have used a stronger creed."[67] In some ways, McLane's story fits within this standard narrative of union corruption. He was being offered a Faustian bargain: mob ties in return for power and advancement.

McLane's reaction, however, points out the problem with this standard narrative. In his description of this episode, he makes it clear that he viewed the prospect of winning an election in these circumstances with great trepidation. Fear, not temptation, was his prevailing emotion.[68] As McLane summarized the situation during court proceedings in 1940, Nitti "gave me to understand that I would run [for the presidency] or I would be found dead."[69]

McLane agreed to become a candidate for president of HREIU but then covertly worked to sabotage his chances in the election. At the union convention where the election took place, he snubbed his fellow delegates. "He did not make any speeches," McLane told the FBI, "and ignored all methods of getting votes." One might dismiss this account as self-serving, but his opponent confirmed McLane's description. Edward Flore, the incumbent HREIU president who defeated McLane at the 1938 convention, told FBI agents, "that he gathered from the way McLane conducted himself that he was an unwilling candidate against him. He [Flore] further advised that he [McLane] did not seem to be mingling with the delegates as one would think and he heard complaints from his own people that he was too cold when he was introduced, that he did not warm up to fellows." Flore told the FBI, "it was rumored that if he [McLane] went back to Chicago without a title it would not be safe for him."[70] In spite of his actions, McLane still received about 36 percent of the votes cast at the convention, a testament to the Outfit's ability to line up support from other delegates.[71] Several delegates told Flore that they had been compelled to vote for McLane.[72]

Perhaps because of his lack of success in this venture, the Outfit next moved to push McLane out of power in Local 278. Sometime after HREIU's convention, Romano, the Outfit's man in Local 278, and Harry Levy, an attorney who worked closely with Humphreys, met with McLane; they "informed him that they were going to take over." Places would now be reversed and Romano would run the union while McLane simply collected a salary. Choosing passive resistance yet again, McLane left town, staying away for three months. In his absence, Romano had Local 278's officials vote to dismiss McLane from his union position.[73]

When McLane came back to Chicago in early 1939, he was finally determined to resist the Outfit. Meeting with Romano and the Outfit's attorney, Levy, McLane warned them that he would devote himself to getting in their way. He would, he told them, "make them so sick of hearing McLane's name that every time they heard it they would become very sick." He hired a lawyer and filed for an injunction against his removal from union office.[74] At the resulting civil court proceedings, he testified at length, providing vivid details of how the Outfit had schemed to gain control of the local. Making good on his threat to Romano and Levy, McLane's sensational testimony drew widespread news coverage. Those press reports in turn put pressure on the state's attorney's office, which was compelled to conduct a grand jury investigation into his charges. Here too McLane testified at length, and his testimony led to criminal conspiracy indictments against six Outfit leaders, including Nitti and Humphreys.[75]

But McLane soon realized the state's attorney's office had no real interest in either protecting him or in winning this case; he was very much on his own and he and his family faced dangerous consequences because of his actions. Just when he became aware of how closely tied the state's attorney's office was to the Outfit is unclear. In his statement to the FBI, McLane recalled that information he gave to the prosecutors, especially to the state's attorney's chief investigator, Captain Gilbert, "was in the hands of the Mob within four hours." As the trial got under way, McLane saw that the prosecution was such a farce that Nitti never bothered to show up in court. Another defendant in the case, Louis Compagna, was not even arrested although he had taken no steps to flee the jurisdiction. Meanwhile McLane and his family were threatened repeatedly. The police posted guards at McLane's house to protect his family and assigned him a bodyguard.[76] But given his experiences with Captain Gilbert, McLane must have had his doubts about the quality of this police protection.

In the end he backed down. When the time came for him to testify against Nitti and the other defendants at the criminal trial, McLane claimed his Fifth Amendment privilege against self-incrimination and refused to answer any questions. His silence led to the acquittal of all of the defendants.[77] Speaking to the FBI, McLane offered no direct explanation for his change of heart, but his attorney later provided more information. McLane had told him, the attorney explained to FBI agents, "that Captain Dan Gilbert of the States Attorney's Office called him in to his office prior to the first session of court, and in a threatening manner told him not to testify."[78]

Two decades later, an illegal FBI listening device picked up Humpreys describing the precise nature of the threat made to McLane. Unaware the room was bugged, Humphreys bragged about how he had gotten McLane to take the Fifth. The union official had been told that should he testify, his wife would be kidnapped and, as one of the agents listening in to the conversation later recalled Humphreys's words, she would be "kept alive as her husband was daily sent one of her hands, then her feet, then her arms." She would be slowly tortured to death.[79]

With no effective ally, McLane's efforts at resistance came to naught. Nitti and Humphreys and the other Outfit defendants were acquitted and, because of double jeopardy, those criminal charges could never be reinstated. The civil proceedings McLane had instituted created only a temporary obstacle for the Outfit. The national union imposed a trusteeship over Local 278 and purged Romano as well as the other local officials with reputed ties to organized crime. When the trusteeship ended a few months later, the Chicago police oversaw the voting to elect new officers in Local 278. But in effect this only meant that, according to McLane, "The votes were counted in the office of the State's Attorney and the decision electing Crowley [McLane's opponent] was announced by Captain Daniel A. Gilbert, chief investigator for the State's Attorney's police." McLane complained that the votes had been miscounted but to no avail. Immediately after his election, Crowley reappointed the mob-connected officials that had been ousted during the union's trusteeship.[80] McLane and his faction were out and the Outfit and its faction were in. In the decades that followed, the Outfit dominated the HREIU locals in Chicago and taxed restaurant employers through control of the Chicago Restaurant Association.[81]

## Conclusion

This was the setting for the labor corruption that Pegler exposed. A new kind of organized crime had emerged in the 1930s, exemplified by the Outfit and its power in Chicago. The Outfit combined a durable organizational structure with an impressive capability for violence. It also could draw on the assistance of other gangs in other regions, and it had strong ties to corrupt officials in local government and law enforcement. In Chicago in the 1930s, it enjoyed virtual immunity from prosecution. It also received help at crucial moments from police and prosecutors. With this power, the Outfit had moved into licensing—in other words, levying a street tax on various kinds of criminal activity such as gambling—by the late 1920s. The move into labor racketeering represented an offshoot of that trend. With the end of Prohibition in 1933 and the consequent decline of bootlegging, these licensing activities became the gang's mainstays.

Some unions and some union officials had long been involved in collusive arrangements with employers, and these were the Outfit's first targets. Gangsters intimidated union officials in order to gain access to union funds and, if possible, taxed unionized employers through captive business associations.

Organized labor's efforts to resist the Outfit in Chicago were largely unsuccessful, as vulnerable union officials could count on neither the support of mobilized public opinion or local law enforcement in this contest. Some union officials left their positions in the face of death threats; others stayed and were assassinated. With just a few exceptions, those who were targeted by the Outfit, and who remained in office, reached some kind of accommodation with the gang. The Outfit's power in this area set the stage for the rise of Bioff and Scalise, and their activities in turn demonstrated how organized crime's influence changed the scale of union corruption in this era.

The gang's move into this area guaranteed its own long-term survival. In the wake of Prohibition, Nitti faced pressure to find ways to support the Outfit's sizeable organization. Gunmen like "Machine Gun Jack" McGurn, who had engineered the St. Valentine's Day Massacre and was allegedly responsible for twenty-eight murders, guaranteed the power of the gang, but those men required continuing economic support.[82] The Outfit needed sources of revenue to meet its expenses and it needed paid positions to which it could assign its membership. Captive unions provided both. After the Outfit had helped to make him president of the Stage Hands Union in 1934, George Browne recalled a conversation with Nitti about the pressures that the Outfit leader faced. "He explained at some length," Browne recalled, "the difficulties he was having keeping his people supplied with money; [he] mentioned for instance Jack McGurn who has to get $150 a week, and many others, and he says, 'When I can't find places to put these fellows, to earn money, we have to take care of them ourselves.'" A year later, Nitti reminded Browne of the Outfit's need for revenue. "Theirs was a large organization," Nitti said, "and they needed much more money."[83]

IATSE and the other unions that fell under the Outfit's control provided a steady source of money that helped the gang thrive in the post-Prohibition Era. As the special agent in charge of the Department of Labor's Organized Crime and Racketeering Section in Chicago noted in 1983, "Labor racketeering is one of the foundations upon which the great strength, wealth and endurance of the 'outfit' was built." Labor racketeering was, the official explained, "a particular specialty of the Chicago 'outfit,' one for which they have been recognized by other organized crime families, law enforcement, and the media." That year, the federal government's Organized Crime Strike Force in Chicago estimated that "there are approximately eighty-five labor organizations affiliated with twenty separate international, national, or independent parent unions that are suspected of being associated with, influenced, or controlled by organized crime and racketeering elements." Many of those unions had "served the mob [for] well over fifty years."[84]

For organized crime groups in general, labor racketeering after World War II played a pivotal role. Vincent Cafaro, a member of New York's Genovese crime family, explained to a U.S. Senate committee in 1988, "We got our money from gambling, but our real power, our real strength came from the unions."[85] This power brought important financial benefits. In industries such as construction or the garment trades, control over strategic unions provided organized crime figures with lucrative economic opportunities. By avoiding certain union restrictions, mob-connected companies enjoyed profitable advantages over their competitors. Sammy Gravano, the former underboss of

Gambino crime family, described how his construction companies doubled their profit margin on particular contracts because mob-controlled unions allowed him to pay below-scale wages to his workers and skip paying their union benefits contributions. At the same time, cartel arrangements, enforced by corrupt union officials, reserved profitable business opportunities for Mafia figures and their business partners.[86]

Seeking to explain the successes of the Outfit in this area, the top FBI official in Chicago in the early 1980s cited one factor above all others: "the extent of public corruption." Addressing a congressional hearing in 1983, the official asserted, "Public corruption is the seed bed upon which Organized Crime grows and flourishes."[87] It was also a critical part of the context in which the racketeering scandal unfolded.

In his exposés, Pegler never described this context, and the accounts of union corruption that have appeared since his time practice the same omission. By leaving out the power of organized crime and its ability to terrorize union officials, and by leaving out the role played by corrupt public officials, Pegler created a particular kind of narrative for union corruption. It became simply the story of greed and ambition on the part of union officials. Moreover, their misdeeds appear to be more of an aberration than in fact they were in Chicago, or places such as New York City, St. Louis, or Detroit in the 1930s.

Portrayed in this historical vacuum, corruption became a problem peculiar to unions and thus easily blamed on the growth of organized labor. For Pegler and many who have followed his lead since, it was an easy logical step to move from denouncing corruption to opposing unions. However, the misdeeds behind this scandal involving Bioff and Scalise—and corruption scandals like it—were the product of larger circumstances, and efforts to combat union corruption had little chance of success if they ignored those circumstances. Removing the corrupt union official but ignoring the Outfit and its corrupt allies in law enforcement would achieve very little.

Figure 3.1: An exhibit from William Bioff's 1941 criminal trial, the Chicago Police took this lineup photo on October 15, 1931. Bioff is in the middle, numbered "2" in the photo and identified on the back as "Henry Martin alias Wm. Bioff." On his right stands James Adducci [1] and on his left, Phillip Mangano [3]. Source: Westbrook Pegler Papers, courtesy Herbert Hoover Presidential Library.

# 3

## Browne, Bioff, and Scalise

### *The Dynamics of Union Corruption*

In many ways, the three men who personified union corruption did not have much in common. George Browne was "a likeable jughead and a Good-time Charley," a congenial beer drinker with a thirst that reputedly had gargantuan proportions. Witnesses described him drinking seventy-two bottles of his beloved Heineken beers in one sitting, and the talk was that on some occasions he finished off over a hundred bottles.[1] When one thought of William Bioff, however, *likeable* was not a word that came to mind. He was abrasive, boastful, foulmouthed, and as one of his relatives put it, an "egomaniac." Bioff himself told federal authorities that, had he stayed in Chicago, he believed his organized crime associates there eventually would have killed him out of sheer irritation.[2] George Scalise was a polished, self-confident charmer. As his longtime secretary Anna Kimmel put it, "Mr. Scalise always treated everyone nicely, including myself."[3] Browne and Bioff held positions in the International Alliance of Theatrical Stage Employes while Scalise came to prominence in the Building Service Employees Union.

The three men were thrown together by Pegler's exposé, which thrust them into the media spotlight and made them into villainous symbols. The negative publicity was followed by criminal prosecutions and convictions for each of them. Their similar fates belied their differences in style, personality, and background. What they shared, however, were careers that had brought them into connection with the seamy underside of the labor movement. Some unions, by nature of the industries they organized, tended towards corruption. In these economic sectors, the dynamics of collective bargaining allowed the officials in charge of a union to wield control of their members in a way that fostered abuses of power. Local unions operating in those sectors suffered from endemic corruption. Browne's rise to the presidency of the International Alliance of Theatrical Stage Employes (IATSE) owed much to the political influence of these types of local unions within the Alliance. Bioff's earliest experiences with organized labor involved these same types of unions. For his part, Scalise had first ventured into union activity as a kind of entrepreneur who saw the profit-making potential of labor organizing in such settings. Their personal histories highlight a common landscape of union corruption; individual stories might differ, but the bleak, organizational features were always familiar. This was the netherworld of organized labor, where long-term patterns of abuse mocked the movement's historic ideals.

Their careers shared another similarity: all three had become involved in organized crime, although again in different ways. Bioff had spent much of his adult life on the margins of the Outfit. Browne had managed to avoid associating with the Outfit until 1934, when he agreed to a forced partnership with the group. The partnership boosted his union career at the cost of involving him in a much larger scale of corruption. Of the three men, Scalise had the strongest ties to organized crime, although he was connected to a New York Mafia family, not the Chicago Outfit. But Scalise had managed to hide those ties so well that until Pegler's exposé they were largely unknown.

And that was the final bond that united their careers: Bioff, Browne, and Scalise served a vital function for the Outfit. Their links to organized crime were not well-known and especially Browne and Scalise appeared to be respectable union leaders. They were front men. Their air of legitimacy masked the organized crime group's schemes, allowing the Outfit to seize control of national unions without raising alarm and outrage, at least not until Pegler's exposé.

## Willie Bioff and George Browne

Although Bioff and Browne made an unlikely pair, soon after they met in 1933 they formed a partnership that shaped the rest of their lives. Bioff became Browne's de facto agent, the one who brokered the illicit deals and ostensibly protected Browne's interests. These activities led to federal convictions in 1941 with lengthy prison sentences for both men. Bioff, hoping to win an early release, decided in 1942 to cooperate with federal authorities. Browne soon followed his lead. Thereafter, in briefings with FBI agents and in trial testimony, they provided their own versions of their backgrounds and their partnership. These accounts supplemented and balanced the dramatic coverage both men received in the media.

As described in news articles, Bioff fit Central Casting's image of a hood. He stood five foot six and weighed two hundred pounds; one journalist likened his physique to that of a wrestler. "His graying, swarthy head sits compactly on his shoulders, which are wide, thick and powerful," said one magazine article. "His bull torso slithers down to a flat hard abdomen. His neck is almost non-existent, his hands pudgy, but not flabby, with thick muscular fingers, his eyes heavy lidded."[4] In using the term "swarthy," the magazine drew on a stock gangster description. But the FBI's profile of Bioff listed him as "fair skinned," demonstrating the dramatic license common in such news accounts. The Bureau, for its part, noted an "oblique scar [on the] left side of the chin," a detail that heightened Bioff's threatening image as the scar-faced mobster.[5] Bioff himself apparently embraced this role. In the police lineup photos, he wore a dark, pin-striped suit with wide lapels and a white fedora with a dark hatband and a wide brim.[6] Decades later Godfather's Pizza would popularize the same look.

He had hustled on the margins for most of his life, and as a result Bioff was an aggressive conniver, a man with apparently limitless confidence that he could bluster his way through any situation. The Bioffs originally were from a town outside of Odessa, Russia, and Morris Bioffsky, which was William's given name, had been born there in either 1899 or 1900. A few years later, his father, Lazar, brought his wife and five children to America and they settled on the west side of Chicago, which was then a tough immigrant ghetto. Taking work as a glazier, Lazar became known as Louis Bioff, Americanizing his first and last name, and Morris became William, or more frequently Willie. A former landlady remembered Louis as a strict father and Willie as a boy who "always seemed to be a live wire." After the mother died in childbirth, Willie's father remarried in 1914. Willie was unable to get along with his stepmother, and he left home for good.[7]

A third-grade dropout, a teenager living on the streets, he scrambled to get by. Bioff worked as an errand boy and helped out around a neighborhood pool hall. At seventeen, he landed a job driving for Mike Galvin, a local union leader and politician in Chicago's notorious River Ward. As Bioff described it, "I started out as Mike Galvin's driver, chauffeur. He took a liking to me, I don't know why, more from pity, I imagine."[8] Galvin led the largest local union in the breakaway group known as the Chicago Teamsters. As a union leader, Galvin shared the same questionable reputation as most of the other officials in the Chicago Teamsters, which had been notorious for corruption since the early 1900s. Here Bioff would have seen firsthand a typical land-scape of union corruption. Galvin combined his union post with leadership in the ward's Democratic Party committee, giving him an important role in the corrupt local political scene as well.[9]

Bioff described his job with Galvin as his introduction to the labor move-ment, but he soon drifted on to other endeavors. Drawing on contacts he made through Galvin's political club, Bioff drove a beer truck for bootleggers and worked as a bartender at speakeasies, the illegal saloons that emerged during Prohibition. The places were often owned by gangsters, and they typically featured gambling and prostitution along with illegal liquor. Such enterprises needed a particular kind of employee, and Bioff took on the re-quired roles. Bioff described his work this way: "my job was to maintain law and order in the gambling house."[10] He was a bouncer, a drink server, and a procurer. It was in that last capacity that Chicago police arrested him in 1922 and charged him with pandering. He was bartending in a combination of speakeasy and brothel that belonged to Jack Zuta, a prominent organized crime figure on Chicago's west side. It was probably Zuta's connections that saved Bioff from having to serve his jail sentence, the incident that Pegler later uncovered.[11] Bioff continued working for Zuta and by the late 1920s had achieved a measure of success. He moved up to the position of collec-tion agent, visiting the saloons that stocked Zuta's alcohol and collecting the money due.[12]

But Bioff's circumstances changed for the worse when Jack Zuta was mur-dered in 1930. Zuta's territory apparently fell under the control of other gang-sters, and Bioff was left to look around for another opportunity. By early 1933, Bioff and a partner had turned to Chicago's live poultry market and tried to set up a collusive agreement that would limit competition among the Jewish merchants there. In return, Bioff and his associate would get one half cent per pound on all chickens delivered at the market. It was a model of labor relations that Bioff would have learned about during his years working with Galvin and the Chicago Teamsters. But the merchants proved resistant, as did the Poultry Handlers' Union, and the venture went nowhere.[13]

In his early thirties, in the midst of the Great Depression, Bioff was stuck as essentially a low-level hustler. Years later, when faced with allegations about Bioff's racketeering past, his attorney noted, "If he was racketeering in Chicago, he didn't make a lot of money out of it."[14] Unable to develop his own schemes, he was left to do the relatively mundane chores required in others' illegal enterprises.

In Bioff's case, these chores apparently did not involve anything so dra-matic as murder. Unlike the notorious killers who surrounded Al Capone and

Frank Nitti, Bioff's record lacked much in the way of allegations involving violence. Police reports indicate that he had threatened a poultry merchant, but nothing ever came of the threat, and Bioff was apparently not intimidating enough to line up the chicken dealers into his collusive organization.[15] He was tough enough to keep order in a bawdy house and to collect receipts from speakeasies. But for a man who spent his life working among gangsters, Bioff's criminal record included just the one conviction for pandering and no arrests for assault—much less murder or even a weapons charge. Nor did the policemen who came in contact with him in those years recall anything that would belie that criminal record.[16] He was aggressive and he talked tough, but it seems unlikely he was killer.[17] Until he teamed up with Browne, Bioff seemed fated to work the seedy edges of the Outfit, one of the obscure bit players in that world.

It was while trying to set up something in the poultry market that Bioff first met Browne, who also was at loose ends at that stage in his life. Where Bioff fit the stereotyped image of a hood, Browne was the typical Irish-American working man. Standing about six feet tall and weighing two hundred pounds, Browne had dark brown hair, blue eyes, and a ruddy complexion.[18] Born in 1893, he had grown up in rural Woodstock, Illinois, and left school after the fifth grade to labor at various odd jobs, eventually landing work as a millwright's assistant at an amusement park. By 1911, he had become an apprentice in the property department of a Chicago theater. Four years later, he completed a formal apprenticeship and became a card-carrying member of the Local 2 of the Stage Hands Union (IATSE).[19]

Affable and intelligent, he had what it took to do well in union politics. One reporter noted, "Mr. Browne can charm you off your feet if he so chooses, and is as alert as they come." He never became much of a public orator, but in smaller social settings, he shined. This same reporter observed of Browne, "He boasts a rare sense of humor, even if it works to his personal disadvantage and [he] is not being fooled very often." News correspondents considered him "a square shooter, and when he gives them his word, he stands by it." With these traits, Browne won election to local union office in his early twenties and also served one term as a vice president in the national union.[20]

The onset of the Great Depression proved devastating for Stage Hands' Local 2 and also for the modicum of success that Browne had achieved. Where fifteen theaters had operated in Chicago, by the early 1930s only three remained open, and they demanded drastic wage cuts from their stagehands. The unemployed members of the local let their dues payments lapse and, with almost no money coming in, the union's two salaried officers, one of whom was Browne, stopped getting regular paychecks. Perhaps in search of a more dependable salary, Browne ran for president of IATSE at the union's annual convention in 1932 but lost.[21]

Like Bioff, Browne had reached a sort of nadir and was looking for a new opportunity. In the wake of his election defeat, Browne accepted an offer from a group of poultry merchants who asked him to help them organize an association to limit competition in their industry. The effort brought him into contact with Bioff, who was pursuing a parallel effort among the Jewish poultry dealers. For a while they teamed up, trying unsuccessfully to build a viable association. Though they were quite different in style and background, something between them clicked. Even as the two men watched their endeavors in the poultry market come to naught, they decided to maintain their working relationship. Browne offered to split what there was of his salary from Local 2. "Bioff was a, what I would say, rather a nimble-witted, aggressive fellow, and I thought I could well use him, and asked him to come with me." The upcoming Chicago World's Fair, Browne explained, would improve prospects for the Stage Hands Union, but it would also bring jurisdictional disputes with other unions. He thought Bioff's assistance would prove useful.[22]

This explanation may have been disingenuous, especially given how events turned out; Browne probably envisioned other roles for Bioff to play. Although Browne was a bona fide union leader, one who had worked in his craft and won election to union office, his conduct had not been spotless. Where Bioff's criminal record involved no violence or weapons charges, Browne could not make a similar claim. In 1924, police found two guns on Browne when they arrested him for taking part in a street fight. A year later, he was admitted to a hospital with a gunshot wound, claiming he could not identify his attacker. During Prohibition, Browne helped bankroll a couple of speakeasies.[23] Finally, in 1933, as he and Bioff initiated their partnership, Browne was receiving a $150 a week from the owner of burlesque theater who paid him to help make sure no competing theaters would open on his block.[24] It was, Browne claimed, the first time he ever took money from one of his local union's employers. He began splitting this money with Bioff, and so their partnership began.[25]

Their first big score came in early 1934, when Local 2's contract with the Balaban and Katz theater chain was up for renewal. A subsidiary of Paramount Pictures Corporation, the Balaban and Katz chain included the premiere movie palaces in Chicago. The company employed stagehands to work the curtains and run the switchboards in those palaces. Local 2's previous contract with Balaban and Katz, negotiated during the onset of the Great Depression, had provided for a temporary wage reduction, but the old pay level was now scheduled to be restored. In discussions with Browne, Barney Balaban, the chain's Chicago representative, argued his firm could not afford to pay such a raise. Revenues had improved and the number of stagehands involved was minimal, but Balaban claimed that granting a wage increase to Local 2 would then lead to similar demands from the projectionists' union and the musicians, and those raises would bankrupt the chain. Balaban offered Browne a bribe in return for continuing the members' pay cut. Browne remembered Balaban coming to see him and saying, "Why don't you let us take care of you, and we'll do like we did for some other fellows. We'll give you $100.00 per week and put you on the payroll under an assumed name or cash or handle it any way you like."[26]

When Browne described the offer to Bioff, his new partner smelled a bigger opportunity. Browne remembered Bioff saying, "We can get a lot more money than that and get it all the time." Bioff told Balaban it would cost the theater chain $50,000 to get this concession and Balaban responded by sending in the firm's attorney to negotiate with Bioff. They settled on the figure of $20,000 and worked out a way to disguise the payoff as legal fees. It was for the time period a large amount of money, and as partners, Browne and Bioff split it down the middle.[27]

They celebrated at a fancy café, the 100 Club, and in the process of blowing $300 in one night they drew the attention of the club's owner, Nick Circella, a high-ranking member of the Outfit. Bioff and Circella had known each other for a long time, an acquaintanceship that stretched back to the days when Bioff drove a bootlegger's beer truck. Their time together back then had not made them friends—apparently the result was just the opposite. This was a pattern for Bioff. Always an eager self-promoter, he seized the chance to flaunt his recent score. Bioff recalled that he did not mention Balaban's payment to Circella, but, "I tried to give him the impression of my prosperity, braggadocio, so I would say." Apparently it worked. Circella was intrigued, and he checked up on Browne and Bioff.[28]

Soon afterwards, Bioff received word that he and Browne were to meet with Circella's boss, Frank Rio. One of the leaders of the Oufit, Rio had been Al Capone's bodyguard, perhaps his closest associate and certainly one the scariest. News reports credited Rio with a triple homicide in 1929 of an alleged cabal of plotters within the Capone organization. All three men were beaten to death at a banquet Capone had held ostensibly in their honor. The *Chicago Tribune* reported that "Rio was believed, rightly or wrongly, to have been the executioner." It was a shockingly brutal crime. Every bone in the victims' bodies had been broken, and then, apparently still alive, all three men had been shot several times at point-blank range. The corpses were dumped on a rural road in Indiana. The coroner who investigated the case said that in his thirty years of experience, he had never seen that kind of damage done to a human body. According to the *Tribune*, "Rio became known as the 'heavy man' for the Capone gang."[29]

Following instructions they had received, Bioff and Browne went to a downtown saloon where they were split up. While Bioff waited at another location, Browne was driven to a secluded spot along the Chicago lakefront. A second car pulled up and Frank Rio got out, walked over to where Browne was sitting, and explained the union leader's new situation.[30] As Browne later recalled the conversation, Rio noted that the Outfit had left him alone. "We have never bothered you," Rio said. "You have always been alright with us." But now things were different. Browne was teamed up with Bioff, and the two men were making significant money out of a struggling stagehands' local, an organization that previously had been unable to pay the salaries of its two officials. Even if he did not know about Balaban's payoff, it would have been apparent to Rio that Bioff had helped Browne conduct some kind of criminal scheme. The Outfit demanded a share of this money, a version of the street tax it levied on others involved in illegal activity. According to Browne, "Rio told him that if Bioff was to be with him, that the mob was going to be 'cut in' and that was all there was to it." The gang demanded 50 percent of all their future scores.[31]

Rio's approach combined enticement and threat. According to the FBI's summary, Browne recalled that Rio "stated that he knew Browne and that he [Browne] never had done any harm, and that in some cases he had done some good, and that he probably would be in a position to do some further good if he would be their friend." Becoming "their friend" meant becoming an associate of the Outfit. But although Browne was ready to team up with Bioff and ready to take money from an employer, he was still reluctant to come under the Outfit's control. He sought to put Rio off, claiming he had no need for protection. Rio responded with a simple ultimatum: "You will either go along with us or you will have to step out and we'll put somebody else in there."[32]

Like McLane of the Bartenders Union, Browne's reaction to the Outfit's overture reflected fear more than temptation.[33] He was reluctant to get involved with the Outfit but also unwilling to abandon his career as a union official. Bioff recalled warning against any attempt at resistance, telling Browne, "that he had to do one thing or the other, either go along with these people or step out, and that they were in no position to buck this outfit." Both men knew that the Outfit had made similar moves on other union officials and that the authorities would offer no help. "The police department worked hand in glove with those people," as Bioff put it, "and anyone that made a complaint in the district attorney's office would have his head fractured before he got home."[34] Under these circumstances, Browne decided to keep his union position and to accept what amounted to a forced partnership with the Outfit. Rio assigned Nick Circella to supervise Browne and Bioff.

Browne's reluctance to get involved with the Outfit was not shared by Bioff, who saw the lucrative potential of the situation. Bioff had never worked in the industry covered by this union, and he had no emotional connection to the people employed in it. His involvement with organized labor was purely entrepreneurial: he wanted to get rich. Now that the Outfit had claimed a stake, Bioff saw an opportunity to use the power of this gang to suit his own needs by promoting Browne's career. In the spring of 1934, Bioff approached the Outfit with the proposition of engineering Browne's election to the national presidency of IATSE.[35]

A meeting was arranged with the Outfit's top leadership, including Rio, Frank Nitti, and Circella. According to Browne, "The sense of the conversation was just this, that Bioff was there to enlist their aid in helping me become the International president, as he said that he thought they had connections in different places that they could probably use to get some influence to bear that would get me some votes [at the union convention]. He said that there was much money to be made."[36] Indeed Bioff dangled the prospect of what—at the time—was a huge amount of money. "Bioff told them that they would make a million dollars."[37]

Nitti and the other Outfit leaders saw the appeal of this venture. They had already gained influence over other prominent union officials; Bioff recalled that at this meeting, they mentioned Jerry Horan of the Building Service Employees Union and Mike Carrozzo of the Laborers as union leaders whom they already controlled. Browne's background added to the appeal of this proposition. "They said they could use a man like him," Bioff remembered. "He has a nice clean background, and they need a front man like him, it is very important to them."[38]

To make Browne president, the Outfit could draw on its nationwide connections with other gang leaders in other cities to help steer the IATSE election. Browne had been defeated in his 1932 bid for IATSE presidency when delegates from locals in St. Louis, New York City, Cleveland, and New Jersey voted for his opponent. Bioff testified that Nitti offered to use his contacts in those cities to bring those delegations around to support Browne at the next convention.[39] It was a classic example of the kind of interregional cooperation that organized crime groups had sought to facilitate through the creation of the national commission.

## IATSE

This strategy succeeded because several local affiliates of the International Alliance of Theatre and Stage Employes Union already had ties to organized crime. The origin of those ties has to do with the history of the union and the range of occupations that it included. Certain locals in the IATSE suffered from perennial problems with corruption, and organized crime groups had gained influence over some of those locals. Although they were scattered across the country in different cities, they tended to exist in similar situations. That pattern revealed much about the dynamics of union corruption in IATSE but also in organized labor in general.

The forerunners of IATSE dated back to the late 1800s, when the teams of craftsmen who accompanied traveling theatrical companies first organized local unions. Several of those locals came together and formed the national union in 1893. The new union claimed jurisdiction over all the men who worked behind the proscenium arch in theaters, from the carpenters who built sets to electricians who did the wiring and worked the lights. When the motion picture industry emerged in the early 1900s, IATSE expanded its jurisdiction to include both the motion picture operators, that is, the projectionists, and the craftsmen employed in the Hollywood studios.[40]

By the 1920s and 1930s, several local unions composed of projectionists had become notorious for their corruption.[41] The roots of the problem lay in the vulnerability of movie theater owners and in the power that union officials wielded over their membership. These conditions made abuses in union governance endemic.

The employers' vulnerability stemmed from the fact that when faced with a strike, movie theater owners had fewer options than their counterparts in other industries. A factory owner, for instance, might try to outlast a strike or relocate his operation to a place where organized labor was weak. If he stayed put, he could hope to draw enough revenue from accumulated inventory to get by and wait out the strikers, especially because the factory's operating costs dropped during a shutdown. But a movie theater owner lacked those options. He could not afford a significant interruption of his business because typically he faced high fixed costs in the form of film rental fees, which were usually paid a year in advance. At the same time, any job action completely cut a theater's revenue. Nor could a theater operator present the union with a credible threat to relocate to some other region.[42]

Given the employers' vulnerability, it required minimal resources for the union's leadership to wage a strike against a movie theater. The local did not need to mobilize a large number of men, only the one or two employees who worked in the projectionist's booth. Unlike labor organizations in other industries, the projectionists did not have to maintain extensive picket lines over long periods of time. A theater usually could not afford to stay closed for very long. And should a theater try to operate with nonunion projectionists, it often suffered from stink bombs or similar tactics, which were quite effective at discouraging customers. Fear of such events would drive families away and ruin a theater's business.[43] As one theater operator in Chicago explained to the FBI, "it would be impossible for his company to survive if the parents and children who entered his theatres did not have every feeling of security for themselves when patrons."[44]

The vulnerability of the employers enhanced the power of the union's leadership. Other unions needed to rally large numbers of members to the cause in order to win a strike, and that fact provided an implicit and continuing check on abuses by the union's leadership. Union officials knew that members who disapproved of their leaders could not be counted on in a time of crisis. But in the projectionists' locals, the leadership needed only the support of a handful of men to win a strike. Given the kinds of tactics that won a theater strike, those supporters might well have disreputable backgrounds.[45] Not everyone knew how to make a stink bomb or was prepared to throw one into a crowded theater.[46] In other words, the union leader in a projectionists' local might successfully organize the industry with the help of a few individuals with backgrounds in strong-arm work and no real connection to the workforce.

Other features of the projectionists' work further increased the power of the union's leadership. Members labored in isolation from each other in projection booths spread across the city, one or two men to a booth. While union members in a manufacturing plant might easily congregate at the workplace and organize in opposition to their union's leadership, the only common meeting location for projectionists was the union hall, a place controlled by the leadership. This made it hard to organize an opposition group to challenge incumbent officers. Because a city had only a limited number of theaters, the projectionists' locals were small, typically numbering a few hundred members. This too discouraged opposition. Potential opponents had little chance of avoiding detection by union officials, who could easily monitor and move against a nascent opposition effort.[47]

The leadership's most powerful weapon, however, was their control over the available jobs. Work assignments usually came from the union hall, and even if a member found his own job at a movie theater, the union's leadership could arrange to have it taken away from him. Members known to oppose the leadership found it impossible to get steady work. Without a regular paycheck, they invariably had to let their union dues payments lapse, and soon they no longer belonged to the local. Those members seen as loyal supporters, however, obtained not just steady work but the best jobs available. This was a significant incentive since wages and hours varied dramatically. Union contracts typically had a range of pay scales and hours to fit the various kinds of theaters, from the first-run movie palaces to the smaller, independent neighborhood theaters. In Boston, for example, weekly pay ranged from $40 to $100 a week for projectionists' jobs. As a result, the leadership could wield an effective array of rewards and punishments to quell potential opposition and build up a group of devoted followers.[48]

The lack of tenable opposition fostered the abuse of power by officials in these locals. Members in several projectionists' locals complained that they had to pay bribes to their leadership in order to gain their union cards or to acquire a job. Members working at the better jobs often had to kick back part of their salary to the local's officials. The union's funds went unaccounted for, and periodically members were pressured to vote for bonuses to supplement the leadership's regular salary.[49]

In many locals, there emerged what was known as the permit racket. Instead of bringing new members into the local, the leadership charged a fee, as much as a $1,000, for a permit to work in unionized theaters. Typically, the union required that in addition to the initial fee, the permit holder had to pay 10 percent of his salary to the union. Permit men, as they were known, often remained stuck in this situation for years, contributing large amounts of money to a union that would not grant them membership or give them any kind of security. Meanwhile, the permit fees, which added up to substantial money, fell under the control of the local's leadership, who used the money to supplement their income.[50] Finally, the same leaders who engaged in such malfeasance tended also to collude with employers because in neither case did they have to fear a backlash from their membership.[51]

Chicago's IATSE Local 110 typified the climate of corruption, intimidation, and violence that could exist in projectionists' locals. Thomas Maloy controlled the local for most of its history until his death in 1935. At five and a half feet tall, Maloy was not a big man and he carried himself in a quiet, "almost deferential manner."[52] But he had gained a well-earned reputation for toughness that went back to Local 110's early days. In 1916, he literally battled with officials in the Electrical Workers Union for jurisdiction over the men working as motion picture projectionists: the dispute was settled only after open gun fights in the city's streets.[53] From that turbulent beginning, he built the union into a thriving institution that included almost all of the city's movie projectionists and that held collective bargaining contracts covering every movie house in Chicago.[54]

The atmosphere of violence continued even after the union was well established. Maloy hired bodyguards and others who might be described as professional toughs or simply gunmen. Ralph O'Hara was one of those men. Officially listed as an organizer on Local 110's payroll, FBI agents who interviewed O'Hara in 1941 described him as "one of Chicago's former outstanding muscle men" and "a polished hoodlum type individual who has been connected with Chicago rackets for quite some time." They noted that his business card read, "Every insurance protection," and commented in their report that the phrase "speaks for itself when the background of O'Hara is considered."[55] In 1933, O'Hara shot and killed the leader of an insurgent group within Local 110. The shooting took place in the union headquarters, where O'Hara claimed the man had pulled a gun on him. Two years earlier, another one of Maloy's opponents was killed the day before he was scheduled to testify before a grand jury investigating Local 110's affairs.[56]

The local's history and the character of its leadership added an element of physical risk to reinforce the economic intimidation that members faced. In 1933, several members complained to the president of the American Federation of Labor, William Green, about the presence at union meetings of "professional gunmen and killers."[57] A Local 110 permit man wrote to Westbrook Pegler that the members "are constantly shoved around, without any voice in the organization. . . . As you know, the least attempt to express your rights, and if you weren't slugged or beaten up, you naturally would have to move to an entirely new industry."[58]

Meanwhile Maloy used his domination of Local 110 to become a wealthy man. He accepted payments from theater owners, and he had a stake in companies that did business with them, for example a cleaning contractor that specialized in deodorizing movie theaters. With a couple hundred permit men paying 10 percent of their salaries, the union generated considerable revenue, and Maloy apparently embezzled freely from the local's funds. After his death, an audit of the union's financial records showed a $500,000 short-age.[59] Taking two of the most egregious years as an example of his activities, the Internal Revenue Department of the U.S. Treasury charged that in 1930 and 1932, Maloy's income was $114,837 and $150,174, enormous amounts back then; when adjusted for inflation, $150,174 would be equivalent to over $2 million in 2003. Maloy's official salary made up only a small portion of that money.[60]

But the illicit source of this wealth left Maloy vulnerable. Like individuals in other illegal enterprises he could not depend upon the police to protect his wealth, and the scale of that wealth made him a target. As a result, even an intimidating figure like Maloy's bodyguard Ralph O'Hara found Local 110 a scary place to work. According to the FBI, O'Hara recalled that "the Operators Union [Local 110] was always in a turmoil, and that frequently Maloy would get a telephone call stating, 'Well, we're going to knock you off.' In fact every day you would think you were going to be killed."[61]

In these circumstances, it was practically inevitable that Maloy would form a relationship with the Outfit. The exact origins of that relationship remain unclear, but Circella, the Outfit leader who came to oversee Bioff and Browne, later told the FBI that it had been well-known that Maloy "acted generally on his own responsibility while maintaining more or less friendly relations with a few members of the Chicago mob."[62] These "friendly relations" had a financial component; Bioff reported that Maloy shared his payoffs with the Outfit.[63]

The situations in other large cities followed a similar pattern. In New York City, Sam Kaplan, the longtime leader of Motion Picture Operators' Local 306, had a squad of bodyguards and used them to stifle opposition within the local. The permit racket flourished, and after Kaplan was ousted in 1932 a union audit found $200,000 missing from the funds.[64] His successor as the head of Local 306 quickly came to terms with Louis Buchalter, a promi-nent Jewish organized crime figure. In May 1933, AFL president William Green received a report that the new administration of Local 306 had paid Buchalter's organization $125,000. In addition, Green's source said that Bu-chalter's people now were "on the payroll" at Local 306.[65] Reports indicate a similar kind of relationship in other cities. In Newark, Louis Kaufman led Newark's Local 144 in partnership with Abner "Longie" Zwillman, a former bootlegger who had become the most prominent gangster in New Jersey.[66] FBI informants described the same pattern in Detroit and St. Louis.[67]

The similarities were more than coincidence. The dynamics of collective bargaining in the industry created conditions that fostered corruption in the projectionists' locals. At the same time, corrupt local union leaders were likely to form relationships with the dominant organized crime group in their area. These relationships amounted to a kind of licensing by organized crime, which taxed union corruption in a manner comparable to the way it taxed other illegal activity, such as gambling and prostitution.

These various local arrangements gained new significance in 1934. Following Bioff's suggestion, the Outfit drew on its nationwide contacts with gangs in other cities to help influence IATSE's election. Browne and Bioff attended a second meeting to plan his election as head of IATSE that spring in which the Outfit leaders were accompanied by Buchalter, the New York gangster.[68] By virtue of his control over IATSE Local 306 in New York, Buchalter held a pivotal position in the upcoming union election. As the largest IATSE local in the country, Local 306 would cast the most votes at the convention.[69]

According to Bioff, Nitti asked Buchalter to contact the New York Mafia leader Charles "Lucky" Luciano, "and deliver this message to him: That Local 306 is to go for Browne." Bioff recalled, "Buchalter's answer to that was, 'I don't have to see Lucky [Luciano] on that, Frank, I can handle that myself, I will take care of it.'" Buchalter also promised to contact the Newark gangster Longie Zwillman and "see to it that Longie delivers" the votes of the union under his control, IATSE Local 244.[70] Arrangements with other gang leaders in other cities presumably followed, although Bioff and Browne were not privy to them.

Perhaps because of these preparations, the actual IATSE convention in 1934 was anticlimactic. The Outfit had sent five men to accompany Browne and Bioff to the convention, and given their backgrounds, it seems clear their job was to intimidate any opposition. Robert "Big Bob" McCullough, who was one of this group, allegedly had been one of the gunmen who killed an assistant state's attorney, William McSwiggin, in 1926. He was also the suspect in three other murders.[71] The other members of this team had similar backgrounds, and IATSE delegates later told the FBI that the presence of these men at the convention did create an impression. But beyond making their presence known, the men from the Outfit did nothing more than lounge around the convention hotel.[72]

Nothing else, it turned out, was required. The incumbent president of the union, William Elliot, had authorized a disastrous strike in Hollywood the year before and chose not to run for reelection. Browne had the support of the New York City and Chicago delegations already sewed up, and he was therefore a very strong candidate. No one decided to run against him, perhaps because he already had a commanding lead, perhaps because of the presence of McCullough and his colleagues, or perhaps a combination of the two. Either way, Browne was elected by a unanimous vote. The Outfit now had installed their choice as the president of IATSE. Browne promptly named Bioff as his personal representative, making him a powerful figure in the union.[73]

## George Scalise

Three years later, in 1937, Scalise too would become the president of a national union with the assistance of the Outfit. The details of his journey to that position differed in specifics from Browne's, but throughout his career Scalise had been involved in unions that resembled the projectionists' locals of IATSE. Scalise's personal history also highlights the local-level dynamics that fostered union corruption. Compared to Browne, though, Scalise was less a labor leader than he was an organized crime figure, albeit one that did not fit the popular profile of a mobster.

By all accounts, Scalise was a pleasant, even a charming man, who unlike Bioff did not look the part of a menacing gangster. The press referred to him as a dapper dresser, and news photos show him round-faced, invariably smiling, wearing tasteful formal attire.[74] In one photo he was proudly standing behind a seated Mayor Fiorello LaGuardia during a set of collective bargaining negotiations; not publicity shy, he offers the camera a friendly look.[75] He was married, had a teenaged daughter, and lived in a modest house in Brooklyn near his parents, whom he helped to support.[76] Internal union correspondence reveals a man comfortable committing his thoughts to writing, who displayed a sure grasp of the bureaucratic intricacies of his organization.[77] He cultivated his contacts in the AFL, presenting influential people like the Federation's general counsel Joseph Padway with generous Christmas gifts.[78] This was a man who sought respectability, so much so that he worked to gather influential supporters for a presidential pardon that would restore the civil rights he lost because of his one criminal conviction, twenty-seven years earlier.[79]

That desire for respectability is apparent from the biography he provided to BSEIU's journal in 1940. It told the story of a hardworking immigrant who achieved success by helping his fellow working man; he was a union idealist, he asserted, despite his youthful mistake.[80]

Scalise was indeed an immigrant, but beyond that the self-portrait tended to obscure rather than reveal the true nature of his career path. He had been born in the province of Calabria in southern Italy in 1897. Named Gaspare, he was the twelfth of thirteen children. The family immigrated to the United States when he was a year and a half old and settled in Brooklyn, where he took the Americanized name George. By his own account, he left school at the age of fifteen and tried a number of jobs, including clerking at a Manhattan jewelry store. He worked there, he claimed, until the time of his arrest on a Mann Act violation in 1913. Scalise's self-portrait had little to say about that incident, but according to his probation report, the arrest stemmed from two separate trips he had taken to Boonton, New Jersey, with an eighteen-year-old woman from Brooklyn. Trial records indicated that he forced her to have sexual relations with several men and then took the money they paid her. The harsh details of the crime spurred the trial judge to issue a stiff prison sentence; Scalise served four years and six months in the federal penitentiary in Atlanta.[81] Upon his release, he returned to Brooklyn where, according to his autobiography, a series of working experiences drew him gradually into the union movement.[82]

Police records and the recollections of his associates provide a different story. In the Bath Beach section of Brooklyn where he grew up, Scalise had been one of a group of young men who allegedly shook down local store owners.[83] His Mann Act conviction also suggests involvement in some type of organized prostitution ring. By the early 1930s, he was firmly connected to the Mafia. He had also moved into a specific kind of criminal activity, and it was this that led to his involvement in organized labor: he had become a professional fixer. He used that skill to make his way in a part of the labor movement where arrangements and side deals, backed up with the threat of violence, offered businessmen stability and security for a price. This was a marginal area in the world of organized labor, largely unwritten about by labor historians but still a significant part of the union movement in New York and other cities in the 1920s and 1930s.[84] Here organized labor gained a firm foothold through collusive arrangements that benefited employers but often sacrificed the interests of the workers.

He could play a role in this world because of his links to the Mafia. The specific nature of those ties—whether he was an associate or a member—remain unknown, but clearly he was connected. His most important relationship was with Anthony Carfano, also known as Little Augie Pisano or sometimes just "the Kid." Allegedly a *capo*, or captain, in what became known as the Genovese crime family, Carfano ran a crew in Brooklyn. In the early days of Prohibition, Carfano had accompanied fellow Brooklyn crime figure Al Capone to Chicago and spent some years there working in Capone's organization. Back in Brooklyn, he had a reputation for toughness, but he also maintained a much less flamboyant appearance than his old associate Capone. Carfano dressed conservatively and, as the *New York Times* put it, "in appearance, resembled a business executive." He apparently cultivated that image, making his headquarters in a downtown Brooklyn office building.[85]

Scalise once explained his relationship with Carfano this way: "We're partners." Carfano got half of everything that Scalise received.[86] In return, Carfano provided Scalise with influential backing and a range of connections. With Carfano to vouch for him, Scalise maintained contacts with a number of other prominent criminal figures. He had close contacts with the Lower East Side gang leader Louis Buchalter. He allegedly had ties with Joey Amberg, a leading figure in the Brooklyn gang scene who was later pushed aside by the Jewish-Italian organized crime group dubbed by the press Murder, Inc.[87] These were relationships that Scalise could draw upon to serve his needs. A police wiretap on Scalise's office in 1934 picked him up using Carfano's contacts to arrange for James Plumeri, a Lucchese crime family member, to damage some trucks in lower Manhattan, apparently as part of Scalise's efforts to organize Teamsters Local 272.[88]

These connections and his personal style apparently made him a skilled fixer. While this might not be an expertise commonly put on resumes, it was for that time and place a valuable asset. In the world of illegal arrangements—such as offering or accepting bribes, or making collusive agreements to limit competition—participants risk legal and financial repercussions if one party to the deal proves untrustworthy. Moreover, should the deal go sour, the individuals involved cannot seek legal remedies. It takes a particular type of person to instill trust and to offer the needed assurances that the agreed-upon conditions of the deal will be met. A fixer does not have to be a tough guy, but he must have access to the kind of extralegal force that all parties know can be called upon should circumstances warrant it. Scalise was both well connected and charming, and the police wiretap on his office in 1934 revealed a range of people calling on him to broker their illegal arrangements. For instance, in April 1934, Louis Block, later an official in the Butchers Union, called Scalise to ask him to use his contacts at the Brooklyn district attorney's office to fix the case of his brother, Max Block, who was facing trial on a murder charge. What precise action Scalise took remains unclear, but a year later court records showed that a Brooklyn judge entered a verdict of not guilty in Max Block's case.[89] Scalise was practiced at making such arrangements. Four days before Block's phone call, the wiretap recorded Scalise explaining to a Jimmy Sabella that "it would cost five bills to get a case thrown out in the Coney Island Magistrate's Court."[90]

Scalise's activities do not fit the standard, cinematic depiction of organized crime, but they exemplify a mainstay of what groups like the Italian American Mafia actually do. Crimes of violence, such as extortion and robbery and vice, garner attention in most popular accounts of the Mafia. But in these endeavors, organized criminal groups have little advantage over more temporary bands of criminals who may have a greater willingness to engage in violence or better access to illegal goods and services. As brokers of illegal arrangements, however, organized criminal groups do enjoy real advantages. Their relative longevity, the geographic reach of their contacts, and their ability to adjudicate potential disputes all enhance their ability to serve as a dependable brokerage service in a wide array of settings.[91] Labor racketeering exemplified just such an opportunity, and in the 1930s organized crime figures like Scalise moved in.

It was as a broker, not as an aggrieved worker, that Scalise came to play a role in the labor movement. Louis Marcus, a labor lawyer who became a close associate of Scalise, testified that in 1929 Scalise asked his help in setting up a Brooklyn branch of Teamsters Local 272, a union of parking garage workers. This marked Scalise's first involvement in organized labor. According to Marcus, Scalise told him he would get the local's charter from "the Dutchman," a reference to the gangster Arthur Flegenheimer, also known as Dutch Schultz, who controlled Local 272's Manhattan office. Over the next couple of years, Marcus did the legal work as Scalise built up the Brooklyn branch of Local 272, setting its offices up in the same downtown office building where Carfano made his headquarters.[92]

Unions of parking garage employees attracted gangsters because organization could quickly be achieved through selective acts of violence. Damage to cars parked in nonunion garages—ice-pick punctures to the tires or slashed upholstery—could quickly force an employer to sign his employees into the union. And union organization in turn provided a cover for corralling the businessmen into an employers' organization whose dues could be tapped by organized crime. In spite of the use of force against employers in such an organizing campaign, this was not a case of out-and-out extortion; employers enjoyed some real benefits. The collusive arrangement between a union and an employers' organization offered parking garage owners a way to manage competition. Employers' associations could set uniform rates and limit the entrance of new competitors.[93]

For the average union member, on the other hand, such a union often brought little change except the addition of regular dues deducted from their pay. Indeed, the way the union was built made such conditions likely.

As union organizers, Scalise and others of his type went into the labor movement to make money; they came from outside the ranks of workers in the industry, with whom they did not really identify. Nor did they depend upon those workers to organize the union through mass picketing and long strikes. Instead they used selective acts of violence committed by a few individuals who probably had links to organized crime. The situation in the parking garages was similar to what existed in the projectionists' locals of IATSE. Free from having to depend on a mobilized, united membership, the union's leadership could safely ignore the members' needs or sacrifice them to the interests of the employers. As a result, as unskilled workers scattered across a wide area and laboring in small shops, garage employees had little knowledge of their union and often no say in its affairs.

Police reports indicate that in the early 1930s, Scalise worked closely with Louis Levine, a Brooklyn parking garage owner, to build up the Kings County Garage Association at the same time as Local 272 steadily enrolled the borough's garage employees. This twofold organizing campaign was marked by occasional reports of violence and property destruction.[94] Levine's participation suggests the benefits that at least some employers saw in the collusive organization. Comments from the newly enrolled union membership, however, indicate that they failed to enjoy similar gains; the union's wage rate often amounted to less than what nonunion workers made.[95] One member, writing to the AFL and referring to Local 272, complained, "This is a racket all over." He described an organization where members were enrolled without their knowledge by employers who simply began deducting the men's dues and never informed them about the union pay scale. Members had no say in the affairs of their union; according to the letter, "this bunch of racketeers . . . run this Union, just as they please."[96]

The organization of garage workers in Brooklyn stemmed not from any emerging worker militancy but rather from an effort among employers to control competition. Scalise's history draws attention to this aspect of the important workplace changes of the Great Depression. The standard explanation of union growth in the 1930s highlights the workers' quest for stability in response to the sweeping economic uncertainties they faced.[97] A parallel quest on the part of many small employers, however, also played a role, as bosses were willing to corral their workers into organizations they believed could bring market stability.[98] While genuine union organizers used this opportunity to achieve significant gains for workers, Scalise and others responded in a more entrepreneurial fashion. The needs of employers and the more hospitable organizing environment of the 1930s offered a chance to make money.

Like a businessman seeking new opportunities for growth, Scalise pursued a range of ventures within organized labor. According to the labor lawyer, Marcus, in 1930, a year after he began working on Teamsters Local 272, Scalise hired him to set up a beautician's local in Brooklyn on the understanding that in this operation Scalise would be partners with the gangster Joey Amberg. A couple of years later, he told Marcus he was going to acquire the charter for a nonkosher butchers local. He explained that the venture would be a shared undertaking with Carfano, who would help finance it.[99] The collusive nature of this enterprise became clear a couple of weeks later when Scalise asked Marcus to form an association of Italian-American butchers, an employers' association to go along with the new union.[100] Later, Scalise arranged for another associate, Isidore "Izzy"Schwartz, to get a charter for a window cleaners' local from the Building Service Employees International Union (BSEIU). Union pickets then worked to support a strong employers' association among Brooklyn's window cleaners. The association policed the industry, forbidding contractors from taking any members' customers and imposing a regular schedule of dues payments.[101]

## BSEIU and Organized Crime

Through his associate Schwartz and the window cleaning venture, Scalise began his rise in the Building Service Union. To get Schwartz a charter from BSEIU for a window washers' union, in 1932 Scalise had turned to his Mafia sponsor, Carfano, asking him to use his influence. By this time, the Outfit had forced BSEIU's president Jerry Horan to accept their control, assigning Capone's brother-in-law Francis Maritote to supervise Horan. Carfano drew on his old ties with the Capone gang in order to gain Scalise the union charter he wanted.[102]

In the years that followed, Scalise used those same ties to gain an official position in the Building Service Union and then quickly move up the ranks to president. When the BSEIU's representative in New York City retired in 1934, Scalise asked Carfano to help him get the job. According to Schwartz, Scalise told him, "that he would get in touch with Augie [Carfano] and let Augie go to work out there [in Chicago] and see what he can do for him." A couple of months later, BSEIU's President Horan appointed Scalise to be the union's eastern representative. Scalise explained to Schwartz that a deal had been arranged with the Chicago mob for Carfano and Scalise to get 50 percent of the union's proceeds from any newly organized members in the East: they would be operating the BSEIU in the East on a commission basis.[103]

In April 1937, Scalise got word that President Horan was ill and thought to be on his deathbed. Schwartz later testified that talking with Scalise, he raised the possibility of Scalise becoming the next president. "Well, we laughed at it—he laughed at it for a moment and then he thought of the possibilities about it there, he would try for it; so he called Augie then." Carfano agreed to help, but he was not hopeful. After hanging up the phone, Scalise told Schwartz, "Augie told him 'O.K.' he will see what he can do, but not to bank on it."[104]

In the end, Scalise became president because of the political problems that beset Thomas Burke, the candidate originally sponsored by the Outfit. Burke had gained power in a Chicago BSEIU local after the murder—apparently by the Outfit—of its previous leader, Louis Alterie. Burke's ties to the Outfit were a matter of common knowledge within the union, and several of the BSEIU board members, who would be voting to pick Horan's replacement, viewed him with distaste. In addition, another candidate from Chicago, William McFetridge, had greater seniority within the union, and he threatened to divide the vote of the Chicago officers. Scalise became a compromise candidate. Since his ties to organized crime were not well known, he did not cause the same objections as had Burke. An outsider, he offered a face-saving alternative to the Chicago officers, and in the end he won the presidency by a unanimous vote of the board.[105]

## Conclusion

Like Browne and Bioff, Scalise was a valuable asset to the Outfit. All three men had relatively clean criminal records that obscured their current strong connections to organized crime. As front men, they could hold powerful positions in national unions without drawing undue attention. At the same time, the Outfit could use the official positions of Browne, Bioff, and Scalise to promote a variety of illegal schemes, such as generating illicit payoffs from employers and embezzling union funds. Such schemes offered profitable new ventures for organized crime. The ability to gain control of a national union also reflected the evolution of organized crime in this era. The Outfit had demonstrated the continuing utility of the interregional connections that organized crime groups had developed over the course of the 1920s and 1930s.

Nor were these the only two unions in which the Outfit had become interested. The effort to engineer McLane's election to the presidency of the Hotel and Restaurant Employees Union had failed, thanks at least partly to McLane's sabotage. But Bioff told the FBI that the Chicago mob wielded control over top officials in several other national unions, including the Laborers, the Laundry Workers, and the Operating Engineers.[106] In other words, Browne, Bioff and Scalise were part of a larger trend. Organized crime's involvement was changing the nature of union corruption, from being only a problem that beset particular local unions to one that could affect members of a national union all across the country. The infiltration made the problem of union corruption worse. Regardless of how well their own local union was run, if the national officers of a union were tied to organized crime, as Browne and Scalise were, corruption would impact every member in every local.

The careers of these three men also offer useful lessons about the problem of union corruption at the local level. The projectionists' locals of IATSE and Scalise's Teamsters Local 272 shared basic similarities that fostered corruption. Especially in fields where mass picketing was not necessary to achieve organization and where workers labored in small numbers at widely scattered worksites, an exploitative union like Teamsters Local 272 or IATSE's Local 110 could emerge. This opportunity was further pronounced in small locals where the leadership controlled the work assignments of their members. These union leaders faced no effective check on their power, a situation that invited abuses. The officials who capitalized on these opportunities were better seen as union entrepreneurs, eager to profit from a labor organization in whatever way was possible. In a collusive setting like the parking garage industry, this would mean creating only the most minimal labor organization while pitching the union as a tool to help the employers. In the projectionists' locals, a union entrepreneur could profit from permit fees, kickbacks from workers, and graft from theater owners. The dynamics of collective bargaining in these situations created a kind of netherworld of organized labor, a network of locals that had long betrayed every ideal of the larger labor movement.

By engineering the elections of Browne and Scalise, the Outfit was attempting to pull national unions into the same netherworld. But in doing so, they faced significant obstacles. The dynamics of collective bargaining were different outside these perennially corrupt locals. The employers were not as vulnerable or as eager for assistance in controlling competition, and the members were not as easy to cow. And as Pegler would demonstrate, corruption at the national level would generate public outrage in a way that local union corruption never had.

Figure 4.1: On June 26, 1938, Hollywood's business leaders came to the White House to meet with President Franklin Roosevelt and discuss cooperation between their industry and the government. This photograph, taken on that occasion, includes several of the film industry leaders who would later testify that William Bioff and George Browne had extorted half a million dollars from them. From left to right: Barney Balaban (Paramount), George Schaefer (United Artists), Harry Cohn (Columbia), Sidney Kent (Twentieth Century-Fox), Nicholas Schenck (Loew's-MGM), Nate Blumberg (Universal), Will Hays (Motion Picture Producers and Exhibitors Association), Albert Warner (Warner Brothers), Leo Spitz (RKO). Courtesy Bison Archives.

# 4

## The Hollywood Case

### *Racketeering in the 1930s from a Business Perspective*

One aspect of these racketeering scandals garnered the lion's share of media attention: the way union corruption affected employers. The criminal indictments and high-profile racketeering trials that followed Pegler's exposé placed the most dramatic emphasis on the plight of the businessmen. This emphasis may have been only because they provided prosecutors with the testimony necessary to make criminal cases. This was true for the biggest case, the federal government's prosecution in 1943 of seven Outfit leaders, a case that drew on the testimony of Hollywood's most powerful executives.

Looking back at that racketeering trial as it was coming to a close in December 1943, the *New York Sun* reminded its readers why the case had attracted so much notoriety. Partly it was a matter of who the witnesses were. "They included a good cross-section of who's who among movie producers in Hollywood." But even more, it was the stories they told. "The stories, fantastic in the extreme, many of them pictured heads of huge industries literally quivering in their boots as men of Bioff's ilk talked out of the corners their mouths and demanded huge sums on pain of having their vast enterprises smashed by strikes and labor troubles. And tribute was paid many times."[1]

In the *Sun*'s article, one particular episode received special attention. "One of these stories was told by no less an individual than Nicholas Schenck, president of Loew's, Inc., who related how he and another movie executive went to a swanky New York hotel and in a room occupied by Bioff and Browne tossed large packages on the twin beds. While they stood there uneasily, Bioff and Browne each opened a package and slowly counted out the $25,000 which each contained."[2] Other news reports highlighted the same episode, as have most subsequent accounts.[3]

The scene's appeal stemmed from the fact that it encapsulated what many saw as the significance of the scandal—union corruption had brought about a dramatic reversal of roles. Otherwise powerful businessmen made craven visits to the "swanky" hotel room of a couple of two-bit hoods, who had the executives wait while they sat on their beds and counted out the money and only then gave the studio heads permission to leave. As one account noted, the executives were reduced to the role of "messenger boys."[4] They submitted to this treatment and offered up "tribute" out of fear; for all of their power and wealth, their businesses were vulnerable to threats made by Bioff and Browne. Union corruption gave men of Bioff's "ilk" a dangerous amount of power.

In the case of Scalise, the victimized businessmen were less glamorous—mainly cleaning contractors—but the story followed the same outline. When Scalise's indictment was announced in April 1940, the New York district attorney's office and the newspapers focused on allegations that Scalise had extorted vast sums of money from New York's employers. The front page headline in the *New York Times* read, "Scalise, Union Head, Seized in $100,000 Extortion Plot."[5] Other reports referred to this amount as a "$100,000 levy" that Scalise had exacted from employers over a period of three years. The story from the Associated Press included in its lead a reference to "Scalise's alleged tribute-fixing activities."[6]

But if the plight of the employers was the most prominent aspect of the scandal, it was also the most misunderstood. The trial testimony of employers misrepresented the dynamics of union corruption. An element of coercion did exist, but outside of the trial context, employers often cited economic gain when they explained why they made payments. To put it simply, they seized the chance to buy off a union leader because the alternatives, including engaging in honest collective bargaining, cost more and provided less security. Businessmen willingly dealt with organized crime because gangsters who controlled unions provided employers with a valuable economic service. Employers were less victims than they were customers.

## Employer Payoffs: Bribery vs. Extortion

Employers who pay money to union officials do so for a variety of reasons, but for prosecutors those payments fall into one of two categories: bribery or extortion. The difference lies in the motivation of the employer when he makes the payment. If the employer makes the payment in hopes of encouraging the union official to betray his responsibilities to his membership, then the money is deemed a bribe, and the employer is as culpable as the union official. But if the employer pays because of threats made by the union official, then the employer is a victim of extortion. The gray area is what constitutes a threat and what actually motivates the employer to make a payment.

Some degree of coercion occurs in any kind of collective bargaining. Even an honest union official, attempting to represent his membership and build the organization, must threaten employers with strikes and attempt to unionize nonunion businesses. And the success of a strike, or a threatened strike, depends upon the degree to which it will have an impact on the business in question. Job actions that do not appear likely to hurt a business do not bring results in collective bargaining. Employers often cite excessive collective bargaining demands by a union as a form of coercion; they are forced, as they put it, to make a payoff to get relief from these demands. But the difference between reasonable and excessive wage demands often depends on whether one is the employer or the employee, as anyone familiar with collective bargaining negotiations knows.

The haziness of the distinction between bribery and extortion means that how an exchange of money gets portrayed often depends on little more than who comes forward first to cooperate with prosecutors. This cooperation is pivotal because a criminal conviction in this type of case requires the testimony of one of the transaction's participants. For prosecutors, the difficulty lies in eliciting such testimony. Like other kinds of transactional crimes such as prostitution, neither party to a payoff is likely to be a willing witness for the prosecution.

In the Hollywood case, the employers came forward first, albeit reluctantly, and that fact shaped the direction of the criminal trials. The movie executives, who had made payments to Browne, Bioff, and their Outfit supervisor, Nick Circella, provided crucial testimony to federal prosecutors. But the executives did so only after one of the leaders in their business community, Joseph Schenck, had been convicted on tax charges in 1941. In exchange for leniency in his prison sentence, Schenck offered to help prosecutors develop a case against Bioff and Browne. Such an offer had much appeal because by this time Pegler's columns had made Bioff notorious.[7] To the U.S. attorney's office, it was worth some horse trading on Schenck's three-year jail sentence for tax evasion.

For his part, Schenck had the wherewithal to bring the other movie executives on board with the prosecution. Known as "Uncle Joe" in Hollywood circles, the *New York Times* observed in 1943, that "Mr. Schenck has always been recognized as a power behind 'the throne' in Hollywood matters generally."[8] He was the chairman of the board of Twentieth Century-Fox and, as another newspaper put it, "one of the most powerful figures in the movie world."[9] Schenck also chaired the producers' committee, which conducted labor relations for the Hollywood studios.[10]

His brother, Nicholas Schenck, led the largest movie company, Loew's, Inc., which controlled the most successful film studio, Metro-Goldwyn-Mayer (MGM), as a corporate subsidiary.[11] Nicholas was the younger of the two brothers but by all accounts an even more commanding presence. Longtime associates called him "General," and as one historian of Hollywood in this era noted, "he cultivated his power and enjoyed exercising it."[12] As the head of Loew's, he had plenty of power to exercise. According to another study of Hollywood in the 1930s, Loew's was, in terms of its assets and its profits, the "King of the Big Eight [studios] and of the motion picture industry of America."[13] The Schenck brothers made a potent combination, and together they exerted their influence to get other Hollywood studio executives to come forward.[14]

As a result, the case against Bioff and Browne became a kind of team effort. In the summer of 1941, federal prosecutors built their case against the two men by working hand in glove with George Z. Medalie, the former U.S. attorney in Manhattan who now represented Nicholas Schenck. Prosecutors told the FBI that "Medalie is 'acting in a super advisory capacity.'" Medalie, drawing on the Schencks' influence, contacted the various studio executives and arranged for their cooperation.[15] Normally prosecutors would be wary of this role being exercised by an outsider, who might be able to coordinate and steer the stories of potential grand jury witnesses. In this case, the U.S. attorney's office had no choice but to accept the involvement if they hoped to win a conviction.[16]

The testimony of the studio executives led to Bioff and Browne's convictions on extortion charges in the fall of 1941. It proved crucial again in the 1943 trial of the Outfit leaders. In return, none of these businessmen faced prosecution for their actions. Indeed, when the Treasury Department proposed filing tax charges against the studio executives in 1941, after Browne and Bioff's convictions, the federal prosecutor handling the case objected vigorously. He told the FBI agents working the case, "The assistance of the corporations was absolutely essential in convicting Bioff and Browne and will be essential in convicting other persons now being considered for prosecution."[17]

The criminal trials, as a result, promoted a simple, one-sided explanation of the payoffs. Drawing on the testimony of the studio executives, the prosecution portrayed the money exchanges between the union leaders and the employers as clear-cut examples of extortion. The Justice Department's indictment of Bioff and Browne in May 1941 charged that the two men had received payments from employers that were "induced by wrongful use of force and fear." The employers made these payments, according to the indictment, "for protection; viz., to prevent and dissuade said defendants from restraining, impeding and obstructing the production, interstate distribution and exhibition of motion pictures . . . and otherwise injuring and destroying and attempting to injure and destroy the business of said victims [the employers]."[18] Two years later, the indictment in the case involving the leaders of the Outfit used the same language.[19]

Nailing down this charge in court led the prosecutor to ask questions about the witnesses' state of mind. Thus, in questioning Loew's head Nicholas Schenck, the prosecutor in the 1943 trial asked, "I am not certain, Mr. Witness, if it is entirely clear when you said previously that if you did not pay your business would be ruined. Just would you explain that, how would your business be ruined if you did not pay, what was in your mind at that time?" Schenck emphasized the vulnerable position of his company: "The reason I made the two payments is, as I explained before, because we had to pay it or destroy our business, and I felt that it is my duty to our company and stockholders to pay rather than destroy our company."[20]

For prosecutors, this was the crucial point that had to be established by their witnesses. The judge presiding over the case explained to the jury in the 1943 trial, "Ample proof has been submitted that money was obtained. It is for the jury to decide whether this money was obtained by extortion or by bribery. If you find this money was obtained by bribery, you must acquit."[21] Under such circumstances, the prosecution needed testimony that offered a one-dimensional view of what took place. The movie executives obliged; so too did Browne and Bioff when later they chose to cooperate with federal authorities in the 1943 trial of the Outfit leaders in hopes of having their prison sentences reduced.

But if one looks at other sources besides the trial testimony, a more complex story emerges. In the months before the 1941 trial and then again before the 1943 trial, FBI agents interviewed potential prosecution witnesses, staking out who paid what amounts and why they paid. The FBI contacted a wider range of individuals than those who testified at trial, and the agents asked the kinds of follow-up questions that no prosecutor would raise in court. These accounts provide a very different picture of the payoffs. Similarly, the initial interviews with Bioff and Browne, after they decided to cooperate but before their trial testimony, offered a different explanation of the payoffs. Even the government itself, when it later pursued tax charges against the Outfit leadership, depicted the payments in a different light than it had in the trials of 1941 and 1943. In contrast to the trial testimony, the line between extortion and bribery was blurred in these accounts. Outside of court, the payoffs were represented as business transactions in which executives knowingly purchased a service from men who they understood were organized crime figures.

## Payments by Movie Theater Chains

The first payoffs in this scandal were by theater chain operators in Chicago and then New York in the spring and fall of 1935. The precipitating event in Chicago was the sudden death of Thomas Maloy, the notoriously corrupt head of Local 110, the IATSE movie projectionists' local. Maloy died after two blasts from a sawed-off shotgun and a volley of pistol shots were fired from a car that passed him as he drove on a busy highway towards Chicago's downtown on February 4, 1935.[22] No one was ever convicted for his murder, but most people concluded the Outfit had had him killed. An internal FBI report in 1941 noted, "Chicago police officials believe that Circella is probably actually responsible for the death of Thomas Maloy."[23] Almost immediately after Maloy's death, Circella ordered Browne to use his authority as president of IATSE to assume control over Local 110. In the resulting union trusteeship of the local, every member of Maloy's administration was ousted, and for all practical purposes Bioff and Circella now ran the union.[24] These maneuvers had a simple goal: the Outfit gained direct access to the sources of revenue that had made Maloy a wealthy man.

Frank Nitti, the head the Outfit, then sent Bioff out to generate some payoff money. The pretext for Bioff's demands was the language in Local 110's collective bargaining contract that governed how many employees a theater had to use to staff its projectionist's booth. Up to the mid-1920s, the standard had been one man in the booth, but that changed when movies with sound first emerged around 1926. Early sound films used a separate phonograph player that needed to be synchronized with the film in the projector. IATSE locals could reasonably argue that the new technology required the addition of a second man in the booths, and this became the requirement in many local union contracts. Around 1929, the technology shifted again with the proliferation of sound-on-film systems that no longer needed a separate, synchronized phonograph player. At the same time, the Great Depression cut movie theater revenues, forcing them to look for ways to reduce costs.

The result was a wave of labor strife involving projectionists' locals across the country as theater owners struggled to eliminate contract language requiring the second man in the booth.[25]

In Chicago, this dispute resulted in a bitter ten-week strike in 1931 involving Local 110. City authorities intervened to negotiate a compromise settlement that allowed smaller theaters an exemption from the two-man requirement. The larger theaters would still have to have two men in the booth, but in return Local 110 granted a 20 percent wage reduction. Continued discontent among theater operators led to a later modification of that compromise, allowing theaters who were in financial trouble to appeal to have the second man removed from their projection booths.[26]

This compromise provided a financial windfall to Maloy. By granting him the discretion to decide which theaters deserved an exemption from the two-man rule, the settlement led to widespread payoffs by theater operators. Maloy even negotiated a standard payoff amount with the head of the Chicago Exhibitors' Association, the leading employers' group for movie theater operators. In return for $1,060, a theater operator could remove one man from a booth. There was a straightforward financial logic to that amount of money. Projectionists averaged a weekly wage of $106, so $1,060 was equivalent to ten weeks' salary: consenting to the payoff saved the operators forty-two weeks of salary, or $4,452. In effect Maloy was charging a 24 percent commission.[27] His take from these payoffs was quite large. To cite one example, Warner Brothers, which operated a chain of theaters in Chicago, paid Maloy $26,600 in 1932 to reduce its labor costs.[28]

In the spring of 1935, with Maloy no longer among the living, Nitti ordered Bioff to tap the same vein. According to the FBI summary of Bioff's account, the Outfit leader directed Bioff to tell the theater operators "that Browne had been elected President on a program assuring members of I.A.T.S.E. that it was his purpose to restore two projectionists in each of the theaters." Bioff acknowledged "that this was merely a threat" but claimed that Nitti had said "it must be carried out until the representatives of the theatre companies saw fit to compromise by offering to pay graft as a consideration for avoiding the necessity of employing more than one projectionist."[29] Bioff approached the executives at the three largest theater chains in Chicago: Balaban and Katz, Warner Brothers, and S and S Theaters.[30]

Noting their recent transactions with Maloy, the executives complained about double billing. But after some negotiations to reduce Bioff's demands, they agreed to a $100,000 payment. Each theater chain would contribute to the $100,000 in proportion to their size, with Balaban and Katz putting in

$60,000, Warner Brothers $30,000, and S and S $10,000.[31] John Balaban, an executive with the Balaban and Katz chain, recalled discussing the demand with his boss at the parent corporation, Paramount Pictures. It was, they decided, the best of two bad alternatives. According to the FBI summary of their interview with Balaban, he explained, "If a payment was not made, they would be forced to absorb a great many operators at high salaries and that such salaries could not be absorbed by the corporation."[32] The stark choice presented to employers makes this look like a clear-cut case of extortion. Bioff himself told the FBI that the demand to restore the extra man to the projectionists' booths was one he knew the theaters could not afford. "They would go bankrupt with the way conditions were at the time," he said.[33]

But subsequent payments by the theater chains in Chicago were more problematic. Over the next several years, from 1936 to 1940, Balaban and Katz made payments totaling $138,000 to Bioff, and then Circella; Warner Brothers paid $91,000, and S and S Theaters $103,000, or a total equivalent to $4.3 million in 2003 dollars.[34] This money was not paid in response to any threats from Bioff to reimpose a second man in the projection booths. Instead, theater executives described these payments in terms of purchasing a particular kind of service.

One of the most detailed explanations came from Morris Leonard, an attorney who took over management of the Chicago Exhibitors Association in 1936. He eventually served as the conduit for the payoffs from Balaban and Katz and Warner Brothers. After the 1935 payment to Bioff, both companies had sought to distance themselves from these transactions by asking Leonard to handle their labor relations with Local 110. In taking on this task, however, Leonard had not intended to be just a bagman. Initially he hoped to avoid offering payoffs, and so he focused on the collective bargaining process, meeting with Labor Wage Scale Board of Local 110 and making the theater operators' case for moderating the union's wage demands.[35]

But he soon found the experience frustrating and turned for help to Circella. Leonard knew Circella socially through contact at Circella's café, the Yacht Club. Leonard would have been familiar with Circella's status in the Outfit. Presumably Bioff had informed Leonard of Circella's role in regards to Local 110, but if he did not know already, Circella explained it to Leonard at their first meeting. Leonard told the FBI that "Circella indicated by his conversation" to him "that he was in complete charge of labor in Chicago in connection with stage hands and [motion picture] operators." He was the man to see, in other words. And although he was a notorious gangster, Circella proved to be a more responsive audience for Leonard than the officials at Local 110.[36]

Leonard continued to meet with Local 110's Wage Scale Board, but secretly he began more earnest negotiations with Circella. "His discussions with Circella," Leonard recalled, "usually consisted of talk about the prices which the Exhibitors Association of Chicago would have to pay Circella for his assistance in helping the Association maintain some semblance of what they considered a fair wage based on practice, experience and precedence." Leonard was bargaining with a notorious organized crime figure for assistance. Specifically Leonard was paying for Circella's ability to force Local 110 to accept what the employers offered. Circella could do this because the local would need permission from the national headquarters of IATSE to go on strike. Browne would never grant such permission without Circella's say-so.[37]

The FBI summarized Leonard's version of the arrangement this way: "Leonard is of the opinion that if the I.A. [IATSE national headquarters] had permitted the local to strike, it would have gone out on strike. The men never got the increase [the local union wanted] and they never went out on strike because the I.A. officials would not give authorization to Local #110 to strike because it was part of the understanding which Leonard reached with Circella when he paid the $35,000 that the I.A. officials would refuse to grant locals permission to strike in order to enforce [their collective bargaining] demands."[38] Without the ability to strike, Local 110's members had to take what the employers offered.

The motive for these payoffs was economic advantage, not fear. Again, from the FBI reports: "Leonard stated that he had no fear of any violence for himself at the hands of Circella or any member of the local. Leonard stated his real fear was that the wage scale would be hoisted to a point where it would be uneconomical for Balaban & Katz Corporation to continue to do business." And if that happened, "It would be necessary for the theatres in Chicago to have [an] open shop." The resulting strike would disrupt business enormously. "Leonard stated that he realized that the expedient way to avoid such conditions was to make the best bargain with Circella that was possible and to make the payments under the arrangement." It was a standard business arrangement in this industry. "Leonard stated that in reference to these negotiations with Circella, that it was the usual method employed in the theatre industry to avoid labor strikes and it was the only way to protect patrons of the theatre from possible harm and discomfort."[39]

For Balaban and Katz, these payments were a smart business move and not a holdup; the same was true for other theater chains who made payoffs. Local 110 members had taken a 20 percent pay cut in 1931, ostensibly in return for keeping two men in the projection booths. By the mid-1930s, however, the booths had only one man and the members agitated to get their former wage level restored.[40] The payments to Circella ensured that would not happen. At Balaban and Katz's parent company, Paramount Pictures, the corporation's general counsel, Austin Keough, explained the math to FBI agents. The company had paid money "to have the union officials refrain from calling strikes when they were making demands for large wage increases usually amounting to 25% to 30%. The payments to Bioff and Dean [Circella's alias] would represent approximately 5% of the payroll instead of meeting the demands to pay the union members a 25% to 30% wage increase."[41]

Money given to Circella amounted to a commission, which he charged employers in return for insuring them substantial savings on wages. In 1938, theater owners forced a further 10 percent wage cut on Local 110, and Circella told Leonard to assess the members of the Exhibitors Association a standard fee of $300 per theater. The terms of this exchange and the role of organized crime were crystal clear to the employers. Leonard told the FBI, "It was well known among the trade that the money was being paid as tribute to Circella and the syndicate." The Bureau's report continues, "Leonard stated that it was cheaper and more convenient for the theater trade to pay tribute to Circella than it was to pursue their legal remedies."[42]

An employer might still call such payments extortion, but his explanation tended to belie such claims. Edwin Silverman, the managing partner at S and S Theaters Corporation, the third-largest chain in Chicago, described his company to the Bureau agents as "a very profitable one." When the FBI asked him to characterize the payments he made to Bioff, he balked at first. According to the Bureau's report, "Silverman was asked specifically how he regarded the payments—whether they were bribery or extortion. Silverman stated that it was a moot question and that he could not answer it specifically, but when pressed for an answer, he stated that in his opinion, it was definitely extortion." Silverman, however, went on to explain that he and his partners believed the money guaranteed "they wouldn't have any labor problems and this was the consideration which he and his partners had in mind when they paid the $16,200." Silverman reemphasized that theme in explaining the later payments the corporation made to the Outfit via the Allied Theater Owners' Association. "He stated that because they made these payments he and his partners figured that they were immune from any labor difficulties." From Silverman's perspective, it worked. There were no strikes and throughout the 1930s, while they were making the payments, there were no pay raises for Local 110's members: instead there were two wage cuts.[43]

A wage dispute involving an IATSE affiliate in New York City, Local 306, triggered payoffs by the two biggest theater chains operating that city, RKO and Loew's. Here the pattern developed in Chicago was repeated. The businesses agreed to pay $150,000 in 1935 and $100,000 in 1937. The companies' top executives in that city—Major Leslie E. Thompson, president and director of RKO Pictures, and Charles Moskowitz, vice president of Loew's in charge of the theater division—handled the negotiations for the payoffs. They also arranged to divide the payments proportionally between their two companies. In the end, RKO cited financial woes to justify holding back part of its share, but both companies still made sizeable payments: RKO handed over $61,500 and Loew's paid $143,500.[44]

In explaining why they made the payments, these executives pointed to immediate concrete results as well as less specific, but still substantial, long-term benefits. In the short term, they were able to force Local 306 to accept a wage cut when the members were agitating to remove a previous pay reduction. Browne had agreed that in return for the money that RKO and Loew's paid, he would deny Local 306 the right to strike. As in Chicago, because the local was unable to strike, it had to accede to the employers' terms.[45]

For the two theater companies, this was a significant achievement. Wages were cut by 26 cents an hour in 1935; a defense attorney in the 1943 trial claimed that this saved Loew's and RKO $10.92 in each employee's weekly wages, or $76,444 in labor cost savings a week for Loew's and $397,488 a year.[46] Extending the logic of those calculations, Loew's payment of $143,500—its share of the total $250,000 payoff—amounted to a 9 percent commission on the $1.6 million it saved in reduced labor costs over four years. In 1942, after the payments became public, a group of rank and file members of Local 306 filed suit seeking compensation for lost wages. The members claimed that by making the $250,000 worth of payoffs, Loew's and RKO had together saved $3 million in labor costs.[47]

Both theater executives, Thompson and Moskowitz, also spoke of broader benefits they expected to get from the payoffs. RKO's Thompson recalled that he believed the money bought him a kind of all-purpose protection by Bioff. According to the FBI's report, "Thompson stated that it was his understanding that he was buying protection from Bioff wherever he might need it; that the company might appeal to Bioff wherever they might get into difficulties." This was important to Thompson because of a surge in worker militancy during the mid-1930s. He referred to "the great deal of difficulty which RKO was encountering with labor organizations in 1935 throughout the United States."[48] Moskowitz described a similar understanding regarding his company's payments.[49]

## Payoffs Connected to Hollywood Studios

The most notorious payoffs came from the major Hollywood studios, which paid over $390,000 to IATSE in from 1936 to 1938. The largest four studios—Warner Brothers, Loew's, Paramount Pictures, and Twentieth Century-Fox—each agreed to pay $50,000 to Bioff in 1936. The two smaller studios, RKO and Columbia, were each supposed to give $25,000. The payments were to be repeated in 1937 totaling a payoff of a half million dollars. But things did not work out that neatly. Columbia Pictures never paid anything, and RKO only paid for one year because it went into receivership in 1937 and so was excused from making a second payment. Warner Brothers also never completed their payments. In another wrinkle, Loew's arranged to make its 1937 payment by having Bioff receive the commission from the company's raw film purchases. Loew's continued giving him these commission payments until 1941, at which point they totaled $238,000.[50] Bioff handed over two-thirds of the Hollywood money to the Outfit leaders, or about $418,000. Corrected for inflation this would be just over $5.4 million.[51]

At the criminal trials, the studio executives described the payments as straightforward extortion. Bioff, they explained, demanded the money during a series of meetings that took place in April 1936. The executives had gathered in New York City for the annual meeting of the parties to the Studio Basic Agreement, the collective bargaining agreement that governed labor relations in the movie studios. As part of that agreement, the heads of the studios and the top officials for the five national union signatories met annually to iron out disagreements and resolve wage issues. Browne attended this gathering as president of IATSE, and in April 1936 he brought along Bioff.

Their presence at that meeting reflected a recent IATSE victory. Three years earlier, under Browne's predecessor, the union had staged a disastrous jurisdictional strike in a dispute with the International Brotherhood of Electrical Workers (IBEW) over who had claim to studio sound technicians. The strike had failed miserably. Working in conjunction with the employers, the other studio unions, especially the IBEW, took over IATSE's jurisdiction; at the same time, IATSE was ousted from the Basic Agreement because its strike had violated a provision in that agreement. IATSE was left with only a couple hundred members in the Hollywood studios and no seat at the table in the studios' collective bargaining arrangement.[52]

Browne's most important achievement as president of IATSE had been getting that jurisdiction back. In December 1935, using his control over Local 110, he staged a brief projectionists' strike in Chicago against the theaters belonging to Paramount Pictures' subsidiary, Balaban and Katz. The walkout lasted only a few hours, but it caused great concern in the movie industry. Browne used the threat of similar job actions against the other studios to leverage IATSE back into the Basic Agreement. The studios were vulnerable to this tactic because they generated much of their revenue through ticket receipts at their theater chains. They could not afford even a brief interruption to the revenue stream from these theaters. So the movie executives agreed to restore IATSE's jurisdiction in the studios, and once again the union had a sizeable membership base of about 10,000 members in Hollywood.[53] With IATSE once more part of the Basic Agreement, Bioff and Browne were in a position to meet with the studio chiefs and, at least according to testimony at trial, make extortionate demands.

Prosecutors used the testimony of Nicholas Schenck, the chief executive at Loew's, as the centerpiece of their case. Schenck described an initial meeting with Bioff and Browne in April 1936 in which the Loew's executive was accompanied by Sidney Kent, the president of Twentieth Century-Fox. Bioff demanded $2 million, Schenck claimed, or he would have IATSE conduct damaging projectionists' strikes against all of the major studios. Referring to Bioff, Schenck testified, "And he says, 'You could not take it. It will cost you many, many millions over again.'" According to Schenck, he and Kent resisted, and Bioff responded by lowering the amount he demanded, eventually asking for a half million dollars in two separate payments over the course two years. "I want $50,000 from each large company," Bioff said, "and twenty-five from each small one." The six movie studios were to make their assigned payments in 1936 and again in 1937. Schenck testified that he and Kent agreed to meet Bioff's reduced demands. "We said, 'All right, now if we have to do it, we have to do it. We can't afford to have our business destroyed so we will have to pay.'"[54] Other executives told similar stories at trial.[55]

Bioff's testimony at the 1943 trial confirmed these accounts. He described, for instance, his encounter with Leo Spitz, the head of RKO. "He [Spitz] says, 'What is this I understand Nick [Schenck] tells me? What is going on?'" "I told him," Bioff testified, "that I was not giving Nick Schenck no idle talk, that they would have to come up with that money or the same thing would happen with other circuits that happened in Chicago with the Paramount Company."[56]

But a year earlier, in May 1942, when he first began cooperating with federal authorities, Bioff had told a different story. Then he said that the initial idea of having the studios make payoffs came from the employers' side, specifically from a New Deal official named Sol Rosenblatt who was close to the studio executives.[57] After this initial approach, according to Bioff, Nick Schenck "communicated with George Browne and indicated a willingness to help Browne collect graft from the moving picture producers but urged Browne to deal with him direct in this matter and not through Sol Rosenblatt, in whom he claimed to lack confidence."[58] Schenck, according to this version of the story, was anything but a hapless victim. "In telling me this," the agent who interviewed him wrote, "Bioff very emphatically asserted that Nick Schenck and the other producers who had given testimony to the effect that he and Browne had extorted money from them testified falsely; that right from the first Nick Schenck took a leading part in helping him and Browne to induce leading representatives of the various moving picture producing companies to participate with him in the payment of graft to them."[59]

Browne also depicted these payments as a bribe. In statements made to FBI agents in the months before the trial in 1943, the IATSE president compared these payments to the ones made in New York by Loew's and RKO in the fall of 1935. Employers paid the money "to see that there were no strikes and further that they [Browne and Bioff] would permit no strikes." According to Browne, Bioff held two meetings "at which Nick Schenck and Sidney Kent attended and everything as to the decision on the part of the employers was left up to the former [Schenck], as he was considered head man in the movie industry problem." They reached an agreement on how much each studio would pay.[60]

At trial, Schenck and the other executives depicted an aggressive Bioff confronting them with threats that any studio that failed to pay would face a nationwide strike of its projectionists. But in their interviews with FBI agents, several industry figures confirmed the alternative accounts of Browne and Bioff.[61] Albert Warner, one of the heads of Warner Brothers Pictures, told the FBI that in the spring of 1936 he "received a call from Nicholas M. Schenck, at which time Schenck advised him that an agreement had been made to pay Bioff a sum of money in order to avoid having labor difficulties in the studios."[62]

The money that Loew's gave to Bioff from 1937 to 1941 in the form of commission payments on raw film purchases appears even less like an example of extortion. First of all, Schenck continued paying after the demands allegedly made by Bioff in 1936 had been satisfied. Moreover, in describing to FBI agents how he had set the payments up, Schenck offered the rationale of a bribe. Schenck told the agents that in 1937 he called Louis B. Mayer, who ran the company's film studios, and told him to make the necessary arrangements for Bioff to get the commission money. In explaining why, Schenck said he told Mayer, "He [Bioff] is all right and he is here and can do favors. It is just as well to have someone friendly."[63] Mayer confirmed Schenck's memory. Mayer told the agents, Schenck "called me and said, 'Louis, I wish you would give this to Bioff's relation—or friend . . . and it will keep him in a good humor and keep him friendly and give you less headaches out there in your operations.'" When the Bureau agents pressed Mayer further, he reiterated the same theme.

Q: Any discussions as to why it would be given to Bioff's relative?
A. Schenck told me at the time it would keep him friendly. It will be more easy to handle the thing.
Q: Did Schenck give you any more definite indication of why?
A: To keep him friendly, life will be easier to operate the plant.

Pressed one last time, Mayer could only offer his own perspective, "I thought Schenck was wise in keeping him friendly."[64]

Instead of "quaking in their boots" with fear of Bioff, the studio executives apparently considered him worth cultivating; in terms of their labor relations, Bioff was their friend in court. As a result, they did what they could to befriend and to protect him. In 1938, Joseph Schenck paid for two ocean cruises for Bioff and his wife, sending them first on a tour of South America and then on a lavish trip to Europe. The producers threw the couple a bon voyage party, and Mr. and Mrs. Harry Warner sent Bioff's wife orchids.[65] The telegram accompanying the orchids read, "Sorry we [are] not on the boat to enjoy [the] trip with you[.] We could certainly use it[.] Take it easy and have a good time[.] Kindest regards."[66]

The producers also worked to bolster Bioff's position in the union. When dissidents in IATSE Local 37, the main Hollywood local, began to challenge Bioff's activities, the studios had the men fired and blacklisted.[67] In 1939, a top executive at MGM studios tried to block the Hollywood Legion Stadium from allowing a group of Local 37 insurgents from using it as a meeting place.[68] In the words of Pat Casey, who represented the studio employers in the Basic Agreement, "the producers were behind Bioff."[69]

Indeed, this was the government's interpretation of the situation, not in 1941 or 1943 but in the fall of 1948, when it pursued tax charges against the estate of Frank Nitti, the Outfit leader. The attorney representing the government in that case depicted the payoffs from the studios not as extortion but as payment "for services rendered." In his opening speech, the government's attorney said, "The heads of the major motion picture producing companies throughout the United States were contacted and their cooperation was elicited in a plan to obtain money in return for which Browne and Bioff were to see to it that the wages of the various locals were to be kept at a comparatively low level and the whole industry was to be kept on a stable and reasonable plan of operation that would be profitable and advantageous to the moving picture executives and the heads of the various major corporations in the moving picture industry."[70]

The government's shift in position from 1943 to 1948 at least partly stemmed from court precedents regarding tax prosecutions. Those precedents made it harder to collect back taxes on extortion rather than bribery payments.[71] But the government's statement in the tax case also offered a version of what happened that accords better with the apparent facts than statements in the extortion cases: the studios did pay for a service rendered. In return for money, Bioff, acting on behalf of the Outfit, guaranteed them IATSE would conduct labor relations in a way that suited the industry's needs.

## The Racketeer-Controlled Union as a Version of a Company Union

Before the National Labor Relations Act of 1935 (better known as the Wagner Act) made the tactic illegal, employers sometimes enrolled their workers into company unions, a term for a workplace organization formed at the company's behest. Employers hoped that a company union would channel worker militancy into controllable directions and forestall organizing drives by legitimate unions. The Wagner Act made company unions illegal at the same time as the country witnessed a dramatic upsurge in worker militancy. Businesses faced the possibility not just that previously unorganized employees might join a union but that those employees might join an organization that would aggressively challenge management prerogatives. It was in this context that organized crime groups like the Outfit provided employers with a new alternative. A union controlled by organized crime would not technically be a company union, but it would offer the same ability to control worker militancy. Payoffs could be seen as a fee that gangsters charged for setting up and running this new kind of company union.

Bioff himself did not use the words company union, nor did the studio executives when they described their transactions with the Outfit's representative. But when the FBI talked to IATSE members and local union officials in Hollywood, those men described Bioff's actions in terms of a company union. Acting at Bioff's behest, President Browne had thrown Local 37, the Hollywood studio workers' local, into trusteeship. Bioff came out to Los

Angeles in the winter of 1936 and assumed direct control over the local at the same time he received the first payments from the studios. For the next several years, Bioff imposed policies on Local 37 that sacrificed the members' needs to the interests of the employers. By his actions, Bioff was "in effect making it a Motion Picture Producers, Inc., controlled union," explained one local IATSE member.[72]

A key issue where the members' interests diverged from the employers concerned the size of the labor pool. The movie companies saved a great deal of money by hiring their studio employees on a casual basis, to work on a particular film, for instance. This meant that the studios' permanent payroll was quite lean. In order for that system to function, the companies needed a large pool of available workers so that they could count on being able to hire studio workers as needed. Bioff accommodated the studios by bringing thousands of new members into Local 37. IATSE members believed that Bioff had conspired with the producers "for the purposes of creating a Producer-IATSE dominated labor pool, one of the largest labor pools ever instituted in the motion picture industry."[73]

For their part, studio employees wanted just the opposite situation. A smaller, controlled pool of available workers would make it easier for studio employees to get enough work on a casual basis to earn a decent living. It also might force the studios to spread their production schedules more evenly over the year, creating steady work schedules. Local 37 members aggressively agitated on this issue, and, had they been in control of their local, they would have pursued very different policies. Instead, they watched their economic situation steadily worsen as their union's leadership betrayed them. Bioff claimed credit for winning a series of raises in the late 1930s, but because the work was spread out among an ever larger pool of workers, the average yearly earnings of Local 37 members declined. By 1938, Local 37 dissidents claimed that average yearly earnings had fallen from $2,500 in 1929 to $1,200 or less.[74]

Bioff also worked with the movie executives to forestall the emergence of more militant labor organizations in the studios. For the producers, this was an issue of some concern because the 1930s witnessed a great deal of labor turmoil in Hollywood. The Screen Actors Guild (SAG) and the Writers Guild both formed in 1933 and agitated for recognition and collective bargaining contracts. At the same time, other trades that had previously been excluded from the Studio Basic Agreement after 1935 could draw upon the provisions of the Wagner Act to pressure the studios into collective bargaining agreements.[75] Added to the mix was the presence of the Committee on Industrial

Organization (CIO), which was active in Los Angeles and apparently interested in gaining a foothold in the studios.[76] Compared to the older unions in the American Federation of Labor (AFL), CIO organizations had a more militant reputation, and most employers, if they had to deal with a union, preferred to deal with the AFL.

In 1937, matters came to a head when the studios faced the possibility of an alliance between the actors in SAG and a coalition of eleven studio craft locals excluded from the Basic Agreement and organized under the name of the Federated Motion Picture Crafts (FMPC). Locals belonging to the FMPC went out on strike in April 1937 seeking a raise and official recognition from the producers. The strikers received support from local CIO organizations, which helped fill picket lines around the studios. Even worse from the studios' perspective, within a week of FMPC's walkout, SAG's membership voted to authorize their leaders to call an actors' strike; the actors had become frustrated with the producers' intransigent refusal to recognize their union. It was a dangerous combination of events. For the studios, any serious interruption of production schedules could be disastrously expensive, but the threat of a possible alliance between the Actors and the FMPC—with its ties to the CIO—was potentially catastrophic.[77]

Bioff provided critical assistance in this crisis. He cooperated with the producers to forestall an Actors' strike, ostensibly exerting the IATSE's influence on SAG's behalf in negotiations with the studios. Privately, as Bioff later explained to the government, "he acted in collusion with Mssrs. [Joseph] Schenck and [Louis] Mayer [the lead representatives for the employers] during their negotiations on behalf of the producers with representatives of the Screen Actors' Guild at Louis Mayer's home on or about Sunday, May 5, 1937." Bioff depicted himself as a double agent at these negotiations. Having already met with Mayer and Schenck, he knew on what terms they hoped to reach an agreement granting recognition to SAG. During the meeting at Mayer's house, however, Bioff, as IATSE's chief official in Hollywood, sat with the SAG representatives, offering support and advice about what terms they should hold out for in their bargaining. He steered them towards the producers' terms. At the same time, because he dramatically threatened a nationwide projectionists' strike if the producers did not agree to recognize SAG, Bioff looked like a labor stalwart.[78]

He played the double agent role so well in fact that after these negotiations SAG's leadership offered public thanks to him for his invaluable assistance.[79] Meanwhile, SAG's agreement with the studios actually gave the producers a strategic victory. The new ten-year contract included a no-strike clause and eliminated the possibility of the actors joining the FMPC strike, a critical goal for the studios.[80]

Having helped the studios deal with SAG, Bioff also supported their effort to defeat FMPC's strike. Joseph Schenck explained to the FBI that in 1941, the studios were dead set against dealing with Federated Crafts. "We didn't want them to get together. We were perfectly willing to deal with them separately, but we didn't want another organization like I.A.T.S.E. because the stronger these people get the more difficult it is for us to deal with them." Schenck told the agents that he "used Bioff in settling my difficulties with the Federated Crafts strike."[81]

One of Bioff's initial briefings with government agents included the same claim, and he described to the agents how he had helped Schenck break the FMPC strike.[82] In order to allow the studios to maintain production, Bioff ordered IATSE members to cross FMPC's picket lines and to do the strikers' jobs.[83] His support for the producers was so transparent that during the strike, according to the historian Gerald Horne, "the L.A. Central [Labor] Council had passed a resolution calling IATSE 'a company union and a scab-herding agency.'"[84]

While this all was going on, in the spring and summer of 1937, Bioff was collecting the second installment of the half million dollar payoff being made by the studio executives. This was the same payoff the executives later claimed at trial that they made out of fear: fear over the destruction of their businesses and fear over dealing with an obvious organized crime figure such as Bioff. Put in the context of the contentious labor relations in Hollywood and Bioff's role in helping to meet the studios' needs, the payments look like a fee for services rendered, not extortion. The service was providing the studios with a company union.

## Conclusion

Typically racketeering in the 1930s is seen as an issue involving labor unions. In the popular press, racketeering often serves as a shorthand way of referring to organized crime's infiltration of unions such as the Teamsters in the 1930s. Much of the concern about racketeering at the time, however, stemmed from the corrupt activity of businessmen in sectors not traditionally linked to organized crime. Observers raised fears of a spreading problem that threatened to engulf the larger economy.[85] While the alarmist tenor of those warnings can be dismissed as hyperbole, criminal cases in Chicago and New York City did reveal widespread connections between businessmen and organized crime; these connections were both significant in scale and relatively recent in their origins.[86]

The example of the motion picture industry indicates that businessmen turned to organized crime in the 1930s because they sought a way to manage the new troubling phenomenon of the 1930s—the growth of organized labor. Worker militancy fed union growth in this decade and organized labor spread to sectors where it had long been excluded. Meanwhile the Norris-LaGuardia Act (1932) and the Wagner Act (1935) robbed employers of tactics such as the injunction and company unions that they previously had used against unions. Businessmen searching for stability in a new era turned to organized crime figures who offered them a way to manage the potentially chaotic influence of unions in their industry.

In the movie industry, executives viewed their arrangements with Browne, Bioff, and Circella as a kind of business transaction. They paid a fee or a commission to these organized crime figures and in return they received specific services: protection from strikes, controlled wage demands, and defense against more militant unionism. In exchange for the money it received, the Outfit gave employers a kind of company union. As the Chicago theater chain operator Edwin Silverman put it, for a businessman like himself the issue of whether or not his payments reflected bribery or extortion "was a moot question."[87] They were fees that he would have preferred not to pay, but he did so because the alternative of depending on collective bargaining was less certain and less advantageous.

The larger issue is not just that the perception of employers as victims was inaccurate. The trial testimony and the media coverage shaped the public's understanding of what this scandal meant, and that had political implications. The image of executives "quivering in their boots" as they paid "tribute" to men of Bioff's "ilk" helped justify an antiunion agenda in a way that a more realistic depiction of what happened would not have done.

# 5

# Union Members and Corruption
## *Exploitation and Disillusionment*

Francis Black worked at Warner Brothers Studios in Hollywood in 1937 when he received word that his union, the International Alliance of Theatrical Stage Employes (IATSE), had levied a 2 percent assessment on his earnings. This requirement came on top of an initiation fee of $100 and the regular union dues of $3 a month. The union's leadership offered no real explanation of why the extra money was needed, and Black objected to paying it. Like other studio employees, he had not chosen membership in IATSE; his employer had assigned him to the union as part of the studios' agreement with President George Browne in December 1935. By the terms of that agreement, Black had been required to join IATSE's Local 37 in order to keep his job as an electrician at the studio.

Although Black paid high dues, he lacked basic citizenship rights within his union. The $3 monthly dues in 1937 were equivalent to about $40 in 2004, and the money paid in by Local 37's 6,500 members amounted to a sizeable sum. According to union records, Local 37 collected just under a half million dollars from its members during the twenty-two months from December 1935 to October 1937. But the members who put in this money lacked a voice in their local's affairs because IATSE's national office kept Local 37 in a trusteeship. William Bioff ran that trusteeship, and for all intents and purposes he exerted complete control over Local 37; all of the other IATSE Hollywood locals were in a similar situation. With Bioff in charge, Local 37 held no regular membership meetings and no elections for union offices. It provided no effective system of shop stewards and offered no accounting of what became of the members' dues money. Local union members viewed the

## Scalise---Then and Now

At the left is George Scalise as he appeared back in 1913 when he was arrested on a white slavery charge. At right is George Scalise today, accused of extortion in what is described as a $1,000,000 racket.

Figure 5.1: The *New York World-Telegram* printed these side-by-side arrest photos of George Scalise on April 22, 1940, the day he was arrested on extortion charges. The caption reminds readers of the labor leader's 1913 conviction for a Mann Act violation, referred to here as a "white slavery charge." Westbrook Pegler had uncovered the 1913 conviction and used it to justify a journalistic campaign against Scalise in particular and union corruption in general. From the *New York World-Telegram*, April 22, 1940.

situation as taxation without representation. For Black, the new 2 percent assessment made this situation intolerable. IATSE's leadership was demanding still more money from the union members but providing neither a meaningful justification nor any record of where the assessment money was going.[1]

Outraged, Black sent in his assessment but accompanied it with a protest. Three days later, Warner Brothers Studios fired him, explaining that it had done so at the request of IATSE officials. When Black applied for work elsewhere in Hollywood, he learned that his union had blacklisted him and no other studio would hire him. He had been a good worker at Warner Brothers, but this fact did him little good. His former bosses at the studio told Black that they would be happy to put him back to work but only after he straightened things out with the union's leadership. He needed to indicate his willingness to accept the assessment, to make it clear he would not rock the boat.[2]

Instead he filed a suit against IATSE's officials in civil court in Los Angeles. The suit detailed Black's complaints about the union's leadership, and demanded the return of his job as well as compensation for his lost wages.[3] Black's plight and his reaction to it formed part of a larger pattern of exploitation and resistance, one that shaped the history of the scandal because it eventually led to Pegler's exposés.

While the Hollywood producers received the bulk of the media's attention, it was the rank and file union members in IATSE and in George Scalise's Building Service Employees International Union (BSEIU) who were the real victims of corruption. Bioff, Scalise, and their organized crime associates devised ways to exploit every member of these national unions. In perpetrating such schemes, the Outfit benefited from the complicity of a wide circle of union officials at the national level. The history of the crimes of Scalise, Bioff, and Browne demonstrated the failure of union governance to live up to the democratic premise upon which it was based: many of the ostensible safeguards against misconduct by national officers proved to be insufficient. As a result, workers like the studio electrician Black found themselves vulnerable to exploitation. For these members, the promise of the union movement was betrayed and Pegler's columns hearkened to their sense of disillusionment.

## Scalise in New York: The Many Profitable Avenues of Labor Corruption

As an avid practitioner of entrepreneurial unionism, Scalise's career in BSEIU showcases the many possibilities for corruption. First, there was the practice of embezzlement. After becoming president of the union in 1937, Scalise coordinated arrangements to siphon money out of the national treasury of BSEIU, acting as the front man for the Outfit and the partner of the New York Mafia leader Anthony Carfano. He split his official salary of $1,000 a month with the Outfit, and he worked with the union's secretary-treasurer to steal money out of the organization's treasury through fake expense vouchers. During the roughly two and a half years of his presidency, prosecutors estimated that Scalise helped the Outfit take about $100,000 out of the BSEIU treasury. In this activity, he seemed to play the part of the accomplice, not the instigator. Helping to loot the national organization's treasury had been part of the deal Scalise had made in order to become president of the union, which was in some ways a nominal position. By the terms of his deal with his organized crime sponsors, his actual authority in the organization was limited to the East Coast, with occasional disputes emerging with the Outfit over what was included in that area.[4]

If for much of the country he was the president of the union in name only, in New York City Scalise's power was far more real. There he benefited from a successful organizing campaign in the mid-1930s that had dramatically expanded the membership of the BSEIU in Manhattan's residential and office buildings and in the city's hotels. Within a few years, the previously unorganized building workers of New York became one of the largest segments of the national union. From 1934 to 1940, the union's membership in New York City rose from 1,200 to over 30,000, while the national union's entire membership that year stood at 60,000. During those same years, BSEIU Local 32B, which stood at the center of this organizing campaign, mushroomed from 300 members to 14,000. By 1940, Local 32B was by far the largest BSEIU local in the country.[5]

Scalise played no significant role in these organizing campaigns except to profit from them. The various accounts of BSEIU organizers in New York all agree that they saw very little of Scalise at this time. He did not attend prestrike rallies or regular union meetings. In these formative years, local union officials organized the members and won the strikes without his assistance.[6]

But then, once the BSEIU locals began to grow, Scalise asserted himself. In Local 32B, he used his influence as a national union officer to gain control over the local and then to begin to drain money out of it. As in the national union, false expense vouchers covered embezzlement from the local's funds. Service providers doing business with the local, such as the union's accountant and a physician doing work for the local's health plan, paid kickbacks that went to Scalise. Local officials were pressured to accept payoffs from businessmen and then to share the proceeds up the chain of command. In this way, Scalise corrupted a local whose growth initially had promised to bring real benefits to the city's building employees.[7]

Scalise also made money by setting up other locals whose purpose from the start would be to drain money from the workers. In April 1938, Scalise set up a charter for Local 94, the Bowling and Billiard Academy Employees Union. The officers he installed to run the new union were operatives for a Tammany Hall political boss, Jimmy Hines, and their chief asset was their experience in stuffing ballot boxes. Scalise arranged for the local to sign a contract with the Bowling Alley Proprietors Association, which granted the union a closed shop and mandated that members' dues be deducted automatically from their paychecks. New York's pin boys suddenly found themselves members of Local 94 and discovered that they now must pay a $5 initiation fee and $2 monthly dues. Since they made only 6 cents a game, these payments to the union constituted a significant financial obligation.[8]

They could see no tangible benefits from this newly imposed union membership. As one wrote to the district attorney's office, "The boys in general are opposed to such a union because it offers nothing in return for the *$2.00 per month* and the academy owners are all inclined to pay the present scale of 6 cents [per] single and 3 cents [per] double [that is, when two pin boys were working one lane] without such a union which is without a doubt a 'RACKET.'" Nor did the members have any real voice in their union. At the local's first election, Scalise's appointees marked 400 ballots for themselves, thus overwhelming the 300 votes cast by actual members of the local.[9] Local 94 was a sham local, never intended to better the lives of its members; it simply conspired with the employers to impose a new tax on workers laboring in the industry. This tax became yet another way for Scalise to profit from his position in the BSEIU.

For employers, these kinds of arrangements with Scalise offered a preemptive strike against the possibility of a more militant union entering their workplace.[10] The changed legal and political atmosphere of the New Deal had undercut previous methods of blocking union organization, including seeking injunctions and forming company unions. However, by allowing Scalise to set up operations such as Local 94, employers dodged these newly erected legal protections. Scalise provided them with a new kind of company union, one for which the employer suffered no legal liability. Better yet, the workers, not the employer, paid for the cost of this "service," in the form of membership dues payments that Scalise or his surrogates then siphoned out of the union funds.

As was the case with Bioff and Browne, the collusive arrangements between Scalise and these businessmen received little attention when his indictment was announced in April 1940. Instead the district attorney's office and the newspapers focused on allegations that Scalise had extorted vast sums of money from New York's employers. These charges depicted the employers simply as victims.[11]

But from the union membership's point of view, the employers were not the victims of Scalise's conspiracies: they were the real winners. Among the companies listed in the extortion indictment filed against Scalise by the district attorney's office was the Handiman Company, a janitorial contractor who testified to making a payment of $11,750. In explaining the indictment to the press, District Attorney Dewey's aides described this as one of the payments made out of fear. Scalise allegedly had used his control of BSEIU Local 32J to pressure Handiman and other cleaning contractors into giving him money. However, an employee of the company writing to the district attorney's office put forward a different scenario. According to this employee, the company bought off the union in order to take shameless advantage of its workers. While the union's contract limited the cleaning women to six hours of work a night, they were routinely forced to stay much longer. "Some of them start at 7 PM and have so much to do they cannot finish until 4 in the morning." Although Handiman was supposed to pay for holidays, it did not. The company deducted money from the employees' wages for damages and other purposes without explanation or justification. The letter closed with the straightforward conclusion about the contractor's relationship with the union: "And also he is a partner to 32J union."[12]

The employers who paid Scalise were, like the producers who paid Bioff, purchasing a service, in this case a compliant union. Scalise and his Mafia sponsor Carfano profited handsomely by taking money from employers in return for betraying the union's role as a collective bargaining agent. The true victims were the union members, many of whom became deeply disillusioned with the labor movement. One BSEIU member in New York wrote to Westbrook Pegler in 1942, explaining how five years earlier she and the other cleaning women at the hotel where she worked were forced to join the union. They paid $2 a month in dues, which she considered a hefty amount. "We were getting only $13—a week." And in return, she and the other members got nothing. "Well, anyway this Schwartz-Scalise gang didn't better our conditions [on the] contrary we were more slaved than before we had no increase in our wages, no vacations, but more work as they laid off people."[13]

## IATSE and the 2 Percent Assessment

Scalise demonstrated the range of labor racketeering schemes that exploited workers, but Bioff and Browne used their control over IATSE to reach a new scale of criminal enterprise. The two men arranged with the Outfit to embezzle over $1.5 million out of IATSE's funds. Corrected for inflation, this would be equivalent to just under $20 million in 2004. This huge amount was more than all of the money that had been received by the Outfit in the other payoff schemes involving this union, and that included the money from the Hollywood producers.[14]

The $1.5 million came from the 2 percent assessment electrician Black had objected to at the cost of losing his job. It was levied for eighteen months on all working members of IATSE. Bioff later acknowledged that only "about 1/10th of 1% [of this assessment] was spent legitimately." The rest of the money went to Browne, Bioff, and the leaders of the Outfit, who divided it up according to a formula worked out with Frank Nitti in 1935. The Outfit received two-thirds of the money and Browne and Bioff split the other third.[15] It was money taken from the paychecks of every working IATSE member, who paid the assessment in addition to the union's regular dues and initiation fees. The scale of this crime raised the issue of complicity, because it could not have occurred without the cooperation of other IATSE officials. Their cooperation, in turn, pointed to fundamental problems with union governance.

IATSE, like other unions, had a formal constitution that promised its members basic democratic protections. Union members elected officers to run their local unions, and every two years they chose delegates to attend a national IATSE convention. Those delegates elected the union's national officers: a general president, general secretary-treasurer, and seven vice presidents who composed the union's general executive board. At these conventions, the incumbent president offered a formal report to all of the delegates, detailing the actions taken by the union's national headquarters during the previous two years. The general secretary-treasurer presented a record of the union's finances, which had been audited by elected union auditors.[16]

Between conventions, the General Executive Board (GEB) made all of the important decisions affecting the union. Sitting alongside the elected national officers at these board meetings—participating but not voting—were a group of appointed officers called international representatives and international trustees, and the collective group informally was known as "the official family." The president's report to the biannual union convention included the official minutes of this group's deliberations.[17]

All of these procedures—elections, audits, and reports—offered the framework for a democratic and honest form of governance. These were fundamental principles for labor organizations. After all, unions originated out of efforts to champion the democratic rights of working people and to protect them from exploitation. Through their convention delegates, members all had a voice in the financial decisions of IATSE, such as how much revenue would be drawn from local dues and how that money would be spent. To guarantee that right, the national officers were duty bound to report financial transactions involving the union's funds.[18]

Thus when the FBI first began investigating Browne and Bioff's activities in the 1939 and 1940, IATSE's other national officers reassured the agents that the members' money was safe. The general secretary-treasurer, Louis

Krouse, patiently explained that "his office gave a receipt for every cent of money received by the union and that every payment made by the union was made by check." All such transactions "had to be accounted for in the books of the general secretary-treasurer," which in turn were regularly audited.[19]

Given such safeguards, one might wonder how Bioff and Browne managed to take $1,513,558.78 out of IATSE's funds, convert it to cash, and split it with the Outfit.[20] To put the matter bluntly, they had help. The members of the "official family"—in other words, the national leadership of IATSE—conspired with Browne and Bioff to circumvent the union's reporting and auditing procedures.

The leadership evaded the procedures for reporting to the membership through obfuscation. In effect, the General Executive Board carried out the letter of the union's rules in such a way as to violate their spirit. For the record, there were reports to the membership on the 2 percent assessment. The printed minutes of IATSE's General Executive Board informed members that it had levied the assessment in order to create a "defense fund" on two occasions, for a total of about eighteen months.[21] But IATSE members reading the minutes learned nothing about how the money had been spent or how much was left in the fund.[22]

The union's national leadership also conspired with Browne and Bioff to convert the 2 percent assessment into cash. The first time this occurred had been during a special board meeting held in December 1935. There had been a brief strike on November 30, lasting only a few hours, by projectionists working in the Chicago area against movie theaters operated by Paramount Studios. Browne had used the threat of similar strikes to convince the studios to bring IATSE back into the Basic Agreement, in other words, to give the union back its jurisdiction in Hollywood.[23] Following this victory, Browne called the members of the "official family" together for a special board meeting. He acted at the behest of the Outfit's leader, Nitti, who wanted Browne and Bioff to draw a sizeable amount of money out of the 2 percent assessment fund. Bioff presided over the board meeting, and he told the officials present that certain expenses had occurred during course of the recent maneuver with the studios and those expenses had to be met with a cash payment. Apparently no further explanation was offered, and no further explanation was requested. To generate a large amount of cash, $125,000 in checks for fictional expenses were drawn on the 2 percent assessment's fund and issued to the members of the "official family." The officials cashed the checks, kept one-fifth for themselves, and returned the remainder of the cash to Bioff.[24]

In the years that followed, the "official family" continued to participate in the process of generating cash out of the 2 percent assessment. Over time an involved system emerged. In addition to receiving checks themselves from the 2 percent assessment fund, the union's vice presidents, international representatives, and international trustees also served as "collectors." They recruited two or three men they trusted in each of their regions, and these men were termed "distributees." The distributees also received regular checks from the 2 percent assessment fund, ostensibly for performing organizing or troubleshooting tasks, work that in fact never occurred. The distributees cashed their checks, kept about 10 percent for themselves, and turned the rest over to the collectors, who passed the money on to its final destination.[25]

For example, William P. Raoul, the international representative based in Atlanta, was responsible for three distributees in his region, one of whom was his son. Each received a weekly check for $110 from the 2 percent assessment fund; those distributees cashed their checks, kept $10 for themselves, and handed the remainder to Raoul. In addition to collecting from his own distributees, Raoul also gathered the cash that was coming into IATSE's international representative in Houston and from a IATSE trustee based in Mobile. Both of those men had their own networks of distributees who were receiving paychecks and turning cash over to them. Periodically, Raoul changed all of this cash into stacks of $1,000 bills and had it delivered to the fund's accountant in Chicago, a man chosen by the Outfit to coordinate the whole operation.[26]

Raoul and the other collectors were paid for their work. In 1938, Raoul received and kept as his own income $4,500 from the fund; in 1939 he earned $3,000 in this way; and in 1940, $3,000. These sums were far from nominal. When adjusted for inflation, $4,500 in 1938 would be equivalent to $60,157 in 2004, and that money came in addition to Raoul's official salary from his union position.[27]

Later, in the wake of Browne and Bioff's convictions, the other IATSE national leaders distanced themselves from what had happened. "We were all deceived," IATSE's general executive board formally declared in 1946, "by the front which Browne had built." Ignoring their own constitutional roles, board members described a scenario in which Browne, as president, wielded the real power. "The history of our organization has proved the necessity and desirability of placing major responsibility in this office and likewise giving him the power properly to discharge that responsibility." Until the revelations at the trials, the other IATSE leaders had simply offered "support [for] Browne in the firm belief that he was handling the affairs of the Alliance in the best interests of its membership." What happened to the 2 percent fund was a mystery to them. Indeed, even today, the history of IATSE that appears on the organization's Web site informs readers that "no genuine accounting of the fund was ever made."[28] The truth was clearly quite different. The general executive board had oversight authority over these funds and the "official family" played an active role in process by which this money was funneled into the hands of the Outfit. What remains unclear is why; specifically why the "official family" violated the trust of the membership and cooperated in this scheme.

In discussions with FBI agents and staff from the U.S. sttorneys office, board members claimed to believe the money from the 2 percent assessment fund was necessary to wage strikes and protect the union's Hollywood juris-diction against incursion by the rival CIO. They ostensibly had accepted Bioff and Browne's rationale for converting it to cash. This kind of off-the-books fund, they were told, would reduce the union's legal liability for actions that might become necessary in waging a hard-fought strike.[29]

IATSE's history in this period, however, belies these justifications. The fact is that the union was involved in almost no strike activity in this period. The motion picture operators' walkout in Chicago in November 1935 lasted only a few hours. The only recorded strike in Hollywood involved makeup artists at the Columbia Pictures studio in 1937, and that strike lasted only one day. Even as a mountain of cash was being accumulated in the 2 percent fund, the union experienced a minimum of strife and opposition.[30] The Commit-tee on Industrial Organization (CIO) did emerge as a rival, and the IATSE did face a jurisdictional battle with a CIO affiliate in Hollywood in 1939. But jurisdictional fights between unions typically involve putting more money into union staff positions: hiring organizers to rally the membership to the cause or attorneys to do battle in the courts. If that was the purpose of the fund, then the members of the "official family" should have asked why it had to be converted into cash.

The justifications being offered just did not add up, and it seems unlikely that the board members accepted them as unquestioningly as they later claimed. The fund was a huge amount of cash being taken out of the pock-ets of their membership. If the money was not going to wage jurisdictional struggles or to support short-lived or nonexistent strikes, where did board members think it was going?

They might have thought the money was going to the Outfit and into the pockets of Browne and Bioff. It would have been a reasonable conclusion to reach. When IATSE's national leadership voted to create the 2 percent assess-ment, the board meetings were presided over by Bioff and attended by the

Outfit's representative Nick Circella. Neither man had had any involvement in the motion picture industry or the union before 1933. Bioff looked and acted like a hood, and Circella was by all accounts an even more intimidating figure, a scarier, albeit quieter, hood. The description in one FBI report on Circella read simply, "tough looking." After Bioff went to oversee IATSE's affiliates in Hollywood, Circella became Browne's constant companion.[31] We know that IATSE officials who interacted with Browne in this period recognized Bioff and Circella as mobsters.[32] IATSE officials also widely believed that Browne took orders from Bioff and Circella. One reporter noted in 1940, "There is a legend in the Alliance [IATSE] that if Circella, Bioff and Browne are in the same room, Circella does the talking. If it is Bioff and Browne, Bioff talks. If it is Browne, Browne talks."[33]

All of the members of the "official family" thus were aware generally of the role of these mobsters, and some of them were also cognizant of the actual scheme. Bioff felt certain that at least two of the board's members, specifically General Secretary-Treasurer Louis Krouse and First Vice President John Nick, "must have known fairly well just what was being done with the money."[34]

Even those board members who lacked specific knowledge would have had to draw troubling conclusions about what Browne's administration was asking them to do: levy an assessment that would raise $1.5 million and put it under the sole control of Browne, who they believed was dominated by Circella and Bioff. Then, as the members' contributions began coming in, these officials helped convert it to the equivalent today of about $20 million in cash and deliver it to an accountant in Chicago, one unconnected to the union.

Their equanimity appears all the more disingenuous when compared with other reactions within the union. IATSE officials in the local unions had strong suspicions that the 2 percent assessment fund amounted to nothing more than a criminal scheme.[35] Some evidence indicates that IATSE members also widely suspected at the time that the money was going to organized crime. A member in Chicago wrote to federal authorities in 1937 about the membership's concerns regarding the 2 percent assessment. In the letter, he informed the authorities that in his IATSE local they referred to it as the "million dollar tax," which was "supposedly for the prospective opposition of the 'C.I.O.'" But the members, he asserted, did not buy this explanation. They had concluded that the assessment was simply a scheme to bilk money out of the union. "A bit of investigation locally soon told us that it [the assessment] has its origins in Alcatraz," he wrote, making a reference to Al Capone, who was imprisoned there and believed by many to still be in charge of the Outfit. "In fact there is a slogan here that its for the 'boy out in Alcatraz'!!"[36]

If members of the "official family" reached the same conclusion, they took no action to stop Bioff and Browne. Despite the amount of money involved, none of the national officials within the union nor the local officials serving as delegates at the IATSE's conventions in 1936, 1938, and 1940 ever publicly challenged Browne and Bioff on this matter. By choosing not to act, all of these officials were complicit in the scheme, perhaps not complicit to the degree of those like International Representative Raoul, who helped convert the fund to cash, but complicit nonetheless. And it was this broad level of complicity that allowed such a huge crime to occur.

This episode points out an important characteristic about union corruption at the level of the national union—that it stems not just from the abuses of a few top leaders but from the decision of the rest of the officials to turn a blind eye towards possible wrongdoing. In the parallel case of corruption within BSEIU, Scalise embezzled as much as $100,000 from the national union. Often he simply chose names out of the phone book and placed them on fictitious expense vouchers that he submitted and converted to cash. In practicing such an obvious kind of embezzlement, Scalise faced no resistance from BSEIU's general secretary-treasurer or from those members of BSEIU's general executive board specifically charged with auditing the national union's accounts. As in the IATSE, the safeguards in the BSEIU constitution proved to be meaningless in practice. Such safeguards depended upon other national leaders fulfilling their responsibilities, and that was not happening.[37]

What explains such a wide level of complicity? Fear must have played a role, although it was only one part of a mix of motives and concerns at work. Interestingly, the only member of IATSE's "official family" specifically to ascribe his actions to fear of the Outfit was Browne. In his debriefing with the FBI, Browne described a tortured existence as president of IATSE, constantly aware that his continued safety depended on maintaining his usefulness to the gang's schemes.

The Bureau reported Browne's account in the third person, a perfunctory effort to disguise his identity. "The informant [Browne] further advised that Browne was in a rather desperate situation all the time; that the Chicago gang were the type of people that wouldn't fool around, and further would not care much about a person's life."[38] The murder of IATSE Local 110's leader, Tom Maloy, in February 1935, was a powerful object lesson for Browne, who had known him for decades. Maloy had cooperated with the Outfit but apparently not enough to satisfy the gang, which murdered him to gain complete control over the lucrative Local 110.[39]

Browne sought to protect himself from the same fate. As he explained, "He put himself in the position of being the best sucker that they [the Outfit] had because he was afraid that if at any moment they could get anybody else, they would do so. By this the informant [Browne] stated he didn't mean that Browne could be put out of the picture, but rather that Browne could be put off the earth." He gave them whatever they wanted and only asked if he could give them more. "If they asked Browne for a check of $10,000, he would ask them, 'What only one check; I'll write you two or three if you like.'"[40]

And he drank a lot. "He became hazy because of the situation," Browne told the FBI, "and he deliberately made himself so by using a great deal of intoxicating liquors, so that he couldn't remember the exact dates or what arrangements were made." Whether he drank to appear even more pliant to his Outfit handlers or to deaden himself to what he was doing, he never explained. He might not himself have known the answer to such a question. It was, of course, a problematic remedy. On the surface, he continued to exhibit a hearty demeanor, and those who met him in this period described a funny, charming man. But he was hospitalized three times in the 1930s with gastric ulcers, and under a pseudonym he began seeing a psychiatrist. He suffered, according to the report of one of the doctors who treated him, "from an acute anxiety state."[41]

By contrast, other members of the "official family" had little to say about their fears. In all of the FBI reports and trial testimony, IATSE's top officials never referred to concerns about the Outfit to explain why they did nothing in response to what was occurring. Less directly involved, they were also in less immediate danger than Browne, but this would have remained true only so long as they presented no obstacle to the Outfit and its plans. The record of union officials murdered by the gang in Chicago made this fact apparent. Fear therefore must have played a part, but acknowledging the role of fear in shaping their actions would amount to admitting their complicity. Such an admission would have carried a political cost in the wake of the scandal, when incumbent board members faced a series of electoral challenges. Instead they referred only to their trust in Browne's good intentions and their ignorance of what he and Bioff had done.[42]

The one exception to this silence regarding fear was an oblique reference made by IATSE first vice president Harlan Holmden. He had worked closely with Bioff in Hollywood from 1936 to 1938. Speaking to FBI agents in 1943, Holmden described passing cash-filled envelopes from Bioff to the Los Angeles gangster John Rosselli. According to the FBI's report, Holmden "advised that he didn't know of any work that Rosselli performed for such compensation, and that he did not inquire of Bioff why Rosselli was getting this money, because he more or less knew it was not a good policy to inquire as to what Bioff was doing."[43]

The statement might be seen as an explanation of the attitude of IATSE's leadership in general towards the 2 percent assessment fund. Something was clearly not right about what was going on, but it was safer to leave it alone and not inquire further. They did not want to know. By maintaining this pretence of ignorance, Holmden and the other members of the "official family" could avoid facing the moral obligation they had to protect IATSE's membership.

Besides fear, of course, another motive shaping the actions of union leaders who betrayed their members was greed. Browne and Bioff received a financial windfall for their roles. The other members of the "official family" profited as well, but to a much lesser degree. They received a fifth of the expense money drawn in December 1935 and a few thousand dollars for their activities as collectors. For them, the money would have worked as an incentive and a constraint. Having participated in the embezzlement, the board members were then implicated in it. Denouncing Browne or Bioff, calling on law enforcement, or any other such response would bring negative consequences for every member of the "official family."

Further down the ranks, the local-level officials who served as convention delegates had to weigh the risks to their careers from speaking out. It was far easier to trust the good intentions of the top leaders and avoid conflict. FBI agents who interviewed Harold V. Smith, a business agent in IATSE Local 695 observed this response. They concluded, "Smith seemed to be willing to cooperate and yet it was evident that his position as business agent for the Sound Local, at a salary of $250 per week, appeared to be more important to him at the present time than jeopardizing that position by [offering] any evidence that he might possibly have in his possession concerning Browne and Bioff."[44]

The nature of union governance also contributed to this pattern of complicity. IATSE was formally a democracy, but in reality, like many other labor organizations, it tended to operate more as a bureaucracy, where power flowed from the top down, from the national office down to the locals. When *New York Times* theater critic Jack Gould attended IATSE's 1940 convention, he was struck by "the virtual divorcement of the average member and delegate from the union's general executive board and ruling hierarchy." Though ostensibly empowered to vote on all resolutions coming before the convention, Gould noted that delegates routinely referred almost all such matters to the executive board to decide as it saw fit. The delegates evidenced no sense of playing a significant role in the organization's governance—just the opposite. "If a local union delegate wanted something from the executive board he spoke of it almost as if it were not part of the Alliance [that is, IATSE] but an autonomous supreme court."

This passivity did not appear to result from any kind of open threats or the presence of nefarious forces at the gathering. The delegates brought their wives and children to the convention, Gould noted, and he detected no outward signs of intimidation at work. To the contrary, he described a convivial gathering of delegates who "represented an average cross section of the American workingman." The convention's proceedings reflected not a climate of terror but a habit of deference to the national union's leadership.[45] Various considerations underlay to that habit of deference. Fear, ambition, and a sense of resignation that this was how things worked in a less-than-perfect world all played a part. None of them necessarily would be apparent to a casual observer, such as Gould, spending a day at the convention.

## Conclusion

The history of the corruption scandals highlighted the problems with union governance and the resulting vulnerability of organized labor's rank and file membership. Scalise's career in BSEIU demonstrated the range of predations that union members might suffer. The 2 percent assessment fund revealed the hollow nature of internal union safeguards. Ostensibly a national union's constitution protected the members' interests from potential abuses by the occasionally corrupt official, but the case of the 2 percent assessment indicated how easily those rules could be evaded. It also revealed the willingness of union officials to overlook evidence of corruption within their organization. Only such complicity made a theft of this magnitude possible.

The claim that complicity of that nature was universal later fueled Pegler's biting attacks on organized labor. But in fact, not everyone in the labor movement had chosen to ignore indications of what Browne and Bioff were up to. Long before Pegler took up the cause, critics had emerged within the Hollywood union community who called for an investigation of Bioff and Browne. Meanwhile, Scalise faced dogged opposition in his own union, and it was these opponents who fed Pegler his exposés.

**EXTRA!** IA Progressive Bulletin **EXTRA!**

107 VOL. 1, NO. 11 P. O. BOX 2102, HOLLYWOOD DEC. 22, 1937, 3c

# BIOFF EXPOSED!

**Looking into the past:**
Two choice views of Wm. Bioff in the file of Dept of Police, Chi.

## SURPRISE MOVE
### DESIGNED TO
#### TRAP LOCALS

Sprung with all the characteristic suddenness of a gangster taking a victim for a ride, the IA officials have announced a series of three meetings for Locals 683, 695, 659 to vote on autonomy.

Called in the midst of the holiday season, with everyone busied with Xmas, the meetings are undoubtedly designed to establish a vote of confidence in the present dictatorship of the International.

The first meeting, which includes Local 695, is planned for Wednesday night in the American Legion Stadium; on Thursday night, same place, Local 659 will be called in; Local 683 is scheduled for Sunday at 11 a. m. in the same hall. No date has yet been announced for Local 37.

Advance meetings of "selected members" of Local 37 indicates that members will be told that re-

(Continued on Page 4)

## POLICE RECORDS
### REVEAL PAST

He is the personal representative in Hollywood of George T. Browne, President of the IATSE.

He is the sole power in control of 12,000 members of the studio locals.

He has been responsible for the collection and disbursement of approximately THREE - QUARTERS OF A MILLION DOLLARS.

He is William Bioff, alias Morris Bioff, alias Henry Martin, alias Willie Bioff.

Chicago police records show that at various times he has been arrested for burglary, pandering (pimping), suspicion of burglary. Police suspected him of complicity in the murders of Thomas Maloy, former business agent of the M. P. O. local in Chicago, and Louis Alterie, a West Side hoodlum who at the time of his death was head of the Theatrical Janitors Union.

Police records show further that Bioff was arrested several times on vagrancy charges, one of the methods Chicago cops used to run known criminals out of the city.

Between Feb. 9, 1921, and the end of December, 1935, when he left Chicago to come to Hollywood, he had become notorious as an associate of gangsters and criminal elements in the Windy City.

The Chicago Tribune of July 19, 1935, in a front page account of the murder of "Two-Gun" Louie Alterie said of Bioff:

". . . police were hunting Willie Bioff and Joe Montana, West Side gunmen, thinking they might have knowledge of the ambush which

(Continued on Page 2)

Figure 6.1: This front page from the *IA Progressive Bulletin* on December 22, 1937, highlights the efforts of rank and file union reformers in the International Alliance of Theatrical Stage Employes. Two years before Pegler's exposé, the IA Progressives sought to draw attention to William Bioff's criminal past in Chicago. *IA Progressive Bulletin*, December 22, 1937, courtesy Herbert Hoover Presidential Library.

# 6

# Union Members and Corruption
## *The Potential for Reform*

In 1937, a group of left-wing union members in IATSE Local 37, the Hollywood studio technicians' local, began a challenge to Bioff and Browne's leadership. At roughly the same time, officials in the Screen Actors Guild (SAG) started a similar campaign. These two groups took up the cause of reform for different reasons, but they came to pursue similar strategies. They mounted what became parallel investigations into Bioff's background. Both groups tried to use the information that they uncovered to curb Bioff's activities in Hollywood. Disappointed with the response from government officials, they turned to the press, and Pegler's exposé represented the culmination of these efforts. Their campaigns demonstrated the potential for reform within the union movement.

This was a side of the story that Pegler downplayed in his columns. He paid scant attention to Bioff's opponents in Hollywood and deprecated the information that they had collected on the corrupt IATSE official. The "somewhat amateurish union of motion picture actors" he wrote in reference to SAG, "had been denouncing Bioff as a hoodlum without actually knowing the facts of his criminal background in Chicago." The columnist's treatment of the IATSE dissidents was even more dismissive: he did not even mention the existence of such a group. Instead he referred to information compiled by their attorney, Carey McWilliams. Pegler tagged McWilliams as "a radical laborite" in the column but did not explain that the lawyer represented an opposition group within Local 37. The columnist wrote that McWilliams, "too, had heard that Bioff had a criminal record but, like the actors and bull-dozed studio workers and others already subjugated by Bioff, lacked exact information."[1]

Partly this dismissive slant reflected Pegler's ego, his unwillingness to share credit for his journalistic coup. But it also had political implications. Deemphasizing Bioff's opponents in the Hollywood unions helped justify Pegler's claims of universal complacency within the labor movement. It made it easier to use this scandal to support an antiunion agenda. Also, Pegler may not have wanted to advertise the real debt of gratitude he owed to the left-wing activists who led the opposition to Bioff in IATSE's Hollywood locals. The columnist was, after all, an unabashed anticommunist, who proudly called himself a red-baiter.[2]

Regardless of Pegler's motives, his treatment of Bioff's opponents was unfair. The information they had gathered was better than Pegler described it and without it his exposé would never have occurred. These union reformers took up the struggle against Bioff's corruption in Hollywood years before Pegler did, and they did so in the face of obvious risks. They acted when the erstwhile victims of Bioff's activities in the business community did nothing. While none of the Hollywood movie executives ever notified authorities of what Bioff and Browne were up to, the union reformers did, repeatedly. They not only called on law enforcement to investigate Bioff's activities, they provided government agents with their first tangible leads in the case. While Pegler minimized the role of these reformers, Bioff did not. He credited them with forcing the Outfit to curb its most lucrative schemes.[3]

But if Bioff's opponents demonstrated the potential for reform within the union movement, the history of their efforts also revealed the constraints under which internal union reform operated. This was true despite the fact that in Hollywood these constraints were less severe than elsewhere in IATSE's jurisdiction. They were still severe enough. By the fall of 1939, the dissidents in IATSE Local 37 were defeated utterly and SAG's leadership was forced to make an accommodation with Bioff. The investigations that the reformers had helped trigger had one by one been stymied. Only after Pegler's exposé in November 1939 and his continuing campaign against corruption in IATSE did law enforcement efforts receive a new impetus. The need for Pegler's intervention demonstrated the limits of reform, even in an environment as hospitable as Hollywood. It also highlighted the poor prospects awaiting union reformers elsewhere.

## Reform Efforts within Hollywood's IATSE

The two men who led dissent within IATSE's Local 37 were dedicated reformers who envisioned a very different kind of union movement for Hollywood's studio workers. Jeff Kibre was a tall, open-faced man who had grown up among the studio workforce. His mother had moved from Philadelphia to Los Angeles in 1908, a divorcée with six children, including Jeff who was two years old at the time. She eventually found work in the film studio art departments. Later she remarried and, with her new husband, set up a prop-making business that served the studios and the local nightclubs. Kibre worked in this business while he was growing up, until, like so many other small enterprises, it went under in the early years of the Great Depression.

Though the failure hurt the family's finances, he still managed to attend college. Kibre studied English at UCLA and planned on becoming a screenwriter. But after graduating, he failed to get work as a writer at any of the movie studios. By 1934 Kibre turned back to the work he had grown up with and took a job as a prop maker in one of the movie studios. In January 1936, when IATSE reasserted its Hollywood jurisdiction, he joined Local 37.[4]

By that time he was also a member of the Communist Party of the United States (CPUSA). His commitment to the radical cause had grown steadily during his college years and afterwards. At UCLA, he participated in various left-wing activities, for instance writing several student newspaper columns in opposition to the mandatory ROTC. But as one of his friends later recalled, during his college years Kibre was more "anarchist and bohemian than radical . . . He was not much of a joiner, not one for taking orders." He became more engaged politically after graduation and apparently more willing to accept discipline. By April 1935, his sense of commitment had grown enough for him to overcome his anarchist tendencies and join the Communist Party, which was in that era a highly structured organization.[5]

It was also an organization that sought to influence the trade union movement. Many Communist Party members in this era worked as organizers for the CIO, seeing that labor organization's growth as a way to champion a range of progressive causes, from workplace rights to civil rights. The party had initially been skeptical about the new labor organization, but it soon became an enthusiastic supporter. As historian Robert Zieger has noted, "The CIO program of energetic industrial unionism, anti-fascism, and coalition with progressive political and social forces coincided with the tactical agenda of the CPUSA."[6] But the party also sought a role in AFL unions, aiming to achieve what party leaders viewed as the reform of these organizations. Communists organized insurgent rank and file groups in a number of conservative AFL unions.[7] Kibre was among those who took on that task in IATSE. For that reason, the party made him a "protected member," officially shielding his status as a CPUSA member in order to facilitate his efforts.[8]

While the party's leadership viewed efforts in the Stage Hands Union with cautious optimism at best, Kibre waxed enthusiastically about his mission. He envisioned Local 37 and the other IATSE locals shaking off the control of the national union, ending Bioff's trusteeship, and creating truly democratic bodies that met the needs of the membership.[9] Kibre argued that the emergence of an authentic union movement in Hollywood offered advantages to progressive unionism, specifically the CIO, across the country. "The motion picture industry is an industry of 'public persuasion,' an industry that moulds public opinion," he wrote, "and as such can be an effective instrument for or against our own organization." "A progressive labor movement in Hollywood," Kibre claimed, "could immeasurably strengthen the forward sweep of Industrial Unionism."[10]

Working alongside Kibre in this campaign was Irving Hentschel, who at five foot five and 120 pounds, was a small but also a determined man. He had trained originally as a machinist, and his first union involvement had been with the International Association of Machinists (IAM). At some point, he became a committed Marxist and joined the CPUSA. Later he would tell people that he was "party educated," which may have sounded more fun than it was. The party had sent him to one of its training schools, something it commonly did with working-class members who had little formal education. There he acquired the academic skills and intellectual background necessary to function as an effective organizer for the party. By the mid-1930s, Hentschel was employed in the movie studios and helping to build an insurgency among the Hollywood IATSE members.[11] It was a cause he believed in deeply. Summing up his criticism of IATSE, Hentschel said, "Unionism is something besides paying money into an organization for which you supposedly get something in return, but which you don't have an active part in." A real union, Hentschel argued, was a democracy that reflected the will of its members.[12]

Both Hentschel and Kibre looked to the CIO for inspiration and support. On the West Coast, the CIO's International Longshoremen's and Warehousemen's Union (ILWU) offered a promising model to follow. Led by Harry Bridges, the ILWU had begun in San Francisco as an insurgent movement within the corrupt International Longshoremen's Association (ILA). Whether or not Bridges himself belonged to the Communist Party has long been a subject of controversy, but clearly he was sympathetic to its ideals. Many of the activists who worked alongside of him definitely were party members. This insurgency within the ILA rose to the forefront during the bitter dockworkers' strike in San Francisco in 1934, when Bridges distinguished himself as an effective leader. In the wake of that conflict, Bridges and his fellow activists took charge of the West Coast ILA locals and created a militant labor movement on the docks, one that tackled the abusive hiring practices and poor work conditions long faced by longshoremen. Shedding the last measure of ILA control in 1937, Bridges directed a secession effort that brought most of these locals over to the CIO. He became the CIO's West Coast director and the new ILWU became a core component of the CIO movement.[13]

Hentschel and Kibre wanted the CIO's help in their efforts to move the Hollywood IATSE locals on a similar path. Writing Bridges in 1937 to ask for assistance, Kibre noted the dissatisfaction that existed among rank and file IATSE members. "As a matter of fact many members openly refer to their organization as a 'company union.'" Although IATSE had won pay raises for studio workers, the union had not addressed problems of underemployment, which dissidents claimed negated the pay raises. Nor had the union done much to address troublesome working conditions by creating an effective system of shop stewards in the studios. The union's inactivity in those matters contrasted sharply with the energy Bioff had displayed in helping producers quell a potentially militant union movement in the form of the Federated Motion Picture Crafts (FMPC) strike in the spring of 1937. Bioff's efforts to break that strike fed perceptions that he represented the movie companies and not their employees. The episode contributed to the already smoldering spirit of dissent within Local 37, and, in the wake of the strike, Kibre, Hentschel, and other insurgents formally organized a group called the IA Progressives.[14]

In time, this group presented Bioff and Browne with a potent challenge. The Progressives' ability to do so highlighted the way in which conditions in Hollywood were more conducive to reform than elsewhere in the union's jurisdiction. Most of the IATSE's membership belonged to projectionists' locals around the country, where the workplace dynamics kept them isolated from each other and easily dominated by the union leadership. But in Hollywood, IATSE members labored together in large groups; each film studio employed from two to three thousand workers. The local unions were comparatively large, with Local 37 having about 6,500 members. This meant that dissent had a better chance to coalesce, as workers on the film lots griped about their union's leadership and listened to insurgents propose solutions. It was possible to build up a critical mass of insurgents who could offer each other emotional and physical support, and most importantly the possibility of success.[15]

As the insurgency emerged in 1937, the IA Progressives pursued a strategy that combined litigation, publicity, and secession. The group filed a suit calling for an end of the trusteeships over the Hollywood locals and asking for the restoration of local autonomy. Kibre assumed from the start that those suits would fail because the national union's legal standing was strong enough to withstand a court challenge. The failure of internal reform, Kibre argued, would build support for a movement to secede to the CIO, as the West Coast dockworkers had done. At the same time, the legal efforts would give the dissidents a more public venue in which to make their case to the IATSE membership. "Evidence will be forthcoming," Kibre assured Bridges in a 1937 letter, "which will publicly indict the leadership of the IA."[16] He referred to the information that would ultimately help trigger Pegler's exposé of Bioff.

The man who came up with that initial evidence was Carey McWilliams. As the legal counsel for the IA Progressives, McWilliams stood at the center of the campaign to combine litigation and publicity to achieve reform. An activist whose involvement on the left included political and intellectual endeavors, McWilliams later became well known as the author of the book *Factories in the Fields*, a searing account of working conditions in California's agricultural regions. Later still he served as the editor of the liberal journal *The Nation*. His active role in these efforts and in representing the IA Progressives was part of the emergence during the Depression of a broad coalition on the left known as the Popular Front. Described by the intellectual historian Michael Denning as an "insurgent social movement," the Popular Front drew together disparate elements on the left including Communists, activists in the industrial union movement of the CIO, antifascists concerned about developments in Europe and elsewhere, as well as those involved in the left wing of New Deal politics. These activists were drawn by a goal of creating change that was more fundamental than just a political shift; they sought as well a meaningful change in American culture and society.[17]

A prosperous attorney and budding author, McWilliams had become active in the early 1930s in the Southern California branch of the American Civil Liberties Union. His work with that group had exposed him to the vigilante tactics California growers were using against union organizers in the state's agricultural regions. The violence of the employers convinced McWilliams that fascism presented a real threat in America, and he turned to a progressive labor movement in the form of the CIO as the best way to hold back the threat. He became legal counsel to a number of CIO groups, and in 1937, as the IA Progressives sought CIO support, he took up their case.[18] He believed that in doing so he was able "to assist in the work of developing genuine trade unionism in the motion picture industry." Given the industry's pivotal role in

Los Angeles, McWilliams saw the effort as critical. "If this can be done," he wrote to a friend in late 1937, "it will make a great difference locally in many ways."[19]

At the same time, he was under no illusion about the leaders of the IA Progressives. Although not a Communist himself, McWilliams knew that Communists played a prominent role in this insurgency and in many of the CIO organizations. He did not wholly agree with the party, particularly regarding its claims about conditions in the Soviet Union. Yet he still worked with Communists because, like other Popular Front liberals, McWilliams believed that only a broad left-wing coalition could effectively promote the kind of real social reform America needed.[20] McWilliams explained his position to a friend. "Don't think that I am a 'convert' or a 'revolutionist,'" he wrote in a December 1937 letter describing his work with the IA Progressives. "I am not a CP member. I have worked fairly closely with them locally because they seemed to be the only people who were doing any work."[21]

McWilliams filed the suit against the IATSE trusteeships for the IA Progressives, but he and Kibre also decided to look into Bioff's background in Chicago, apparently searching for material to use in their publicity campaign. They struck pay dirt. Information provided by the Chicago Crime Commission revealed both Bioff's criminal record and allegations that he was tied to organized crime.[22] The dissidents publicized what they had found in the December 22, 1937, edition of their *IA Progressive Bulletin*. Under the banner headline "Bioff Exposed! Police Records Reveal Past," the article quoted various *Chicago Tribune* news stories that connected Bioff to gangsters such as Jack Zuta and "Dago Lawrence" Mangano. The insurgents also provided details from Bioff's police record for the period from 1931 to 1933, when Bioff had been arrested on vagrancy charges. The article in the *IA Progressive Bulletin* explained that such charges were "one of the methods Chicago cops used to run known criminals out of the city."[23]

Pegler would later draw on the same material in his exposé, but when he did so he offered more than just a recapitulation. The article in the *IA Progressive Bulletin* made only a passing reference to Bioff's conviction in 1921, the conviction that formed the heart of Pegler's piece. "Chicago police records," the *Bulletin* noted, "show that at various times he has been arrested for burglary, pandering (pimping), suspicion of burglary." The *Bulletin* offered nothing more on Bioff's pandering conviction. In three long columns that took up most of the four-page publication, the article never drew directly on the arrest report from the pandering case although it quoted the later arrest reports from the 1930s extensively.[24] Perhaps the Chicago Crime Commission failed to supply McWilliams with the 1921 arrest report. Or perhaps the dissidents did not see the dramatic potential in that case, a potential that Pegler later used to great effect. Obviously the dissidents were unaware that Bioff had failed to serve his six-month jail sentence for the pandering conviction. They would never have passed up the chance to use that information against him.

Still, two years before Pegler's exposé, the IA Progressives earnestly struggled to publicize Bioff's shady background. McWilliams devised a strategy to get the information they had uncovered to an audience much greater than just the studio workers who read the *IA Progressive Bulletin*. He tried to spur a government investigation into IATSE's leadership. In the fall of 1937, soon after he filed the suit against IATSE, McWilliams approached an old law school classmate, William Mosley Jones, who had become the speaker of the California State Assembly. Jones had recently pushed through legislation that created a series of interim investigative committees that were empowered to hold hearings in the period between the assembly's regular legislative sessions. The choice of subjects to be investigated was apparently quite open. McWilliams saw the potential publicity value of such hearings and showed Jones the material he had on Bioff. He hoped Jones would set up hearings on corruption within Hollywood's IATSE and generate news coverage that would strengthen the insurgents' cause.[25]

The plan went awry because IATSE was not the only organization in California plagued by corruption. Taking the material McWilliams had gathered, Jones vigorously urged the Interim Committee on Capital and Labor to begin hearings on IATSE's activities in Hollywood. The speaker even offered to provide investigators from his own law firm, Neblett and Jones, to do some of the necessary digging into the finances of the IATSE locals under Bioff's trusteeship.[26]

Jones's enthusiasm, however, did not stem from concern about the plight of rank and file IATSE members. As the committee investigation got under way, the speaker's law firm partner, William Neblett, paid a visit to one of the leading movie producers, Louis B. Mayer. Neblett offered, for a fee, to arrange the downfall of IATSE and thus rid the studios of a powerful union. Mayer later testified that Neblett told him, "I think you have a darned good chance of getting rid of the I.A.T.S.E., if you take care of us." It was a classic case of legislative corruption. Neblett was peddling Speaker Jones's influence over the investigative committee and the kind of hearings it would hold.[27]

Mayer turned him down, but the producers, it turned out, were not the only potential customers for what Neblett could offer. The Interim Committee's hearings opened on November 12, 1937, with testimony by IA Progressives, including Hentschel, who testified about the local union trusteeships dominated by Bioff, the 2 percent assessment fund, and the retaliation that members suffered when they complained about these conditions. Drawing on McWilliams's materials, the Interim Committee members promised tough questions in the near future for Bioff about his background in Chicago. Desperate to avoid such questions, Bioff arranged to pay Neblett off, and through him, presumably bribe Speaker Jones. At Bioff's direction, IATSE officials wrote Neblett a check for $5,000 for unspecified legal services. Neblett also allegedly received another $20,000 in cash from Bioff. The committee's investigation abruptly concluded, and Bioff was spared having to answer detailed questions about his past.[28] He had dodged McWilliams's planned legislative exposé.

Ironically, the hearings vindicated Bioff's trusteeship over the Hollywood locals. The investigators that the firm of Neblett and Jones had supplied to the Interim Committee on Capital and Labor turned in a report that praised the union's leadership and vouched for the integrity of IATSE's financial practices. "Our investigation indicates that the complaints against these organizations are ill founded," the report concluded. The findings were so positive that one might have believed that Bioff's people had written it themselves. And in fact, one of the investigators later testified, that was exactly what happened.[29]

Meanwhile, the hearings resulted in bad publicity for the union dissidents, the opposite of what McWilliams had hoped for. The press coverage of the hearings came to emphasize revelations that the IA Progressives who testified, especially Hentschel, had ties to the radical CIO. One headline in the Los Angeles Times read, "C.I.O. Trick Suspected in Studio Union Inquiry." The next day's headline eliminated any doubt, proclaiming, "Film Inquiry Laid to C.I.O." The text of that article referred to the "Communistic C.I.O." and charges that it sought to "'muscle into' the [IATSE] alliance field." The news stories focused on testimony by IATSE leaders and their supporters who asserted that the IA Progressives were part of a communist conspiracy to help the CIO seize jurisdiction in Hollywood.[30]

The insurgents enjoyed a measure of revenge a year later. A series of scandals in the legislature triggered a public grand jury investigation in the summer of 1938 into influence peddling in the California State Assembly. When the grand jury looked into the previous year's IATSE investigation, it soon uncovered the $5,000 payment to Neblett. Working out from there, the grand jury's investigators exposed the salient details of how the Interim Committee on Capital and Labor had produced a whitewashed report on IATSE's leadership.[31]

But they also uncovered something even more helpful to the insurgents. Bioff's bank records revealed a $100,000 payment he had received on June 25, 1937, from Arthur Stebbins, a nephew of Joseph Schenck, the powerful Hollywood producer. The nephew's bank records indicated that the money had come originally from Schenck, with the nephew's account used as a temporary midpoint in the transaction in an effort to disguise the source of the payment. At the time Bioff received the money, Schenck was chairman of the board of directors of the Motion Picture Producers' Association. He had just coordinated the studios' efforts to defeat the strike by the Federated Motion Picture Crafts. The strike had ended on June 12, thirteen days before Bioff received the $100,000. The two events appeared connected. Bioff's aid to the studios during the strike had drawn criticism at the time, and the revelation of this payment seemed to explain his actions. Everything about the payment—the timing, the effort to disguise Schenck's role, the amount of money involved—looked incriminating.[32]

But according to both Bioff and Schenck, appearances in this particular case were deceiving. Both men later claimed—after they began cooperating with the Justice Department—that the $100,000 had not been a payoff but instead a sham transaction, a fake loan, that would allow Bioff to purchase an expensive ranch he wanted without creating tax problems for himself. Though rich in cash from his illegal activities, Bioff's legitimate assets were not sufficient to buy the scale of property he sought, and such a purchase, he believed, would draw scrutiny from the IRS. To create paper assets, he asked Schenck to arrange the $100,000 as a loan on paper, and then secretly paid the producer back almost immediately.[33] It was a strategic blunder with serious consequences for Bioff. He must have fumed over the bitter twist of circumstances, as the one transaction that was not a payoff only served to confirm everyone's suspicions about his corrupt ties to the producers.

For the IA Progressives the grand jury's revelation was a publicity coup, and they quickly seized on it to further their cause. Citing the $100,000 payment to Bioff, Kibre and McWilliams on September 8, 1938, filed a formal complaint with the National Labor Relations Board (NLRB) against IATSE's leadership and the studio employers. The complaint charged that the studios had paid Bioff this money in return for gaining covert control over the four IATSE locals that operated in Hollywood. "The producers," according to McWilliams and Kibre, "have simulated a process of collective bargaining in an effort to satisfy the legal requirements of the Wagner Act, but actually, because they have been dealing with their assertedly paid agents, Bioff and Browne, [the producers] have refused to bargain with the employees." The result, the insurgents claimed, was a pattern of sham bargaining between IATSE and the employers.[34] IATSE was in effect a company union. If the NLRB vindicated these charges and ruled that IATSE was indeed no more than a covert company union, the agency could decertify IATSE and take away its Hollywood jurisdiction. The IA Progressives would have taken a giant step closer to their goal of bringing the studio workers into a new CIO union.[35]

For Bioff and Browne, and for the Outfit as well, the IA Progressives represented a serious threat, forcing the gang to curtail—at least temporarily—its activities. Bioff later told federal agents that "he, Browne and others were extremely concerned about the charges made against them before the Labor Board on account of his $100,000 transaction and the stock deals with Joseph Schenck." At the same time, they worried about the fact that, as Bioff explained it, "a number of disgruntled but unidentified members of the locals of the I.A.T.S.E. in California had distributed thousands of pamphlets containing [complaints about] the 2% assessment and alleging all kinds of thievery on the part of Browne, Bioff and others in the organization." "While this so-called 'heat' was on," according to the FBI agent's report, "Bioff had advised Browne to promptly grant autonomy to the locals in the Hollywood area and announce the discontinuance of the [2 percent] assessment in question." The IATSE executive board approved both of those measures.[36]

In September 1938, the board also accepted, with great regret, Bioff's resignation. It was a gesture evidently meant to undercut the force of the charges McWilliams had filed with the NLRB. It did not, however, represent a real fall from power for Bioff. Despite his formal resignation, IATSE's general executive board voted to continue Bioff's salary for another year out of gratitude for his "valuable services in the past." Meanwhile, at the behest of the Outfit's leadership, Bioff continued to act behind the scenes as the dominant IATSE official in Hollywood.[37]

But Bioff had clearly suffered a setback, and the discontinuance of the 2 percent assessment was a major achievement for the reformers. The IA Progressives had done something that the employers, the government, and other IATSE officials were unwilling to: they had interfered with the Outfit's ability to use corrupt officials to exploit IATSE members all across the country.

It was, at this point, a lonely effort. Almost no one else seemed interested in stopping Browne and Bioff. The studio executives later claimed to be Browne and Bioff's victims, but in the late 1930s the relationship looked a lot more like an alliance. The producers worked with Bioff in 1937 to limit the damage done by the California State Assembly's investigation. A year later,

Joseph Schenck advised Bioff on how to respond to the grand jury hearings on legislative corruption; Schenck suggested stonewalling and the use of political influence to limit further investigation.[38] In 1937, federal authorities received complaints from IATSE members about the 2 percent assessment and misrule in their union. But the Justice Department recommended against further investigation and the FBI merely filed the complaints away for future reference.[39] Within IATSE, Browne's administration ran unopposed in every union election. When Hentschel presented a reform resolution on behalf of the IA Progressives at IATSE's 1938 convention, not a single other delegate spoke up in support of it.[40]

For its part, the American Federation of Labor had endorsed Browne's administration in the most symbolically important way that it could: in October 1936, Browne was elected to one of the powerful vice president positions on the AFL's executive board.[41] The Federation also lent Browne its support in the struggle with the Hollywood insurgents. In 1938 and 1939, as Browne and Bioff waged a legal battle with the IA Progressives before the NLRB, the AFL's chief counsel, Joseph Padway, represented IATSE's administration.[42]

## Screen Actors Guild

In this period, only one other group besides the IA Progressives sought to bring down the corrupt administration that was running IATSE. Although their politics differed greatly from those of the IATSE dissidents, the leadership of the Screen Actors Guild (SAG) pursued a parallel course. They too investigated Bioff's background and they too sought to use what they found to challenge Browne's administration. The degree of success achieved by SAG demonstrates one more aspect of how the conditions for resisting union corruption were much more hospitable in Hollywood than elsewhere.

SAG emerged in 1933 out of dissatisfaction with the way that the Academy of Motion Picture Arts and Sciences had represented actors in the face of studio demands for wage reductions and other concessions in the early dark days of the Great Depression. To many in Hollywood, the Academy appeared to promote the interests of the producers. That sentiment spurred a few individuals to organize a new union for screen actors. Led by a core group of actors that included Alan Mowbray, Eddie Cantor, and Robert Montgomery, SAG steadily gained credibility in the Hollywood acting community. These leaders sought support in the wider labor movement by affiliating SAG with the existing umbrella labor organization for actors, the Associated Actors and Artistes of America, usually referred to as the Four A's; the association included such groups as Actors Equity, the union representing theater performers. Through membership in the Four A's, SAG became part of the AFL. Winning acceptance from the employers, however, proved more difficult, and for several years SAG's efforts to gain a contract from the movie studios met with frustration. The producers were obdurate and the other union signatories to the Studio Basic Agreement, including IATSE, offered no assistance, refusing to make SAG's request a part of their bargaining demands with the studios.[43]

The breakthrough came in the spring of 1937. The strike by the Federated Motion Picture Crafts (FMPC) put the studios in a vulnerable position, and SAG appeared poised to stage a walkout in support of the strikers. Had that happened, production at the studios would have ceased, something FMPC on its own had been unable to achieve at least partly because of Bioff's efforts. Several observers since that time have interpreted SAG's move to support the FMPC as a strategic feint in their own interest, designed to put pressure on the employers to recognize the Actors. If it was, it succeeded marvelously. Meeting with Joseph Schenck and Louis B. Mayer at Mayer's beach house on May 9, 1937, SAG's leaders worked out the details for a collective bargaining agreement with the studios. The contract set terms for working conditions and provided minimum wage protections for extras and supporting actors; it also granted SAG a union shop, meaning actors working in the studios would be required to join the union. In return, SAG promised not to strike during the life of the five-year contract, guaranteeing it would play no role in the current FMPC strike. Some in FMPC complained about being double-crossed, but for the actors' union, this was a strategic victory and the leaders celebrated their achievement at a victory rally held on the evening of May 9.[44]

At that same rally, SAG's leaders publicly thanked IATSE for its "invaluable support," by which they meant in particular Bioff's assistance.[45] He had been at Mayer's beach house when they got there on May 9, and at a crucial moment in the meeting he appeared to have put IATSE's support squarely behind SAG's demands, threatening a projectionists' strike if the producers balked. According to one account, as SAG's leaders left the beach house that day, one of them said, "Wasn't that wonderful of Bioff?" But SAG's president, Robert Montgomery, responded by raising a forefinger in warning and uttering two words of caution: "Watch it!" From the start, Montgomery viewed Bioff's motives with suspicion.[46]

Montgomery's instincts were sound. Bioff later admitted to the FBI that he was working with the producers at that meeting, acting as a kind of double agent. Moreover, in the months that followed the meeting at Mayer's house, it became clear that Browne and Bioff planned to take over the actors' union or, failing that, to seize its jurisdiction.[47]

Their plans reflected more than the usual expansionist impulses of ambitious union leaders. In this case, Browne and Bioff represented the Outfit, which desired to co-opt another labor organization. A pretext for IATSE's expansion soon emerged in the form of a dispute within the Four A's, the umbrella labor organization of actors. The governing council of the Four A's voted to unseat Ralph Whitehead, the president of one of its affiliates, American Federation of Actors (AFA), a union of burlesque and nightclub entertainers. Acting in defiance of that ruling, Whitehead asked Browne for a charter to bring his organization into IATSE. Such a move would give IATSE (which had never before included performers) an opening wedge into the actors' jurisdiction.[48] Browne later testified that he mentioned the possibility to Nick Circella, his Outfit overseer. "He came back to me about a day or so later," Browne remembered, "and he said, 'George, I would issue the charter to those people.' He said, 'My people would like to get hold of that union.'" Anticipating the money to be made, Frank Nitti designated an Outfit member, Charles Gioe, to oversee the actors' union in the same way that Circella managed the gang's interests in IATSE.[49]

SAG's leaders knew nothing about Nitti's decisions, but on the ground in Hollywood they soon became aware of Bioff and Browne's aggressive intentions. Bioff announced a plan in the fall of 1937 to bring all of the unorganized crafts in the film industry into IATSE. Among the unorganized crafts he included writers, directors, and actors, all groups of professional workers whose labor organizations were titled guilds.[50] Justifying its jurisdictional claims, IATSE officials asserted that such organizations only masqueraded as unions. A resolution issued by IATSE's 1938 convention asked the AFL "to withdraw charters and any other support it is giving to these so-called guilds falsely parading as Labor Organizations."[51] The common assumption was that working through Whitehead's breakaway performers' organization, the AFA, IATSE would take in the numerous extras and supporting actors in Hollywood. This would leave SAG with a nominal organization that included only a small number of stars. SAG's position would then be untenable as a real labor organization, and its role in collective bargaining in the movie industry would end.[52] SAG officials connected IATSE's expansionism not so much to the greed of the Outfit as to Bioff's collusion with the producers. It appeared to SAG's leadership that the producers wanted to use Bioff and IATSE to rid the studios of a bona fide, and therefore potentially troublesome, actors' union.[53] This reading of the situation reflected the fact that—far from being victimized by him—producers were widely seen as using Bioff to achieve their ends.

As the dispute between IATSE and SAG developed, it appeared to be an uneven contest. Many in the labor movement viewed SAG's leadership as dilettantes and amateurs who would be easily outmatched by tough union professionals like Bioff and Browne. As one official in Whitehead's AFA explained the situation to a reporter, the Screen Actors had "let themselves in for more than they bargained."[54]

The president of SAG embodied the dilettante image of that union and its members. Readers today might be more familiar with Robert Montgomery's daughter, Elizabeth Montgomery, the star of the 1960s sitcom *Bewitched*. But in the 1930s, Robert Montgomery was a popular leading man who specialized in playing the flighty, often inebriated, playboy character in romantic comedies, movies with titles like *So This Is College*, *The Divorcee*, and *Petticoat Fever*. As Montgomery himself explained his acting career, "The directors shoved a cocktail shaker into my hands and kept me shaking it for years." Nor did his appearance off the screen contradict the movie characters he played. One profile described him as "a slim, rather elegant young man who collected first editions, played polo, liked to get into hunting pinks, and refused to carry cigarettes because he felt that their bulk spoiled the drape of his coat."[55] He seemed to be a frivolous dandy who could be easily pushed around or manipulated, and that apparently was Bioff's assumption.[56]

If so, the assumption was a mistake. Soon after the Actors had won their first contract from the studios but before IATSE had announced its expansionist intentions, Bioff called Montgomery about a fairly minor internal matter within SAG; it involved a suspension handed out to a SAG member who had done the work of one of FMPC's strikers. Bioff left a message demanding they "reinstate the girl immediately." Montgomery's response was pointed and assured. "The only way I can explain the stupidity of your message," he told Bioff, "is that some oaf in your office got the wrong number." Montgomery would not be bullied. In another phone exchange, when Bioff lapsed into his usual style of threats and profanity, Montgomery simply hung up. SAG's president was tougher than he looked. As his close friend James Cagney later explained, "The one thing Montgomery loves besides his wife and children and a few friends, is a good fight."[57]

The movie playboy image belied a serious man with strong political convictions. Unlike his movie characters, Montgomery drank sparingly in social settings and was known for having a cutting wit. He took an avid interest in politics, but in contrast to the left-wing activists who led the IA Progressives, Montgomery's political trajectory followed a path similar to Pegler's. Montgomery began as a New Deal supporter but moved to the right politically during the course of the 1930s, becoming an earnest anticommunist, a supporter of Thomas Dewey, and later a member of Dwight Eisenhower's administration.[58]

The depth of Montgomery's commitment, as well as his courage, was demonstrated when World War II broke out in Europe. He was in England for a film shoot in early 1940, and although the United States remained neutral, Montgomery was unwilling to be a passive spectator to the conflict. When the film shoot was over, he abandoned his profitable acting career and joined the American Field Service as a volunteer ambulance driver. He served on the front lines in France that spring as the Allied forces crumbled before the German blitzkrieg. For his courage in evacuating wounded soldiers while under fire from a German machine gun, Montgomery was made a chevalier in France's Legion of Honor. When America entered the war in 1941, he enlisted in the U.S. Navy and served as a PT boat squadron commander in the South Pacific. He saw action in the Solomon Islands and later transferred to the North Atlantic, where he won a Bronze Star for his role in the Normandy invasion.[59]

In 1937 and 1938, Montgomery led SAG's resistance to Bioff, and by extension the Outfit. George Murphy, who was another member of SAG's executive board at the time, later recalled, "Without question, Bob Montgomery is the hero of this story. He inspired the rest of us to stand up to the gangsters threatening our industry. It was no easy decision. These weren't movie tough guys; they were the real thing."[60] A clear sense of danger existed. Murphy remembered, "I began to receive veiled threats. The worst concerned my children. I was warned that if I took them out on the street they would have acid hurled in their faces." Other SAG executive board members received death threats passed on from third parties. In one case, a bomb was found connected to the engine block of a SAG official's car. Montgomery brushed aside suggestions that SAG hire guards to protect him, but a committee of movie stunt men did arrange to accompany him and other SAG officials at public gatherings.[61]

Like McWilliams and Kibre of the IA Progressives, Montgomery suspected that Bioff's background would yield useful information for a publicity campaign. Bioff's appearance and manner betrayed his past. Montgomery went before SAG's executive board and asked for a special appropriation of $5,000 to hire private investigators. He promised that if their research turned up nothing he would reimburse the union for the expense, and he supplemented the appropriation with his own personal funds.[62] The investigators he hired were former FBI agents, who almost certainly worked for the Edwin H. Atherton Agency, a private investigating firm based in Los Angeles. These agents assembled materials that matched the ones acquired by the IA Progressives, newspaper clippings and Bioff's arrest records from the Chicago police.[63] It seems likely the investigators tapped the same source as the IATSE dissidents had at the Chicago Crime Commission.

But the investigators hired by SAG went at least one step further. They were the first to uncover Schenck's $100,000 payment to Bioff. By the spring of 1938, according to SAG's attorney, "We knew the bank where the money went into; we knew the source of the money, and we were positive about of our facts."[64] FBI agents later learned that Montgomery had copies of the checks involved in the $100,000 transaction, checks that presumably he got from the Atherton Agency.[65]

Just how the Atherton Agency came to acquire these bank records is not completely clear, but circumstantial evidence points to a deft political maneuver. Information about the payment first surfaced publicly during the August 1938 grand jury hearings on legislative corruption in Sacramento, and the Atherton Agency was also the firm that did the investigative work for that grand jury. It seems likely that Atherton's investigators used the subpoena power of the grand jury to pursue an investigation into Bioff and his corrupt ties to the producers. Given the grand jury's mandate, this was a tangent. In other words, the investigators took advantage of an investigation into legislative corruption to pursue a case on labor racketeering for a private client. The result affirmed Montgomery's choice of investigators. Because SAG had purchased the assistance of a politically potent investigations firm, they reaped substantial benefits. Not only did the investigators uncover a damaging link between Bioff and one of the leading producers, but the grand jury hearings in August 1938 forced that tie into the news. It was the same strategy that McWilliams had pursued a year earlier, but in this case it succeeded.[66]

In his efforts to bring Bioff down, Montgomery went further still. Perhaps because he was aware of how little had been accomplished at the state level in 1937, Montgomery turned for help to federal law enforcement. He arranged for SAG's attorney, Laurence Beilenson, to meet with the secretary of the treasury, Henry Morgenthau Jr. On July 1, 1938, Beilenson personally gave Morgenthau a letter from Montgomery and a copy of the file put together by SAG's private investigators.[67]

The choice of the Treasury Department may seem odd today, when the FBI is seen as the premier federal law enforcement agency, especially in matters involving organized crime. But the situation was quite different in the 1930s. The FBI then largely avoided such cases, pursuing instead less organized but still notorious bank robbers such as John Dillinger and Alvin Karpis. It was Morgenthau's Treasury Department that made the big federal cases against organized crime and corrupt politicians. Treasury's most noteworthy victories included the convictions of Al Capone and later Tom Pendergast, the political boss of Kansas City.[68]

By going to the Treasury Department, however, Montgomery was resorting to a tactic used in the past by antiunion forces. Historically employers had turned to law enforcement, using corruption prosecutions as a way to blunt the force of organized labor's efforts. SAG's leadership must have worried that their actions in this case would appear similar, so they sought with some success to avoid publicity about their consultation with Morgenthau; no mention of the encounter appears in previous accounts of SAG's dispute with IATSE.[69]

Treasury secretary Morgenthau, however, recorded many of the meetings in his office, including this one, and so a transcript of the encounter survives. The transcript reveals the dilemma facing Montgomery and the Actors officials. In seeking the downfall of Bioff, SAG's leaders acknowledged they also were targeting his nominal boss, Browne, the president of IATSE. And as SAG's attorney, Beilenson, noted, "Unfortunately, Mr. Browne is a Vice President of the A.F. of L." Revelations regarding Browne might therefore tarnish the AFL, and SAG could expect little gratitude for such a result. The investigation they wanted might also cause permanent harm to IATSE's standing, and this too was an issue. "We have nothing against the Union [IATSE]," Beilenson asserted, "and the last thing we want to do is destroy the union, but we would like to destroy the leadership." Given such circumstances, SAG's leadership wanted to make sure that their approach to Morgenthau's office remained a secret. Montgomery himself had chosen not to come, Beilenson explained, because his appearance at the Treasury Department inevitably would have become public knowledge. "Everywhere he goes it is catalogued by the press."[70]

That being said, SAG's leadership still depicted themselves as defenders of an honest labor movement. They had no doubts, Beilenson asserted, about the character of Browne and Bioff. "We do feel, as far as Mr. Bioff and Mr. Browne go, they are the worst type of racketeer." The Actors were certain that a "$100,000 bribe was paid to Mr. Bioff to break the painter's [that is, the FMPC] strike in the motion picture industry." That payment, SAG officials asserted, was part of a general pattern of "racketeering" in Hollywood and elsewhere.[71]

Morgenthau was clearly flattered to be approached in this way, and he made an investigation into corruption in Hollywood a priority for the Treasury Department's staff.[72] Morgenthau kept himself informed as the investigation progressed. Almost a year later, the treasury secretary continued his avid interest in the case, describing its progress to Attorney General Frank Murphy and noting that "it was brought to my attention by Robert Montgomery." Proud of the distinction involved, Morgenthau boasted to Murphy, "And he [Montgomery] wouldn't trust it to anybody else except me."[73]

His comment touches on a distinctive aspect of SAG's reform efforts. Faced with an aggressive labor racketeer who threatened his union's independence, Montgomery had a unique resource upon which to draw: his status as a celebrity. As a movie star, his requests for assistance received serious attention from people in power. Another example of this phenomenon occurred in the spring of 1939: apparently impatient with the pace of the Treasury Department's investigation, Montgomery went to the FBI. By this time he was no longer president of SAG, his term of office having expired, but Montgomery still took an interest in blocking Bioff's activities in Hollywood. The Bureau's Special Agent in Charge in Los Angeles went out to Montgomery's house to meet with him and filed a report directly with J. Edgar Hoover, the head of the FBI. Hoover had met Montgomery before, and the FBI director promptly wrote to him about the investigation. Addressing Montgomery as "Dear Bob," Hoover went on to promise "an immediate and complete investigation of this case."[74]

Montgomery's ability to use his celebrity status highlighted another way in which conditions in Hollywood were especially conducive to reform efforts. Elsewhere in the country, complaints by union members and other union officials about the activities of a labor racketeer such as Bioff rarely received a serious response from law enforcement officials. Faced with pressure from the Outfit in Chicago, for instance, union leaders pleaded in vain for help from the police or the state's attorney's office. For the behind-the-cameras studio workers, the same pattern existed in Los Angeles. IA Progressives had turned to District Attorney Burton Fitts in April 1939 asking for a grand jury investigation into Bioff's local activities. Fitts initially promised a vigorous probe but soon changed his mind. After meeting with several IATSE officials and leading studio executives, including Joseph Schenck, Fitts announced to the press that "most of the controversy was based on a complete misunderstanding." He postponed the grand jury investigation indefinitely and took no further action in the case.[75]

Federal authorities usually were no more likely to get involved. The Justice Department responded with a form letter to requests for assistance from dissidents in Chicago who belonged to IATSE's Local 110.[76] A complaint to the Department of Labor from members of a corrupt BSEIU janitors local in Chicago was forwarded to the AFL.[77] The typical victim of union corruption would never be able to reach through the federal bureaucracy to have a one-on-one meeting with a cabinet-level official. Nor would a cabinet-level official be expected to take such a personal interest in the case. The Screen Actors, and especially Montgomery, were the exception that proved the rule of just how stiff the odds were against the typical union member trapped in a corrupt local.

SAG's case was exceptional in another way as well. The typical union dissident, or even group of dissidents, did not have the resources to conduct the kind of preliminary investigation that SAG had been able to commission. Hiring a team of private investigators would be unlikely; hiring a firm as well connected as the Atherton Agency would be downright impossible. Without the kind of incriminating material that Atherton's investigators unearthed, most dissidents were left to make unsubstantiated charges. Those charges, in turn, were easily dismissed as sour grapes from a minority faction in an internal union struggle.

Being in Hollywood mattered, and this was true for the media as well. Reader interest in movie stars guaranteed news coverage of SAG officials that would not have been as easy for union leaders elsewhere to get. When SAG issued a public denunciation of Bioff's criminal record and decried his efforts to move in on their union, the *New York Times*, for instance, covered the charges extensively.[78]

## Pegler's Intervention

Pegler's role demonstrated the same phenomenon. He was drawn to this issue initially because labor relations in the movie industry made for an interesting news story, and as a daily columnist he was always in search of good potential material. His initial columns on the Hollywood labor situation appeared in February and March 1938. The first piece emphasized the paradox of comparatively wealthy actors and screenwriters being involved in a labor movement. "This item will be a sort of overture," he wrote, "to an attempt to describe a strange class struggle which is taking place in Hollywood, where a union of actors and a union of writers is making belligerent passes at the moving picture industry."[79]

But ever the industrious reporter, his columns indicate that he had made contact with Montgomery and with the IA Progressives. In a subsequent column, Pegler mentioned a conversation with Montgomery and referred to concerns that IATSE "might one day try to absorb the actors and writers." IATSE had made "no formal move yet," he observed. "Nevertheless, the actors are wary and are investigating the careers of Mssrs. Brown and Byoff [sic]."[80]

Pegler came back to the story in mid-May 1938. In the meantime, the columnist had met with McWilliams, the IA Progressives' attorney, who later recalled, "I happened to meet Westbrook Pegler in the St. Francis Hotel in San Francisco. We spent an afternoon discussing the strange careers of Messrs. Browne and Bioff." In an apparent reference to that meeting, Pegler sent a telegram to his publisher, Roy Howard, on March 19, 1938, describing a "great gain of information which [will be] useful later." Pegler's personal papers include a copy of the *IA Progressive Bulletin* from December 1937, the issue that included the article entitled "Bioff Exposed!" It seems likely that McWilliams gave Pegler this publication in hopes that the columnist would provide the kind of useful publicity that the dissidents were always seeking.[81]

If so, then they must have been very pleased with his column on May 19, 1938. Pegler began by informing his readers, "A few critical individuals in the mechanical and unskilled lines of work in the moving picture business in Hollywood are waging a fight against the leadership of George T. Browne, president of the International Alliance of Theatrical Stage Employees, and Willie Bioff, his personal representative on the coast." Echoing complaints of the IA Progressives, the columnist asserted that IATSE "is undemocratic toward its rank and file members." He then referred to allegations of Bioff's ties to organized crime in Chicago, allegations that had appeared in the Progressives' *Bulletin*. Pegler's column closed by noting, "Although Mr. Browne is the supreme boss of the Alliance, the opposition for the time being is concentrated on Mr. Bioff, with his delegated powers as personal representative. There is a feeling that, somehow, Mr. Bioff is not the type and that a more suitable man easily could be found to administer the affairs of thousands of workers in a very wealthy union."[82]

But then Pegler left the story alone for over a year, only coming back to it in late August 1939, when he wrote a column on the SAG's efforts to fend off IATSE's takeover. Comparing Browne to Hitler, Pegler depicted the interunion struggle as a smaller scale version of Germany's effort to annex the Sudetenland in Czechoslovakia. The columnist had little to say about the issue of union corruption at this point, except for the final paragraph of the piece. It proved to be a foreshadowing of his exposé of Bioff in November. "The unfortunate actors have one hope," Pegler wrote. "The Department of Justice has lately begun an investigation of Mr. Browne's union, including the career of Mr. Willie Bioff, personal representative of Mr. Browne, who had some interesting adventures in Chicago in the hoodlum days of Al Capone and left his name on the guest books of the Chicago Police Department."[83] It was by physically checking those police records that Pegler uncovered the fact that Bioff had never served the six-month jail term for his old pandering conviction. Pegler made that revelation the centerpiece of his exposé on November 22, just as he went on to use that exposé to raise widespread concern about the problem of union corruption.

In the end, Pegler's involvement proved pivotal. Because in spite of all the advantages that Bioff's opponents in Hollywood enjoyed, their efforts came very close to failing. By the fall of 1939, Bioff had apparently dealt successfully with his opponents in the Hollywood union movement and the investigations launched by the Treasury Department and the FBI had stalled out.

The fate of the IA Progressives was the saddest. After Kibre and McWilliams had filed their charges before the NLRB, citing the $100,000 payment from Schenck to Bioff, IATSE had sought to mollify the dissidents. It granted Local 37 a degree of autonomy in September 1938, and by January 1939, the local was freed from the trusteeship completely. The former dissidents now held office in the local, but they were stuck waging a bitter fight with a faction within the local still loyal to Bioff and Browne. The political fight was exacerbated by a campaign of harassment. IA Progressives in local union office were followed, as were their wives; they received threatening phone calls at home and at work. Kibre was forced to accept bodyguards to protect his safety. Still the reformers persevered, and in March 1939 the IA Progressives' slate won every single office in Local 37's election. Browne and Bioff responded by declaring a state of emergency and reimposing the trusteeship. In an effort to block the reformers, IATSE's national leadership decided to divide Local 37 up into five smaller locals, in which, presumably, it would be easier to keep a lid on dissent.[84]

Abandoning all hope of working from within IATSE, the IA Progressives reformed themselves as the United Studio Technicians Guild (USTG) and filed with the NLRB for a representation election. They asked the federal agency to allow the studio workers covered by IATSE to vote on whether this new labor organization, the USTG, or IATSE would represent them as their official collective bargaining agent. This was the secession movement that Kibre always had viewed as the reformers' long-term goal. The USTG received support from the CIO, which helped with funding and provided organizers to work among the studio workers. The reformers also received a CIO charter for their new organization.[85]

But this assistance cut both ways. It allowed Kibre and Hentschel to conduct a serious election campaign against the better financed and better connected IATSE organization in Hollywood. But it also allowed Bioff to depict USTG as nothing more than an effort by the CIO to move in on the lucrative movie industry jurisdiction. IATSE officials added this charge to warnings that they had long been making about the Communist ties of the IA Progressives. Bioff and Browne, meanwhile, worked to mend their relations with other AFL unions in Hollywood. As a result, the other AFL unions in Los Angeles came to the support of IATSE in a way that they might not have otherwise. As the AFL's official publication in Los Angeles explained, "Every local union in Hollywood realizes what this attack by the CIO means, and they are rallying around the IATSE."[86]

In this way the NLRB election came to involve more than just what IATSE members thought about corruption. Even studio workers who resented Bioff's activities had to consider the risks involved in supporting USTG. Thanks to the NLRB, the election itself would be free and fair, but the aftermath was another story. Studio workers considering how to cast their vote realized that if USTG won, they might well end up belonging to an isolated, and therefore vulnerable labor organization. The studios had made their hostility to USTG apparent. After the election, the employers and the other studio unions could conspire to strip USTG of its jurisdiction, and then the workers who belonged to the new union would be out of work.[87] And then, on the eve of the election, Bioff announced that he had negotiated raises for the IATSE members of 15 to 20 percent from the studios. As one reporter noted, "The question before the voters was no longer who should represent them, but whether they preferred a contract containing a 20 percent increase to taking their chances with the U.S.T.G. and seeing what it could obtain for them."[88]

The studio workers chose security, and at the end of September 1939 USTG was defeated in the NLRB election by a significant margin, 1,967 to 4,460. Banned from rejoining IATSE, the former USTG activists lost their jobs in the studios and faced the possibility of being permanently blacklisted in the movie industry. Kibre bargained to win leniency for some of these activists by promising to leave the movie industry and never return. Hentschel offered to drop his pending lawsuit on IATSE's finances. In return, Bioff and Browne agreed in November to a partial pardon that permitted some of the USTG adherents to return.[89]

Those who were readmitted into IATSE had to sign a formal apology designed, apparently, to reinforce the humiliation of their defeat. The preprinted document declared that the member did "hereby sincerely apologize to the Alliance, its members and particularly to the International Officers for all the derogatory statements made by me against them. I am profoundly sorry now that I made these statements and committed these actions . . . I have reached the conclusion that my activities were wrong, and that the policies of the Alliance are to the advantage of, and for the best interest of its members."[90] For the reformers, this was a bitter pill indeed. As one of them later recalled, "The idea of apologizing to those bastards was a hard one to swallow."[91] Those who refused to sign—and some did—lost all chance of working in the studios.[92]

Meanwhile, Bioff had dealt with the Screen Actors' Guild by agreeing to drop any plans to annex the Actors' jurisdiction. At Bioff's behest, Browne cancelled the charter he had issued to Whitehead's AFA (the nightclub performers' union) and promised to never again raid the Actors' jurisdiction. This move came as the result of a formal agreement that SAG's leadership had negotiated with Bioff and Browne in early September, just a couple of weeks before the NLRB election involving the USTG.[93]

The Actors paid a price for this agreement with IATSE. Minutes from the meeting of the board of directors of SAG on September 2, 1939, reveal part of that price. "In return for said agreement [protecting SAG's jurisdiction] Mr Bioff asks that a letter of thanks for settling the controversy be written to him." The next day, as required, Kenneth Thomson, SAG's executive secretary, sent a letter on behalf of SAG "to assure you [Bioff] the assistance you rendered is appreciated."[94] Also SAG's leadership had to publicly support IATSE in its NLRB election contest with the reformers in USTG. This meant issuing a press release on the eve of the vote in which SAG's board of directors stated that it "stood one hundred percent behind any movement to maintain the position of the American Federation of Labor against encroachment of the C.I.O. upon its jurisdiction in the motion picture industry. This statement is made without reservation or equivocation."[95]

It was not quite as bad as the formal apology IA Progressives were made to sign, but for someone like Montgomery these must have been unpalatable actions. Just a few a months earlier, he had told an FBI agent that "there must be a show down in the film industry, in order that many of the undesirable executives and gangsters associated with the industry be eliminated."[96] Now, in order to win security for SAG, his union had to walk away from such a showdown. Commentators at the time remarked on the degree to which SAG had backed off from its earlier public rhetoric. In the *New York Times*, a columnist in the entertainment section wrote, "The actors made a great point of Bioff's biography and swore and vowed the issue was whether 'gangsters' and racketeers were to control the amusement world. Never! Proclaimed the actors." And now, this writer pointed out, they had signed an agreement with Bioff and thanked him for his efforts; even worse, they publicly support his campaign to defeat the reformers in the USTG. As the columnist observed, "The actors may now taste a little humble pie."[97]

By the end of September 1939, the only remaining significant threat to Bioff and Browne's role in Hollywood were the investigations launched by the Treasury Department and the FBI. And here as well, Bioff seemed to have evaded his opponents. Investigators from both agencies had tracked down leads and compiled evidence of Bioff's corruption, documenting Joseph Schenck's $100,000 transaction with the labor leader and uncovering stock purchases Schenck made for Bioff and expensive home furnishings provided by one of the studios. They appeared to have evidence for a prosecution involving tax evasion and bribery charges against Schenck and Bioff. In August 1939 the Department of Justice deputized a prosecutor, Charles Carr, to serve as a special assistant to the attorney general and assigned him the task of developing cases in the Hollywood corruption investigation.[98] But with Carr's arrival on the scene, the momentum behind the investigation subsided; it began to look unlikely that any successful prosecution would emerge.

Exactly why this shift occurred was not clear. Carr followed the usual procedure and convened a grand jury to hear the evidence and consider an indictment. This was much more than a formality: typically, grand jury proceedings offered a chance to strengthen a corruption case. Witnesses testified under oath and they could be compelled to answer questions, allowing law enforcement officials to pry damaging admissions out of some of the conspirators in a scheme. But in this case, no such admissions emerged and the studio executives remained obdurate. By mid-October 1939, Carr told the investigators that he could see no viable prosecutions coming out of this case. He reported to his superiors in Washington that "the government was on a hopeless fishing trip."[99]

This was a disappointing finding for the investigators, and they expressed doubts about the sincerity of Carr's efforts. In memoranda sent to their superiors in Washington, D.C., Treasury and FBI agents complained about the way Carr conducted the grand jury proceedings. As one FBI agent put it, "It appeared to the writer that Mr. Carr lacked confidence in developing any successful prosecution against anyone."[100] Another Bureau agent complained that Carr had not even bothered to look at the three lengthy reports the FBI had put together on the case.[101] Treasury Department personnel critiqued Carr's questioning of witnesses before the grand jury, which to investigators seemed to be perfunctory. They complained that he violated standard procedure by letting witnesses who had finished testifying confer with ones who were waiting to appear. This allowed the targets of the inquiry to coordinate their stories.[102]

To investigators, it appeared that Carr's conduct stemmed from more than ineptitude. They wrote their superiors about rumors of corruption and political influence. FBI agents reported an informant's claim, for instance, that a deal had been worked out for Carr to become the next U.S. attorney in Los Angeles in return for not vigorously pursuing the Hollywood corruption cases.[103] Treasury agents pointed at Carr's former law partner, who had received a hefty retainer from one of the targets of the investigation.[104]

It is impossible to know for certain whether these allegations were well founded; clearly they were no impediment to Carr's future career. In February 1940, he resigned his position as special assistant to the attorney general and went into private practice. His new partner was a prominent tax attorney, a former associate counsel of the IRS whose list of notable clients included Joseph Schenck. Three years later Carr was named the U.S. attorney in Los Angeles. He held that position from 1943 to 1946, achieving a measure of fame for his vigorous pursuit of Mann Act charges against Charlie Chaplin.[105]

In Washington, officials in the Treasury Department made no reference to the rumors of corruption, but they did conclude that political considerations had derailed the case. Secretary Morgenthau and his top aides had become convinced that the potent influence of the studio executives in Los Angeles made a successful prosecution there very unlikely. Treasury officials requested that the case be reassigned to another prosecutor in some other city, but the Justice Department was reluctant to follow that advice.[106]

In the end, the case was transferred but only after Pegler's exposé, which made Bioff a notorious figure and reinvigorated efforts to pursue the Hollywood corruption investigation. The chronology of events is significant. Carr had completed his grand jury presentation by mid-October 1939 and formally recommended against prosecution. Treasury Department officials made their complaints at the end of that month, to no apparent effect.[107] But then in late November 1939, Pegler began producing his pieces on Bioff, making the issue of corruption in IATSE a mainstay of his column. Days after Pegler's first article on this subject, Secretary Morgenthau asked his staff to locate his "correspondence with Robert Montgomery in regard to Willie Bioff."[108]

By late December, in a meeting between Justice and Treasury Department officials, the attorney general's top assistant revealed the change of attitude that had occurred at the Justice Department. In reviewing the progress of ongoing investigations, he remarked, "One of the cases is against the notorious labor racketeer, Bioff."[109] A few days later, the attorney general himself told Morgenthau, "Of course the Bioff thing is sort of a national scandal. . . . It's looking bad all over this country. I won't feel right about it unless we can get some action."[110]

In the wake of Pegler's columns, the prosecution received new attention. On January 10, 1940, the Justice Department announced Bioff's indictment on tax charges. The bribery investigation of Joseph Schenck was transferred to the U.S. attorney's office in Manhattan, where it led eventually to criminal indictments on tax evasion charges. Convicted in 1941, Schenck agreed to cooperate with authorities in return for a more lenient sentence, and his cooperation set the stage for the racketeering cases against Bioff and Browne, and later against the leaders of the Outfit.[111]

These cases vindicated Pegler's journalism, but they also vindicated the charges that Kibre, Hentschel, and the IA Progressives had first made in 1937. The prosecutors developed leads initially uncovered by Montgomery's private investigators. The IA Progressives and SAG's leadership both played pivotal roles in Bioff's downfall; they were the largely unknown instigators of this scandal. Leaving them out of the news coverage, however, served a purpose. It allowed Pegler to use this exposé to promote his larger political agenda, in other words, to shape a scandal that discredited the entire labor movement. Pegler's own willingness to stand up to racketeers could be compared to the apparently unbroken complacency within organized labor.

Meanwhile an alternative story remained untold. That version would have pointed out how the opposition to Bioff from within the Hollywood union movement compared to the cooperation he received from the studio executives. It would have noted the difficult odds that union reformers faced. And instead of justifying a legislative campaign to curb organized labor, this version of the story might have convinced the public of the need to pass measures that would protect union democracy.

Figure 7.1: Captioned, "Russia's Not the Only One That Fights Alone," Jay "Ding" Darling's cartoon compares Westbrook Pegler's campaign against union corruption to the Soviet Union's valiant struggle against Nazi Germany. The cartoon depicts a fearless Pegler using his pen to take on labor racketeers while the Roosevelt administration, Congress, and employers cower in fear. The cartoon appeared in the *New York Herald-Tribune* on November 14, 1941, the day after William Bioff received a ten-year jail sentence for his conviction on extortion charges. Courtesy of the "Ding" Darling Wildlife Society.

# 7

## The Newsmen

### *"Molders of Public Opinion"*

Jay Ding Darling's cartoon of Pegler, published in November 1941, celebrates the columnist as a courageous journalist. The caption, "Russia's not the only one that fights alone," referred to the Soviet Union's battle against Nazi Germany unaided in 1941 by allies in mainland Europe. The allusion reinforced the cartoonist's depiction of Pegler as a lone crusader.[1] Pegler portrayed himself the same way in his columns, as the intrepid reporter who was willing to confront the labor bosses in order to protect American workers. "I ventured into this controversy," he wrote in April 1942, "when mine was a very unpopular cause and do not intend to quit now that the real enemies of American Labor [abusive union leaders] are on the defensive and on the run."[2] The language he used depicted this campaign as an actual physical fight. "I love it when these labor skates get sore and start swinging from their heels. Then I stand back and pop them silly, as I will now proceed to do to the editors of a journal of the A.F. of L. called 'The Labor Union.'"[3]

But the image of the lone journalistic crusader was inaccurate. Pegler belonged to a larger effort in this period to use the power of the press to sway public opinion; although he was a crusading journalist, he was hardly on his own. Pegler received support and encouragement from his publisher, Roy Howard, head of the Scripps-Howard newspaper chain. Howard and other important conservative newspaper publishers bitterly opposed the New Deal, and they employed the news pages and editorial spaces of their publications to support their conservative stands. This was a politically engaged brand of journalism. Writing to a member of the Scripps-Howard staff in 1937, Howard asserted, "Unfortunately, for the time being at least the Republican

Party seems to be hopelessly moribund. However, this fact does not seem to me to relieve us from our obligations as journalists who seek to function as molders of public opinion."[4]

Howard and other Scripps-Howard executives came to focus much of their enmity against one particular aspect of the New Deal: the Wagner Act and the changes that that legislation had wrought in the field of industrial relations. As the Wagner Act grew in importance to Howard, he came to see the problem of union abuses as a key issue, a way to rally opposition to the New Deal. In the summer of 1939, executives at Scripps-Howard decided to mount an editorial campaign on this subject. Soon afterwards, Pegler's exposés of Bioff and Scalise appeared and presented a compelling example of that very issue. The columnist's follow-up to those exposés, which became a continuing campaign against union abuses, promoted Howard's conservative political agenda.

Pegler aimed to influence public opinion as well, and this desire shaped his reporting on the scandal. Looking back in 1942 on the stories he had written over the last couple of years, Pegler wrote, "Through my efforts American Labor has now learned that unions, as now constituted and conducted under the existing laws, are a menace to the freedoms and the form of government that this country is fighting to preserve against Hitler and the Japs."[5] Pegler used investigative reporting and his own pungent writing style to raise those concerns. He took on the role of muckraking journalist, achieving a political impact that was similar in scale to his Progressive predecessors'. But the columnist also shaped this news story in specific ways, emphasizing some aspects of what occurred and deemphasizing or ignoring others. In particular, Pegler obscured the sources of his scoops because they undercut one of the central themes of his antiunion argument, specifically the monolithic corruption of organized labor.

Pegler's account of the scandal became the standard journalistic depiction. Other news accounts of Bioff, Browne, and Scalise latched onto the image of duplicitous labor leaders betraying their hapless members. The misdeeds of those individuals, news accounts informed the public, indicated a much larger problem in the labor movement. Meanwhile, the role of organized crime, political corruption, and the complicity of the employers received almost no attention. As a result, the scandal offered a morality tale about the rise to power and subsequent corruption of the labor movement. While that message would prove useful for conservatives seeking to rally opposition to the New Deal, it had less to offer the working men and women who were the real victims in the scandal. Just as the history of this scandal involves the criminal acts of Bioff, Browne, and Scalise, it also reflects the motives of the journalists who transformed that corruption into a particular kind of story.

## The Publishers

Franklin Delano Roosevelt faced bitter opposition from powerful elements within the Fourth Estate; he claimed that 85 percent of the nation's newspapers opposed his administration. Later studies have thrown that percentage into question, although they do suggest that the proportion of opposition was 65 percent.[6] Roosevelt's enemies included an important group of newspaper publishers, among them Roy Howard, who led the Scripps-Howard newspaper chain and who employed Pegler as one of his star columnists. These publishers became early bastions of support for the conservative counterattack against the New Deal. They played active roles in Republican Party politics, but they also used their power in the media to attempt to sway public opinion, seeking to discredit the New Deal. Publishers influenced editorial expressions and news coverage, but in the 1930s and 1940s, they also used syndicated columnists. Ostensibly independent voices of opinion and analysis, columnists offered publishers an avenue of influence at once indirect and potent.

For a time, early in the Roosevelt administration, Roy Howard had been a fervent supporter of the New Deal. His shift into the ranks of the opposition carried important implications because Howard led what had been one of the most powerful media voices on the progressive side of the political spectrum. The Scripps-Howard newspaper chain included twenty-four newspapers strung out across the country from New York City to San Francisco, mostly located in medium-sized cities such as Indianapolis and Memphis.[7]

Edward Wyllis Scripps had built the chain in the late nineteenth century. A legendary pioneer in the newspaper industry, Scripps was also an eccentric. Until late in his life when his doctors made him reform, he chain-smoked cigars and drank gargantuan amounts of alcohol, reportedly regularly consuming thirty cigars and four quarts of whisky in a day.[8] But he was also a canny businessman. In 1878, he had seen the penny press, newspapers that made profits on mass circulation, emerge in the nation's largest urban areas, and he focused his attention on bringing similar publications to medium-sized industrial cities.[9]

His newspapers appealed directly to a working-class audience and featured an editorial policy that championed their interests, what he referred to as the good of the "95 percent" of society who were not powerful or privileged.

Scripps's motto, which explained his papers' principle, was "always opposing the rich, always supporting the working man." This policy included vociferous support for the right to unionize and other causes often inimical to the mainstream press.[10]

Defiantly progressive, even radical, such editorial stands also proved quite profitable, and the newspaper chain thrived. Scripps became wealthy and gradually retired from active management of the chain, taking up the life of a gentleman rancher at his southern California estate. In 1922 he appointed Roy Howard to run the business in partnership with his son, Robert Paine Scripps. The senior Scripps died in 1926. By all accounts his son, only tepidly interested in the newspaper business, played a restricted role in the day-to-day management of the chain; after Robert Paine Scripps's death in 1938, Roy Howard chaired the trust that controlled the Scripps-Howard corporation, thus assuming complete control of the business.[11]

A compactly built man, with a "a high banjo-string voice," "a tendency towards prolix," and a flamboyant taste in clothing, Howard very much enjoyed center stage.[12] As one profile of him put it, "He carries walking sticks, his folded pince-nez invariably swings across his waistcoat, and to see him stride through a city room on one of his best days is to see an army with banners."[13] Howard had reached the center of this particular stage by working his way up the ranks of the newspaper business. The son of a railroad worker, he started out as a poorly paid reporter at the *Indianapolis News*, then wrote and edited for a number of papers until he was appointed to lead the newly founded United Press wire service. His success in building up that operation caught Scripps's attention and secured his fortune as the older man entrusted him to lead his newspaper chain. By the late 1930s, Howard was a wealthy man, earning an estimated a half a million dollars a year in personal income, and determined to wield influence in the political arena.[14]

But as he wielded that influence, his politics shifted. Over the course of the 1930s, under Howard's leadership, the Scripps-Howard chain abandoned its identification with progressive causes and moved decisively to the right. The shift was dramatic. At the start of the New Deal, Howard offered enthusiastic support to President Roosevelt. FDR's press secretary Steve Early informed the president in 1935 that under Howard's leadership the Scripps-Howard newspapers were "truly carrying the flag for the New Deal."[15] But by 1937 support gave way to opposition. In June 1937, Howard wrote to Scripps-Howard's editor in chief, George B. Parker, that under Roosevelt's leadership, "We in the United States are in the process of abandoning the Capitalistic system."

The newspaper publisher now believed that Roosevelt had been led astray by the most radical members of his New Deal administration and was taking the country in a direction that few people wanted. Howard cited the role of New Deal insiders, such as Thomas Corcoran, an influential official at the Reconstruction Finance Corporation, and Benjamin Cohen, a government attorney whose recent biography was subtitled *Architect of the New Deal.* "I think, in a word," Howard wrote to his editor in chief, "that Roosevelt, egged on by the Cohens, Cochrans [sic] and their ilk, is getting away with murder, and I believe that the situation is rapidly developing to a stage that calls for some action on our part."[16] Henceforth the Scripps-Howard papers' editorial policy supported Roosevelt's opponents on a range of issues, from the restructuring of the Supreme Court to the executive reorganization bill. In 1940, Howard vigorously backed the presidential candidacy of Wendell Willkie, Roosevelt's Republican opponent.[17]

Observers at the time offered various explanations for Howard's shift. FDR insinuated that Howard's resentment over paying the higher income taxes needed to fund New Deal relief programs motivated him to join the opposition.[18] Others have noted Howard's concern about the growing power of organized labor, particularly the Newspaper Guild. Formed in 1933, the group evolved over the next couple of years from a professional organization of newswriters into a trade union that engaged in collective bargaining.[19] Howard himself always claimed that he had not changed at all but continued to champion traditional liberal ideals as Roosevelt's New Deal veered away into radical waters.[20]

Whatever the reason for his shift, Howard now joined the ranks of other powerful publishers whose ability—and willingness—to affect news coverage made them dangerous opponents of the New Deal. Critics at the time referred to them as the "press lords," newspaper owners who were politically active, conservative, and capable of shaping public opinion.[21] The so-called press lords included men like Frank Gannett, the conservative owner of the nation's third-largest newspaper chain.[22] In 1937, after Roosevelt announced plans to reorganize the Supreme Court, Gannett set up the National Committee to Uphold Constitutional Government, which played a leading role in blocking FDR's efforts.[23] Three years later, Gannett ran in the Republican Party's presidential primaries as a dedicated opponent of the New Deal and all that it stood for.[24] Ideologically ranged alongside Gannett stood prominent publishers such as William Randolph Hearst, whose newspapers reached as many as 30 million readers a day, and Colonel Robert R. McCormick, outspoken owner of the *Chicago Tribune*, a paper read daily by as many as a million residents of the greater Chicago area.[25]

Critics at the time and since have highlighted examples of the ways publishers openly worked to influence the news.[26] In 1935, a memo sent to all Hearst editors and Universal News Service bureaus read, "The Chief [Hearst] instructs that the phrase 'SOAK THE SUCCESSFUL' be used in all references to the [Roosevelt] Administration's Tax Program instead of the phrase 'SOAK THE THRIFTY' hitherto used, also he wants the words 'RAW DEAL' used instead of 'NEW DEAL.'"[27]

As Roy Howard joined the ranks of the opposition, he took similar steps to mold the news that appeared in his chain's papers. In a letter to the executive editor of Scripps-Howard's flagship paper, the *New York World-Telegram*, Howard wrote, "I think it should be our definite policy to print everything cogent and understandable that is calculated to impress the public with the fact that the government is demonstrating a drunken sailor's attitude towards the billions gathered from the taxpayers."[28]

Such anecdotes highlight the most extravagant examples of how conservative publishers sought to shape the news, but the more effective forms of influence were both mundane and ubiquitous. In the mid-1930s, Leo Rosten conducted a comprehensive study of the Washington Press Corps, and one of the issues that he focused upon was how publishers influenced the reporting of their correspondents. In talking with reporters, Rosten found few examples of direct orders being issued to write a certain way. Instead he cited the role of institutional incentives that worked indirectly but constantly to steer reporters in particular directions.[29]

Through these incentives, writers learned to respond to issues in a way that matched their publishers' priorities. "As a human being," Rosten wrote, "the reporter adjusts himself to the tastes of other human beings who pass judgment on his work." Correspondents whose views accorded with those of their superiors received the better writing assignments. They watched and saw how stories written one way were relegated to the back pages and stories written with another slant made the front page. Reporters tailored their articles accordingly, without ever receiving an overt order to do so.[30]

Syndicated columnists offered conservative publishers another venue through which to try to influence public opinion. Such efforts had a surreptitious quality to them because although these columnists made no claim to objectivity, they did present the appearance of independence, and that fact constituted an important part of their appeal.

Open censorship, once again, played a less important role than more indirect but consistent methods of influence. Publishers at times killed columns they found unacceptable or excised offensive sections, but such overt acts were comparatively rare.[31] Roy Howard managed a stable of columnists through a corporate subsidiary of Scripps-Howard, and his correspondence reveals his reluctance to take such dramatic actions. That kind of overt censorship cost money, in the loss of columns that were already paid for, and it undercut the value of the product Howard's company sold by sullying the columnists' reputation for independence.[32]

Instead Howard's correspondence indicates an ongoing campaign to encourage cooperation. This included getting columnists to focus on particular subjects and not others as well as steering them to approach a subject from a particular angle. In 1941, Howard wrote Scripps-Howard's editor in chief about his management of General Hugh Johnson, a popular political columnist of the day. "I must say that in all fairness Johnson has been extremely tractable recently. I have explained to him my plan to move into this fight on the blank check bill gradually, and to have the pitch of our fight rise gradually. I have had a hundred percent co-operation on suggestions I have made to him on topics to be covered."[33]

Given their status as the stars of the editorial page, with the resultant egos and individual agendas, Howard did not always achieve that level of cooperation with his columnists. But he worked towards it tirelessly, handing out flattery here, avuncular advice there, and at times stern warnings.[34] For the columnists, as professional writers, this constant stream of criticism and guidance coming from their employer had a significant impact. Raymond Clapper's wife recalled how even as her husband acquired growing popularity and critical acclaim for his columns in the early 1940s, he remained especially sensitive to Howard's criticism. Clapper told her at one point, "If I ever got a swelled head you can trust Roy to take it down."[35]

Pegler's situation in this respect was no different. Scripps-Howard executives did view him as their most talented and most troublesome columnist, but they still made every effort to win his cooperation. Howard had given Pegler his big break, hiring him to write a column in 1933, and that early support helped justify the publisher's regular practice of critiquing Pegler's columns. Suggestions came in the form of tips on style and content. Howard framed the input as helpful and well-meaning advice, putting himself forward not as a censor but as one who sought to foster and then guard Pegler's success. A strong friendship between the two men, who had known each other for decades, eased Howard's task. Moreover, the men shared similar political views, both coming to oppose the New Deal by the end of 1936. Their closeness—aided by Howard's assiduous coaching—meant that the views expressed in Pegler's columns reflected Howard's politics. In a 1941 profile of the publisher, A. J. Liebling wrote that through Pegler's columns Howard "had found his voice."[36]

This close tie between the publisher and his star columnist formed the backdrop to Pegler's crusade against union corruption because by the late 1930s Howard was focusing attention on the rise of organized labor. By the winter of 1936–37, internal correspondence between Howard and other executives at Scripps-Howard showed increasing hostility to the Wagner Act. Tense relations with the Newspaper Guild formed the backdrop for this hostility, but so too did the wave of sit-down strikes, which began that December 1936 in Flint, Michigan. In February 1937, Howard wrote privately to one of his columnists, Hugh Johnson, "I think the Wagner law is a very faulty and poorly constructed piece of legislation. I'm not sure but the best thing that could happen would be to have it knocked out." A year later, while having lunch with President Roosevelt, Howard insisted that revising the act should be at the top of the administration's agenda.[37]

In the spring of 1940, Howard explained to Scripps-Howard's editor in chief his rationale for targeting the issue of union abuses and their connection to the Wagner Act. The issue would highlight the way the New Deal expanded the power of the executive branch by catering to particular interests, among them the leaders of organized labor. "The fundamental criticism to be levied against the Roosevelt administration," Howard wrote, "is that it has advanced government by man as against government by law. If we are going to continue to deserve rating as liberal newspapers we have an obligation, it seems to me, to wage unending warfare against government by man instead of government by law and I think the Wagner Act furnishes as good a stage and as good a setting as we could expect to find for making this fight."[38]

Thus as the 1930s came to a close, Howard and his colleagues at Scripps-Howard viewed the Wagner Act not just as a political issue of great significance but as the best grounds on which to battle the New Deal. They believed that their newspapers could and should draw public attention to the issue. In late August 1939, Howard encouraged his staff to prepare a series of editorials that would indict the law for making labor conditions worse and for ignoring the concerns of working people.[39] Three months later, Scripps-Howard's star columnist, Howard's good friend and informal spokesman Westbrook Pegler, offered his exposé of Bioff, and by early 1940, that exposé had evolved into a major campaign against union corruption.

## The Exposé and Pegler's Anti-Union Corruption Campaign

Pegler's initial stories in 1938 about tensions between the Stage Hands Union and the Screen Actors Guild mentioned Bioff's criminal record, but the columnist did little at that time to pursue the Bioff angle. At that point he was not working to develop the theme of union corruption as a way to denounce organized labor. Instead Pegler tried to use his early reports on the Hollywood labor scene to highlight the aggressive empire-building of an AFL union and to raise the specter of left-wingers controlling the content of America's films.[40]

But he soon became frustrated with efforts to shape that story out of the events unfolding. In March 1938, he wrote in his column that if his readers found the stories on IATSE and the actors boring, "you have nothing on me, because for some reason it doesn't jell, and after today to hell with it." The story he hoped to find was not there. "I doubt that the Writers Union will grow enough muscle to impose a closed shop and an indirect but effective form of censorship, and it seems unlikely that the alliance of stagehands, gaffers and other block-gang [that is, IATSE] will ever take over the beautiful dilettante-laborites of the Actors' Union and cut a 10 per cent slice right off the top of those $200,000 and $400,000 salaries."[41]

A year later, Pegler came back to the subject of IATSE's leadership in Hollywood. He did so as his publisher planned a series of editorials that would use the theme of union abuses to attack the Wagner Act. Pegler's own columns increasingly had taken on the same issue, and in August 1939, he had denounced labor leaders by comparing them to Chicago racketeers who sold "'protection' to businessmen." That fall he pursued a story that could demonstrate this comparison; Pegler went back to work on the allegations surrounding Bioff's past. This time the columnist took the trouble to visit Chicago and track down the court records involved in Bioff's 1922 conviction. He also talked to policemen who remembered Bioff. Pegler found specifics both on Bioff's arrest and the fact that Bioff had never served his prison sentence.[42]

It was a story that ideally suited Pegler's current purposes. On November 22, 1939, his column opened on a dramatic note. "Willie Bioff, the labor dictator of the entire amusement industry of the United States and Canada and sole arbiter, on the union side, of problems affecting the 35,000 men and women of the mechanical crafts of Hollywood, was convicted of pandering in a trial before Judge Arnold Heap of the Chicago Municipal Court in February, 1922." Pegler revealed that although Bioff had been sentenced to serve a six-month jail sentence, he in fact had been released on bail after serving only seven days and had never been called back to complete his sentence. The column went on to report in vivid detail the crime for which Bioff had been convicted as well as the assertions by Chicago police officials that Bioff was a longtime associate of the Capone gang. He was a bona fide racketeer. In the weeks that followed, Pegler came back to the story, hectoring the State of Illinois to force Bioff to finish serving his sentence and mocking Bioff's attempts to defend himself.[43]

During these first couple of months, as the columnist turned again and again to this story, the outline of Pegler's campaign gradually took shape. Initially it focused on bringing Bioff to justice, an effort that Pegler warned was likely to be stymied by the IATSE leader's ties to Hollywood employers and the assistance he received from corrupt political figures. "There has been so much failure and evasion by public officials up to now that it must be assumed that the investigation and prosecution will be thorough only if the officials are kept in the glare of public scrutiny and suspicion constantly until the job is done."[44]

Also in this initial stage, Pegler raised the issue of the employers' complicity. He referred to the role of Hollywood studio executives, which was in striking contrast to the columns he produced later in the scandal. In December 1939, Pegler wrote, "Further developments—if the officials, in both California and Illinois, are closely watched and not allowed to sneak over any fast ones—might show why it was that the movie industry—that is to say, the employing side—liked to sit across the table from Bioff in the role of labor's man." Pegler highlighted the inaction of the movie industry executives who "never made any move to discredit Bioff," despite the fact that his criminal past had been "common knowledge in Los Angeles for years."[45] These references to political corruption and the role of the employers demonstrated the issues Pegler might have developed in his reporting on this story.

But he soon stopped pursuing such angles. Instead, by January 1940, Pegler came to focus exclusively on union abuses and the complicity of union leaders. The columnist picked up the new theme on January 6 when he denounced William Green, the president of the American Federation of Labor (AFL). Pegler argued that Green was complicit and that his failure to police the AFL had allowed not just Bioff's entrance into the house of labor but in fact a larger process of racketeer infiltration. "A roster of the officials of A.F. of L. unions presents a number of candidates for a rogues' gallery," Pegler charged. "To the extent that he persistently declines or neglects to interfere Mr. Green is himself a party to a state of affairs which is not only a disgrace to his organization but a much worse menace to organized labor than all the Girdlers and the Communists together."[46] (Thomas Girdler, the head of Republic Steel, was notorious for his ruthless opposition to unions.) The problem, Pegler concluded, was the corrupt nature of much of the union leadership and the complaisant attitude of the remainder.

A week later, this new line of emphasis shaped Pegler's report on Bioff's indictment for income tax evasion on January 10, 1940. The tax charges stemmed mainly from Joseph Schenck's $100,000 loan to Bioff in 1937. The Internal Revenue Bureau viewed that transaction as a bribe and legally therefore unreported income for Bioff. Pegler briefly reviewed the reasons why the film studios would have wanted to reward Bioff, but the columnist avoided referring to Schenck, or any other movie executive, by name. "If he [Bioff] had been bargaining hard for the workers, no magnate would have been likely to give or even lend him $100,000." Pegler also avoided labeling this $100,000 transaction with the harsh term *bribery*. In the same article, however, he treated the union side quite differently. Referring to the high dues and initiation fees charged by some IATSE locals, Pegler denounced the whole organization as a "union which extorts an income tax from American workers amounting to 10 percent of their gross earnings and has been known to extort an initiation fee of $3,000."[47]

And in that article reporting on the alleged $100,000 bride paid by Schenck to Bioff, Pegler closed by asserting that episode demonstrated the guilt and the complicity of the AFL's president. "This is one of William Green's most important unions, and Mr. Green's comment on the revelations concerning Bioff, therefore constitute a resounding affirmation of the policy of the A.F. of L. on the subject of racketeers in the labor movement. Mr. Green has said exactly nothing. That is what makes the comment so resounding."[48]

For the next several years, Pegler hammered at away at that theme. The columnist alternated between examples of corrupt union officials and denunciations of Green and other leaders for their allegedly uniform complicity. Pegler's focus on this theme became so frequent that he came to refer to it as "Topic A." As he put it at the start of a column in November 1941, "Here we are back on Topic A, but no subject interests more people than the union thing just now."[49] Any variation was so unusual that it drew attention. *Newsweek* reported on a Pegler column in 1943 that took the form a whimsical poem about selling an unused suit. The article concluded, "Next day Pegler was back in his familiar groove, castigating racketeering labor unionists."[50]

And it was invariably the labor unionists, not the employers, who he casti-gated. Between 1941 and 1944, Pegler reported on the role of the Hollywood executives in the scandal on only three occasions. During Browne and Bioff's racketeering trial in November 1941, Pegler wrote skeptically about the testi-mony of studio executives who claimed that Bioff had extorted money from them. Pegler noted that these same executives had stonewalled him when he was first researching his exposé on Bioff. The column concluded, "Well, the story is still no more than half told, but when the trial is over there will be further dispatches, you may be sure, about the business morals of the men in the movie industry."[51] When the trial concluded, however, no such dispatches appeared.

Two years passed before he touched on this part of the story again, in one column in May 1943, and then one final time in January 1944. On the latter occasion, Pegler wrote about the Hollywood employers at the conclusion of the racketeering trial of the Outfit's leadership. Again he cast doubt on the testimony of the studio executives who claimed to have been victimized by Bioff and the Outfit. "I insist," he wrote, "that there was a meeting of the minds in which the employers willingly collaborated to get an advantage over the workers of the industry and profit for themselves."[52]

It was an aspect of the scandal that he had never developed in his report-ing, but Pegler took no responsibility for that omission. "It has sometimes been charged that I am partial to crooked employers in scandalous rela-tions between unions and industry. I have never been, and this is one case in which I am convinced that the employers deserve the official attention of the United States Department of Justice." He eschewed taking on any such project himself, however, and he offered no explanation of why the matter had gotten such negligible attention in his columns.[53] Pegler never mentioned this angle to the story again. These three columns were the exceptions that proved the rule; they demonstrated a road not taken in terms of his journal-istic campaign and the way he had shaped the story of the scandal.

Similarly Pegler refrained from pursuing stories about the political cor-ruption in Chicago. Such corruption, especially within the city's law enforce-ment community, had allowed the Outfit to flourish and facilitated the gang's move into labor racketeering, which had set the stage for Bioff's activities in Hollywood. It was a central part of this scandal's history. Pegler's lack of coverage could not be explained by a lack of familiarity with conditions in Chicago. He had grown up there and throughout the late 1920s and early 1930s worked for the leading Chicago newspaper, the *Tribune*. Nor was the columnist without useful sources in the city's law enforcement community.

Pegler's reportage on the Bioff scandal drew on information provided by investigators in the Chicago prosecutor's office, specifically the subordinates of Captain Daniel Gilbert, the chief investigator for the Cook County state's attorney. These subordinates gave Pegler access to police records and offered background information on Bioff and his union associates.[54] Despite—or perhaps because of—his use of those sources, Pegler's columns did not cover the allegations of organized graft that swirled around State's Attorney Thomas Courtney and Captain Gilbert in the early 1940s.[55]

About the actual racketeers—in other words, the Outfit—and its role in this scandal, Pegler did offer his readers some information. In early April 1940, he wrote a couple of columns about Frank Nitti, "the boss criminal or regent of the new Capone mob in Chicago." The columnist was one of the first journalists to publicize Nitti's actual role in the gang hierarchy. Pegler referred to the gang's move into labor racketeering in the same column, writing of "the new Capone mob which has now muscled into Labor with a capital L." That June, Pegler neatly summarized the position of IATSE's president, George Browne. "Mr. Browne is not his own man. He was picked up out of obscurity by a Chicago mob and placed in the union presidency as a dummy for the racket."[56] In these columns, Pegler offered a general outline of how the Outfit had co-opted a corrupt leader like Browne to aid in their schemes.

But generally, Pegler's columns offered a less informative and less balanced depiction of organized crime's role. A column in August 1942, for example, depicted the union movement in general in Chicago as never having been anything but an adjunct of organized crime. It was, he wrote, "a city where organized labor always has been a racket dominated by criminals and where the few honest leaders have silently condoned such evil conditions either out of fear of the underworld or in an uncourageous belief that to drive the rascals out would be to cause scandal and harm to the cause of labor."[57] More common, however, were the columns where Pegler simply equated IATSE with organized crime by describing it as "the Stage Hands' and Movie Employees' Mob."[58]

In the end, the columnist appeared uninterested in the role of Nitti or the Outfit in this scandal. He referred to them in only a handful of columns. And when he did mention them, he blurred the difference between actual organized crime figures and labor leaders he viewed as complicit. Despite his careful explanation in June 1940 of Browne's role as a front man, a year later Pegler wrote, "Now I suppose everyone knows that George Browne, the Chicago gangster, is a vice president of the A.F. L."[59]

Pegler had decided that the story to be pursued in the Bioff scandal was the menace of corruption in the leadership of organized labor, that and nothing else. It was in that light that on January 19 Pegler's column took the form of an open letter to William Green. In it Pegler dramatically revealed that George Scalise, president of Building Service Employees International Union, had been convicted in 1913 for violating the Mann Act, engaging in "white slavery" as Pegler referred to it. Similar to the column on Bioff, Pegler included allegations that Scalise associated with organized crime figures, in this case Frankie Yale, and other Brooklyn mobsters. The columnist emphasized the similarity between the two labor leaders. Addressing Green, Pegler wrote, "There is your colleague George Scalese [*sic*], to keep your noted co-worker Willie Bioff company. They have everything in common."[60]

Pegler offered this revelation as proof for his assertion that "the roster of officials" in the AFL "contained the nucleus for a good, major league rogue's gallery." But it also represented a challenge and a rebuke. Pegler wrote Green, "I can't see how you can fail to know what he [Scalise] is or, if you do know what he is, why you haven't had him thrown out of the American Federation of Labor. Do you think it is doing the American Federation of Labor any good to permit such a man to be president of one of your big international unions or doing the rank and file working stiffs any good to subject them to the rule of a vicious mobster?"[61]

For Pegler, the unmasking of Bioff and Scalise had a wider significance. It demonstrated the corrupt nature of the entire leadership of the AFL and justified efforts to amend the Wagner Act. In February 1940, Pegler wrote, "I have recently named two racketeers in control of two big A.F. of L. international unions, but I could name a hundred thieves and gangsters, embezzlers and terrorists who hold office in unions of the American Federation of Labor. They infest the A.F. of L. to such a degree that the organization has negligently lost its right to public respect as a labor movement and has become the front for a privileged terror obviously comparable to the Mafia of Sicily."[62] For those who thought he made such charges for effect, Pegler claimed just the opposite. "Unfortunately for the A.F. of L. and labor, I do not exaggerate the facts. On the contrary, I speak only of my own knowledge and I don't know the half of it. Next year, barring war, the national government will have to take action. This kind of thing can't go on and the means of reform apparently do not exist from within."[63]

By asserting that the means to reform unions did not exist from within, Pegler bolstered his claim that the Wagner Act needed to be amended, but at the same time the columnist was discarding a central part of the history behind this scandal, one he consistently neglected in his reporting. Pegler largely ignored the opposition to Bioff and Scalise that existed within the union movement. This was particularly ironic given the debt that the columnist owed these union reformers. His exposé of Bioff could not have occurred without the efforts of the IA Progressives in Hollywood, or Robert Montgomery, the president of SAG. Similarly, the revelation of Scalise's criminal past came directly from his opponents within BSEIU, a group of local officials who denounced their president's malfeasance and his ties to organized crime. Pegler downplayed the role of Bioff's opponents in Hollywood; the columnist never admitted his debt to Scalise's opponents. In doing so, Pegler enhanced his own image while contributing to a monolithic depiction of organized labor as either corrupt or complaisant.

## Opposition to Scalise

Pegler's exposé on Scalise had its origins in a court complaint filed in San Francisco in late December 1939. Members of several BSEIU locals in that city charged that Scalise wanted to stop their local leadership from demanding an accounting of how the national president was spending the union's money. Scalise, they complained, violated BSEIU's own constitution by submitting no financial statements to the membership. The members claimed that they could not even find out what Scalise's salary was. They asked the judge to block any further per capita payments by their locals until a court-appointed auditor had conducted an accounting of the BSEIU's funds. They also wanted the court to restrain Scalise from imposing a trusteeship over any San Francisco locals. Finally, the complaint asked the court to block Scalise from removing Charles Hardy Sr. from his union offices; Hardy was a vice president in the national union and the most prominent BSEIU leader in San Francisco.[64]

The suit was a response to a move several days earlier by Scalise, who had filed internal union charges against Hardy and two of his sons, who were also local BSEIU officials. The charges included allegations of malfeasance with local union funds, but the central complaint was that the Hardys had engaged in a "campaign of vilification" against the BSEIU's national leadership, meaning Scalise.[65]

That campaign of vilification consisted of pamphlets that had begun circulating in late 1939. The pamphlets informed union members that "George Scalese [sic] was convicted of violating the Mann White Slave Act and paroled from the United States Penitentiary at Atlanta, Georgia." This revelation preceded Pegler's exposé by several months. The pamphlets emphasized Scalise's role as a newcomer both to the BSEIU and the industry in which its members labored: "He [Scalise] never worked as a building service employee, but was in the undertaking business in our city of New York up to 1929." The pamphlets continued, "That is the kind of man that orders the International Union to pay him over $120,000 a year, without counting bills for expenses which run another $25,000 a year." And in what could be labeled either prescience or cynicism vindicated, the pamphlet claimed, "Any local union which fights his gangster control, he seizes control of by asking for an accounting. He has stooges in the local accuse honest officials of the local which fight him."[66]

The pamphlets' publishers described themselves as "hard working building service employees, who believe honest unions can do a lot for working men." They chose, however, not to give their names. Scalise believed that Hardy and his sons were responsible. As a result, BSEIU's president moved to drive these opponents out of the organization by using the union's disciplinary process, a system in which he could file the charges and appoint the board that would hear them. If the board Scalise appointed agreed with the charges Scalise had filed (which did seem likely), it could expel the Hardys from the union. According to the pamphlets that denounced him, Scalise had adopted the same technique to remove union opponents on three previous occasions.[67]

In the case of the Hardys, Scalise faced a particularly determined group of opponents who used every resource at their disposal to resist this fate, and one tactic they resorted to was feeding information to Pegler. Charles Hardy Sr., usually referred to as "Pop" Hardy, had emigrated from England to Canada, where he took a job on the Canadian Pacific Railroad and worked as a teamster in Manitoba. He served in the Canadian military during World War I and was wounded. Returning to civilian life, he moved to Portland, Oregon, with his wife and their two sons. He worked in the shipyards until postwar cutbacks left him to look elsewhere for a living. The family ended up in San Francisco, settling down in the working-class district of Hayes Valley. Pop Hardy took work as a janitor and in his free time avidly played soccer in the Bay Area ethnic teams that were common in the 1920s. As his sons grew up, he coached them and their friends in youth league teams. In 1926, he joined BSEIU Local 9, a small theater janitors' local, and with his forceful personality quickly moved into a leadership post.[68]

As his sons grew up, he brought them into the union movement. "My dad had us trained from infancy to be union men," George Hardy later recalled. "He'd assign us to picket lines and other tasks, even though we were just kids." The two sons, as they became older, brought along their friends from the

Hayes Valley. This group became a corps of union activists in the 1930s, as the Hardys conducted a series of successful organizing drives among the Bay Area janitors. In addition to Theater Janitors' Local 9, a number of new Building Service locals emerged in San Francisco. These new locals included the cleaning staff who labored in offices, apartment buildings, and department stores, as well as hospital workers. The Hardys even reached out beyond the Bay area to organize janitors in Los Angeles and elsewhere across the state of California. As George Hardy remembered it, "Organizing in those days was both for survival and decency. Nobody gave us any money, and yet those unions were all formed by us, the guys from the [Hayes] Valley. Most of the organizing in the entire state of California came out of little Local 9." Charles Hardy Sr. became a vice president in BSEIU, thus a member of its general executive board, and its most prominent leader on the West Coast.[69]

He broke with Scalise sometime in late 1938. A dispute over an AFL jurisdictional ruling apparently played a part in this conflict. Hardy balked at an order from Scalise to obey the AFL and turn over a group of San Francisco hotel industry janitors to the Hotel and Restaurant Employees International Union. But there were other issues at work. In the court proceedings meant to forestall BSEIU's internal disciplinary process, Hardy testified about the origins of the conflict. He described a conversation with the national union's secretary-treasurer, Paul David, who had told him that in addition to the BSEIU president's salary of $20,000 a year, Scalise was taking $8,000 to $10,000 a month "for expenses."[70]

Hardy's interference apparently led Scalise to threaten his life, and those threats revealed Scalise's mob background to the San Francisco leader. In one episode, according to court testimony by Hardy, Scalise warned him, "You rotten ____, you'll do what I tell you and like it or I'll put you out of the way."[71] On this occasion and others, Scalise was accompanied by Thomas Burke, a BSEIU vice president from Chicago with strong ties to the Outfit. On the stand, Hardy recalled, "I was really scared, because Burke is Scalise's gunman." Burke "goes everywhere with Scalise," Hardy testified.[72] Hardy's attorney told the court that the rest of BSEIU's general executive board "is under the control, domination and dictation of George Scalise, president of the international."[73]

Hardy was the only one on the board who dared to challenge what Scalise was doing. Having done so, however, the San Francisco labor leader faced union disciplinary charges and almost certain expulsion. Hardy could appeal to the courts to block that process, and he did, but precedent favored Scalise because the courts deferred to internal union governance. In the end, the

California Supreme Court ruled that BSEIU's disciplinary procedure could go forward, a decision that would have sealed Hardy's fate. But that ruling did not come until May 1940. In the meantime, Scalise had been "Peglerized." The columnist's exposé in January 1940 was followed by a campaign directed at Scalise, and then in late April the New York district attorney, Thomas Dewey, indicted the BSEIU president. Soon afterwards, Scalise resigned as president of the union. Scalise's precipitate downfall saved Hardy from expulsion and validated his opposition efforts. The columnist and the San Francisco labor leader had done each other a big favor.[74]

But the connection between the Hardys and Pegler has long remained a hidden part of this scandal's history. Unlike Bioff's opponents in IATSE, the Hardys were reticent about the details of their anticorruption efforts. This was true despite the fact that subsequent events vindicated their actions. After Scalise's conviction and imprisonment, an internal BSEIU hearing in July 1941 acquitted the Hardys on all of the charges that Scalise had filed against them.[75] Pop Hardy resumed his post as vice president of BSEIU, and when he died in office in 1948, his son George Hardy took over that position. George Hardy later became president of the national union (by then titled the Service Employees International Union), serving from 1971 to 1980.[76] The account of their role in the Scalise scandal that appears in George Hardy's union biography simply reads, "When Eastern mobsters—who also ran a strikebreaking 'security' company [a reference to Scalise]—tried to muscle in on BSEIU, the Hardys used the courts, the press, and honest BSEIU unionists across the country to defeat them." Though rich in detail on other aspects of Hardy's career, the booklet provides no further information about this pivotal episode.[77] One might think that, having rescued the union from organized crime, the Hardys would have wanted to say more, a lot more, about their role.

But their careers in BSEIU undoubtedly militated against any such desire. As long-term members of the union's national bureaucracy, both father and son would have had reasons to obscure their actions in 1939 and 1940. In a time of desperation, they had adopted the tactics of union dissidents. They turned to the courts for an injunction to block the union's own internal procedures and denounced the leadership with privately distributed fliers. Union leaders routinely excoriate such tactics as the divisive acts of a disloyal minority. In an even more problematic maneuver, the Hardys had fed information to an infamous antiunion journalist, Pegler.

As a result, written records on this episode are scarce. There are the newspaper reports of the court battle the Hardys waged in early 1940, attempting to block Scalise from ousting them and taking over their locals. Those are supplemented by a few cryptic records included in a set of papers that George Hardy took with him when he retired from the union in 1980 and that his daughter later donated to a university labor history archive. And finally, the New York district attorney's case file on Scalise includes a few more union documents from this time, including a copy of the pamphlets that appeared in late 1939 denouncing Scalise.

From this material, we can piece together a tentative account of what happened. None of the records prove conclusively that the Hardys authored the pamphlets denouncing Scalise in late 1939. But Scalise obviously believed they did, and we can assume he had good reasons for this belief.[78] As for the origins of the charges contained in those pamphlets, Pop Hardy referred to his discovery of Scalise's malfeasance during the trial testimony in early 1940; apparently the San Francisco union leader had questioned BSEIU's secretary-treasurer about Scalise's financial practices.

The pamphlets also included allegations about Scalise's criminal background. The source of those allegations is obscure, however. Threats from Scalise and Burke probably indicated to Hardy the two men's ties to organized crime, but the details regarding Scalise's much earlier Mann Act conviction, which took place in 1913, would not have been easy to come by.

George Hardy's papers suggest a possible source. In a file of union correspondence from 1939 to 1981, Hardy included only one record from the period 1939–1942, a letter from a private investigation firm in San Francisco dated November 10, 1939. The correspondence itself is uninformative; it simply contains an agreement regarding the employment of an operative from the firm but provides no details on the actual assignment of that operative.[79] Still, its inclusion in Hardy's papers and the date on which it was written both seem significant. They raise the possibility that the Hardys employed a private detective to track down details about Scalise's background. In doing so, they would have followed a course of action similar to Montgomery and SAG in seeking to reveal Bioff's past. The employment of such a detective would explain the information in the pamphlet, not just about Scalise's conviction but also the detail that he had served his sentence at the federal prison in Atlanta.

The trail from the Hardys to Pegler is equally obscure. The Hardys never spoke about giving this information to Pegler, and Pegler referred in only the most general terms to his source for the exposé on Scalise. In a 1940 magazine profile of the columnist, Pegler mentioned receiving tips about Scalise. According to the article, "Some of the tipsters were members of the building-service union who wanted to get out from under Scalise's domination. In letters to

Pegler, they repeated an item of common gossip in the union to the effect that Scalise had once served a Federal prison term."[80] Pegler offered nothing more about these sources and denigrated the information he received as "common gossip." The information in the pamphlets was better than that.

Pegler's debt to the Hardys appears more clearly if one reviews the time-line of events in his exposé. After Scalise had moved to expel the Hardys in late December 1939, their loyal supporters among the San Francisco BSEIU locals organized a Voluntary Defense Committee for Local 87 Officials. This group sent out a flier dated January 11, 1940, and addressed it to local union officials across the country. Signed by Jack Foley, who identified himself as a member of BSEIU Local 117 in San Francisco, the flier described Scalise's recent actions against the Hardys and asked for help. The flier included a copy of the text from the earlier pamphlet, which had revealed Scalise's Mann Act conviction.[81] Pegler came out with his exposé on that conviction eight days later, on January 19. Several weeks after that, in early March 1940, Pegler wrote to Foley, "I have read with interest several communications received from you and your committee." That letter was filed among George Hardy's cor-respondence, suggesting his involvement in this transaction.[82] Subsequently, in two other columns that winter, Pegler referred to Scalise's move to oust the Hardys for spreading "malicious propaganda."[83]

But beyond that, the columnist and Scalise's opponents within BSEIU kept their distance. Pegler did not take up the Hardys' cause in his columns and the San Francisco labor leaders did not praise Pegler's reporting on the scandal. Neither side apparently saw any advantage to publicizing their connection to each other. Especially as Pegler's conservative reputation waxed over the subsequent years, the Hardys would have gained nothing by revealing their role in his exposé of Scalise. For his part, Pegler's account of the exposé em-phasized his intrepid researching skills, which led him to the federal building in Brooklyn where Scalise's old court records lay waiting to be discovered.[84] Citing the contributions of others to that discovery only risked diminishing his accomplishment. Also, the columnist had little interest in describing an example of vigorous opposition to corruption from within the union move-ment. That angle offered less support for Pegler's efforts to use this scandal to justify limits on union power.

## News Coverage of the Corruption Scandal

Instead of writing about the Hardys or the IA Progressives and their struggles against corruption, Pegler focused on Bioff, Scalise, and the top AFL leader-ship. His coverage centered on the misdeeds of union leadership and offered a rallying point around which to gather support for new restrictions on organized labor. Scalise's arrest and then conviction in 1940 not only vindicated Pegler, it drew wide coverage in the news media. Bioff and Browne's convictions the following year kept the scandal alive, and so too did the racketeering trial involving the Outfit's leadership that stretched from late 1943 to early 1944. This news coverage followed Pegler's lead and depicted the scandal as a morality tale that offered a warning about the dangerous power union leaders had achieved. In developing that theme, the news media largely rejected other potential interpretations.

Pegler created the model for most of the news coverage that followed his initial exposés. He emphasized the theme of the hypocrisy of union leaders throughout his reporting. Their private acts, he asserted again and again, contradicted the public image labor sought to project. Despite their pious claims of concern for the workingman, Pegler charged, union leaders were nothing more than cynical, grasping officeholders, the worst of them petty criminals, the best of them timid time servers, afraid to rock the boat.[85]

To take one example, in mid-April 1940, the columnist discovered that Scalise had secretly purchased a mansion on the shore of Lake Mamanasco in suburban Ridgefield, Connecticut. While the house had fallen into disrepair and the original asking price of over $100,000 had dropped to $20,000 by the time Scalise purchased it, the story still provided Pegler with a lot of good material. Reminding his readers that the mansion had ten master bedrooms, a seven-car garage, five bathrooms, and extensive servants' quarters, Pegler contrasted this symbol of luxury with Scalise's claims of a humble life of devotion to the cause of union labor.[86]

A subsequent column took the form of an open letter to the members of the Building Service Employee's International Union. "Greetings," Pegler began. "Your honored international president, George Scalise, who learned the trade of bargaining agent in the same school that was patronized by Willie Bioff, the dictator of the amusement craft unions, which is to say as bargaining agent for prostitutes, has recently bought a country mansion far from the crowded slums in which most of you live." Scalise's salary of $20,000 a year, his unlimited expense account, and the fact that he had never labored in the trade his union represented were contrasted with the working lives of the membership. "Many of you—that is the chambermaids among you—are caring for upward of 20 rooms every day in hotels ranging in character from mediocre to bad, for wages of $14 a week, and $20 a week is considered to be good pay for the most prosperous of you. Out of this you pay your initiation fees and dues, plus occasional fines for such offenses as speaking disrespectfully of your union officers."[87]

Pegler's tack in this reporting fit within a convention that exists in news coverage of scandals. This coverage taps reader interest by highlighting the way that a transgression violates the stated ideals of an individual or an institution. The fact that such transgressions are usually hidden, or covered up, heightens the dramatic effect of the exposé while also giving the journalist a central role in the resulting scandal. But the revelation of such hypocritical transgressions also can have important political results. Such revelations sap the prestige of the affected institution and provide an opening for those who charge that its idealistic claims are self-serving cant. For those institutions whose authority stems from their claim to some moral purpose, and unions are among such institutions, scandals can have serious results. They can drain away the moral authority that gives union power public legitimacy.[88]

In this case, Pegler's revelations about Scalise's luxurious life demonstrated the hypocrisy of the BSEIU leader's claims to be a selfless champion of the workers. Because Pegler always asserted that Scalise was representative of other union leaders, his reporting tainted organized labor in general. Pegler made an impact with this angle. The *Washington Post*, in reviewing the success of the columnist's campaign against Scalise, noted, "His account of the union leader's lavish mode of living, supported by dues collected from charwomen, chambermaids, and other hard-working low-paid workers, was a telling bit of publicity."[89]

As the scandal unfolded, this issue of hypocrisy, the disjuncture between the egalitarian claims of organized labor and the reality of Bioff and Scalise's crimes, became a recurring theme in the coverage offered by a range of news outlets. For instance, *Time* magazine's article on Scalise's arrest focused on the charge by a New York prosecutor that "the union is to Scalise what a jimmy is to a burglar." The article pointedly quoted Scalise's letter of resignation in which he had addressed his members as "Dear Brothers and Sisters," a commonplace example of how union leaders harkened to the egalitarian ideals of organized labor. The article nailed home its implicit point about the union leader's hypocrisy with a caption under his photo, which read, "George Scalise: were his brothers & sisters a jimmy?"[90]

In addition to hypocrisy, news coverage of the rise and fall of Bioff and Scalise often contained elements of a morality tale. Accounts of Scalise's arrest invariably emphasized the evident luxury of his lifestyle, the silk pajamas, the expensive hotel room, and the mansion in Connecticut. Newspapers carried prominent photos of his personal secretary, Anna Kimmel, described as "about thirty years old, brunette and attractive." Much more than one would expect, the stories referred to Scalise's clothing, often in great detail. Describing his garb at the arraignment, for example, the *New York Herald-Tribune* reported Scalise "was dressed in a gray herringbone woolen overcoat and double-breasted blue suit. He wore a gray Homburg hat, a white shirt with sharply pointed collar and a flowered print tie."[91] At the same time, news coverage emphasized his immigrant background. As if descriptions of his "swarthy" or "olive complexion" were too subtle, reporters reminded readers that the "Italian born defendant," came of "Italian born parents."[92] His was a tale of great success, a poor immigrant living the life of a wealthy executive. "Over a period of some twenty years," the *New York Herald-Tribune* observed, "Scalise developed from a hoodlum, panderer and hireling of notorious labor racketeers to a person of affluence and power, who as head of an international labor union, controlled the destiny of 70,000 low salaried workers."[93]

But this success was achieved through immoral means, much like the fictional gangsters of the popular crime films of the era such as Tony Carmonte of *Scarface* (1932). They, too, rose from immigrant backgrounds to achieve wealth and power. They, too, enjoyed the accoutrements of an upper-class lifestyle.[94] To the extent that Scalise's eventual downfall resembled the dramatic fate of those fictional gangsters, it delivered a similar moral message about the wages of sin.[95] Newspapers were careful to emphasize that lesson in their accounts of Scalise's conviction and sentencing. The *New York Sun* sententiously concluded, "Thus it comes about that Scalise, once a bootlegger, a gangster's bodyguard and a panderer, who rose to a measure of respectability as a union leader, falls again into the shadows of prison bars which are likely to confine him for some years."[96]

If this morality tale validated conventional morality, it also offered a warning about the type of men who had come to power with the rise of organized labor. "On its face, the Scalise conviction simply means that another thief has been caught," the *New York Herald-Tribune* admitted. But, the paper's editorial continued, the story's "larger implication" included concern that had to be raised by the fact that "a man of Scalise's stripe—the former bodyguard of gangsters, the ex-bootlegger, the convicted panderer—could lift himself to the seats of the mighty and obtain virtually absolute control over the funds paid into a union by one of the poorest and most defenseless group of workers."[97] Pegler had made Scalise into a symbol. As such, he represented the danger that men of his "stripe" had achieved power in the newly renascent union movement.

All of this news coverage followed Pegler's lead by focusing on the misdeeds of the union officials, their hypocrisy, their rise and fall from wealth and power. Left out almost completely were the other participants in these events, the employers, who used Scalise to maintain a quiescent labor supply in a time of union militancy. Only on one occasion did a newspaper, the *New York Herald-Tribune*, raise a question about this matter. When the district attorney's office suggested in late April 1940 that the amount extorted by Scalise might have amounted to as much as a million dollars, the newspaper wondered about the silence of the employers, the alleged victims. "Further mystery was thrown about the affair by the refusal of the eleven firms and twenty hotels involved in the charges to say in what way they had been victimized, if so."[98] But the paper offered no follow-up, and no other publications took up a similar line of inquiry.

The reporting on Bioff followed the same pattern with, once again, a single exception to demonstrate an alternative angle that the news media might have taken. While other publications emphasized Pegler's role in exposing Bioff and then focused on the testimony by studio executives about how the Chicago union leader had extorted from them, the *New Republic* provided the lone dissenting perspective. The magazine ran an article by Carey McWilliams, the attorney who had represented the IA Progressives and who also wrote on the California scene for a number of liberal publications. He offered a corrective to the mainstream press coverage, emphasizing the "complex developments" that lay behind the Hollywood extortion trial. He described how the same studio executives who now testified to fearfully making extortion payments had worked tirelessly in 1936 and 1937 to bolster the power and position of Bioff and Browne. McWilliams asserted that the two men had offered the employers a bulwark against the possibility of more radical unionism. The article documented the active and willing role played by the employers. It was the studios that forced the other Hollywood unions to readmit IATSE into the collective bargaining agreement, overnight placing some 12,000 workers back under the Stage Hands' jurisdiction. The studios granted Browne and Bioff a closed shop agreement. Then the employers fired the union dissidents who had opposed Bioff's leadership and publicly questioned where the money raised in IATSE's 2 percent membership assessment had gone.[99]

This was, McWilliams argued, a mutually beneficial arrangement. "Browne and Bioff policed the 12,000 members of the IATSE for the producers and the producers policed the same members for Willie and George." In turn, the half million dollars in payments referred to during Bioff and Browne's racketeering trial, McWilliams wrote, should not be labeled as simple extortion. "The reason the Motion Picture Producers 'paid off' is obvious: they wanted the 12,000 members of IATSE in Hollywood held in check, and Browne and Bioff were just the men to handle this assignment."[100]

Once again, following Pegler's lead, no other publications pursued this alternative line of reporting. Instead, Bioff and Browne's trial and convictions in the fall of 1941, and the trial and convictions of the Outfit leaders in late 1943 on similar charges, became simply a reason to condemn the immorality of the union movement. The *Newark Evening News* asserted, "The trial of these racketeers, following on the conviction of Browne and Bioff, offers convincing proof of the danger to which both unions and the public are subject from the lack of laws adequate to insure decent management within organized labor."[101] The *New York Daily News* offered similar commentary in the wake of Bioff and Browne's conviction. "Not all of organized labor is run and robbed by racketeers, by a long shot. But a good part of it is, and it is time, we believe, for the situation to be cleaned up, for the benefit of all organized labor and of the general public."[102]

As charges were followed by trials and then convictions, editorial writers across the country joined with Pegler to assert that these revelations demonstrated the rotten nature of the AFL's leadership. After Scalise's arrest, the *Washington Post* asserted, "The distinguishing feature of the charges in the present instance is that they bring into question the effectiveness of the A.F. of L. leadership in dealing with the problem" of labor racketeering. And like Pegler, the *Post* viewed the problem of labor racketeering as "a public issue of tremendous importance." An editorial cartoon in the *New York Herald-Tribune* from that date, entitled "Before the Bar," shows Scalise facing a judge who holds "extortion charges," and behind the labor leader looms a ghostly figure labeled "A.F. of. L."[103]

National news magazines also drew on the stories of Scalise and Bioff to offer a similar indictment of the labor movement. On the eve of Bioff and Browne's trial in the fall of 1941, *Time* magazine ran a story headlined, "Holdup Men of Labor." The article charged, "President William Green's federation is infested with racketeers as the C.I.O. is plagued with Reds."[104] Stories in *Newsweek* and *Life* magazine repeated this charge while crediting "Columnist Westbrook Pegler's tireless exposés of union racketeering."[105]

These articles gathered together disparate episodes of corruption in a variety of unions, some occurring decades apart, and depicted those episodes as part of a current crisis revealed by the scandal involving Bioff and Scalise. In doing so, the stories followed Pegler's lead. They also used a journalistic practice commonly employed to heighten reader interest by linking a single news event to a larger pattern of similar events. A random shark attack becomes part of a wave of random shark attacks, however unlikely it is that the events are in any way connected.[106] Making such value-laden connections, however, also reflects editorial priorities, which in this case included promoting a scandal that challenged the place of organized labor in society.

The Scripps-Howard chain published its own series of articles over the summer of 1940, building on Pegler's exposés by profiling a range of other examples of union corruption. Walker Stone, the editor who oversaw the series, explained in an internal memo that it would require minimal further investigation. They could simply have a reporter draw on the news files from the Scripps-Howard affiliates in various cities for stories of past abuses. There would be little that was new. Instead, Stone explained, "What we need to do here is to draw all the isolated instances into one picture 'to point a moral and adorn a tale.'"[107] The intended moral was that corruption within organized labor had created a national crisis. One headline in this series, for instance, drew on events overseas to depict corruption as a threat to national security; it read, "How 'Fifth Column of Criminals' Penetrates High Places of American Labor Movement."[108]

## Conclusion

Pegler's exposés of Bioff and Scalise and his campaign against union corruption represented a latter-day example of muckraking journalism. The muckrakers of the Progressive era had pioneered the exposé. As historian Richard L. McCormick has written, the muckrakers used investigative reporting to expose widespread political corruption and to arouse public indignation. The muckrakers' impact, McCormick concluded, stemmed from their ability to connect detailed revelations to a larger pattern of corruption that demanded reform. "The point is not simply that more people than ever before became aware of politico-business corruption," McCormick explained, "but that the perception of such a national pattern itself created new political understandings."[109] Pegler too offered detailed revelations and warned Americans of a dangerous pattern of corruption that demanded political change. But whereas the muckrakers usually had targeted the power of corporations, Pegler applied their techniques to warn about the dangers posed by unions.

In mounting this crusade against union corruption, however, Pegler left out important parts of the scandal he had uncovered. He wrote little about the role of the employers and essentially nothing about the political corruption and organized crime that had set the stage for Bioff and Scalise's misdeeds. The columnist also minimized the opposition that these two corrupt labor leaders had faced within the union movement. The result was a skewed portrayal of a real problem, union corruption.

To the extent that other news outlets followed Pegler's lead, the American public received an alarming but fundamentally flawed account of this problem. To read these news reports, one would conclude the scandal revealed that many—if not most—labor leaders were criminals and those who were not did nothing to restrain their corrupt colleagues. A columnist in one union publication commented sarcastically on the character of this news coverage in November 1941, as Bioff and Browne's racketeering trial came to a close. "As every newspaper reader knows by now, unions are bad because they are run by crooks, Communists or tyrants—or a combination of all three."[110]

If this kind of news coverage did little to promote needed reforms in union governance, it did justify calls to amend the Wagner Act in ways that would restrict union power. In that regard, Pegler's publisher could look at the results of his columnist's campaign against union corruption with great satisfaction. In October 1941, Howard wrote to Pegler, "I am convinced that you, more than any single individual or any single journalistic force in this country, have furnished a crystallization point for public indignation, resentment and uprising against the super-racket masquerading under the title of 'labor union leadership.'" Howard asserted that the legislative results would be forthcoming, especially if the news media continued its current campaign. His letter continued, "I believe you have set in action forces which, properly stimulated and backed up by the American press, will force on Congress a course of action that will yet rescue the American labor man from a new form of serfdom."[111]

Howard saw this campaign as a political opportunity for the opponents of the New Deal. In a letter to Scripps-Howard's editor in chief that same October, Howard observed, "A tidal wave of popular disgust with and opposition to the arrogance of union labor leadership is building up." Referring to the Republican presidential candidate of 1940, Howard asserted, "If [Wendell] Willkie could be made to see it, and could get his political surfboard up on the crest of that wave, it would I am certain carry him on a long and successful ride."[112] Although Willkie never did seize this opportunity, other opponents of the New Deal did.

Figure 8.1: The *Chicago Tribune* ran this cartoon by Joseph Parrish on April 23, 1940, the day after George Scalise's arrest on extortion charges. Defending himself from Westbrook Pegler's attacks, Scalise claimed he was singled out because of his devotion to labor's cause. In contrast, this cartoon depicts a labor racketeer using "The Cause of Labor" to mask violent, criminal activities motivated by greed. It suggests that Scalise represented a pattern of criminality and hypocrisy in the labor movement, as Pegler had contended. Courtesy *Chicago Tribune*.

# 8

## The Scandal's Political Impact
### *Pegler and Antiunionism*

President Franklin Delano Roosevelt launched his second reelection campaign on the evening of September 11, 1940, making a speech that was broadcast nationwide. He chose a setting and a topic that reinforced his ties to his most important constituency, working-class Americans. Roosevelt spoke that night from a meeting of the International Brotherhood of Teamsters, whose delegates had gathered in Washington, D.C., for the union's convention. According to *Time* magazine, "two thousand neatly dressed, ham-fisted delegates" had crowded into Constitution Hall where they "sat with eyes glued on the stage." Roosevelt's choice of setting demonstrated his political acumen. The delegates and their wives made an enthusiastic audience, jumping to their feet to cheer the president with shouts and whistles.[1]

Roosevelt praised the recent growth and achievements of a union whose notoriety in later years often made it a byword for labor corruption, and he placed his administration's New Deal reforms squarely at the center of the burgeoning union movement. "Much of this progress [by organized labor] has been due, I like to think, to the one thing that this Administration from the very beginning has insisted upon," Roosevelt said, "the assurance to labor of the untrammeled right, right, not privilege, but right to organize."[2]

Then, in the midst of a talk that his aides had labeled in advance as his "labor speech," he raised an issue that risked alienating his intended audience. While he was explaining why working Americans should vote to defend the New Deal from its Republican opponents, Roosevelt brought up the subject of union corruption.[3] He made a reference that listeners following the ongoing criminal trial of George Scalise would have understood immediately. The president observed that "we all know that internal obstacles to the growth of labor unions have come in those rare instances where the occasional scoundrel, it's a good word, old fashioned, the occasional scoundrel has appeared in a position of leadership." He described such scoundrels as small in number. He decried the fact that the great mass of union members suffered because of the misdeeds of a few "selfish and guilty" individuals. But Roosevelt also acknowledged the political importance of the issue, and he sought to reassure that his administration's prolabor policies did not mean it was complacent. The president warned, "Labor knows there is no room in the labor movement for the racketeer or the strong-arm man. Government, your government, is determined to help labor unions clean their own houses of those few persons who try to betray them."[4] Less than a year after Pegler's exposé of Bioff, union corruption had become a national scandal, and that national scandal had begun to change the political landscape for organized labor.

The scandal unfolded even as organized labor realized startling gains and enjoyed a strong political alliance with the Roosevelt administration. Many union members and their families recognized the importance of Roosevelt's support for labor and deeply appreciated it. Mrs. Hammond Miller, writing from Jersey Shore, Pennsylvania, where her husband worked on the New York Central Railroad, congratulated the President on his September 11 speech to the Teamsters. She went on to laud his contribution to organized labor. "The laborers have received more the last 7 years than ever before. You, as the head of our nation and a very great leader, have done more through your untiring efforts to promote the general welfare of unionized labor than any predecessor."[5] For people like Mrs. Miller, the New Deal's ties to organized labor demonstrated its concern for the welfare of working Americans. In return they voted Democrat, and their ballots formed the heart of the party's new electoral dominance.[6]

But the union corruption scandal triggered by Pegler's exposés promoted a different view both of organized labor's gains and of the New Deal. The scandal contributed to public suspicion of union power, an historic problem for organized labor. News reports on Bioff and Scalise portrayed labor organizations not as part of an idealistic cause but as greedy rackets that exploited working Americans. Joseph Parrish's political cartoon printed in the *Chicago Tribune* the day after Scalise's arrest, offers one illustration of this unsavory image (figure 8.1). Parrish depicts organized labor's mask being lifted to show a grinning racketeer, for whom "The Cause of Labor" was nothing more than a bandit's disguise.[7]

To the extent that this scandal promoted that negative image of the labor movement, it left the New Deal politically vulnerable. Instead of guarding the interests of working Americans, critics charged that Roosevelt had placed them under the control of racketeer-dominated unions. Thus while many letters to the president congratulated him on his speech to the Teamsters, there were those who had less kind things to say. W. L. Rifenbrick, for one, wrote in from southern California to denounce Roosevelt's New Deal, which he argued was far from a boon to the working man. "You have raised the hourly wage rate of workers but you failed to mention the workman's pay envelope contains less money every month than in 1939. You also forgot to mention the fact that the workmen have lost their constitutional right to work, but now have to pay tribute to labor racketeers."[8] For Rifenbrick and a growing number of others, the New Deal's ties to organized labor became a central justification for their opposition. The issue of union corruption formed a leading wedge for opponents of the New Deal, who had found a way to attack organized labor while still depicting themselves as sympathetic to the plight of the working classes.

Pegler's exposés thus triggered a scandal with important political results. As Scalise, Bioff, and Browne went to trial and were convicted in 1940 and 1941, Pegler built on those stories, offering follow-up revelations. At the same time, the columnist expanded the terminology of corruption to redefine broad swaths of union activity as illegitimate. His efforts combined with an ongoing antiunion movement that had existed long before the scandal but that now followed Pegler's lead in important ways. The arrival of World War II also shaped the political effects of this scandal, feeding a popular backlash against unions. For the opponents of organized labor and for the opponents of the New Deal, who were almost always one and the same, this shifting public opinion offered an opportunity to attack the New Deal's greatest electoral strength, its support from working Americans. It also offered a chance to begin cutting back the legislative gains unions had recently won, most importantly the Wagner Act. During the 1940s, the most important victories being scored against the New Deal, not just in blocking its further progress but in rolling back reforms already won, occurred in the field of labor legislation.

## The Rise of an Anti-New Deal Coalition

As the 1940s opened, union leaders had many reasons to rejoice. During the previous decade, organized labor had enjoyed phenomenal growth. By 1939, 25 percent of non-farmworkers belonged to unions, double the proportion of 1929. In comparison to the relatively narrow range of industries organized in the 1920s, by the end of the 1930s unions had established themselves across a wide swath of the American economy, from manufacturing to mining, maritime, and transportation sectors. Geographically, organized labor had broken out of its earlier areas of concentration and, with the exception of the South, membership was more evenly distributed across the country than ever before. Old bastions of antiunionism had fallen. In Los Angeles, for instance, the Merchants and Manufacturers' Association for decades had kept union organization at bay, only to watch its bulwarks crumble in the face of New Deal era organizing drives.[9]

Legal victories matched these membership gains. Through the late 1930s and early 1940s, a Supreme Court more and more responsive to the New Deal's priorities rendered a series of decisions that bolstered organized labor's cause. The Court held up the constitutionality of the Wagner Act and supported the efforts of the National Labor Relations Board to force employers to obey the law. It rejected efforts to apply antitrust restrictions to organized labor, thereby denying union opponents a tactic that had proved devastatingly effective in earlier decades.[10] As the economy improved in late 1940, unions redoubled their organizing efforts, winning landmark victories in the steel and auto industries. From June 1940 to December 1941, they gained one and a half million new members. Stubborn corporate hold outs, such as Ford Motor Company and Republic Steel, capitulated and signed collective bargaining agreements.[11]

And yet, there were troubling signs of change in the political landscape. In the 1938 elections, voters had ousted prolabor governors in Wisconsin, Pennsylvania, and Michigan, and their replacements pushed through new state-level restrictions on union activities. This trend continued, until by 1943 a dozen states had passed laws that ranged from restricting picketing to forbidding union political contributions. In Congress, the end of one investigating committee and the creation of very different ones foreshadowed the shifting political fortunes. Since 1936, Senator LaFollette's Subcommittee Investigating Violations of Free Speech and the Rights of Labor had investigated the abuse of civil liberties that stemmed from employer efforts to block union organization. The committee publicized everything from the espionage network funded by GM to violence practiced against farmworker families and their representatives in California's Central Valley. In 1938, however, efforts to renew the committee's funding failed, a sign of decreasing congressional support for labor's agenda. At the same time, Congress voted funds for a new House Committee on Un-American Activities, which promptly began a campaign to publicize Communist infiltration in the CIO. In the summer of 1939, Congress created a new subcommittee to investigate the National

Labor Relations Board, a move widely seen as a precursor to attempts to amend the Wagner Act. As historian Howell Harris has observed, "Clearly, labor's moment was passing, the window of opportunity which had swung open in 1935–37 was slowly being shut."[12]

The new political climate affected more than just organized labor; the changing public mood also strengthened conservative opponents to the New Deal. For much of the 1930s, they had remained a relatively small and ineffectual group. The wealthy industrialists who had abandoned the Democratic Party to form the American Liberty League in 1934 had expected to create a mass organization opposed to the New Deal. By 1936, however, the League had fallen far short of that mark. An estimated 125,000 people belonged, and they came overwhelmingly from the wealthier classes. Few in number and tagged as rich elitists, they exerted little influence in the 1936 election.[13] The Republican Party itself did so poorly in that election that some questioned its continued existence.[14]

In Congress, conservative members dwindled down to a handful by the middle of the decade. Republican legislators were few in number and split by serious ideological divisions. The most active voices of conservative opposition came from Southern Democrats, but even they practiced self-restraint, wary of Roosevelt's overwhelming popularity. These congressional conservatives scored their first important victory in 1937 when they blocked Roosevelt's efforts to reorganize the Supreme Court. That legislative battle saw the emergence of an effective, though informal, alliance between conservative Southern Democrats and newly reunified Republicans. The economic recession that struck in the fall of 1937 strengthened that coalition by undercutting the New Deal's popularity, and the 1938 mid-term elections significantly increased conservative numbers in the House and Senate. By 1939, congressional conservatives offered stubborn resistance to Roosevelt's efforts to expand the New Deal.[15]

That November, the political columnist Raymond Clapper observed the changing public mood and the gathering forces arrayed against liberal reform. "The days of the New Deal as such appear very likely to be drawing to a close," he wrote. "Roosevelt may drive on for a short time longer but already the page is being turned on him."[16]

Still divided by party and region, Roosevelt's opponents in Congress waged a selective battle against the New Deal. On certain measures, such as public works spending, opponents found their fellow congressmen unwilling to risk the ire of constituents who stood to benefit from these government programs. On other issues, successful coalitions could be gathered in spite of pressure from the administration.[17] Conservatives, for instance, could rally legislative and public support by decrying the dangerous growth of executive branch authority. The battle over the reorganization of the Supreme Court was one such issue. So too was Roosevelt's proposed executive branch reorganization bill, which went down in defeat in 1938. "Opponents could, and did, relate the 'dictatorial' ambitions of the President to the failure in business confidence," historian James Patterson noted. "The issue provided conservatives of both parties with an excellent club with which to batter presidential prestige."[18]

The growing power of organized labor offered another issue around which a strong conservative coalition could be built. The issue united conservative Republicans from the East and the Midwest with their Democratic counterparts from the South and generated passionate feelings among them.[19] In his private correspondence, a Republican congressman from Michigan, Clare Hoffman, suggested dealing with a strike in his district in 1939 by resorting to brute force. "The only thing left is to swear in a sufficient number of citizens as deputy sheriffs and apply the same kind of medicine to these lawless agitators as they are in the habit of dishing out."[20] One of his Democratic colleagues from a border state that same year dramatically referred to unions by asking, "Are we going to permit this fiery dragon to continue to suck the blood of American business and destroy American institutions and ideals?"[21]

But in spite of their strong personal feelings, the opponents of the New Deal approached the labor issue warily. Republicans especially worried about the political costs they might incur. Roosevelt's astounding landslide reelection in 1936 stemmed from the support of working-class Americans, and any hopes of Republicans to reclaim their majority status would remain unrealized until they could win back at least some of those votes. Thus in 1940, the Republican presidential candidate Wendell Willkie courted the endorsement of John L. Lewis, head of the CIO. In exchange for receiving it, Willkie's campaign announced its support for the Wagner Act and the system of collective bargaining that it had created.[22] In Congress, Michigan's Hoffman privately chafed at the cautiousness of his fellow Republicans as his party's leaders held back from endorsing direct legislative attacks on the Wagner Act.[23]

But as the union corruption scandal garnered ever more public attention, it offered conservatives a way to attack organized labor while at the same time proclaiming their concern for working-class Americans. Hoffman was one of those who saw the opportunity. The feisty conservative Republican represented a rural district in southwestern Michigan, one dotted with medium-sized industrial towns such as Benton Harbor. A small-town lawyer, he had worked his way through school, attending Valparaiso College in northern Indiana, and he looked back on his youth with a nostalgia and pride that girded his conservative beliefs. "In spite of the 'starvation wage,'" he recalled, "I had all I wanted to eat and all I needed to wear, and I frequently went fishing and hunting, I cannot complain of my country, its system of government or the way it used me."[24]

He could complain about the New Deal's efforts to change that system of government, and he did so loudly and frequently. Hoffman was labeled "one of the most reactionary Republicans on Capitol Hill," and he voted uniformly against every New Deal measure.[25] Like many other opponents of the New Deal, hostility to organized labor was his ideological passion. He began proposing amendments to the Wagner Act as early as 1939, becoming one of the point men on the issue among the Republicans in the House.[26] By 1947, he served on the six-member conference committee that ironed out the final details of the Taft-Hartley Act, which achieved the first permanent amendments to the Wagner Act.[27]

In 1940, like many of his conservative colleagues, Hoffman eagerly used the Bioff and Scalise scandals to justify his position. In a speech in May 1940, in the immediate wake of Scalise's arrest, Hoffman charged that the cases Pegler had exposed demonstrated how the "millions of dollars [that] have been collected from the workers in the way of membership fees, dues, and special assessments has found its way into the pockets of racketeers."[28]

That November, Hoffman stood on the floor of the House to argue for a series of amendments to the Wagner Act, justifying his stand by referring to the activities of Bioff and Scalise. "I am for the man who works," Hoffman asserted, "not for the man who collects from the workingmen, not for labor racketeers. I am against men, such as Scalise and Bioff, that Westbrook Pegler has been writing about." Hoffman used the corruption scandal to claim that the real friends of the working class were conservatives like himself and not the New Dealers. "The administration claims that it is friend of the laboring man. I charge that it permits the laboring man to be exploited by and for the benefit of political labor organizers and racketeers."[29]

He was not the only congressman to invoke Pegler or the scandal that the columnist had nudged onto the national stage. Nor was his attack in November the first to pair the scandal with a legislative proposal. In August 1940, Senator Robert Reynolds, a Democrat from North Carolina, had placed a Pegler column on Bioff and Browne into the *Congressional Record* and used it to support a proposed amendment to the Wagner Act.[30]

## After the Exposé: Pegler's Continuing Campaign

Even as Hoffman, Reynolds, and others seized on the political opportunity presented by the scandal, Pegler continued his campaign against union corruption. As he did so, the columnist expanded his targets, seeking to prove that Bioff and Scalise represented a widespread problem in organized labor. Pegler's denunciations now frequently included the activities of left-wing union leaders from the Congress of Industrial Organizations (CIO). But the columnist also came to use the terminology of corruption in ways that would label much of what all unions—conservative, progressive, and everywhere in between—did as illicit. In doing so, he contributed an important element to antiunionism in the 1940s.

The successful prosecutions of Scalise in the fall of 1940, and then of Bioff and Browne the next year, vindicated Pegler's journalism, winning him a Pulitzer prize for reporting in 1941 and making him a hero to many Americans.[31] But these convictions also potentially resolved the scandal. At this point, Pegler might have declared "mission accomplished" and moved onto other issues; he chose instead to continue his campaign. The columnist explained this decision in early 1942, as Bioff and Browne were committed to federal prison. "The AFL has not reformed," the Pegler charged. "Some spectacular criminals have been sent to prison, no thanks whatever to William Green or the AFL, but Green and the entire executive council sat with George Browne [who had served on that body] throughout his evil career, and Green and Joseph Padway, the general counsel [of the AFL], praised and upheld him." Guilty by extension, neither Green nor Padway had left office, and so Pegler claimed that real reform had yet to occur.[32]

In this same column, he argued that other cases similar to Scalise and Bioff remained prevalent in the AFL.[33] Throughout 1940, his column featured cases of individual labor leaders with criminal records, often involving an arrest unrelated to their union post that had occurred decades earlier. Essentially these columns were efforts to repeat the dramatic unmasking he had achieved with Bioff and Scalise. As such, they were not entirely successful. Some of the union officials profiled in this fashion lacked any subsequent arrests, had no apparent ties to organized crime, and evidenced no misconduct in union office. Except for the long-ago conviction, they did not resemble Bioff or Scalise. In a column on one such case in July 1940, Pegler wrote that union officials "surely will denounce this revelation as another attempt to discredit the leadership of certain A.F. of L. unions, which is exactly what it is."[34]

He did eventually find compelling cases involving other corrupt officials in other unions. But Pegler never repeated the dramatic act of unmasking an apparently respectable leader, which had been a potent aspect of his exposés of Bioff and Scalise. Pegler's best follow-up cases involved union leaders already notorious when he began writing about them. One of them was Mike Carrozzo, a powerful figure in the Chicago branch of the Laborers' Union. Others included Mike Boyle of the Electricians Union in Chicago and Joe Fay and William Maloney, vice president and president respectively of the Operating Engineers Union.[35] In all of these cases there were allegations of ties to organized crime and of misconduct in the union offices held. But the key themes in the columns were always hypocrisy and the AFL's complicity.[36]

There was one significant shift in his reporting on organized labor in this period—he began paying more attention to the CIO. In the wake of his exposés on union corruption, Pegler began to write regularly about the threat of communist influence within certain CIO affiliates. In June 1941, he warned that thanks to such influence, "today Communists can tie up factories whose products are urgently needed to defend the United States against Stalin's partners in conquest."[37] And while the Nazi invasion of the Soviet Union changed matters dramatically, Pegler still cited the danger of having disloyal communists control CIO unions. Writing in September 1941, he referred to them as "Muscovites" "who lately stabbed this nation between the shoulders and then abruptly whooped it up for war, but in defense of Russia, not the U.S.A."[38]

At the same time, he branded a range of legal union activities with illicit labels, expanding the category of corruption to cover activities that all labor organizations, of any political stripe, did. Thus he labeled union dues "tribute" and applied that usage to include all labor organizations in general. "It is a notorious fact," Pegler claimed in a column in November 1941, "that many billions of dollars, stet [that is, *correct*], many billions, not mere millions, have been wrung from the workers by professional unioneers and that only pennies of this enormous tribute have been accounted for in the last eight years."[39] In other columns, he chose the harsher term "extortion" to label all union income, including dues. "But union income is not made up of gifts. It is obtained largely by extortion in the guise of dues, fees and assessments."[40] Pegler used this language to denounce both AFL and CIO unions; in fact, he applied it to any labor organization that had union shop agreements that obligated an employee to join the union. "The C.I.O. is not required by any law to account for the money thus taken, or extorted, from members who submit only because they must submit or go jobless."[41]

The columnist similarly employed an expansive definition of the term *racketeering*. He applied it to unions such as the Teamsters or the Carpenters, which used tactics such as secondary boycotts to pressure employers to sign collective bargaining agreements. Such tactics were legal, but Pegler still equated them with racketeering. "This will take some time," he wrote in October 1941, "but I have plenty of time and some of it will be devoted to the leaders of the Longshoremen and some to those of the Carpenters and Teamsters who think that antisocial and anti-American rackets are legitimate if conducted according to their own constitutions whatever the damage to the rights of ostensibly free Americans."[42]

When used in this way, these terms denigrated every labor organization. All unions—affiliates of both the AFL and the CIO as well as independents—charged dues or required initiation fees. Almost every labor organization sought to include union shop provisions in their collective bargaining agreements. Such provisions helped protect a union's security, by blocking, for instance, an employer from favoring nonunion members. Similarly, almost any union that could employ secondary boycotts did so; it allowed them to avoid costly and often unsuccessful organizing campaigns that employers would resist fiercely.

But for Pegler, all that this meant was that unions in general could be labeled "rackets." As he put it in a column in early 1940, "This is the swollen national racket which calls itself the body of Labor with a capital L."[43] His universal application of the term can be seen in a piece written two years later, in which Pegler denounced AFL and CIO efforts to broadcast their concerns on a weekly radio program. Pegler wrote that access should be given instead to "the man or woman who joins or refuses to join up as another unit of power in the hands of the master racketeers."[44]

His use of language in this way was quite purposeful. Pegler openly acknowledged that the specific terminology employed in news reporting had the power to legitimize or delegitimize unions. He explained his views on such matters in a column that he addressed to "my revered bosses, the newspaper editors," but that he also recommended to "a variety of other persons dealing in public expression, such as radio speakers, magazine editorialists and occupants of or candidates for public office." Pegler explained to this audience that a union official should not be called a "Labor Leader," because the term conferred an unwonted respectability. "'Labor leader' is inaccurate and misleading when applied to most of the professional unioneers of both big camps [AFL and CIO] and the term 'Labor' is equally deceptive when applied to unions." The columnist asserted, "When you speak or write of such a man as Wrong John Lewis [the head of the United Mine Workers Union], for example, as a 'Labor Leader' you are suggesting that he is a popular leader of voluntary followers." Pegler considered that suggestion to be both inaccurate and politically wrongheaded.

A better term, Pegler instructed the editors, was union "boss," or, as he put it, "They are not leaders but bosses and most of them, dictators." The word *boss*, in turn, conveyed a central assumption about the nature of organized labor, which Pegler believed he had demonstrated in his columns. "It should be recognized now and kept in mind," Pegler instructed the editors, "that the union bosses may be and, in the absence of knowledge to the contrary, should be presumed to be, a boss if not an oppressor and exploiter of 'Labor.'"[45]

## Pegler's Ties to the Wider Antiunion Movement

Pegler was not the first person to deploy language in a way that would delegitimize unions. As far back as the turn of the twentieth century, antiunion forces denigrated union power by using terms like *czar* and *tyrant* to refer to labor leaders.[46] The term *racketeering* itself originated out of the same kind of exercise. Its root, the word *racket*, had emerged in the early twentieth century as a generic label for illegal activity. By the mid-1920s, newspapers used the word *racketeer* to apply to individuals, often bootleggers, who made their living through illegal activity. Drawing on the popularity of that term, officials at the Chicago Employers' Association, an antiunion organization, created the new gerund *racketeering* as part of a campaign designed to weaken the city's labor organizations.[47]

Andrew Cohen traced this linguistic maneuver in his book on the history of labor relations in Chicago. Cohen described a system of craft governance that had emerged in Chicago during the early twentieth century. This system allowed many unions to exercise a powerful role in the city's marketplace via collusive agreements to control competition, which they made with groups of small local employers. Antiunion corporations, the main supporters of the Employers' Association (EA), resented this system and the power it gave to union leaders. The new term *racketeering* emerged out of the EA's efforts to break this system. Cohen writes, "In 1927, Employers' Association secretary Gordon L. Hostetter conceived the term to direct growing public concern about bootleggers like Al Capone against the officials who enforced prices and wages in trades like construction, laundry and kosher foods." Hostetter's goal, Cohen explains, was to weaken the city's unions. "He sought not to expose the power of men like Capone within the labor movement, but rather to compare craft governance to extortion." In calling the activity *racketeering*, the EA was "comparing union officers to mobsters."[48]

Pegler's deliberate use of the word *racketeering* highlights the fact that the columnist's efforts fit within a larger history of antiunionism. Pegler's exposés, however, gave his critique of organized labor a distinctive credibility and an impact that made him an especially important part of the antiunion movement. Since the turn of the twentieth century, businessmen and corporate lawyers had been leading organized opposition to unions. The themes they used resembled those taken up by Pegler. Groups ranging from the National Erectors' Association to the National Association of Manufacturers had criticized unions on issues such as picket line violence and closed shop contracts for decades. These employers' groups also had levied charges of corruption against union leaders as a way to discredit them. The obvious self-interest of the employers, however, undercut the credibility of their attack on union abuses. In 1920, for instance, the humorist Finley Peter Dunne mocked open shop employers for asserting that they supported "properly conducted" unions. His fictional Mr. Dooley explained that this meant, "No strike, no rules, no contracts, no scales, hardly any wages, an 'dam' few members."[49]

As a professional journalist, not a businessman or a corporate lawyer, Pegler could appear more disinterested while at the same time his investigations yielded startling revelations that validated his criticism of unions. He used ferocious language in his reporting, but at this point in his career that style did not detract from his credibility. Indeed the downfall of Bioff and Scalise had just vindicated his journalistic acumen. In 1941, *Printers' Ink*, an advertising industry journal, praised Pegler as "a hardboiled reporter who knows what he is talking about, who checks and double checks his material before printing it." The same article also claimed that his impact stemmed from his "slam-bang" writing style. "The fact that he uses a meat ax rather than a rapier does not discount in the least from the strength and logic of his position. In fact, his slam-bang, almost cruel, handling of the matter is all to his credit; drama and plenty of it is needed in order that the issue may be presented in its true colors."[50] The combination of Pegler's occupation and writing style, therefore, meant that his charges had more impact on public opinion than the previous efforts of antiunion employer associations.

In same way, Pegler was not the first prominent voice to call for reform of the Wagner Act, but he played an important role in shaping the direction that these efforts took. Proposals to amend the act dated back to the spring of 1937, when the Supreme Court had declared the law constitutional. By 1938, both the Chamber of Commerce and the National Association of Manufacturers had begun calling for reform. They and other critics in this period, however, focused their efforts on a congressional investigation of the

National Labor Relations Board (NLRB), the agency created to administer the act. Critics hoped to prove both the board's prounion bias and the need for amendments to the act.[51]

Howard W. Smith, a conservative congressman from Virginia, led the resulting investigation in late 1939 and early 1940. So dedicated were Smith's conservative political convictions that they found expression even in his style of dress, which was flamboyantly old-fashioned. He used a pince-nez rather than glasses and wore wing-collared shirts, affecting the look of a small-town attorney from the previous century. A former judge who had been elected to Congress in 1931, Smith was a strict constructionist who opposed the expansive government being created under the New Deal. As historian James Patterson has noted, "No man was more stridently opposed to the New Deal." The congressman especially abhorred unions, which he believed had been granted a dangerous amount of power under the Wagner Act. His committee's investigation of the NLRB received assistance from employers' groups who supplied Smith's chief counsel with promising leads. The resulting hearings generated publicity and pressured Roosevelt to reorganize the NLRB.[52]

But the efforts to amend the Wagner Act in response to the investigation failed. By early 1942, Smith and others had turned away from the NLRB and began to draw on theme of union corruption and misconduct, which Pegler had promoted in his exposés. In April that year, Smith released to the press a letter he had written to William Green denouncing the labor leader for the abuses and corruption that existed in the AFL. Smith warned Green that "public opinion will no longer tolerate boycotts, jurisdictional strikes and unconscionable initiation fees which, as you well know, are prevailing practices protected, defended and encouraged under present A.F. of L. policies." And like Pegler, Smith emphasized the issue of corruption: "That racketeers and gangsters dominate and fatten on many of your locals is a fact well known to you and to the public at large."[53]

Pegler had ties to another prominent union opponent in this period, Congressman Martin Dies, of the House Un-American Activities Committee (HUAC). Formed in 1938, HUAC quickly focused on the alleged threat of Communist infiltration within the CIO and held hearings to publicize the danger. Pegler wrote columns in support of Dies's efforts and in the early 1940s devoted increasing space to the issue of Communist influence in the CIO. In turn, Dies drew on Pegler's example. In December 1941, in a speech before Congress, HUAC's chairman dramatically revealed that his investigators had discovered that the CIO was being infiltrated not just by Communists but criminals as well. Submitting a list of CIO leaders with criminal records, Dies claimed they represented only the tip of the iceberg, making an argument that paralleled Pegler's condemnation of the AFL. Dies asserted, "It is un-American to force workingmen into the shackles of labor bosses who strive to build up personal power for themselves through the use of the communist and criminal elements that gravitate toward them." Like Pegler, Dies depicted the union membership as unwilling victims. "I am profoundly convinced that the overwhelming majority of labor would, if it were articulate, join me in this solemn protest against the criminal and the racketeer in unions."[54]

The emphasis on union abuses, the broad definition of corruption, and the universal tag of racketeer to cover all labor leaders—left, right and center—became the themes of antiunionism in the 1940s. Pegler's campaign promoted these themes, but they took hold in the particular political context of World War II.

## The Wartime Context

Formally the United States entered the war in the wake of Japan's attack on Pearl Harbor on December 7, 1941. But the country had begun to mobilize for war about a year earlier, as Congress passed the Selective Service Act in September 1940. The Lend-Lease Act came in early 1941, and soon after Congress began approving huge new military appropriation bills. This spending helped bring the country out of the Great Depression, and unemployment rates plummeted. That economic recovery, however, also spurred a renewed wave of strikes in 1941, as unions seized the opportunity to push through organizing campaigns in basic industries such as automobile and steel production. Coming amid efforts to achieve a defense build-up, those walkouts generated much controversy. Many Americans resented unions for pursuing their own interests at the apparent expense of the nation's efforts to prepare for an impending war.[55]

Controversy continued in the wake of Pearl Harbor even as the government's involvement in labor relations increased dramatically. The federal government set up a wartime agency, the National War Labor Board (NWLB), to oversee labor relations, and the board imposed a pivotal policy in 1942. The NWLB's maintenance-of-membership rule required a business with an existing union contract to enroll all new workers into the union, unless they specifically requested otherwise within the first fifteen days of their employment. The rule basically imposed a union shop on all wartime employers. The NWLB sweetened this measure for organized labor even further in 1943 when it required employers to deduct their workers' union dues directly from payroll, enforcing what usually is referred to as the dues checkoff system. The government's policy meant that the waves of workers flooding into the war industries flowed as well onto union membership rolls. Organized labor grew significantly as a result, from about 10 million members at the start of the war to almost 15 million by the war's end.[56]

But public hostility over wartime strikes probably tempered satisfaction union leaders might have enjoyed as a result of the gains in membership. In order to bar a repeat of the inflationary spiral that occurred during World War I, the NWLB imposed a cap on wage increases, known as the Little Steel formula, which limited raises to no more than 15 percent. Both AFL and CIO leaders had adopted no-strike pledges in the wake of Pearl Harbor, but frustration among rank and file members often boiled over into wildcat walkouts. Members bridled over wages that were not keeping up with price increases; they also resorted to walkouts in an effort to resolve workplace disputes with their employers. As a result, although there was little industrial strife in 1942, the number of strikes began to grow in 1943 despite the no-strike pledges of national union leaders. The most notorious examples were a series of walkouts in 1943 by members of the United Mine Workers Union, led by John L. Lewis. During the next two years, the number of strikes—and man-hours lost to strikes—continued to rise.[57]

The wartime setting offered Pegler new arguments to bolster his anti-union stand. At the simplest level, Pegler adapted to the emerging context by adding a new series of epithets to his indictment of union leaders. Now, in addition to comparing union officials to gangsters, Pegler likened them to the fascist enemy. In early 1942, referring to the "thugs and extortioners holding union charters," Pegler noted, "I have often pointed the similarity between these bands and the Black Shirts of the Duce and the Brown Shirts of the Fuehrer."[58]

This language allowed him one more way to depict the union membership as innocent victims. Union officials like Green argued that the cases of corruption Pegler had found were the exception and AFL members were on the whole law-abiding citizens. Pegler responded, "It is the vicious minority in command of the unions, which holds the power. It could be said with equal truth that the Germans are not bad people. Of course they are not bad people, but just as a small, unspeakable group of bad men control the Germans, so do a relatively few individuals in the A.F. of L. wield the power for evil."[59]

The war also offered Pegler additional grounds to condemn union activities he had long found objectionable. As more and more Americans in 1940 and

1941 encountered union shop contracts at various defense projects, Pegler integrated their experiences into his ongoing denunciation. In early October 1941, he opened his column by writing, "To all the American workers, men and women, who have been compelled to give up various sums of money to the licensed extortioners of unions as the price of jobs on cantonments, factories and other works in the national defense or war program, Greetings."[60] After the United States formally entered the war, Pegler continued this line of attack, giving it—if possible—a tone of even greater outrage.[61]

Claiming that rapacious union leaders put their interests ahead of the nation's, Pegler loaded one more charge into his ongoing indictment of union leaders: the charge of treason. He argued that organized labor was taking advantage of the wartime emergency and its political ties to the Roosevelt administration to expand its power and wealth. "The whole nation, with no exception worth bothering about, accepted the war as a fight for life after Pearl Harbor," he wrote in April 1942. "And the assumption was that in the face of the common enemy we would suspend for the duration the domestic social and political program of the national government." But instead, the Roosevelt administration supported organized labor's demands, including closed shop contracts on defense projects and dues checkoffs. "The bitter fact is that the whole American people in all economic grades is fighting an array of terrible foreign military foes who threaten to enslave and partition this country are never allowed to forget that they are being used to create a new internal force [unions], governed by a few personalities who are contributing nothing to the war, which plans to inherit the government after the war is won."[62]

Indeed, according to Pegler, union leaders frequently stooped to "sabotage" of the war effort in order to promote their selfish agenda. "I presume that nobody will argue against the notorious fact that there has been vast sabotage of the war effort through union strikes in ship yards, airplane plants, steel mills and the like, while young men by the thousands have been vanishing from home into the army and navy and most of the civilians have been fumbling for something helpful to do beyond paying heavy taxes and doing without," Pegler wrote in August 1941.[63]

The war, he asserted, heightened the need to amend the Wagner Act and curb the power of union leadership. Most American workers "are normal American citizens, loyal to their country and elected government and willing to work for reasonable pay under fair treatment." Given their patriotism and the fact that "many of them have relatives in the army and navy," they could not possibly have been willing participants in strikes involving defense projects. Thus, Pegler charged, the strikes at war plants offered a poignant example of the abusive power wielded by labor officials under the Wagner Act. "Strikes against the national defense continue, even though many individual workers who go on strike would prefer to stay at their jobs, so we find that the real trouble is an abuse of power by union leaders who were given that power in the first place by President Roosevelt." And if the war highlighted their abusive power, it also justified immediate action to curb it.[64]

Pegler's campaign formed the leading edge of a broad sweep of news coverage and commentary that was hostile towards organized labor. Much of this coverage drew on the scandals Pegler had first publicized, and much of it echoed his allegations of widespread corruption. Similarly, news coverage often emphasized the wartime context and used that context to depict labor's leadership as disloyal. Radio news commentators like H. V. Kaltenborn, one of the most popular of the 1940s, demonstrated this pattern.[65]

Although Kaltenborn originally had taken a moderate stand regarding organized labor, in early 1942 he began attacking unions, sharply condemning union leaders as corrupt and unpatriotic.[66] During his regular evening broadcast on March 17, 1942, Kaltenborn told his listeners, "Today the labor unions have power without responsibility. No man can produce war material in any of the major plants of the United States without first paying tribute to a labor union." This money went into union treasuries, and Kaltenborn echoed Pegler by noting that union officials faced no legal requirements to account for these funds. Many unions were honestly administered, but the radio commentator explained many others were not. "In instance after instance, the courts have convicted union racketeers who abused the privileges which a friendly administration has conferred upon them."[67]

In other broadcasts, Kaltenborn claimed that "labor union practices are injuring and destroying America's war effort."[68] He cited demands that "war workers pay work permit fees for the privilege of doing war work," a practice long excoriated by Pegler.[69] Complaining about wartime strikes, Kaltenborn contrasted rank and file members, who he asserted were "more patriotic than their [union's] International President." "Unless these workers are egged on by unpatriotic leaders to vote in favor of a strike, they vote against a strike."[70] Charging that organized labor was "fattening on the opportunities provided by the needs of America in time of war," he called for revisions to labor law that would curb union power.[71]

The proliferation of such critical news commentary struck some observers as equivalent to an organized campaign. A 1941 article in the liberal *New Republic* referred to "a campaign in the press and in newsreels, to stir public indignation against the interruption of the defense effort." Citing growing hostility to unions, the article continued, "Among many of the lower-middle-class groups, as well as the higher income brackets, the press campaign has taken its toll."[72]

Working-class union members also felt the impact of this press coverage. In March 1942, O. A. Knight, an official with the CIO Oil Workers Union, described how: "Members of my own organization have told me that when they go into their homes of an evening after doing their day's work they find their wives and children and other members of their family, who have been reading this stuff, plead with them to get out of the union movement, because they have been convinced the union movement is vile and doing something to disturb and disrupt the war effort of this nation."[73]

Current research cautions against overstating the degree to which media content directly controls public opinion. But studies do tend to agree that the news media can shape public priorities by providing coverage that emphasizes a certain issue, essentially defining it as a crisis.[74] In the early 1940s union abuses became such a crisis. The crisis emerged in the wake of the scandals that Pegler had exposed, and it attained greater significance as the country shifted to a wartime footing in the early 1940s.

## Public Opinion

That crisis, in turn, affected perceptions of organized labor. Opinion polls showed that support for organized labor fell in this period. In May 1940, when asked, "Are you in favor of labor unions?" 74 percent of Americans responded yes, and 26 percent said no. A year later, in August 1941, 67 percent declared themselves in favor of unions and 33 percent were opposed.[75] The drop was significant if not disastrous. The polls indicated, after all, that a majority of Americans still expressed support for organized labor.

Such continued support, however, belied growing concerns about union abuses. Americans, by 1941, viewed unions as potentially dangerous and often corrupt. Asked about organized groups that presented a threat to the American form of government, people ranked labor unions third, after the Nazis and Communists.[76] In the spring of 1941, 75 percent of Americans believed that "there is too much power in the hands of the leaders of labor unions." By way of comparison, only 59 percent said yes to the question "Do you think there is too much power in the hands of a few rich men and large corporations in the United States?" Even fewer worried about the growing power of the government.[77]

Polls indicated that much of the public's concern focused on union leadership. A lot of Americans were concerned about the radicalism of union leaders: 61 percent thought that "many labor union leaders are communists." But more Americans worried about the corruption of union leaders. In October 1941, 73 percent believed that "many labor union leaders are racketeers."[78] Seven months earlier they were asked a similar question—"Westbrook Pegler, the newspaper writer, says that many union leaders are racketeers. Do you agree or disagree?"—and 72 percent agreed. The polls showed that this conclusion was shared by a majority of Americans across all major demographic groups, regardless of economic class and age. Even a majority of union members agreed with Pegler's conclusions.[79]

The concerns expressed in these poll numbers emerged at the same time as the Bioff and Scalise scandals blossomed, but also in the midst of the 1941 strike wave. It was not the case, however, that the average American weighed those issues in isolation. Rather, these concerns tended to coalesce, emerging in a hostile stereotype of union leaders whose allegedly selfish, unscrupulous ways were summed up in the term so avidly promoted by Pegler, *racketeer*.

When average Americans put their distrust of union leaders into their own words, writing letters to politicians and newspaper editors, they demonstrated connections that the opinion polls only suggested. These letters interweave allegations of widespread corruption with other issues that generated hostility and suspicion towards organized labor.

Many of those who raised the subject of corruption, for instance, also emphasized the political power of unions and criticized the selfish motives that they ascribed to labor strikes. Robert E. Price, who had been a union member for over three decades, wrote to the conservative congressman Clare Hoffman, "We now have labor organizations, not devoted to the promotion of and protection of the workers rights, but labor organizations that through political license are engaged in the same type of racketeering as the booze racketeers of the prohibition era."[80] Their racket, Price explained, was "shaking down the workers and extorting loot from industry." By loot, Price—echoing Pegler—included legal, but from his perspective exorbitant, union dues and wage gains. "Their purpose is not to secure a fair day's compensation for service performed but to extort from the members as heavy an assessment as they can get away with and to placate the members by forcing industry to pay arbitrary wage scales."[81]

As the United States prepared for war and then, in December 1941, entered it, these personal expressions of concern about union corruption increasingly included allegations of widespread disloyalty on the part of union leaders.

Mrs. Henry Tredwell wrote Congressman Hoffman in May 1943 in support of wartime legislation to limit strikes. In doing so, she denounced the selfish attitude of organized labor. Referring to American troops overseas, she wrote, "Boys who are giving their lives as sacrifices in North Africa are only getting $50 a month, and these union laborers are not forced to work under the awful hazardous conditions existing on the above mentioned front." This concern then blended into her outrage about racketeering: "I think the general public are getting good + tired of these strikes and the labor racketeers who are getting plenty of gravy—ask *Westbrook Pegler* about it. He knows and express[es] plenty of such work going on in unions."[82]

In a letter to the editor of the *New York Times*, Thomas H. Greene asked, "We fought the first World War to make the world safe for democracy. Are we to join the second World War to make America safe for labor racketeers?" He went on to complain that while soldiers, consumers, and taxpayers all made sacrifices in the name of national defense, union leaders called strikes for "such racketeer privileges as the closed shop in defense industries."[83]

In popular parlance, racketeering came often to refer to more than just criminal behavior. As a label, it came to include a range of unpopular union activities. Louis Schaeffer, an insurance agent from Columbus, Ohio, used the term in the more expansive way when he wrote to Congressman Howard W. Smith in November 1941. Schaeffer sent his letter to express his disapproval of closed shop contracts. "I feel that it is about time this government said that it would not be compulsory for a man to join a union before he could get work." In calling for legislation banning the practice, Schaeffer labeled it a form of racketeering. "I think that this is the most outrageous thing in our entire labor question, and I as well as many of my friends always have said that they did not understand why some thing was NOT done by this government that would protect a man from this union racketeering."[84]

Denunciations of wartime strikes often invoked the word racketeering. Letter writers blamed such walkouts on union leaders, who were described as having dictatorial control over their organizations. Average citizens used the term in reference not just to AFL leaders implicated in criminal activity but also to their ideological opposites in the CIO.[85] Writing to Congressman Hoffman in 1943, A. G. Dobbins of Wheaton, Illinois, concluded, "In summing it all up, Mr. Hoffman, our beloved country is suffering a lot from the communistic labor agitator racketeers. With the coddling of them by the New Deal they are seriously undermining our national morale."[86]

When United Mine Workers president John L. Lewis defiantly led controversial strikes in 1941, he became the most unpopular man in America.

Seventy-two percent of Americans disapproved of the CIO leader's actions, and pollsters reported that, when asked why, a significant proportion labeled him a racketeer. A typical expression, pollsters noted, was, "He is a racketeer, out for as much money as he can get."[87] The charge did not refer to any allegations that he extorted payoffs, but rather that he put his ambitions ahead of the good of the nation.

The broad use of this term indicates the suspicion with which many Americans viewed important aspects of union power. In itself that was not a new phenomenon. But the popularization of the term racketeer took that historic suspicion a step further by implicitly coloring important aspects of union power as illicit. The scandals of Bioff and Scalise had contributed to this view, as had the way news coverage depicted those scandals. Wartime concerns also fed public resentment of labor. Pegler's role had been to create a lexicon of denunciation that linked individual cases of abuse to a menacing depiction of union power in general.

## Antiunionism and Anti-New Deal Conservatism

Pegler led the way in linking concerns about the growing influence of organized labor to arguments against the New Deal and its vision of a more expansive role for the federal government. The columnist had turned against the New Deal in 1937, in the same period when he began consistently to criticize organized labor. Over the course of the following years, his attacks on the Roosevelt administration often cited the New Deal's support for unions.

The gist of Pegler's conservative argument was that the New Dealers had taken advantage of the crisis caused by the Depression to dramatically expand the power of the executive branch of the federal government. The seemingly haphazard nature of the New Deal's reforms, Pegler charged, was in fact a tactical misdirection that allowed the Roosevelt administration to avoid the opposition that a true understanding of their program would create. In the short run, the New Deal used federal relief funds to build a kind of national political machine, where the allocation of strategic favors guaranteed political allegiance. And like the corrupt political machines of Boss Hague in Jersey City and the Kelly-Nash administration in Chicago (who, Pegler noted, were loyal allies of the Roosevelt administration), the New Deal used selective enforcement of the law as a way to win supporters and punish opponents. In the long run, these developments would lead, Pegler warned, to a fascist dictatorship along the lines of those in Soviet Russia or Nazi Germany.[88]

For Pegler, the Wagner Act formed a key part of this New Deal fascist conspiracy. Viewed in combination with the increasing restrictions that the New Deal placed on business, this labor legislation exemplified the intolerance of totalitarian states towards free enterprise. Attacking the Roosevelt administration in August 1939, he asserted, "We haven't gone all the way to fascism in our hostility to business, but the New Dealers aren't through yet."[89]

Pegler charged that the Wagner Act allowed the Democrats to forcibly enroll America's working class into state-sponsored bodies that operated as auxiliaries of the New Deal. "This is a law," he warned in mid-October 1940, "which drives millions into unions against their will, under the rule of unioneers whose character the government disclaims any right or responsibility to investigate." In return for forcing workers to join their unions, "the labor bosses . . . naturally string along with the administration which delivered to them so many new members and so much revenue in fees, dues and assessments." And in turn, these loyal unions handed over a portion of the money to the party in power. "So these labor bosses put through resolutions levying political assessments on the members, including the unwilling ones, and turn the money over to the political treasury of President Roosevelt's Social-Democratic party."[90]

Further down the road, once the party was secure in its power, the unions would be taken over by the government, Pegler predicted, and the fascist model would be complete. Union members, he wrote, "then would find themselves in a government labor front almost identical with those of Italy and Germany."[91]

In making this conservative argument, Pegler emphasized that government expansion under the New Deal menaced the rights not just of the well-to-do but of working-class Americans. By helping unions to enforce union shop agreements, Pegler claimed, the New Deal stripped workers of a fundamental right and put them at the mercy of exploitative union leaders. Explaining the importance of this right, he wrote, "It is the right to deal individually as a free man, the right to the rewards of one's toil and not to share that reward with any unofficial, irresponsible taxing and grafting authority." Pegler depicted the New Deal, and its expansion of government's role, as part of a scheme that would gradually destroy this right to work and thus diminish individual freedom. "Mr. Roosevelt's administration," the columnist charged, "has been conniving at wholesale violation of that right."[92]

Pegler placed his warnings about government expansion in the same columns that profiled the plight of workers caught up in corrupt locals, arguing that union corruption was one aspect of a larger threat posed to individual rights under the New Deal.[93]

## Antiunion Politics

As Pegler plied these arguments in his columns, opponents of the New Deal mounted a campaign in Congress against the Wagner Act. They were motivated both by hostility to organized labor and by the belief that this issue could be exploited to undercut the New Deal. In 1941 and again in 1943, conservatives used the issue of union abuses to win important political victories, for the first time rolling back a key part of the New Deal's legislative achievement. For the Roosevelt administration, public hostility toward union leaders became a growing political problem, one linked to their declining strength in Congress.

The tactical advantages of this line of argument against the New Deal became clear in late November and early December 1941, as conservatives in the House of Representatives put a series of amendments to the Wagner Act to a vote. The legislative contest came amid growing resentment of strikes in the defense industries. The stubborn refusal of John L. Lewis to give up demands for a union shop in the coal mines operated by steel companies also had raised tempers, both in Congress and among the general public.[94]

But the rhetoric that emerged during the lengthy congressional debate constantly returned to the issue of union corruption. Conservatives proclaimed their desire to protect American workers from the "racketeer" leaders who would exploit them and endanger the nation's security. Representative Martin Sweeney from Ohio said, "The real friends of labor are those who would free and emancipate labor from the designing and selfish labor leaders and dictators." He went on to assert, "Congress is determined to save honest labor from its racketeering leaders."[95]

Congressmen such as Eugene Cox deployed the term "racketeer" to denounce union leadership in general, branding both AFL and the CIO officials with the label. Ranked by the *New York Times* as "one of the most prolific and fiery of the Southern Democrats," Cox had represented his district in southeast Georgia since 1925. He held a powerful post on the House Rules Committee and consistently used it to oppose New Deal legislation. A bitter opponent of organized labor, according to the historian Gilbert Gall, Cox was "regarded by many as industry's self-appointed House watchdog." As a former judge, Cox was capable of measured, even "Ciceronian" delivery in his speeches on the floor of the Congress, but he also was known for slipping into a more hyperbolic style. In the midst of one such speech in 1943, he reached out and pulled the hair of a nearby congressman to emphasize his point. On another occasion, he started a fist fight on the floor of the House.[96]

Given the tone of his speech on December 1, 1941, one suspects that his fellow congressmen tried to keep well out of arms' reach that day. Speaking in favor of amendments to the Wagner Act, Cox denounced Harry Bridges, a West Coast leader of the CIO Longshoremen's Union, who was widely alleged to be a Communist Party member. "The goons are here," Cox announced. "The alien Harry Bridges is in the capitol giving orders to his henchmen. Greedy, brutal, racketeering labor leaders have made a pawn of the safety of the people."[97] By using the word racketeering this way, Cox was not alleging that the left-wing Bridges had ties to organized crime or that he took payoffs. Instead, he meant that Bridges and other union leaders exercised dictatorial control over their labor organizations, and that they used this power to promote their interests, not their memberships, and certainly not the interests of the nation at large.

This broad construction of corruption followed Pegler's lead, and Cox tapped a number of the issues that the columnist had raised. Most union members had not joined willingly, Cox argued. Once forcibly enrolled in a union, members had no real voice in the government of the organization. The leaders "levy tribute, any tribute they please—as they do now—on the free wage earners of America." The resulting situation cried out for a legislative remedy. "Mr. Chairman," he told the House, "the security of this Nation, the very safety of our people is being opposed and hamstrung by a handful of rapacious, audacious racketeers, lustful for power and greedy for profit."[98]

Organized labor's allies quickly noted the argument's similarity to what Pegler had promoted in his columns. Congressman John Flannagan of Virginia referred to the supporters of the Wagner Act amendments as "Peglerites." He pointed out how the recent corruption scandal had made these legislative proposals possible. "I realize that public opinion, aroused by the acts of a few misguided labor leaders and the revelation that other unscrupulous labor leaders have prostituted their leadership into racketeering, is demanding anti-labor legislation." But he also charged that labor's opponents had fostered this sense of alarm to suit their political needs. "These Peglerites, with Jeremiah complexes, daily giving birth to spasms of fear, I am constrained to believe, have done as much, if not more, to disrupt public-industrial-labor relations, than all the irresponsible labor leaders and racketeers combined."[99]

But the force of public opinion aroused by the scandal and the controversial strikes could not be denied, even by labor's legislative allies. "Gentlemen, a rising tide of public opinion is demanding that Congress act to curb the arbitrary use of unlimited power granted labor unions and various racketeers masquerading under the protection of labor unions," warned Congressman Francis Walter of Pennsylvania.[100] Walter, who later chaired the House Un-American Activities Committee, probably used that claim to justify a vote he would have cast regardless, but his colleague Jerry Voorhis of California acknowledged the situation with evident chagrin. One of the most liberal members of Congress and an ardent New Dealer, Voorhis later was unseated by Richard Nixon, who charged that the congressmen had communist sympathies. In the debates over labor legislation in December 1941, Voorhis described himself as prounion, but explained that "given all the anti-labor feeling that unquestionably exists," some legislation had to be passed. His only hope was to make the amendments that went into law as constructive as possible.[101]

In the end, in early December 1941, the House of Representatives passed the most stringent set of proposals that had come before it, the Smith Act, thereby delivering a stinging legislative defeat to organized labor and the Roosevelt administration. The bill drew on the war emergency to invoke new limits on union activity, but many of its provisions also reflected the charge that irresponsible, "racketeering" leaders were causing industrial turmoil. The legislation banned strikes in the defense industry that aimed to achieve a closed shop contract. A thirty-day cooling-off period was mandated before any strike or lockout could occur involving a defense contractor. Should conciliation fail during that period, the law mandated that workers have a secret ballot, overseen by the government, to determine whether they did indeed support a strike. Congress intended to protect workers from being dragged into disputes against their will by their leadership, a practice believed to be widespread.[102]

Many of the other provisions read like a shopping list of Pegler's proposals over the previous two years. Unions were barred from waging jurisdictional strikes or practicing secondary boycotts against defense contractors. Although the law itself did not use the words "goon squad," a favorite term of Pegler's, it implicitly raised the issue in two of its provisions. First, threats and violence by labor's forces during all strikes were made specifically illegal. Second, pickets at job disputes were required to be bona fide employees of the company involved in the dispute, not persons sent in by the union to achieve its aims. The act imposed new rules for union governance that paralleled Pegler's suggestions. All unions were required to register with the government, and in so doing file public reports on their membership, dues, and finances. Highlighting the way that scandal had made the character of labor leaders a key political issue, the law set out new restrictions for union officers. It banned any member of the Communist Party, Young Communist League, German American Bund, and anyone convicted of a felony involving moral turpitude.[103] Thus without specifically using their names, the law directly dealt with the cases of the convicted panderers Bioff and Scalise.

Having passed in the House by a wide margin (the vote was 252 to 136), the measure still had to win assent in the Senate.[104] Roosevelt's ability to have labor legislation bottled up in the Senate's Education and Labor Committee promised to make the task of conservatives difficult, but unions still had plenty of cause for alarm. Given the climate of public opinion, even staunch senatorial allies of organized labor such as Florida's Claude Pepper indicated their intention to back some kind of legislation in the coming weeks. "I say this as a champion of labor itself," Pepper asserted, "for labor needs to be defended against some its own embittered and avaricious leaders by its real friends."[105] It was unlikely that Roosevelt's supporters could have prevailed for long.[106]

In the end, however, events on the international front intervened. The day after Senator Pepper made his comments and before the Senate could begin considering this legislation, the Japanese attack on Pearl Harbor dramatically swept such matters off the public agenda. In the climate of national unity that followed the attack, the Smith Act was pushed to the side. Instead, Roosevelt called for a national labor-management conference in which both sides agreed to the peaceful resolutions of disputes as well as a wartime ban on strikes and lockouts. In January 1942, the president set up the National War Labor Board to administer this new system of collective bargaining.[107]

For a while, the comparative calm that settled over industrial relations forestalled further calls to amend the Wagner Act. But strikes began to increase in number in late 1942 and 1943 as workers and some unions defied the no-strike pledge, and so the Smith act reappeared, winning passage in June 1943 in a modified form as known as the Smith-Connally War Labor Disputes Act.[108] Many of the provisions in the earlier version, such as the requirement that unions register with the government, were left out of this bill. Smith-Connally, however, did maintain its predecessor's emphasis on regulating strikes at defense industries. It empowered the president to seize critical industries affected by strikes and imposed criminal sanctions against job actions at such government-controlled facilities. The premise that union members needed protection from their leaders was maintained by a provision that called for mandatory thirty-day cooling-off periods and government-run strike votes before all walkouts. Finally, this act stole another page from Pegler's legislative proposals by banning unions from making political contributions.[109]

In retrospect, critics of this legislation have noted the ways in which the Smith-Connally Act failed to achieve its apparent goals. President Roosevelt remained a staunch supporter of unions, and those sentiments shaped the way he used the powers the act had granted him to seize plants. On the rare occasion he invoked those powers, for instance in the government's seizure of Montgomery Ward in 1944, he acted to protect the workers' rights and to penalize an obstinate employer.[110] The new provisions for government-run strike votes actually worked to legitimize wartime walkouts, which now could be initiated through a federally sanctioned procedure. In contrast to the claims of legislators, union members did not prove reluctant to vote for strikes. Indeed, so willing were members to approve strikes that such ballots became part of the bargaining strategy by labor organizations, which sought to demonstrate the solidarity of their membership to employers. Nor did the new restrictions stymie the political role of unions. That summer, the CIO formed its Political Action Committee to raise voluntary funds from its affiliates' membership, and by 1944 organized labor once more provided important campaign support to New Deal Democrats, including the president.[111] Moreover, as a wartime measure, the act's provisions would go out of existence at the end of the current national emergency.

But labor leaders at the time marked the legislative battles in 1941 and 1943 as bad omens. The United Mine Workers' official journal referred to the Smith Act's passage in the House in December 1941 as "one of the blackest days in American legislative history." Union officials recognized the powerful symbolic importance of the legislation.[112] If the restrictions placed only a light restraining hand on union activities, the language of the measures helped to engrave a negative image of labor on the public mind. These bills proclaimed that union members had to be protected from their leaders, who were irresponsible and self-interested. It tarred the political influence of organized labor as illegitimate, the result of funds mulcted from the dues of the rank and file whose views had little role in how their money was spent. That the reality of union practice and affairs differed dramatically from this image mattered less than the fact that the image had achieved this level of political currency.

For the same reasons, delegates gathered for a convention of the National Association of Manufacturers (NAM), a leading anti-union group, celebrated the legislative victory in December 1941. According to a press report on the gathering, delegates described the Smith Act as a "godsend." "When its sponsor, Virginia's wing-collared Representative Howard W. Smith, turned up at yesterday's session, he entered as a conquering hero. As one man, the NAM rose and gave him a thunderous ovation."[113]

## Long-Term Political Costs of the Scandals

The air of scandal that enveloped organized labor had political results beyond the legislative arena. For Roosevelt's New Deal administration, its strong ties to organized labor began to exact a political toll. Instead of these links demonstrating the administration's concern for the welfare of working Americans, to more and more people they indicated a calculating alliance, one that sacrificed national interests to political expediency. Republicans were quick to exploit this change in views.

We know something about these political ramifications thanks to President Roosevelt's keen interest in gauging public opinion, an interest that he maintained throughout his years in office. By the early 1940s, he encouraged his aides to explore what was then the emerging field of public opinion polling. At his request, staff members commissioned a number of private polls on a range of issues, showing him the results in confidential memos.[114] The changing public attitude toward labor became one of the main issues examined by these polling studies.

In November 1941, his aides passed on to Roosevelt a lengthy compilation of these polls, entitled *Public Opinion and Labor Problems: Confidential Report*.[115] The study's authors warned the president about the danger of his administration losing working-class support because of growing public concern over union abuses. The polls indicated a widespread belief of a majority of Americans that unions should be more strictly regulated to protect members and that many union leaders were either Communists or racketeers. The authors of the report emphasized that most union members held the same beliefs; indeed, most union members even agreed with Pegler's charges.[116] These findings revealed a growing disaffection with organized labor even among working Americans, and that shift in public opinion had baleful implications for the New Deal, given its prominent political ties to unions.

If Roosevelt was doubtful of these private findings, he had only to consult the similar results being reported by George Gallup's polling organization. Gallup also pointed out the political implications of the findings. "While Republicans in Congress have focused their attacks on New Deal foreign policy," he wrote in October 1941, "actually one of the greatest criticisms which the American people have against the Roosevelt Administration today is not its handling of foreign policy, but its handling of strikes and the labor situation." He pointedly observed, "During the last year the New Deal labor policy has, in fact, been farther out of line with public opinion than any other major New Deal policy."[117]

As the 1944 presidential contest approached, Republicans decided to capitalize on the issue. Thomas Dewey, the Republican nominee, had built a nationwide reputation as an anti-racketeering district attorney in New York, and his successful prosecution of Scalise in 1940 had contributed to that reputation. Like Roosevelt, Dewey was an aficionado of opinion polls, and the Republican candidate's staff also noted the changing public attitudes towards labor.[118] Dewey's polling research indicated that Roosevelt was losing support among American workers, including union members. "While Roosevelt still commands a 2 to 1 majority in union ranks," one report noted, "the trend of his popularity among union men is down."[119]

A memo by a key member of his campaign staff argued that Dewey should aggressively pursue working-class votes by emphasizing union scandals and abuses. "I know that candidates have considered it practically political suicide to attack labor on any score," asserted Ray Rubicam, the vice chair of the Advisory Committee on Publicity and Public Relations. "But by now it is plain that the country is sick of labor dictatorship, sick of labor's frustration of democratic processes." The situation had been different, he acknowledged "when the chief victim was industry." But now, "when the worker himself begins to feel victimized," the Republicans should respond. "The situation is crying for attack," he urged.[120]

This opinion became the consensus. Dewey's chief speech writer, Stanley High, explained how he intended to emphasize this issue by ensuring that every speech candidate Dewey made emphasized this point: "Thanks to the New Deal—and its alien supporters—the future of organized labor in the U.S. is a desperate race between European-minded labor leaders and corrupt labor racketeers, on the one hand, and the great mass of intelligent American workmen who want an American chance, under American auspices to get ahead in an American way."[121]

Although the Republicans lost the presidential contest in 1944, the party adopted the issue of union abuses, including labor corruption, as a mainstay in its appeals to the electorate. The issue gave the conservatives a trump card to play against the New Deal, a way to claim that the real friends of working Americans would protect them from the corruption and abuses of labor leaders. It also allowed conservatives to frame concerns about individual rights and the dangers of collectivism in ways that included working-class Americans. As historian Melvyn Dubofsky has noted, a leading postwar conservative figure, Senator Robert Taft, defended his effort to amend the Wagner Act in 1947 as a measure "to liberate the industrial worker from industrial thralldom by guaranteeing his constitutional rights as American citizen to do as he pleases."[122]

Pegler had invoked this language of rights in the same context as early as 1940, when he wrote of the AFL and CIO: "The danger to the people's liberty lies in the fact that both of these big unions take it for granted that they have a vested right to govern millions of citizens . . . all in flagrant, brutal disregard for the rights of the victims."[123] By demonstrating that some union officials, such as Bioff and Scalise, were in fact criminals who exploited their organizations' membership, Pegler gave this conservative use of rights language a potency that it otherwise would have lacked. It was one of the most important long-term political effects of the scandal.

The columnist's political impact was palpable. It was for that reason that in Congress, both the supporters and the opponents of organized labor cited Pegler, alternatively damning and praising his efforts. Labor leaders certainly took Pegler's efforts very seriously, and they searched for an effective response.

# "Labor Must Clean House"

## The Challenge of Responding to Pegler

The FBI maintained a substantial file on Pegler. Most if it consisted of letters denouncing him for his attacks on President Roosevelt or for his criticism of the FBI, an agency that the columnist felt was overrated. But Pegler's FBI file also contained a transcript from a Bureau wiretap in August 1943 on the New York City offices of the National Maritime Union (NMU), a left-leaning union that represented members of the Merchant Marine. Pegler had written a series of columns attacking the NMU and its president, Joseph Curran, for—among other things—alleged Communist connections. Angry and determined not to let Pegler's columns go unanswered, NMU officials in New York debated how to word their reply. Although the FBI has blacked out the names of the union officials on the transcript, the conversation still offers a firsthand perspective on labor's attempt to respond to Pegler.

Earlier the NMU office had phoned the press to announce that tomorrow they intended to picket the *World-Telegram's* building "in protest against the treasonable statements by columnist Westbrook Pegler against the valiant men of the Merchant Marine." But as one official explained on the phone, they considered modifying the press release. "We're worried about that word treasonable."

The official at the other end, who apparently had been called for advice, responded, "Yeah, I think it should come out. I don't think you can take a chance on it."

"See, we feel here in the office that we have a case against the guy."

"You have a case against the guy, but it's a very strong statement in time of war. I know you feel like making it, so do I, but I would want it in some

Figure 9.1: This cartoon by John M. Baer appeared on March 9, 1940, as labor leaders and their supporters sought to respond to Westbrook Pegler and the criticism of the American Federation of Labor that his exposés had generated. The cartoon tags such critics and their use of the term *racketeer* as part of a "smear" campaign. From *Labor: The Railway Men's National Weekly*, March 1940.

other way so that there could be a looser interpretation. Unpatriotic is not strong enough for your purpose, huh?"

"No, vile would be more like it."

"Vile is all right."

"Vile is all right?"

"Sure."

"You cannot call a guy a traitor," the second official explained. "It's awful strong stuff. If you want another opinion, why, call around a little more, but I would very much hesitate before issuing a statement of that sort."[1] Another call that shortly followed this one confirmed the advice, and presumably the NMU dialed back the voltage of its response out of fear of a libel suit.[2]

Pegler's vituperative campaign against union officials hurt. It hurt politically and, as the FBI transcript reveals, it hurt on an emotional level as well. But finding an effective response proved difficult. With his writing skills, the vigor of his charges, and his access to a nationwide audience, Pegler made for a tough opponent. For its part, labor was divided and ill-equipped to wage a media counteroffensive. No coherent strategy emerged, and the existing divisions—between AFL and CIO, between conservative and progressive unionists—were reflected in the range of responses.

Meanwhile, their liberal allies warned organized labor of the stakes involved. In February 1940, just weeks after the Bioff and Scalise scandals had broken, the *New Republic* printed an editorial entitled "Labor Must Clean House." "The tide of hostility to labor in this country is steadily mounting," the liberal magazine warned, "and it is more than time that the workers and their friends should realize the situation." With the New Deal in decline, antiunion forces were gathering strength for an effort to amend the Wagner Act. "All the available evidence shows that in the battle for control of public opinion on this issue, labor at present is running behind."

The editorial emphasized the impact of Pegler and the scandals he had uncovered: "The most spectacular charges against labor have to do with racketeering and with an inferior or dubious quality of leadership. Mr. Westbrook Pegler has recently got a good deal of attention when he showed that Willie Bioff, Hollywood leader of the stagehands' union, was a fugitive from justice, having been convicted in Chicago many years ago of being a panderer." New charges against Bioff for income tax evasion exacerbated the situation, the *New Republic* explained, as did Pegler's revelations regarding Scalise's criminal past.[3] The editorial warned organized labor against the complacent attitude of "the public be-dammed" that it had taken in the past. In the era of the New Deal, public opinion mattered. "Today labor no longer depends wholly on its own strength; it has been aided very materially by national and state legislation such as the National Labor Relations Act, the anti-injunction and wages-and-hours laws. But government depends in a substantial degree on public opinion. If the unions sulk in their tent, or depend on the efforts of a few moth-eaten and elderly lobbyists of the slap-your-back and have-a-cigar type, they are likely to take an awful beating."[4]

The challenge, as the *New Republic* saw it, was for unions to both mount a successful public relations campaign and wage a vigorous effort against racketeering. "The racketeering leaders should be swept aside and the racketeering unions with them. The kind of labor movement this country needs should have no place for a leader who talks about a prison sentence for having been a panderer as a mere boyish peccadillo, or turns up with thousands of dollars of income he can't explain." Failure to respond adequately risked "seeing the trade union movement in this country set back a generation." And failure to achieve the necessary internal reforms would provide an opportunity for labor's enemies. "If labor doesn't clean its own house, the job will be done by someone else in a way that neither labor nor its friends will like."[5] In this way, the *New Republic* offered a warning and a standard by which to measure the success or failure of labor's response.

For a variety of reasons, organized labor failed to meet this challenge. It was never successful at getting its side of the story to the public. And the American Federation of Labor failed to make the sweeping reforms that would have convinced the public, or even its liberal allies, of its willingness to tackle the problem of corruption. One measure of this failure can be seen in the decision of many liberals to support greater government regulation of unions. In so doing, the erstwhile liberal allies of labor publicly distanced themselves from union leaders, and this division foreshadowed one of the sources of labor's political decline in the years after World War II.[6]

## Denial: Not Just a River in Egypt

For the AFL, the first stage of its response to Pegler amounted to denial. They refused to acknowledge that anything significant had been uncovered. The organization's leadership initially offered support to both Bioff and Scalise and attempted a kind of column-versus-column debate with the columnist. Both moves proved disastrous. But both also reflected the particular perspective that AFL leaders brought to the problem of union corruption. They also stemmed from the nature of Pegler's attack, which made a point of lumping all union leaders, what he called "unioneers," together. His columns insinuated that they were all crooks. If AFL leaders reacted defensively, if they proved unresponsive to his call for action, in some ways Pegler had made that reaction inevitable.

In all of this, AFL president William Green was a central player. He was both the target of much of Pegler's vituperation and the man ultimately responsible for answering the columnist. In his late sixties by the time the Bioff scandal broke, Green's appearance belied the dark, menacing, stereotypical racketeer that Pegler made the mainstay of his depictions of union leadership: Green was anything but menacing. According to a biographer, the short and plump Green "had a solemn, but well-fed appearance. Conservative suits, pince-nez glasses, and a gold watch chain all lent an air of respectability and trustworthiness. His well-scrubbed, rosy-cheeked, fat face, combined with his ever present smile gave him a sincere and submissive semblance."[7] A journalist's description in 1941 emphasized Green's "apple-cheeked, sedate, and neat" appearance and likened him to a "benign professor." But the placid, genial, professorial mien was in some ways misleading. He was, in fact, a dedicated union leader who had spent most of his adult life working in the labor movement. This was not the first labor scandal he had seen, nor was Pegler the first critic he had encountered. The same journalist who had likened Green to a professor noted, "He listens to you courteously, but with an air of resignation, as if he had heard it all a hundred times before—as, no doubt, he has."[8]

He had come up through the ranks of the labor movement. The son of an English miner who had immigrated to the Ohio coal fields, Green had been raised a devout Baptist, and for a while in his youth aspired to the ministry. Family circumstances made that impossible, and at age sixteen he went to work in the mines. By the age of twenty-one he had won local office in the United Mine Workers Union (UMW), and over the course of the early 1900s he steadily rose up through that organization from regional to national office. In 1924, UMW president John L. Lewis helped engineer Green's election to replace the recently deceased Samuel Gompers as head of the AFL. Green was a compromise candidate, agreeable to the various factions involved. After his election, he promised to follow Gomper's precedent and leave control of AFL policy in the hands of the executive council.[9]

Descriptions of the federation's internal politics in the 1920s and early 1930s depict Green as a figurehead rather than a strong president. Real power rested in the hands of an inner circle of veteran union presidents with large and stable memberships, such as Daniel Tobin of the Teamsters and William Hutcheson of the Carpenters. These men hashed over issues at regular late-night poker games held during the evenings when the executive council was in session. The teetotaling, religious Green did not belong to this poker-playing inner circle and apparently did little to set the federation's agenda.[10]

His inactivity, however, may have also reflected the degree to which the conservative Green agreed with the policies that the AFL pursued in these years. His conservatism matched that of the other federation leaders. As a group, they had come of age in the late 1800s and had helped bring their organizations through bitter employer counteroffensives in the first part of the twentieth century. These union leaders were the survivors. They had learned a cautious aversion to taking risks with their institutions, and they viewed with skepticism the periodic waves of worker militancy, which had proved all too inconstant in the past.[11] For Green, this experience was colored by his deep religious faith. Historian Craig Phelan's biography depicts Green as a nineteenth-century religious idealist who placed his faith in moral appeals to employers for cooperation. Phelan wrote, "He remained forever the Baptist minister calling on the sinner to repent."[12] As a result, Green accepted the cautious, conservative policies of the AFL executive council.

By the mid-1930s, with a new upsurge in worker militancy and with the New Deal's support for labor, some AFL officials had come to see the need to take risks. Led by UMW president Lewis, in 1935 a group of union leaders formed a Committee on Industrial Organization (CIO), whose goal was an aggressive organizing drive directed at the nation's mass production industries. Unlike the AFL, which typically had organized workers by their craft and had focused more on skilled employees, the CIO brought all of the workers in a plant into one union that had an industrywide jurisdiction. In steel plants, auto factories, and meat packing yards across the country, the CIO reached out to workers whose new enthusiasm for unions had been viewed so warily by Green and other AFL leaders.[13]

The emergence of the Committee for Industrial Organization roused Green to action, and he led the AFL in a strident counterattack against the threat of a rival labor federation. At his instigation, the AFL's attorneys provided a new interpretation of the federation's constitution that allowed Green to suspend the CIO unions. In 1937, he engineered the passage of a one-cent assessment on all AFL members, this new war chest to be used to pay for an aggressive organizing drive aimed at CIO jurisdictions. The AFL staff was purged of anyone with CIO ties, and he led the way in forcing city and state labor federations to expel CIO affiliates. When the CIO responded by holding a founding convention in October 1938 to make its temporary committee a permanent, independent entity, the Congress of Industrial Organizations, Green supported even bolder moves against it. John Frey, head of the AFL's Metal Trades Division, publicly testified before the House Un-American Activities Committee that Communists had widely infiltrated the CIO.[14] Meanwhile the AFL's lead counsel, Joseph Padway, began meeting with employers groups, such as the National Association of Manufacturers, to coordinate efforts to amend the Wagner Act in ways that would help to slow CIO growth.[15] In all of these actions, Green showed himself capable of vigorous, aggressive leadership.

By 1940, the AFL had demonstrated that under Green's leadership it would weather the storm and survive the CIO's secession. Spurred by competition, AFL affiliates had mounted ambitious organizing drives that increased their membership rolls dramatically. The federation boasted 4.3 million members, roughly double the size of the rival CIO.[16]

The CIO secession had significant consequences for the AFL's ability to respond to a corruption crisis. The most progressive elements of the labor federation had left to join the CIO and as a result, the influence of the conservative unions, especially in the construction trades, had increased proportionately.[17] Efforts to take a hard line in demanding reform with any AFL affiliate were now tempered by the fear that the affiliate could, if it chose, simply switch sides and join the CIO. Finally, AFL leaders who were making charges of communist infiltration in order to undercut their rivals in the CIO were prone to interpret charges of racketeer influence in the AFL as inspired by similar partisan motives.[18]

The secession of the CIO restrained organized labor's reaction to the scandal, but so too did the tradition of hostile media coverage of unions. Labor publications put the matter bluntly: one headline in the Chicago AFL's *Federation News* read, "Daily Newspapers Hostile to Labor."[19] Another article in the same paper reviewed how this coverage depicted a union official as a villain no matter what he did. "If he does his job, protects his membership in their difficulties and permits no digression on the part of employers from the contracts agreed upon, then he becomes a 'terrorist' and a 'goon' in the daily press. If he sits tight, does nothing and permits his members to be sacrificed, then he is a 'racketeer' who collects dues and does nothing further."[20] From organized labor's perspective, prominent news commentators such as Pegler exacerbated the hostile coverage.[21]

To many inside the union movement, the news coverage amounted to a conspiracy. It was an effort, the *Federation News* asserted, by "the daily press to tear down the confidence of the trades unionists in the labor movement."[22] A sense of being under attack, by a hostile news media and by the secessionist CIO, encouraged a wary, defensive posture on the part of the AFL when the Bioff and Scalise scandals broke, and this helped lead to the mistaken decision to deny the significance of what Pegler had uncovered.

Both Bioff and Scalise took advantage of the AFL's wariness to win an early show of support from the Federation in the face of Pegler's revelations. When Pegler's first columns on Bioff came out in November 1939, the Stage Hands official was in the midst of contract negotiations with Hollywood studios. Bioff quickly depicted himself as the victim of a conspiracy by the employers to dig up an old charge and thus block his efforts on behalf of his union members. Pegler's column, he asserted, was a "plot to blacken my character and get me out of the way, now that the battle of the film unions for higher wages is on with producers." The studio heads, who in fact had done their best to build Bioff's power up, could honestly deny the existence of such a plot.[23] But despite the dramatic stretch required, Bioff blithely took on the role of a martyred union official done in by nefarious employers. "I represent 30,000 people who are fighting for better wages, conditions and hours," he told reporters after his extradition to Chicago. His valiant efforts, he claimed, had made him a target. "The money interests want me out of the picture." And playing to the AFL's suspicions of its rival labor federation, he continued, "so do the C.I.O. and the Communists."[24]

Back in Los Angeles, AFL officials demonstrated their continued support for Bioff by refusing his resignation as chairman of the Conference of Studio Unions and instead voting a resolution declaring their confidence in him. They claimed to want him to keep his chairmanship, even if he had to conduct negotiations from inside an Illinois prison cell.[25] While AFL president Green took no active part in this show of support, it had at least his tacit approval. The telegram announcing the resolution was sent out by Meyer Lewis, the AFL representative on the West Coast and Green's direct subordinate.[26]

Scalise also assumed the role of a dedicated union official. In the wake of Pegler's exposé, Scalise called a meeting of the executive board of BSEIU, presenting them with both his written defense against the columnist's charges and the offer to resign. While not denying the conviction, Scalise emphasized how long ago the crime had occurred and asserted that in the years since he been an upstanding citizen and a devoted labor leader. His efforts to build BSEIU had brought him enemies, and those enemies, he implied, were behind Pegler's exposé. Scalise made one theme central to his defense. "I have paid my debt to society for the act I committed as a youth. Is it the American way to brand a person forever, even though that person has been punished and has learned a sufficient lesson to lead an honorable life?"[27]

For BSEIU's executive board, the answer to that question was a resounding no. They refused to accept his resignation and issued a unanimous resolution stating their continued confidence in his leadership.[28]

Scalise had sent a similar written defense to key leaders in the AFL, and he followed up by making a personal appearance before the AFL's executive board.[29] Like their counterparts in BSEIU, the AFL leaders found Scalise's defense convincing. Writing privately to Scalise, Joseph A. Padway, the AFL's general counsel, reassured him that Pegler's exposé of his "boyish indiscretion" had done him little harm. "In the few comments I have heard around here, not a single derogatory statement was made about you, but everyone damns and curses a writer who will resurrect an act of a young lad, which has long since been forgotten."[30]

At a press conference in early February 1940, Green responded to questions about Scalise by saying that he had had a long talk with the embattled BSEIU president. According to Green, Scalise "challenges any one to attack his record since he committed the crime for which he was convicted when he was 18 years of age." It was unfair, Green asserted, to continue to punish a man for a crime committed so long ago. The AFL president acknowledged that he supported Scalise's application for a presidential pardon, an executive action that would free Scalise from the legal disabilities that followed from a felony conviction, for instance, restoring his right to vote. "All I can say is that as far as I know, and I have known him only since 1937," Green told the press, "Mr. Scalise has gone straight, that his conduct has been satisfactory, that he has been punished enough and that as a matter of simple justice, he having paid a penalty twenty-seven years ago, his civil rights should be restored."[31]

In this very public way, Green offered support for Scalise in the face of Pegler's allegations. The AFL president was more careful in his comments regarding Bioff, and this perhaps revealed that Green had his doubts about the conduct of affairs in the Stage Hands' Union. At one press conference following his defense of Scalise, Green had added, "Mr. Bioff, on the other hand, is a perfect stranger to me."[32] But in neither case did Green voice concern about the men's criminal pasts or express a willingness to investigate seriously allegations made against them. Instead in the immediate aftermath of Pegler's exposé, in January 1940, Green criticized the columnist, referring to him by implication as one of "the enemies of labor, taking advantage of the division which was created in the ranks of organized labor" and "becoming shrill in their abuse." There was, Green boldly asserted, no serious problem with union corruption. "The American Federation of Labor has full and complete confidence in the integrity of the 4,000,000 working men and women who are its members and the men and women they have chosen to be their leaders."[33] By supporting a pardon for Scalise, Green put his own reputation on the line, explicitly vouching for the Building Service president's good character and current honesty.[34]

This proved to be a costly mistake. As the true nature of Bioff and Scalise's activities came to light, this early show of support appeared to vindicate Pegler's claim that Green and the rest of the AFL leadership were complicit. The news of Scalise's indictment spurred the *Washington Post* to publish an editorial condemning Green. "One would expect President Green of the A.F. of L. to take an active part in efforts to rid his organization of all parasites and criminals." But instead, the editorial noted, Green had criticized Pegler. Green was "apparently satisfied with Mr. Scalise's personal assurances that he was leading an exemplary life, and intimated that the columnist lacked a sense of decency in exposing a 'sordid story' of the labor leader's past." As result, the editorial argued, Scalise's indictment amounted to an indictment against Green's leadership. "The public is beginning to wonder to what extent lack of initiative on Mr. Green's part is responsible for continuance of racketeering in A.F. of L. unions."[35] The *New York Herald-Tribune* noted that "apparently, the only action taken by Green has been to have a talk with Scalise and get his assurance that since his release from prison he had 'gone straight.' Pretty feeble."[36]

AFL officials ruefully acknowledged that a public relations disaster had occurred. In May 1940, John Frey, president of the AFL's Metal Trades Division, wrote in a private letter to longtime friend and fellow AFL official Victor Olander about the "Pegler articles." "We do not need to minimize their harmful effect," Frey observed. "They did us much damage so far as public opinion is concerned."[37] Daniel Tobin, president of the Teamsters Union, observed in his union's official journal, "One thing is certain; that the articles written by Mr. Pegler have injured the American Federation of Labor substantially."[38]

In what must have been a bitter hindsight, President Green himself described the scandal's impact on public opinion in a private letter. "The American Federation of Labor and unions affiliated with it are being charged on every hand with being governed by racketeers and criminals. These charges have resulted in the development of a very hostile public opinion in some places which is reflecting itself in the Congress of the United States and in state legislatures." Having learned a painful lesson, Green was writing to a local union official urging him to oust an officer of his local who was recently convicted of a crime. "This [hostile] feeling will be intensified if local organizations such as yours stand up and defend men with criminal records and insist such men with criminal records remain officers of their organizations."[39] He was in effect asking the local official not to repeat his own mistake in mishandling the Scalise revelations.

The AFL's decision to support Scalise and Bioff played a central role in giving the scandal the significance it came to assume. It vindicated one of Pegler's main assertions that the AFL's top leadership refused to acknowledge the problem of corruption and, when pressed, defended racketeering officials rather than putting the needs of the vulnerable rank and file first. Having been wrong in his public assessment of Scalise, Green's assurances regarding the general honesty of other AFL officials came into question. It was a damaging political misstep.

The episode raises the question of why Green and other AFL leaders made such a blunder. They were not, after all, political novices. Why in particular had Green taken the risk and staked his reputation on Scalise's good character? There were several reasons for the AFL leaders to discount Pegler's attack. As Scalise claimed, his criminal record showed only that one arrest and conviction, which had occurred decades earlier. For "a criminal of the vilest type that it is possible to imagine," as Pegler had described him, Scalise did not have much of a rap sheet.[40]

Additionally, the AFL leaders must have weighed Pegler's animus against organized labor, including the columnist's tendency to lump broad categories of union leadership under the label *racketeer*. He displayed that tendency again a couple of weeks after his exposure of Scalise, before the AFL's leadership had made a public pronouncement on the BSEIU president. On February 1, 1940, Pegler explained in his column that he disagreed with those who argued that, while there might be a few bad apples, the AFL was generally an honest organization. "From that opinion, " Pegler wrote, "I have to dissent to the extreme of saying that, in my opinion, the American Federation of Labor is rotten with extortion and racketeering."[41] Six days later, he used the words "criminal scum" to refer to the AFL's top officials, insinuating that the label fit the organization's entire leadership.[42] The tone of these attacks was vicious, and they clearly stung. The abstemious Green, who had aspired for the ministry early in life, privately bridled at Pegler's denunciations.[43]

Having spent a lifetime in the labor movement, Green and other union officials might well question the columnist's basis for assessing any particular union official. If Pegler saw just another racketeer in Scalise, union officials like Green would have noticed that the Building Service Union apparently had flourished under Scalise's leadership. It was during his tenure as the

BSEIU's East Coast representative that the union had made its big organizing breakthrough in New York City, and those gains continued once he became the national president. From 1934 to 1940, the union's membership in that city had risen from 1,500 to 30,000.[44]

Then, too, Green apparently had come to know Scalise on a personal basis. Pegler described Scalise as a former bodyguard for a gangster, presumably a tough guy, but Green would have encountered a likeable, well-spoken family man.[45] The two union officials had dined together, and Scalise had agreed to serve on a charity committee that Green chaired.[46] Indeed, Scalise assiduously cultivated his contacts among the top leadership of the AFL, presenting influential people like General Counsel Padway with generous Christmas gifts.[47] In these and other ways, Scalise acted less like a gangster than an ambitious union official, a type with which Green would have been familiar.

Finally, AFL officials reacted to the scandal in the context of their current struggle with the CIO, and this cast further shadow of suspicion on Pegler's motives. Daniel Tobin, president of the Teamsters Union, observed that "not one word [in Pegler's revelations] has been uttered against any of the C.I.O. unions." As a result, he explained, "Some of the men of the Labor side of the American Federation of Labor are of the opinion that the C.I.O. is indirectly responsible for the [Pegler] writings."[48]

For all of these reasons, Green followed the wrong impulse and defended Scalise against Pegler's attack. For similar reasons, the AFL failed to separate itself from Bioff when the first allegations emerged about his criminal past in Chicago. In so doing, the federation's response to Pegler only fed the scandal. Later efforts to answer the columnist proved equally unsuccessful, and this was particularly true of the AFL's attempts to bring its case before the public.

## The AFL Public Relations Effort

In February 1940, the AFL's executive council debated whether or not to mount a public relations campaign in response to Pegler. President Tobin of the Teamsters described the debate that had taken place in an editorial he wrote for his union's official journal. "As a member of the Executive Council I favored the Federation giving greater publicity to its position in answer to the charges made in the series of articles written by Mr. Pegler."[49] But, the Teamsters president explained, "A majority of the Executive Council took a different attitude." The council members had a number of reasons for their reluctance to take on such an ambitious effort. "Some believed the more attention given to this writer's attacks the greater publicity would be given the writer. Others believed it would be impossible to get our side of the question before the public." And, Tobin noted, some were afraid of drawing Pegler's fire towards themselves. "Others believed that to continue to answer Mr. Pegler in a series of articles might arouse him, his bitterness and ability, and might bring about attacks on other leaders in the Labor Movement." And so the AFL mounted no major public relations campaign.[50]

Instead, Green made an effort to respond to Pegler in kind. The AFL president wrote three columns in which, with careful prose and mild tones, he answered key elements of Pegler's attack.[51] Where Pegler described union members as unwilling victims, Green depicted a vigorous rank and file membership who enjoyed real benefits and actively policed their organizations against the occasional bad actor. The fact that Pegler had unearthed the dubious pasts of Bioff and Scalise, Green argued, did not discount this roseate picture of union governance. "Would it be fair to condemn American democracy because of the Teapot Dome scandal and the disclosure that even a Cabinet officer has been corrupt?"[52]

Green responded as well to "Westbrook Pegler's charge that the American Federation of Labor condones and protects dishonest unionism." The AFL president labeled the claim "a deliberate falsehood." "We call upon our affiliated unions to root out and expel any individual found guilty of a betrayal of trust. In addition we call upon the constituted public authorities of our cities, states and nation to enforce the law that applies to all our citizens without fear of favor." Such exhortations fell short of exercising active oversight among the AFL affiliates, but Green explained that the federation's constitution enshrined the principle of autonomy for its constituent members. Referring to the national and international unions, Green wrote, "Their relation to the A.F. of L. is like that of the states to the federal government. Their elected officers are responsible to the members of the union, not to the A.F. of L." Thus in cases of official wrongdoing by national union officials, "the officers of the A.F. of L. have no legal or constitutional authority to supersede the officers of a national or international union or to give them orders."[53] Green could not remove an official like Bioff from his position in IATSE even if he wanted to. While this kind of autonomous structure limited the AFL's anticorruption efforts to a kind of moral suasion, he argued it protected real democracy in the federation.[54]

Green's private papers are sparse, and he left no indication of what exactly he wanted to achieve with these columns. Clearly he hoped to counter some of Pegler's contentions, but in choosing this format he inadvertently placed himself in a lopsided contest. Unlike Pegler's nationally syndicated columns, Green's three columns reached a very limited audience. He apparently sent letters out to newspapers that published Pegler asking them in the interest of fair play to print his response.[55] There is no indication that any except Pegler's home paper, the *New York World-Telegram,* actually did so. And for its part, the *World-Telegram* buried these replies in the back pages. Nor did Green's columns appear in the nation's labor papers, such as Chicago's *Federation News.* Most people would have learned of Green's response only by reading Pegler's summary and rebuttal of it, and therein lies the irony. Without actually making himself heard, the AFL president had provided Pegler with more material to write on, giving the columnist one more way to keep the scandal alive and to justify his condemnation of the AFL.

Pegler took full advantage of the opportunity in a series of columns in early April 1940. In Pegler's version, Green had launched a personal attack on him and so justified the kind of pugnacious response that Pegler had made his specialty. "My little dispute with William Green regarding the activities and influences of criminals in the American Federation of Labor has been impersonal and factual to date, but Mr. Green will not have it so. He gets personal and erroneous, if not untruthful, and makes it necessary for me to feed him some crow."[56]

Pegler depicted Green's defense as yet another indication of the unwillingness of the AFL's leadership to address the problem of union corruption. Instead of going after Pegler, Green should have been going after the crooks. "I may be naïve," Pegler wrote, "but if I were president of the A.F. of L. I would find somewhere in the [AFL] Constitution legal authority to disown and throw out of the movement not only Willie Bioff and George Scalise, the convicted vice-mongers who never were workers and always have been racketeers. . . . I would not wait for reporters or public prosecutors to delouse my organization, but, out of devotion to the A.F. of L. and its good name in the interests of the rank and file, I would raise pluperfect hell until all criminals and grafters were driven out." Because he made this his goal, Pegler claimed to be not an enemy of organized labor or of the AFL, but in fact a better friend to it than President Green. "I am not hostile to the A.F. of L. or any of its component unions, and I am much more sympathetic with the underpaid and oppressed rank and file than many of the union officials are."[57]

But Pegler's most telling point had to do with the disingenuous quality of Green's depiction of organized labor. Green's portrayal of union governance,

where an informed and active membership oversaw their organization's finances, had the whiff of a Platonic ideal. With busy lives and plenty of other
commitments, most union members knew little about how their unions were
run. Green could have argued that relatively few union officials engaged in
the blatant betrayals of trust—such as embezzling large sums from their
membership or taking bribes from employers—and still recognized that
corruption was a problem. But he did not.

Pegler cited all of these as examples of Green's efforts to evade responsibility by pretending not to see the problems that existed. Throwing Green's
words back at him, Pegler asserted that many of the so-called "autonomous
unions are themselves dictatorships which could be broken up by the federation authority but cannot be overthrown by their own members." In these
cases, Pegler argued, fear kept members from playing the kind of governance
role that Green had pictured, and these were conditions, Pegler insisted, that
Green must have known existed. "I can't persuade myself that Mr. Green is
ignorant of these facts or that he really believes these dictatorships can be
conquered by the little people."[58]

Indeed, it seems safe to conclude that Green did know real problems existed. Certainly his colleagues acknowledged as much privately, and though
his sparse private papers leave no record of it, we can assume Green shared
their perspective and their concerns. Among those colleagues was John Frey,
the president of the AFL Metal Trades Division. Like Green, Frey was a
longtime union official, a conservative, who worked in the same AFL headquarters in Washington, D.C., as Green. In a letter written in May 1940, Frey
admitted, "The facts going out concerning Bioff, Scalaise [sic] and others are
merely an evidence that racketeering is rampant in some of our International
Unions." Frey described his own firsthand contact with this phenomenon.
"I am compelled at times to be in contact with trade union representatives
whom I feel certain are racketeers and gangsters. I feel assured because the
home they live in, the type of automobiles they own, and their many other
expenditures make it clear that the source of income must be largely outside
the salary they receive as trade union officials."[59]

It seems likely Green would have been meeting similar officials and reaching comparable conclusions. In an undated speech, probably from 1933, Green
described the growing problem of "gangsterized unionism" and alluded to
organized crime's growing influence "not only in Chicago, New York, Detroit, and Philadelphia, but in a dozen other of our industrial centers."[60] As
president of the AFL, he received letters from rank and file members caught
up in these locals, just as Pegler did. These letters belied Green's description

of an empowered union membership that could rise up to oust corrupt leaders.[61] The disingenuous quality of Green's response not only left him open to Pegler's riposte, it undercut the AFL's effort to make its case.

## The Second Stage of the AFL's Response: Avoidance

There was another venue in which the AFL might have made its case, the courts, and although the executive council considered this option, it chose instead a policy of avoidance. President Green proposed the possibility of suing Pegler for libel in May 1940, in the wake of Scalise's indictment. At a meeting of the executive council, he cited Pegler's column of February 17, 1940, which had asserted, "The A.F. of L. is not the body of Labor with a capital L at all, but a great, arrogant, corrupt, hypocritical, parasitic racket which preys on union men and the public, and persecutes non-members and has been getting away with many varieties and all degrees of crime, up to and including murder, for years." With the executive council's approval, Green asked two AFL attorneys to study the feasibility of a suit based on that column.[62]

Both attorneys advised that a libel suit was feasible because the columnist had crossed the lines protecting journalistic free speech in the viciousness of his attack. The AFL could sue both the columnist and the papers that had published his columns, and the federation reasonably could ask that punitive damages be assessed. Both attorneys, however, warned that a trial judge might allow the other side wide latitude in presenting its defense. This would permit Pegler's attorneys to air some of the AFL's dirty laundry by bringing into the trial evidence regarding Scalise, Bioff, and other examples of corruption. The result would be embarrassing, but the attorneys concluded that the AFL would probably still win its suit.[63]

And yet, neither attorney urged the AFL to follow this course, and one, the federation's influential general counsel Joseph Padway, strongly advised against filing a libel suit. In his brief, Padway warned, "My own opinion is that Pegler is anxious to be sued." The suit "would furnish him the opportunity to keep alive this form of attack and to invigorate what may soon become less interesting to the reading public." Instead Padway advised waiting Pegler out. "Personally, I feel that Pegler's 'undigested venom of his spleen' will in time become nauseating to the general public because of its repetition and sadistic foundation. Therefore the effects of his attacks upon individuals and their organizations will soon disappear." Apparently agreeing with Padway's conclusions, the AFL's executive council followed his advice. They tabled consideration of filing a libel suit and the proposal faded away.[64]

The AFL's leadership had chosen avoidance over conflict. In so doing, they passed up the opportunity for a different kind of public debate with the columnist, one that would have taken place in a courtroom, not the pages of a newspaper. Their decision reflected a chastened assessment of Green's earlier attempt to make his case, and it may well have saved the federation from further negative publicity. But it also left Pegler's continued claims against the AFL essentially unchallenged and so enhanced the columnist's credibility with the reading public. Thus, for example, in 1943 one of Pegler's readers, Mrs. Henry A. Tredwell of Brooklyn, wrote to a congressman advising him to consult Pegler for information about disloyal racketeers running America's unions. Noting the charges made by the columnist, she wrote, "It must be God's truth or they would have sued him long before this."[65]

## Dubinsky's Reform Proposal

One who strongly disagreed with the AFL's response to Pegler's allegations was David Dubinsky. The president of the International Ladies Garment Workers' Union (ILGWU), Dubinsky became the most prominent voice in the labor movement to call for a vigorous anticorruption campaign. A short, intense, ebullient man who spoke with a "blurred Yiddish accent" and a cigar habitually perched in his mouth, Dubinsky was an idealistic labor leader who ran the ILGWU as a model union. He kept official salaries modest, including his own, and maintained an exacting account of union finances, which he then made public to his members. One labor expert noted, "The ILGWU published . . . the most detailed financial statements of any union in the United States." Behind these policies lay an abiding faith in the potential of the labor movement. As historian Irving Bernstein explained, "Dubinsky's philosophy was uncomplicated. He was deeply devoted to democracy, political and industrial, and believed that the union was indispensable to both."[66]

Born in Brest-Litovsk, in what was then Russian-controlled Poland in 1892, Dubinsky had become a union activist as a teenager. Jailed by Tsarist police, he was exiled to Siberia at the age of sixteen for his involvement in organized labor. He escaped and immigrated to America, where he went to work in New York City's garment district. There he became involved in the ILGWU, eventually helping to lead an anti-communist faction in the union and emerging as president of the organization in 1932. He took over a union on the brink of dissolution and led it through a dramatic comeback. The ILGWU went from a nominal 40,000 members when Dubinsky assumed office to 250,000 by 1938.[67]

Having seized the moment with his own organization, Dubinsky was one of the leaders in 1935 who urged the AFL to respond to the opportunity presented by the New Deal and launch an organizing drive in the basic industries. When those appeals proved fruitless, he joined other industrial unionists in forming the Committee on Industrial Organization. But he opposed making this division between the AFL and CIO permanent, and by 1939 he was ready to bring the ILGWU back into the AFL, where its return would be welcomed by the federation's leaders as a sweet symbolic victory and perhaps the start of a trend.[68]

For his part, the politically savvy Dubinsky saw reaffiliation as a chance to prod the AFL into reform. In early 1940, he believed that organized labor must respond constructively to the controversy aroused by Pegler and the scandals encircling Bioff and Scalise. The ILGWU president had a firsthand perspective on the problem of union corruption, and this reinforced his sense of imperative. Organized crime figures had long played a role in New York's garment industry, and they had exercised that role by dominating key unions, including the ILGWU's Local 102, which had jurisdiction over garment trucking. Dubinsky had fended off efforts by gangsters to gain a greater hold over his union even as he was forced to tolerate their continued presence in particular locals. These encounters left him with an appreciation of the danger presented by organized crime's growing influence in the labor movement. As he later recalled, "Because our experience made us conscious of how readily a union could be converted into an instrument for extortion, especially in a fragmented industry, we felt a special responsibility to demand that the labor movement as a whole be vigilant in preventing corruption from thriving in its affiliated units."[69]

Dubinsky believed that the leadership of the AFL had become complacent about this problem. "Leaders like William Green, Matthew Woll and George Meany, though themselves untainted, preferred to look the other way. 'Live and let live,' was their philosophy," he recalled. "That was just the way hoodlums George Scalise of the Building Service Employees International Union and Willie Bioff of the International Alliance of Theatrical Stage Employees, along with all their fellow graduates of the Capone mob and Murder Inc., preferred to have it." As a result, corruption had thrived as organized crime's presence grew in various union affiliates. "Their thievery and thuggery became so brazen that it eventually threw a heavy blanket of filth over the whole

A.F.L." In addition, he felt the AFL's complacency threatened organized labor's future. The corruption that existed in some unions left a taint on all unions in the public's mind. "This was not just a matter of idealism. The good name of all of labor was endangered by the extent to which racketeers held power in the teamsters, the building trades and many of the service unions."[70]

Protecting the good name of labor, Dubinsky argued, meant challenging the traditional autonomy enjoyed by AFL affiliates. President Green had cited that autonomy, guaranteed by the federation's constitution, and depicted it as a bedrock principle that made real anticorruption oversight impossible. But by early 1940, Dubinsky denounced that as an outdated policy that needed to be changed. He told ILGWU delegates at the union's May 1940 convention that changing that principle of autonomy would be one of the ILGWU's demands in return for reaffiliation with the AFL.[71]

Following Dubinsky's lead, the ILGWU convention voted to reaffiliate with the AFL and to propose a resolution to the 1940 AFL convention calling for reforms in the federation's constitution. The most revolutionary part of their reform proposal would give the AFL's executive council the authority to remove any national union officials "convicted of using their official position in their unions for personal gain, or/and convicted of any other acts which cast discredit upon the labor movement."[72] Correspondence between Dubinsky and the ILGWU's attorney indicates that this amendment was made with Bioff's case specifically in mind.[73]

The two other amendments proposed by the ILGWU did far less violence to the AFL's tradition of autonomy for national union affiliates. One would put the AFL officially on record as urging national unions to create rules in their constitutions "for adequate disciplinary action against such of their officers as may be charged with the above acts." The other called for the AFL's executive council to exert its moral authority in cases where an affiliated union failed to act. "Whenever the Executive Council has valid cause to believe that a union official is guilty of any such offense and the union in question fails to institute proceedings in accordance with its constitution, the Executive Council shall be empowered to use its full moral influence to achieve the institution of such proceedings."[74]

These reform proposals received little support from the AFL's leadership as it gathered at the organization's annual convention in November 1940. When the *New York Times* reporter A. H. Raskin talked to AFL convention delegates, he reported, "They agreed that labor should do its own housecleaning lest it forfeit public confidence or open the door for government intervention, but few evinced any enthusiasm for proposals to center disciplinary power over the officers of international unions in the hands of the A.F. of L. executive council." Nor did President Green and other executive council members express support for changes that would decrease the autonomy of national union affiliates. As a result, the ILGWU's reform proposal met tough resistance at the convention in the crucial Resolutions Committee.[75]

Then, on the third day of the AFL gathering, Dubinsky was attacked in the convention's hotel bar by Joseph Fay, a vice president in the Operating Engineers. Fay was a power broker in the New York area construction industry and allegedly had connections to organized crime. He also had a reputation for violence that included accusations of involvement in the murder of a rival labor leader. In 1945 he was convicted on charges that he had taken payments amounting to $350,000 from construction contractors.[76] He was, in fact, an AFL leader very much like Scalise, Bioff, and Browne, and earlier that evening he had been drinking with Browne. According to the *New York Times* reporter who witnessed the encounter, Fay approached Dubinsky's table and urged him not to push forward his anticorruption resolution. Asked to leave, Fay came charging back a few minutes later with another official from his union, and before it was broken up by bystanders, the resulting melee had spilled out into the hotel lobby.[77]

The incident was widely covered in the press, where it served to highlight the AFL's resistance to reform. A page 1 story in the *New York Times* opened, "The bitterness created in some American Federation of Labor circles by the introduction by the International Ladies Garment Workers Union of a resolution condemning racketeering by labor officials came to a head early this morning in a free-for-all battle in the lobby of the Hotel Roosevelt." A story in the *Washington Post* described how Fay "registered his opposition to the Dubinsky resolution with his fists." Ironically, Fay had done Dubinsky something of a favor: his attack and the publicity it generated put pressure on the AFL convention to make concessions to the Garment Workers' reform proposal.[78]

As a result, the convention did ratify an anticorruption measure, but only after it had been watered down substantially by the Resolutions Committee. The committee eliminated the first part of the ILGWU's proposal, the one that would have given the AFL executive council the authority to remove a national union officer convicted of using their union position for personal gain or a crime involving moral turpitude. This had been the only provision with real teeth. The committee left untouched the two other parts of the resolution. These called for the executive council to urge national unions to include anticorruption provisions in their own constitutions and asked the council "to apply all of its influence" on any recalcitrant national union which failed to act against a corrupt official in its ranks.[79] These two provisions essentially continued the existing practice of the AFL, which had limited its role in fighting corruption to the use of moral suasion.

This limited gesture was further undercut by the fact that the AFL chose to reelect the IATSE's president, George Browne, to serve on the executive council. Aware of the bad publicity it would create, President Green had not wanted Browne to stand for reelection. When Browne chose to run anyway, however, Green backed down and took no steps to stop him. The ILGWU delegates refused to vote for him, but like all the other members of the AFL executive council, Browne ran unopposed, and so he was elected unanimously despite his involvement in the Bioff scandal. The *New York Times* report emphasized the irony of the AFL's actions. "Mr. Browne, whose organization has been criticized because of the presence among its officers of Willie Bioff, convicted panderer, and other men with criminal records, will serve as a member of the AFL executive council charged with responsibility for the enforcement of the anti-racketeering resolution adopted by the convention last Tuesday."[80]

An editorial in the same newspaper expressed disappointment with the AFL's apparently limited commitment to reform. Referring to the resolution that had been passed, the editorial stated, "It is at least a formal recognition that evil exists and should be stamped out. But further than that it does not venture. Without the provision of machinery to make a housecleaning effective the [AFL's] report as it stands remains hardly more than a pious reaffirmation of sentiment previously expressed by most of labor's responsible national leaders." The *New York Times* also noted the problematic logic behind the AFL's proposal. "Individual unions are encouraged to protect themselves and expel criminals within their own ranks, though just how they are going to do this, once they have been captured, is not made clear."[81]

This sense of disappointment was widespread. The *Federation News*, a Chicago labor publication, observed in December 1940, "Unfortunately, the position assumed by the New Orleans convention of the A.F. of L., as expressed in the above recited disposal of the subject of labor racketeering, does not seem to impress the public in general and the daily press in particular, especially the pro-administration newspapers."[82]

Dubinsky had hoped for more, and in the months that followed he became further disillusioned regarding the AFL's commitment to reform. He later recalled, "We had to be satisfied with that [what the convention had passed], and it quickly became plain that the Federation had no intention of making anything at all of this new grant of power."[83] He did not even bother to attend the 1941 AFL convention, and the ILGWU submitted no further reform proposals. According to a newspaper report, "Associates said he was 'saddened' by the lack of any apparent disposition on the part of leaders of the A.F. of L. to come to grips with the racket problem."[84]

Dubinsky never believed that his proposed reforms would eliminate union corruption. His own experiences in New York's Garment District had taught him how embedded corruption was in certain sectors of the economy. But the passage of strong anticorruption measures and the vigorous enforcement of such measures would have sent the membership and the general public a message. Referring to a more vigorous effort in the 1950s, he said, "It restored faith that idealism was not dead in the labor movement. People knew that we were not asleep or indifferent to corruption."[85] The lack of such action in the 1940s sent the opposite message.

## The CIO's Response

In contrast to the AFL, CIO reactions to Pegler shifted dramatically during the early 1940s, from initial support of the columnist's crusade to active opposition. When Pegler's first revelations appeared, CIO publications covered them extensively and favorably, treating them as yet more evidence of the rival AFL's corruption. Thus the *UE News* (the official publication of the United Electrical, Radio, and Mechanical Workers of America) on February 3, 1940, reported Pegler's exposé on Scalise in a section of the journal entitled "Crime News from the AFL" and gave the story the headline "William Green Pleads for White Slaver."[86] Other CIO publications followed a similar line. In response to Scalise's conviction, the *CIO News* printed a story that repeated many of Pegler's ongoing themes. "Though Scalise's shady past was well known—he served 4 1/2 years in Atlanta federal penitentiary for Mann Act violations—President Green of the AFL consistently refused to take action against the racketeering union official and even furnished a testimonial on his character to the Attorney General Jackson."[87] Such stories bolstered the CIO case against the AFL and the federation's devotion to craft unionism. As an editorial in the *CIO News* explained in March 1940, "They [AFL leaders] like craft unionism, because the many small craft groups offer a maximum opportunity for racketeering and graft. They are opposed heartily to unity with the CIO, because that too would put an end to their rackets."[88]

CIO leaders made similar claims in public statements that emphasized the significance of Pegler's exposé. In late January 1940, Harry Bridges, head of the International Longshoremen and Warehousemen's Union (ILWU) and the West Coast director of the CIO, used the scandal to denounce President Green of the AFL. "The Bioffs, the Scalises and the Joseph P. Ryans [head of the AFL's notoriously corrupt longshoremen's union] speak only too well of Mr. Green's ideals in the labor movement." Bridges urged Green to "spend his time cleaning out the AFL and doing a real service to labor."[89]

But by 1941, CIO publications changed their tack dramatically. The *UE News* dropped its "Crime News from the AFL" series, stopped reporting on the scandals Pegler continued to uncover, and ignored Bioff's conviction that fall. Instead, an article in November 1941 denounced Pegler as a "scandal monger" who constantly rehashed the same stories and gave "the impression that the halls of labor are overflowing with crooks and racketeers." Now the *UE News* sought to minimize the significance of corruption; this same article asserted, "The fact is that the number of crooked men in labor is as nothing compared to finance, business and even politics."[90]

The change in attitude reflected concerns about the passage of antilabor legislation, a possibility that the *UE News* informed its readers stemmed from the hostile press coverage organized labor was receiving. An article in December 1941 explained, "The newspapers are chiefly responsible for this clamor for antiunion legislation. For more than a year they have been bombarding organized labor with the vilest and most incendiary misrepresentations."[91] The shift against Pegler may have been helped along by the columnist's increasing attacks on the CIO leadership for its alleged complacency regarding communism.[92]

Concern within the CIO about the effects of this negative press coverage grew over time, as did the conviction that it reflected a coordinated campaign in support of antiunion forces. At a conference of representatives of CIO organizations held on March 23, 1942, CIO president Phil Murray told delegates, "As you doubtless know, the organized labor movement in America has been subjected to a most vicious attack by the interests inimical to the welfare of the labor movement. Manifestations of national hysteria designed to destroy the standards of labor, and designed also to destroy the labor movement itself, have been evident within recent weeks. The columns of almost every newspaper throughout the country have been teeming with vitriolic attacks on labor leaders."[93]

In their efforts to counter this campaign, CIO officials denounced several media figures, from the radio commentator Kaltenborn to the conservative columnist David Lawrence.[94] But, in an implicit acknowledgement of his significance, Pegler received particular attention. In 1943, James Carey, the secretary-treasurer of the CIO, took Pegler on in a printed debate in the *Ladies Home Journal* entitled "Is Pegler Fair to Labor?" It was the only encounter of its kind during the war years. Pegler and Carey were allotted a preset amount of space to respond to the title's question. Carey opened by referring to several recent cases of corporate corruption involving shoddy materials sold to the military. He continued, "If I were Westbrook Pegler I would cite these cases to prove that American Big Business is willfully endangering the lives of American troops for profit." Mocking Pegler's method while at the same time emphasizing its effects, Carey explained that he would then cite those cases again and again. "After a few months—if I had access to the columns of a national syndicate—I would probably have convinced a large section of the people that the great majority of American businessmen are sinister characters, undermining the war effort, risking American lives."[95] In the same way, Carey charged, Pegler had convinced a large number of people that such a description fit the country's labor leaders. The CIO secretary-treasurer viewed Pegler's columns as important weapons in an antiunion campaign. Privately, Carey fumed, "Pegler's crime is not his campaign against racketeers and traitors, but in his use of the Communists and racketeers as a convenient handle to beat all of organized labor."[96]

While Carey engaged in a printed debate, other CIO leaders took a more direct approach. Joseph Curran of the National Maritime Union, for instance, described Pegler as a "hireling" of labor's enemies and an example of the fact "that the press lies, distorts, and suppresses the news to give unions a black eye."[97] Beginning in May 1943, Pegler had written a series of columns that depicted Curran as a disloyal Communist, whose current vociferous support for the war reflected his devotion to the Soviet Union and belied his willingness to use his union position to dodge the draft. NMU members, Pegler charged, mocked the Navy personnel with whom they served while their leaders plotted with "Harry Bridges and his Communist Fifth Column" of disloyal union officials.[98] In response, the NMU launched a nationwide picketing campaign denouncing Pegler and demanding that newspapers in port cities drop his column. A directive sent out by the national headquarters ordered the union's port agents to "Please make arrangements for mass picketing of any newspaper that carries his column in your port."[99]

On the West Coast, Harry Bridges, head of the CIO's longshoremen's union, went where the AFL executive council had feared to tread and filed a libel suit against Pegler and the Hearst Syndicate, which now distributed his columns. Bridges's suit cited two particular columns that had appeared in September

THE CHALLENGE OF RESPONDING TO PEGLER · 229

1944 and that had accused him of imposing his radical political agenda on his rank and file membership.[100] He asked for general damages of $400,000 and another $200,000 in punitive damages.[101]

In other words, the CIO adopted a more confrontational approach to Pegler than had the AFL, but this strategy also had its drawbacks. The CIO's secretary-treasurer, Carey, expressed satisfaction with the results of his printed debated with Pegler, but the impact of one piece in a woman's magazine, compared to Pegler's steady stream of newspaper columns, was necessarily limited.[102] Nor did Bridges' libel suit constitute much of a victory; the case never made it to trial.[103] At his publisher's behest, Pegler offered a limited retraction. He submitted a proposed column to Bridges' attorneys that modified his charges, retreating from the problematic claims while repeating the most biting insinuations about the labor leader's communist connections.[104] Finding such a retraction unappealing but faced with a difficult case in court, Bridges' attorneys agreed to withdraw the suit in return for court costs.[105]

Bridges encountered the same obstacle that the National Maritime Union's attorney had observed when he advised Curran not to sue Pegler for similar attacks. As the attorney explained, "The technique employed by Pegler is truly an ancient one, except that he has become a master of it. He seasons a large batter with truthful statements with a pinch of falsehood. If you resent the seasoning, you must have the entire batter examined." The result was a weak legal hand for the labor leader and a trial that might generate only more bad publicity.[106]

The NMU's picketing campaign backfired as well. It simply generated more negative coverage in the media, which depicted the union as a dictatorial force trying to stifle the freedom of the press. The *New York Times* story, for example, described an NMU official threatening the *World-Telegram's* editor. The article presented a scene in the editor's office right out of a bad movie script: "'You people better watch out,' Mr. Rogan [the NMU official] said. 'If you don't remove this guy [Pegler], you'll have more than picket lines around this office. We're giving you warning now.'" The story went on to quote Pegler explaining, "Everything that I said was true. This is a communistic front organization which also picketed the White House until Hitler attacked Russia. During all that time this organization was Hitler's ally." The *Times* article vouched for Pegler's assertions, explaining "the National Maritime Union and its leaders followed the Communist Party line on the question of the war, national defense and the characterization of President Roosevelt as a 'war monger.'" The article ended with a description of how, at the conclusion of the picketing, "each marcher had his union book stamped to show that he had taken part in the demonstration."[107] The final detail left the implication that the men had been coerced into participating.

An editorial in *Collier's* magazine described the incident as an example of the intolerance of left-wing union leaders. "It is the totalitarians who feel that we'd be much better off if the press were permitted to print only what some American counterpart of Dr. Paul Josef Goebbels said it might print." The magazine claimed that the NMU and other unions sought to avoid responding to Pegler's valid criticisms. "Instead of answering Pegler's charges with facts, the NMU leaders habitually content themselves with spreading personal abuse of Pegler—the old, familiar name-calling tactics for which the Communists in this country have long been famous."[108]

Frustrated, the NMU's director of public relations, Leo Huberman, wrote to the editor at *Collier's* to complain about one-sided quality of news coverage, which made it impossible for a union to get its side of the story to the public. "You publish an editorial upholding Pegler and denouncing the National Maritime Union," Huberman wrote. "You have had countless opportunities to read Pegler's side of the case. Have you, in all honesty, ever read the union's? If so, where? What section of the 'free press' ever gave the NMU an opportunity to present its side?" Huberman noted that *Collier's* had never asked the NMU if they had a response to Pegler's charges. "Had you done so, you would have learned that we do have an answer. We tried to get that answer printed in the *New York World-Telegram*, but we did not succeed." Huberman's letter included copies of correspondence from the NMU to the *World-Telegram* offering a point-by-point rebuttal to Pegler's claims and a request to have their response printed in the paper. The newspaper had turned them down. Huberman concluded, "What the NMU leaders, whom you criticized, are after is not *less* free speech, but *more* of it. What we want is a press that would be truly 'free' in the sense that it would be open to us when we're under attack. What we want is a press such as you described, one which gives everybody 'the right to speak his mind.'"[109] *Collier's* never printed Huberman's letter, thus further demonstrating his point. His complaint summed up the obstacles that organized labor, both AFL and CIO, confronted in making its case to the public.

## Conclusion

The reaction of labor leaders in both the AFL and the CIO reflected a grim realization that negative media coverage was contributing to a dangerous shift in public opinion, and that shift in turn offered aid and encouragement to labor's political opponents.[110] As one letter to the AFL president put it, "Unless we put forth some effort to give the soldiers in the field and the public the right picture; it will be appalling what will happen after the close of the war."[111]

But in spite of the fact that they could perceive the harm being done, the AFL leadership did not take a different public position. In the wake of Browne and Bioff's convictions in November 1941, the Federation's publicity director, Philip Pearl, even wrote an article describing how the convictions vindicated the AFL's policy of standing pat. "The Browne-Bioff case proves what the American Federation of Labor has all along contended—that the laws on our statute books today are all that is needed to wipe out racketeering."[112]

Not just the public, but organized labor's liberal allies were reaching a very different conclusion, however. The same month that Pearl's article appeared, the *New Republic* referred to the Bioff case and concluded, "There is much in labor's house that needs mending." The editorial continued, "The racketeering in some of the AFL unions has been notorious, and the evidence of it disclosed in the current trial of Willie Bioff has only served to fortify the ordinary middle-class American in his fantastic conviction that all labor leaders are racketeers." Now, almost two years after issuing its warning when the scandal first broke, the *New Republic* expressed support for legislation to regulate unions. It referred specifically to a set of proposals appearing that month in the *Atlantic Monthly*.[113]

Other calls for regulation appeared, among them an article by Oswald Garrison Villard, recently retired as editor of the *Nation* and a longtime liberal supporter of unions.[114] Writing in 1944, Villard complained that unions had done little to correct the abuses that were feeding public bitterness against labor. "It is a cause for profound discouragement that the heads of the AFL, for example, not only consort with crooks within their leadership but have never yet taken any striking action to drive unworthy men out of their ranks." As a result, he concluded, government regulation was required. "The workers themselves therefore need regulation of unions, and millions of them will welcome it; the only question is how to do it in such a way as not to constitute government control."[115]

The challenge that had confronted labor in January 1940, when the scandal unfolded, had been twofold. First, as the *New Republic* had warned, labor needed a public relations campaign that would make its side of the story heard. Secondly, the American Federation of Labor needed to convince the public that it could and would clean its own house and tackle the problem of union corruption. The fact that even liberal sympathizers like Villard criticized labor's response demonstrated just how short of the mark the response had been.

Figure 10.1: Rube Goldberg's cartoon, bearing the caption "A.F. of L. Nursery Rime," appeared on April 24, 1940, at the time of George Scalise's arrest and indictment. Goldberg modified the words of the traditional nursery rhyme to indict William Green and by implication the rest of the American Federation of Labor for indifference to the corruption revealed by the Scalise scandal. Courtesy Rube Goldberg, Inc.

# Conclusion
## *Opportunities Lost and Opportunities Taken*

Pegler aspired to use his union corruption exposés to achieve real reform, but instead the scandal and columnist's campaign did little to help the cause of workers caught in corrupt unions. The result was the necessary drawback to the kind of crusade he had mounted. His distinctive style of writing generated a potent reaction among the nation's newspaper readers, spurring outrage and making labor racketeering an issue of national concern. But over time, this same style worked against him. His exposés devolved into repetitive screeds, alienating readers who might have shared his concern for the average working man but who did not embrace his larger conservative agenda.

Despite such limits, Pegler did continue to have a political impact. The campaign against union corruption became the keystone of conservative opposition to the New Deal, a goal that had become very important to Pegler. Conservatives seized the issue and followed Pegler's lead in wielding the label of racketeer against the entire organized labor movement. They scored important political victories, but what they called labor reform did nothing to help rank and file union members.

Meanwhile, in the netherworld of the labor movement, where Bioff and Scalise's counterparts continued to operate, little changed. After winning convictions in the cases that Pegler had helped uncover, federal law enforcement efforts flagged. No wider campaign to curb mob infiltration of the union movement emerged, and union members were left once more to the dubious protection of local law enforcement agencies. Nor did Pegler's campaign lead to practical reform from within the labor movement. Even union leaders who agreed with him that union abuses existed and corruption needed to be dealt with, viewed the columnist with such a level of distrust that there was no possibility of meaningful dialogue.

David Dubinsky was a case in point. A union official who might have been a potent ally for reform, he came to see Pegler as inimical to the labor movement. Initially, in 1940, the two men had appeared to engage in a kind of implicit collaboration. Dubinsky, as president of the International Ladies Garment Workers' Union (ILGWU), drew on Pegler's exposés to push hard for reforms in the AFL, chiding federation leaders for their apparent complacency. In turn, Pegler wrote glowing praise of the ILGWU president. In July 1942, the columnist referred to Dubinsky as "one of the few men in the AFL leadership with the honor and the courage to fight racketeers."[1]

By the end of that year, however, Pegler began lumping Dubinsky in with all of the other union leaders whom he denounced in his columns. Unable to cite any evidence of corruption and faced with the fact that Dubinsky was a committed anticommunist, Pegler still found grounds to criticize. He attacked the Garment Workers Union for collecting contributions from its membership to support relief and underground resistance efforts in Nazi-occupied Europe. Using language that gave these payments the sound of extortion, Pegler wrote, "Like it or not, American workers have to shower down." In fact, the contributions were voluntary. But for Pegler neither the fact that the contributions were voluntary nor that Dubinsky gave his members a detailed accounting of union funds mattered. "Accountancy doesn't guarantee legitimacy in the use of union funds accounted for," Pegler asserted.[2]

Dubinsky tried reaching out to Pegler through a personal letter, explaining to the columnist why his criticisms were ill-founded. But when Pegler's attacks continued, the Garment Workers' president wrote to Pegler's publisher, Roy Howard, in July 1944 complaining about the tactics that Pegler resorted to in his reporting on organized labor. In this letter, Dubinsky repeated the explanations he had offered Pegler and asked Howard to treat his correspondence as "not intended for publication." He concluded by invoking the title of Pegler's column, "Fair Enough." Dubinsky wrote, "Any fair-person, I judged, would have accepted that explanation as 'fair enough.' Not so Mr. Pegler, a man with a mission to smear and break down trade unions right or wrong."[3]

Howard responded by acknowledging his columnist's faults but defending Pegler's goals. The publisher argued that Pegler was a crusading journalist dedicated to the cause of union reform. "I know him to be sincerely convinced of the existence of corrupt and subversive forces within the labor movement. I am sure that he is convinced that these menacing forces are not going to be dealt with until an aroused public demands action after the fashion in which it forced cleanups in insurance, banking, railroad practices and the Stock Exchange."[4]

Dubinsky was unconvinced. Writing back to Howard, he offered an epitaph for Pegler's crusade: "Westbrook Pegler has rendered valuable service to the community in exposing racketeering in several labor unions as well as labor leaders who use the labor movement for self-aggrandizement, but Pegler has cancelled the value of his contribution by attacking unions indiscriminately." Judged by his writing, Pegler's intent was destructive, not constructive, Dubinsky asserted. "When one reads Pegler's attacks upon unions, one cannot help feeling that he is interested not only in correcting abuses, but in breaking down unionism, that he is hitting below the belt, and that he would throw the baby out together with the bath."[5]

## Pegler's Decline

Howard refrained from mentioning it in his exchange with Dubinsky, but the publisher had been warning Pegler of just such an outcome for the previous two years. He had urged Pegler to vary his subject matter and change his writing style to protect the effectiveness of his crusade. As early as July 1942, Howard wrote Pegler about complaints from newspaper editors around the country "against the heavy overloading of your product with stories confined to the single subject of the activities, Communistic and racketeering, within the ranks of organized labor." Invoking these editors to justify his advice to a columnist he knew to be proud and stubborn, Howard wrote, "Their hope is that you will vary your topics sufficiently to hold all the audience which you have already attracted."[6]

A year later, he added to this warning a remonstration about Pegler's writing style. Using a boxing metaphor, Howard wrote, "You are losing a lot of points because of low swinging, heeling your glove and employing a few of the tactics of a journalistic Elbows McFadden." Howard described a "more or less brutal bar-room fighter quality" that was overtaking Pegler's columns. "I think it is bad because it gives people the impression that you're in a grouch with yourself and the world and that, consequently, anything you say can be discounted on the grounds that your effort does not spring from a sincere desire to redress a wrong, but rather from a grouch's desire to kick a cat."[7] In the spring of 1944, the publisher wrote, "Your job on the racketeers in Labor is not done. But your effectiveness in getting it done will be measured by your success in holding your audience."[8]

Pegler bristled at this advice. He took it as an attempt to shake him from his crusade against union abuses, and he saw that effort as too vital, his role too unique, for him to accept guidance from others on how to conduct it. "I am sure I was the first to perceive and attack the faults of the Wagner Act and the Labor Relations Board and unionism," he wrote, "and this at the time when the slightest breath of complaint against the practices and some of the personalities of unionism was heresy and one could be stoned for breathing such." Now was no time to relent, Pegler argued. "The evils are not cured yet and they will not be until the laws are revised and because I started this thing and have a better grasp of the elements of the controversy than any of you and a knowledge of the personalities and records as good as any in the country, I will not drop it."[9] His passionate concern and his sizeable ego led him to shrug off suggestions that he modify his reporting and rethink his crusade.

Similarly, Pegler rejected suggestions that he balance coverage of union corruption with stories on abuses that existed within the business community. He was aware that this was a common critique of his columns. In a letter to Howard, Pegler referred to an editorial that "said, as so many others have, that I ought to devote some attention to the misdoing of employers." But Pegler's next sentence conveyed both his impatience and his unwillingness to consider such advice. "If he [the editorial writer] knows about such misdoing, why the hell doesn't he write it? Why is he covering up, anyway? I just don't know of such misdoing. I hear a lot of talk about it but none of these people ever give me chapter and verse."[10] Such a response belied the pride that Pegler took in his skills as an intrepid reporter, one who had uncovered misconduct repeatedly in the past. It is hard to believe that Pegler himself found this response convincing.

Although Pegler refused to accept it, Howard's advice had been sound. Constant repetition, failure to present a balanced perspective, and the steady stream of insult and innuendo all changed the way that readers saw Pegler's reporting. It was not that his readership abandoned him en masse. As one of the editors on the Scripps-Howard newspaper chain explained in May 1944, "He still has a good following. Among industrialists and certain other elements of business he is our number one feature, with anti-administrationists [that is, opponents of the New Deal] he is also tops." But Pegler's claim to write on behalf of the average working man, the rank and file union member, now rang hollow. The editor's report continued, "Labor—rank and filers as well as leaders—dislike and distrust him. They feel he is prejudiced and unfair." The repetition of his columns had also taken its toll. "Certainly he has done a grand job against labor's abuses and racketeers but I believe too frequent treatment of the subject makes his stuff deadening and less effective."[11]

A survey of columnists written in 1944 by Charles Fisher offered the same negative assessment. Fisher referred to "a deterioration of style" in Pegler's columns, which had "come to depend more frequently upon vituperation." Pegler's exposés of Bioff and Scalise had been an important achievement, Fisher acknowledged, but in subsequent years his writing on racketeering had degenerated into simple antiunionism. Fisher observed that Pegler "had used the case [of Bioff and Scalise] to damn all labor and to suggest that the 12,000,000 American trade union members were probably in the hands of racketeers." The result was that Pegler's columns now served mainly to feed the antiunion sentiments of readers who were already hostile to organized labor. "Any newspaper reader with a dislike of unionism is delighted to be informed daily that shocking doings a thousand miles away are connected directly to his own shop steward's request for fresh towels in the washroom," Fisher observed. Pegler's columns confirmed the suspicions of such an anti-unionist, who was "encouraged to regard each strike of which he hears as a cunning device of racketeers."[12] The devotion of these kinds of readers, however, would do little to win internal reforms within the union movement.

The lack of such reforms was telling, even for Pegler. Though he rejected criticism about the methods he employed in his crusade, the columnist rue-fully acknowledged how little he had achieved. In an interview in 1943, he downgraded the significance of the convictions of Scalise, Browne, and Bioff. "'There's not much accomplished in knocking down punks like those birds,' he remarked, 'so long as men like Green and [AFL general counsel] Padway, who really run the AFL, don't accept the responsibility of protecting honest union men from exploitation by vermin.'" Criminal convictions alone achieved little. "You can send a hundred crooks to prison, but another hundred will take their place unless the conditions are cured under which crooks can get control and keep control of labor unions."[13]

What Pegler wanted was a set of guarantees for the basic democratic citizenship rights of union members within their labor organizations. As he envisioned it, the federal government could establish a broad oversight role to ensure that union governments protected their members' rights. He called for federal regulation of union finances, to guarantee that dues, fees, and assessments set by labor organizations were fairly levied and the funds thus raised were administered honestly. He also demanded guarantees against racial discrimination and political retribution within unions. "The membership must be wide open to any citizen engaged in the trade of that union without restriction. This means that if I am a Negro the union cannot bar me on account of my color." Union members, Pegler argued, should have the right to free speech and dissent within their organizations. The federal government should not "permit the union to throw me out for criticizing its officers, methods or constitution. As a citizen I am allowed to criticize the officers, methods and constitution of my state and nation, and the same rights must be guaranteed as to this minor citizenship in the union." What he was describing, although he did not use the term, was a kind of bill of rights for union members.[14]

He paired these proposals up with others that had less to do with the democratic rights of union members but reflected instead his own wary view of organized labor. Thus he argued that unions should be restricted from playing an active role in politics. Here he cited the fact that many union members had joined only because the collective bargaining contract at their workplace required them to. A labor organization with such involuntary members, Pegler argued, "has no right to indorse any political ticket, platform or candidate . . . or contribute one cent of the money I am compelled to pay as dues, assessments and fees for any purpose to which I am opposed." He argued that unions should not be able to deduct member dues straight from their paychecks, because such practices granted unions an illegitimate taxing power. "Only my government has the right to tax me." Pegler also called for tighter restrictions on union picketing in order to protect nonmembers and employers from acts of violence and intimidation.[15] These proposals reflected his desire to limit union power.

His reform proposals for union governance did not constitute a perfect solution to the problem of union corruption. Among other problems, they were vague. The details of how such regulations would be implemented would determine whether they were effective. Such details would also determine whether these regulations did more to weaken unions or to strengthen union democracy. Indeed, critics of such efforts, then and now, view the intent of union democracy proposals with skepticism. The protection of individual rights, on the one hand, and the disciplined unity that labor organizations need to engage in collective action, on the other hand, can come into conflict. That conflict, in turn, explains why conservatives often adopt this issue. Proclaiming the need to protect workers' individual rights offers a politically appealing avenue for attempts to sap the strength of unions. Thus antiunionists seeking to ban union security clauses assert that they are protecting the worker's "right to work."[16]

But the goal of union democracy amounts to more than the narrow promotion of individual rights. Thus not just conservatives but many liberals also have supported efforts to promote union democracy, arguing that by empowering the rank and file of unions, one energizes the labor movement. In the 1940s, Pegler's calls for new regulations to protect union democracy were echoed by the American Civil Liberties Union.[17] Meanwhile employers voiced their wariness over such proposals. As the *New Republic* noted in an article in 1947, "George Romney, director of the Automobile Manufacturers' Association, plaintively remarked last year that 'responsible' rather than 'democratic' unions were the need of the motor car industry."[18] Such examples show that it is wrong to reject all calls for union democracy as ploys to weaken organized labor. In Pegler's case, the changes that he sought to make union governance more democratic were separate from the ones he believed would constrain the power of organized labor.

Whether or not the proposed reforms would have solved the problem of union corruption is, however, another question, and one worth asking. Would they have stopped the kinds of activities in which Bioff, Browne, and Scalise were involved? As with any counterfactual, a definitive answer is impossible. Still, we can say at the very least that empowering a democratic opposition within the Building Service Employees' International Union (BSEIU) and within the International Alliance of Theatrical Stage Employes (IATSE) would have been helpful. In both unions, there were members and officials who dared to criticize what was going on in their organizations. Such opposition might have had more impact had these reformers enjoyed legal protections against the retribution that they suffered. Without fear of reprisal, more members might have dared to join these reform efforts and more officials might have stood up to question how their national leaders were managing the union's funds. To the extent that complaisance stemmed from fear, Pegler's reform proposals offered an important palliative. An active and protected democracy within unions would limit the damage that could result from the Outfit's ability to subvert a handful of national leaders.

Still, Pegler's reforms would not have been a cure all against corruption. We know this for certain because two decades later Congress passed a "Bill of Rights for Union Members," as part of the Landrum-Griffin Act (1959), and this included many of the protections Pegler had described. Proponents at the time argued that it would allow members to police their own unions by voting out corrupt leaders. The results, however, were disappointing. Insurgent movements did arise to challenge entrenched regimes, most notably in the United Mine Workers Union and the Teamsters Union in the 1970s. But organized crime remained able to dominate the national leadership of several unions, including the Teamsters. Many local unions, as well, remained firmly under the control of corrupt forces. Landrum-Griffin's limited impact stemmed from a number of factors, including weak enforcement efforts by federal agencies and the narrow changes it called for in union electoral procedures. Real change required a more forceful intervention. Not until the 1980s and 1990s, when federal law enforcement mounted a sustained campaign against organized crime, harnessing powerful new legal tools such as the RICO statutes, were many of these unions freed from mob control. And even with the broad criminal conspiracy provisions and civil remedies provided by RICO, government efforts have often fallen short of complete success.[19]

If Pegler's reform proposals did not amount to a magic silver bullet that would have ended union corruption, they still represented part of a larger set of missed opportunities. As constructive reform measures, they would have been helpful in empowering union members. The columnist also might have combined his reform proposals with a more accurate account of the scandals, writing reports that gave newspaper readers a clear sense of the role of organized crime, corrupt machine politics, and employers. He might have credited the efforts of union members and local officials, such as Jeff Kibre and George Hardy, who demonstrated the potential for internal reform. This balanced reporting might have done more to encourage prominent labor leaders such as Dubinsky, or even Green, to trust Pegler; union leaders might then have seen some value in reaching out in the interest of reform. Such a response would have undercut the efforts to cast the entire the labor movement under the shadow of the term *racketeer*. It would have mitigated the concerns the American public felt about the power that unions wielded, and that would have hampered the efforts of organized labor's opponents to play on those fears.

But none of that happened. Instead Pegler continued to ply a steady offering of denunciation in his columns through the war and into the postwar era. In 1946 and 1947, he was still hearkening back to his original exposés of Bioff and Scalise and applying the same formula to new exposés.[20] The effect was deadening, and even Pegler came to tire of his columns on this subject. In a private letter, written in 1948, he admitted, "I feel that the stories that I have written recently about unionism in breadth and in particular are weary work."[21] It was a rare moment of honest self-appraisal for someone who had never been prone to modesty.

He continued to write for many more years, switching to the Hearst syndicate in 1944 and producing a daily column for them until 1962. He was less widely respected than in 1940–41, but Pegler remained a popular columnist throughout the 1940s and into the early 1950s. As late as 1954, his column appeared regularly in nearly 200 newspapers that reached a readership estimated at 35 million and that earned him close to $100,000 a year.[22]

More than that, Pegler spawned a series of imitators, journalists who also focused on the subject of union abuses. The best known of these was Victor Riesel; his widely syndicated column "Inside Unions" decried the role of communists and exposed cases of corruption from 1942 until Riesel's retirement in 1990. He essentially became Pegler's successor.[23]

## The Shadow of the Racketeer

Pegler's less tangible but more potent legacy was a language of suspicion for organized labor, a language that he had helped popularize in his reporting on the Bioff and Scalise scandals. This was the shadow of the racketeer, a menacing depiction of organized labor's power that antiunion forces invoked throughout the postwar era. Its rhetorical center was the word *racketeer* itself. The term proliferated in post–World War II references to unions, providing conservatives with a convenient way to play on public fears about the power wielded by the leaders of organized labor. The racketeer was a mainstay in accounts that pictured a nation menaced by unscrupulous union bosses, either criminals or communists, who used their unwitting union membership to achieve their own selfish ends. In one dramatic example, in 1947, Senator Alexander Wiley of Wisconsin claimed, "We are confronted with a situation in which the American Garden of Eden has been invaded by the serpent of racketeering, which threatens to make this earthly paradise a European-like scene of chaos and conflict."[24]

The concern about union power and union leaders was in itself not new, but previous expressions of this concern lacked a term with the criminal overtones that racketeer had. For instance, congressional debates in the spring of 1937 held in the wake of the sit-down strikes featured strident denunciations of unions by conservative critics. The speeches made in that earlier era rang with warnings of mob rule, anarchy, and radical schemes, but not the danger of the racketeer. In this earlier era, for instance, Congressman Clare Hoffman's frequent denunciations of unions made not a single reference to racketeering. Instead, in a typical speech on the sit-down strikes, Hoffman warned in January 1937, "Today in Michigan there exists a situation where there is already at hand all of the elements which go into a revolution, all of the elements which make for civil war."[25] These earlier antiunion denunciations centered entirely on the CIO, which was depicted as a radical organization. The implication, and sometimes the actual claim, was that the conservative union leaders of the AFL presented no threat to the nation and even perhaps provided a useful service.[26]

Some ten years later, in the wake of Pegler's exposés, when critics invoked the shadow of the racketeer, they warned about the danger of all types of unions because of the power labor organizations granted to their leadership. In May 1947, the *Saturday Evening Post* published an editorial entitled "Unbridled Union Power Threat to Security." The editorial called for legislation that would ensure "no aggregation of good Americans would long be led in any direction by racketeers, radical doctrinaires, demagogic exhibitionists or potential traitors."[27]

As a method of denunciation, the shadow of the racketeer blurred the distinction between the left and the right wings of the labor movement. Wilbert Lee "Pappy" O'Daniel, a senator from Texas, demonstrated this in 1947 when he spoke against "the communistic labor-leader racketeers, who do not toil, but who live in luxury at the expense of those who are honest and who toil to make an honest living." Labor leaders, he was asserting, were at once radical ideologues and greedy criminals.[28] A flamboyant, politically savvy populist, O'Daniel served as a spokesman for a right-wing group, the Christian Americans, who were dedicated opponents of the New Deal's prolabor policies. In this role, he found it useful to invoke the menace of the racketeer. On the floor of the Senate, he described how he had called for "legislation which would protect the honest workman of this Nation, who sought to follow a lawful vocation, from the assaults of the goon squads and the labor racketeers."[29]

As O'Daniel demonstrated, the shadow of the racketeer allowed conservatives to pose as protectors of working Americans even as they pushed for new restrictions on organized labor. More broadly, the tactic offered political cover for attacks upon the New Deal. Republicans especially indulged in this strategy because the GOP pinned its postwar electoral hopes on winning back at least a portion of the working-class vote.[30]

In speeches that they gave in support of legislation to amend the Wagner Act in 1946 and 1947, Republican congressmen depicted workers as persecuted by union leaders. Senator Joseph Ball of Minnesota, a leading figure among the antiunion members of Congress, asserted, "There is no question about the fact that today individual employees are kicked around in American industry even more by unions and their agents than they are by employers."

Representative Hoffman denied that legislation proposed by Republicans in 1947 was "an anti-labor bill." He asserted, "Why this bill is a bill to protect the union man himself." He continued, "The only one who is condemned in this bill is the racketeer, the extortionist, the man who is hiding behind the cloak of unionism, masquerading as a union official, who is, after all, nothing but a crook carrying on a crook's business." Another House Republican, Fred Hartley, explained, voting for the proposed amendments to the Wagner Act was "a vote for the rank and file within the labor movement."[31]

Citing the need to "stop labor racketeering," a Republican congressman from Indiana claimed that union leaders oppressed not just their membership, but the general public as well. "Our big job," he asserted, "is to protect the public from union leaders who have misused their power."[32] As historian R. Alton Lee observed, "Republicans campaigned for office in 1946 principally on the issue of curbing union power." They scored major victories that year, gaining control of both houses of Congress.[33]

The newly empowered conservatives offered protection to union members, and the general public, in the form of new regulations on organized labor that would restrict closed shop contracts and secondary boycotts, among other things. These restrictions formed the centerpiece of the Taft-Hartley Act, which the anti-New Deal coalition pushed through Congress in the spring of 1947. According to the *Chicago Tribune*, Minnesota's Senator Ball justified including a ban on the closed shop because, he said, "its abolishment by law would enable union members to oust 'racketeering and communist' leadership." The *Tribune* left the logic of that claim unexamined. Similarly, Senator Robert Taft, a cosponsor of the act, justified a proposal to restrict secondary boycotts by referring to them as a "kind of racketeering activity."[34] In what might be called a happy coincidence for conservatives, these measures to protect the rank and file worker—bans on closed shop contracts and secondary boycotts—were the same measures sought by employers' groups, such as the National Association of Manufacturers (NAM). In fact, NAM attorneys had played a role in drafting key sections of this legislation.[35]

Not every proposal to protect the rights of workers was so vigorously sought by NAM, and not every proposal survived the legislative process. A combined House and Senate conference committee, dominated by Republicans, worked out the Taft-Hartley Act's final language in May 1947. This committee dropped a proposed bill of rights for union members from the final version of the law. As a result, Taft-Hartley did nothing to promote union democracy for organized labor's rank and file. An actual union reformer, faced with another corrupt union leader such as Scalise or Bioff, still had little if any chance of mounting a successful insurgency in the wake of the new law's passage. To his credit, Pegler had seen this coming. In late 1946, he wrote about the legislative proposals then being circulated, "Not one of the reforms thus far offered would compel unions to respect the civic and human rights of the workers and to conform [union governance rules] to the Constitution of the United States." Judged by legislative results, the expressions of concern for the union rank and file that were voiced by Taft-Hartley's proponents were more rhetorical than real.[36]

It was rhetoric, however, that both sides in this legislative contest believed had strategic value. Historical accounts of Taft-Hartley's passage have noted the range of issues and events that helped Republicans push this bill through. These events included a wave of strikes that followed the end of the war, especially the controversial walkouts by coal miners under the leadership of John L. Lewis.[37] But in the congressional debates over the Taft-Hartley Act, labor's supporters noted the frequency with which conservatives invoked the menace of the racketeer. "Stirring speeches have been made about injustices and racketeering," asserted Robert Twyman, a representative from Illinois, "as well as the inroads made by communism into the labor organizations." Or as Donald O'Toole, a Democrat from New York, put it, "You talk on the floor of this House as though labor was composed of villains, thieves and cutthroats."[38] Others pointed out the conservatives' tendency to label a wide range of union practices, such as secondary boycotts, as examples of racketeering. An article in the *New Republic* cited "the persistent efforts of anti-labor Congressmen to expand the anti-racketeering laws, and to justify the expansion by listing a large variety of alleged offenses which are not 'racketeering' in any strict sense of the word."[39]

Citing the political value of this language, one congressman, Vito Marcantonio, even sought to turn the term back on labor's opponents. Marcantonio represented a New York City district made up largely of poor and working-class immigrants, mainly Italian and Puerto Rican. He was possibly the most left-wing member of Congress in the postwar era and a spokesman for a host of causes that enjoyed little popularity in the increasingly conservative atmosphere of Cold War America. He challenged the assumptions upon which the foreign policy of containment was based, and he protested the legal tactics emerging in the postwar red scare. In the debates over labor legislation in early 1947, he questioned the conservatives' definition of the term racketeering.[40]

Referring to the legislation that would become the Taft-Hartley Act, Marcantonio observed, "You say that you are going to do this to get rid of the

Communists in the unions, to get rid of the racketeers." It was a claim, he asserted, that was based upon dubious motives and a politicized use of the word racketeer. It was also a rhetorical game that two could play. "Now about this talk of racketeering, let us see who are the real racketeers." If racketeers victimized working people, Marcantonio argued, then "we find the real racketeers are the gentlemen who asked for free enterprise in order to raise prices." He referred to spiraling inflation, which had been exacerbated after conservatives in Congress forced an end to most government price controls after the war. Citing the punishing effects of that inflation on working Americans, Marcantonio shifted the label of racketeer to profiteering businessmen and their political allies. "They made billions and billions of dollars in wartime. Now these are the men who are destroying the purchasing power of the American people and seek to destroy the rights of American workers. They are the real racketeers."[41]

But here, as usual, Marcantonio was on the losing side. Touted by its supporters as a law that "meant the end of the day of the labor racketeer," the Taft-Hartley Act passed, even overcoming a presidential veto.[42]

As an omnibus act, it amended the Wagner Act in a number of ways, some more important than others. In many ways the new act codified an existing pattern of labor relations that had emerged over time, the product of accumulating court decisions and National Labor Relations Board rulings. Thus, when Taft-Hartley specified "new" rules for NLRB procedures, one scholar has noted, it largely "formalized past practices" already instituted by that agency.[43]

Other changes amounted to nothing more than empty gestures of reform. A new requirement that unions file financial reports with the Department of Labor (DOL), for instance, included no mandate for how those reports would be used. Ostensibly it would foil racketeers such as Scalise, who embezzled union funds. In reality it did nothing of the kind. The provision had no connection to any union democracy mandates and lacked a meaningful enforcement mechanism. Seeing through the legislative pretense, Pegler had denounced the filing requirement as empty posturing. He was right. When the law went into effect, the mandated financial reports simply gathered dust at the DOL. They were not available to the public or to members of the unions that filed them. As one congressional investigator later discovered, both the DOL and the NLRB policy was that "as far as their departments were concerned, the reports did not even have to be true. It was necessary only that they be filed each year, regardless of their accuracy."[44]

But other provisions of Taft-Hartley had greater significance. There were restrictions on the right to strike, which included bans on jurisdictional strikes and secondary boycotts. The attorney general now had authority to obtain an eighty-day injunction to halt any strike that he declared would present a danger to the nation. Closed shop contracts became illegal, and states could now pass legislation to ban union shop contracts as well. A number of states, particularly in the South, took advantage of this latter provision, creating a Southern tier of so-called right-to-work states where unionism remained weak. The ban on union shop contracts presented one more barrier to union organizing efforts in the region. As one textile union organizer complained, with such laws in place "any mill that wanted to could beat the union."[45]

Taft-Hartley also placed limits on which types of workers unions could organize. Specifically the law denied supervisory employees the right to collective bargaining under Wagner Act protections. This effectively separated them from the union movement and made them potent allies in management's efforts to resist union organizing campaigns.[46]

In the name of restoring balance, Taft-Hartley lifted some restrictions on what employers could do or say during the course of an NLRB-supervised election. At the same time, the act imposed new limits on union conduct in such proceedings. The stated goal here was to curtail unions from engaging in coercive tactics against employers, tactics that could force a company's employees into a union against their will; this practice was sometimes called top-down organizing. The result of the new legislation, however, was to offer employers a way to string out NLRB proceedings by filing a series of unfair labor practice charges against a union engaged in an organizing campaign. The NLRB had to investigate and rule on each charge. Those rulings could be appealed, and in this way an employer could blunt a union's organizing campaign while also forcing it to incur prohibitive legal expenses.[47]

In assessing the impact of all these provisions, labor leaders eschewed understatement. Asked by the *New York Times* to comment on the law's passage over a presidential veto, union officials offered responses ranging from "a step toward fascism" to "a triumph for reaction." On the West Coast, the longshoremen union's leader Harry Bridges said that for organized labor, the day of the bill's passage was "Labor's Black Monday, the worst day in its history."[48]

Despite such rhetoric, the law's immediate impact was muted. It did not wreak immediate destruction on organized labor. In fact, unions continued to grow throughout the 1940s and into the 1950s. But the new restrictions circumscribed union efforts to organize in areas outside the manufacturing heartland or in the expanding professional and service sectors of the economy. In the words of one labor historian, "The legal straitjacket imposed by Taft-Hartley ensured that the unions reborn in the New Deal would now be consigned to a roughly static geographic and demographic terrain, an archipelago that skipped from one blue-collar community to another in the Northeast, the Midwest, and on the Pacific Coast." In time, employers would exploit this relative isolation, mechanizing more and more jobs and shifting the factory work that remained out of this union archipelago. The disastrous effects of Taft-Hartley then would become manifest.[49]

Meanwhile, the menacing depiction of organized labor, which Taft-Hartley's supporters had invoked so vigorously, remained an effective political weapon. The shadow of the racketeer grew throughout the postwar years as the left wing of the labor movement faded. Taft-Hartley required all union officials to sign an affidavit that they were not members of the Communist Party. At roughly the same time, an internal purge of communists and alleged communist sympathizers took place within the CIO. That anti-leftist campaign culminated in 1949, when the CIO expelled eleven unions because of their alleged communist affiliations. Labor historian Nelson Lichtenstein describes this succinctly as the "amputation" of the "trade union left." In its aftermath, it became harder and harder for antiunionists to raise concerns about union power by invoking the threat of a radical CIO.[50]

Instead conservatives found that warnings against the role of organized labor were best framed by throwing the spotlight on the racketeer. Congressional investigations offered antiunion politicians a way to publicize that menace, and the pattern for such investigations emerged in 1947. That year—for the first time since 1930—Republicans held a majority in Congress. They promptly used that majority to shift the investigative priorities of Congress and launched that body's first ever hearings on union corruption. Representative Fred Hartley, the cosponsor of the Taft-Hartley Act, chaired this initial probe, which looked into the alleged abusive practices of a Philadelphia local of the Teamsters Union.[51] Pegler had long called for such a congressional investigation, citing the potential political benefits it could bring.[52]

The report issued by Hartley's committee came out in April 1947, just as the Taft-Hartley Act was working its way through Congress. Invoking the image of the racketeer who donned the mask of labor's righteous cause, the report strongly supported the ongoing campaign to amend the Wagner Act. "That such lawlessness masqueraded under the guise of union activity only serves to illustrate the ease with which, in the present state of Federal laws, persons of evil intent may falsely pose as benefactors, protectors and exponents of the cause of labor, while simultaneously using labor's banner as a cloak to shield their own extortionate objectives."[53] This was Pegler's depiction of racketeering union leaders; they were men who assumed a righteous pose only to serve their own criminal ends.

From 1947 to 1960, there were a dozen congressional investigations into union corruption. The leading conservative antiunionists in the postwar era, from the perennial stalwart, Hoffman, to the rising conservative star of the 1950s, Barry Goldwater, served on these investigating committees. In this same period, New York State, under Governor—and two-time Republican presidential candidate—Thomas Dewey, held widely publicized hearings on corruption in the longshoremen's union. The 1954 blockbuster film *On the Waterfront* dramatized those hearings for millions of American moviegoers. That film, and the extensive media coverage of the various hearings, promoted growing public concern, if not fascination, with the menace of the labor racketeer.[54]

This trend reached its apogee at the end of the 1950s. From 1957 to 1959, the McClellan Committee in the Senate held the era's most extensive hearings on union corruption. As had been the case with its predecessors, political considerations shaped the course of its investigation. Conservative senators—Southern Democrats and Republicans—dominated the committee and thus controlled what was the largest staff yet assembled for a congressional investigation. That staff's investigative agenda reflected the committee leadership's hostile views of union power. Thus, in spite of the fact that the committee's official title was the Select Committee to Investigate Improper Activities in the Labor or Management Field, the staff focused their attention on labor, not management; employer misconduct was ignored or glossed over. The resulting hearings were widely publicized in print media and on television, and they transformed James R. Hoffa, the president of the Teamsters Union, into a national celebrity, a symbol of the problem of union corruption.[55]

Hoffa's prominence, in turn, greatly aided the efforts of antiunionists. A 1959 editorial by the *Wall Street Journal*, entitled "The Virtue of Mr. Hoffa," highlighted the way in which the Teamsters' notoriety helped the campaign to impose new restrictions on organized labor. "The difficulty in curbing labor union power thus far," explained the *Journal*, "has been that the people have not clearly seen, or believed, the danger." Hoffa, made into the embodiment of the racketeer, solved that problem. For the same reason, the U.S. Chamber of Commerce savored the effects of these hearings, which aided that group's efforts to win tighter restrictions on union secondary boycotts. As a member of one of the Chamber's legislative lobbying committees put it, "The McClellan hearings gave us the train to ride on; they were the bulldozer clearing the path." In 1959, conservatives drew on public concern about Hoffa to win a new round of amendments to the Wagner Act, further limiting union activity.[56]

## The Absence of a Federal Response to Racketeering

Hoffa's career demonstrated one more reason why the shadow of the racketeer shaped public perceptions about organized labor in these years. Organized crime continued to wield influence in a number of unions, including, by the 1950s, the Teamsters, which was the nation's largest labor organization. Mobsters exercised this influence with little danger of interference from the government. Despite all of the denunciations of racketeering, federal law enforcement remained inactive in this area. In the postwar era, there was no concerted campaign to use federal prosecutions to deal with the problem of mobbed-up unions.[57]

The history of the Justice Department's prosecution of the Hollywood racketeering cases demonstrates the lackluster federal efforts in this area. Robert Montgomery, of the Screen Actors Guild, had helped spur the initial Treasury Department investigation in 1938, providing evidence of the producer Joseph Schenck's $100,000 payment to Bioff in 1937. Later, when the case had stalled out in the grand jury stage, Pegler's exposé on Bioff had pressured the Justice Department to find a way to restart it. The attorney general transferred the case to a different U.S. attorney's office, one more removed from the enervating influence of the film industry. In early 1940, he sent it to the U.S. attorney's office in Manhattan.[58]

There the case came under the direction of a young assistant U.S. attorney named Boris Kostelanetz. Twenty-eight years old in 1940, Kostelanetz was "a slight young man" with "smoothly brushed brown hair," a conservative taste in clothing, and a polite but reserved air. He was the brother of the famed conductor Andre Kostelanetz, and both brothers had fled, with their family, from Russia's Bolshevik revolution. A lawyer who was also a certified public accountant, Kostelanetz specialized in cases involving complicated financial transactions. He successfully handled a series of fraud cases and despite his relatively junior status, he was a natural choice for the high-profile assignment of prosecuting Schenck for tax evasion and perjury.[59]

For the next several years, Kostelanetz lived the Hollywood racketeering case. He worked with a team of investigators from the Treasury Department and the Federal Bureau of Investigation, first convicting Schenck and then using that conviction to win the cooperation of the Hollywood studio chiefs for a prosecution of Bioff and Browne. When those two union officials agreed to cooperate in 1942, Kostelanetz had them transferred to the Federal House of Detention in Manhattan, located right next to the U.S. attorney's office. Browne and Bioff became essentially adjunct members of the investigating team, spending nearly every workday at the prosecutor's office. They provided copious information on the Outfit's activities in Hollywood and its control over a number of Chicago unions. Bioff, taking to his new role with his typical flair for self-aggrandizement, offered suggestions for ways to approach potential grand jury witnesses and on occasion took part in the meetings with them. Many of those witnesses, when threatened with perjury and contempt citations, supplied further leads. Kostelanetz's team filled fourteen filing cabinets with information on this case and material for potential future prosecutions. The young assistant U.S. attorney acquired a unique level of expertise about the Outfit and its labor racketeering activities.[60]

All of this hard work apparently came to fruition in 1943. Faced with federal indictments for extortion and mail fraud, Frank Nitti, Capone's successor as the head of the Outfit, committed suicide in March, before he could be arraigned. Six other members of the Outfit, including the men thought to dominate its ruling council, surrendered to federal authorities. Tried on the extortion charges, all of them were convicted in late December 1943. For Kostelanetz, who had faced a battery of the best criminal defense lawyers in the country, this was a brilliant achievement. The judge followed his recommendation and sentenced the Outfit members to serve ten years, the maximum sentences allowed for the charges.[61]

At the time, it looked like this was just the beginning. An indictment for mail fraud still hung over the heads of the recently convicted Outfit leaders; those charges stemmed from the embezzlement of IATSE's 2 percent assessment fund. The four counts of that indictment each carried a five-year sentence, and so, combined with their current prison terms, the Outfit defendants might find themselves looking at a total of thirty years in jail. Even hardened criminals, when faced with such sentences, sometimes turn state's evidence in return for leniency. It seemed to be a real possibility in this case. Indeed, the trial judge made a point of indicating his willingness to consider sentence reductions if any of the defendants chose to cooperate. And, if one of them had, prosecutors might have cracked open any number of cases involving labor racketeering, municipal corruption, and murder.[62]

Nor was that the only avenue available for further prosecutions. Kostelanetz told FBI agents that he hoped to pursue cases against the various Chicago attorneys who had served as bagmen in the movie studio payoffs to Bioff and Browne. Such spin-off cases had strategic value. Respectable white-collar professionals such as those Chicago attorneys often decided to cooperate when confronted with the possibility of even minimal jail time. Kostelanetz had also talked with the FBI about drawing information from the movie studio chiefs regarding payoffs to IATSE officials in other cities, such as Boston and Washington, D.C.[63]

Thus the convictions of the Outfit's leadership in December 1943 appeared to be the start of something bigger. In the wake of his court victory in December 1943, Kostelanetz told reporters that the federal investigation would continue. News reports predicted that more indictments of other Outfit members were just around the corner. In one of the more hyperbolic expressions of the hopes raised by this case, a *Chicago Daily News* article on the original indictments in March 1943 exclaimed, "The whole Chicago mob now faces obliteration, literally. The defendants in the indictment returned today, if convicted, can be sent bye-bye for up to 30 years."[64]

But as it turned out, those defendants served only three years, and no wave of prosecutions arose to obliterate the Outfit. Kostelanetz never got a chance to pursue any follow-up cases; instead, in early 1944, the Justice Department sent him to Scranton, where he oversaw an investigation into corruption involving a couple of federal judges. In this new assignment, he would have little call to draw upon his accumulated expertise on the Outfit. In Kostelanetz's absence, no other prosecutors took up the subsidiary cases involving the Outfit's bagmen. There was no investigation of payoffs to other IATSE officials in other cities. The Justice Department kept postponing prosecution of the mail fraud indictments until early 1947, when the Outfit defendants hired an additional lawyer. This one happened to be a close friend of Attorney General Tom Clark. After billing his clients $15,000, the new attorney convinced the Justice Department to dismiss the mail fraud indictments. With those indictments out of the way, the Outfit defendants were eligible for parole. Another set of politically connected attorneys went to work, and in August 1947, the three members of the U.S. Board of Parole, all appointed by Attorney General Clark, voted unanimously to release the defendants from jail and allow them to finish their sentences while on parole.[65]

This proved to be a controversial decision. The *Chicago Tribune* published an exposé on the early release and the political machinations that lay behind it. Congressional hearings followed and the Justice Department mounted a belated effort to reverse the Parole Board's decision, but despite the controversy the paroles remained in effect. In the end, this first serious federal effort to curb organized crime's role in labor racketeering resulted in the absolute minimum jail time possible for the Outfit's top leadership. As an object lesson on the federal government's commitment to free unions from the scourge of racketeering, it was a disappointment.[66]

The other shoe dropped in 1955. Soon after the Outfit defendants had completed their sentences, the gang apparently took its revenge on Bioff. Any earlier attempt at retribution posed the risk that the Outfit leaders' paroles would be revoked; this could have been done merely on suspicion of their involvement in murdering the key witness from their trial.[67]

Knowing the gang would seek revenge, both Bioff and Browne had gone into hiding after their release from prison in 1944. Bioff and his wife moved to Phoenix, where they went by the last name of Wilson. The former boot-legger turned union official now assumed the role of a retired businessman. But still full of bluster, he began spending time in Las Vegas, and this prob-ably was how the Outfit tracked him down. On the morning of November 4, 1955, Bioff went out to his driveway, waved to his wife who was looking out the kitchen window, and got into his pickup truck. When he turned on the ignition, a dozen sticks of dynamite attached to the engine block blew up. Bioff's vehicle disintegrated and, as one news report put it, "pieces of his body were scattered throughout the yard of his $40,000 home."[68]

The local sheriff's office issued a statement that suggested the murder was in revenge for Bioff's testimony against the Outfit. It was a reasonable assumption. And if it was true, it called for federal action, at the least to pursue an obstruction of justice charge against those responsible but also, one might think, to demonstrate the government's commitment to curbing racketeering. The Justice Department formally asked the FBI to conduct a "preliminary investigation" in order "to determine whether there is in fact any basis for the statements ascribed to the investigators of the Sheriff's Office that the planting of the bomb in Bioff's pick-up truck was a 'revenge killing,' in retaliation for Bioff's having testified at the aforementioned trial."[69]

The resulting FBI investigation was brief and, in a way, straightforward. A Bureau teletype from the Phoenix office reported (in telegraphic shorthand) that agents had interviewed the local sheriff. "He advised investigation to date has not developed any evidence that killing of Willie Bioff was in retali-ation for his having testified in anti-racketeering trial in forty-three [1943]. He stated only basis for statement attributed to his investigators that it was retaliatory killing was speculation on their part." The agents asked the sher-iff to contact the Bureau if any specific evidence did turn up. And thus the investigation was completed; the Phoenix office's teletype concluded, "No further inquiry being made."[70]

The Maricopa County Sheriff's Office never did manage to build an effective case against the Outfit for Bioff's murder. The deputies remained stymied, the federal authorities stayed out of the matter, and the crime went officially unsolved. Along with the outcome of the Hollywood racketeering cases, this sent a public signal about the very limited nature of the federal commitment to fight organized crime's involvement in labor unions. The task was left to local authorities, in Maricopa County or in Chicago's Cook County.[71] The results were no different than they had been in the 1930s, when Murray Humphreys first led the Outfit's move into labor racketeering. Any union member or official considering taking a stand against the mob was reminded of the very real risks involved.

For the local union member, the scandals—and the resulting political outcry against the shadow of the racketeer—had brought no meaningful change. To cite just one case, the Outfit remained in control of Maloy's old projectionists' local, IATSE Local 110 in Chicago, throughout the postwar era. Members told the FBI that the arrests made in the Hollywood racketeering case had done nothing to improve their situation. As one put it, he "could expect no better treatment now than before the indictments were handed down in New York, the only effect of the indictment was to substitute the collection men."[72] Almost two decades later, in 1960, another member of the local complained to the Department of Labor (DOL) that his union was controlled by "crooks and racketeers." The DOL asked him to gather evidence to substantiate his charges. On the day that seventy-two-year-old Herman Posner, a longtime dissident in Local 110, was scheduled to meet with DOL personnel, he was stabbed to death. His murderer took the documents Posner had gathered on the corrupt conditions in the local. Chicago police investigated the killing, but officially the case remained unsolved.[73]

Posner's death was a sad reminder of how Pegler's campaign had failed to bring meaningful changes for rank and file union members. Conservatives had seized the opportunity offered by this scandal and Pegler's depiction of racketeering to score important political victories. But the opportunity to do something about the plight of union members trapped in mobbed-up unions went unrealized. While the shadow of the racketeer cast a pall over the labor movement in general, in places like Local 110, meaningful reform remained as distant as it ever had been.

# Notes

## Abbreviations

Dewey Scrapbooks = Thomas E. Dewey Scrapbooks, microfilm edition, reel 2, University of Rochester, Rochester, N.Y.

FBI Bioff File = Federal Bureau of Investigation, William Bioff File, acquired through Freedom of Information Act

FDR Papers = Franklin Delano Roosevelt Papers, Franklin D. Roosevelt Library, Hyde Park, New York.

Howard Papers = Roy W. Howard Papers, Library of Congress, Washington, D.C.

IBT Papers = International Brotherhood of Teamsters, Chauffeurs, and Warehousemen Papers, State Historical Society of Wisconsin, Madison, Wisc.

ILGWU Papers = International Ladies Garment Workers Union Papers, Collection 5780/002, Kheel Center for Labor-Management Documentation and Archives, Cornell University Library, Ithaca, N.Y.

McWilliams Papers = Carey McWilliams Papers, Collection 1319, Department of Special Collections, Charles E. Young Research Library, University of California, Los Angeles

Morgenthau Diaries = Henry Morgenthau Jr. Diaries, Franklin Roosevelt Presidential Library, Hyde Park, N.Y.

NARA = National Archives and Records Administration, College Park, Md.

NMU Files = National Maritime Union; William Standard, General Counsel's Files, 1937–1949, Collection Number 525, Kheel Center for Labor-Management Documentation and Archives, Cornell University, Ithaca, N.Y.

NYDA Papers = Papers of the New York County District Attorney's Office, New York City Municipal Archives, New York, N.Y.

Pegler Papers = (James) Westbrook Pegler Papers, Herbert Hoover Presidential Library, West Branch, Ia.

Pegler-Bisch Collection = Pegler-Bisch Letters, St. Louis Mercantile Library, University of Missouri–St. Louis, St. Louis, Mo.

Pegler AEF Correspondent File = Records of the American Expeditionary Forces (WWI), National Archives and Records Administration, College Park, Md.

*People v. Scalise* trial transcript = Record on Appeal, People of the State of New York against George Scalise (1940) Appellant Division, First Department

Scalise Trials Clipping File = Lillian Goldman Law Library at Yale Law School, New Haven, Conn.

*U.S. v. Campagna* trial transcript = Transcript of Record, United States Circuit Court of Appeals, United States of America against Louis Campagna, Paul De Lucia, Phil D'Andrea, Francis Maritote, Charles Gioe, John Rosselli and Louis Kaufman, Docket No. Cr 114–101, box 5808, Record Group 276, Northeast Region, National Archives and Records Administration, New York, N.Y.

## Introduction: "Peglerized"

1. *New York Herald-Tribune*, Apr. 22, 1940; *New York Sun*, Apr. 22, 1940; both clippings in "The Trials of George Scalise, President of the Building Service Employees' International Union, and James J. Bambrick, president of Local 32–B of that union, who were charged with federal tax evasion, forgery and grand larceny" (Newspaper Clipping File, 1940–41, Scalise Trials Clipping File). Also, *New York World-Telegram*, Apr. 22, 1940, 1; *New York Times*, Apr. 22, 1940, 1; *Chicago Tribune*, Apr. 22, 1940, 1; *Philadelphia Inquirer*, Apr. 22, 1940, 1; *Washington Post*, Apr. 22, 1940, 1; "Scalise, Union Head, Jailed for Extortion," *San Francisco Chronicle*, Apr. 22, 1940, 1; "A.F.L. Union Chief Seized in Extortions," *Los Angeles Times*, Apr. 22, 1940, 1.

2. "Racketeer Scalise," *Time* 35 (May 6, 1940): 20–21.

3. Westbrook Pegler, "Fair Enough," Jan. 19, 1940, box 120, Pegler Papers.

4. Pegler, "Fair Enough," Jan. 26, 1940; Jan. 31, 1940; Mar. 1, 1940; Apr. 2, 1940; Apr. 12, 1940; Apr. 16, 1940; Apr. 18, 1940; Apr. 24, 1940, in box 120, Pegler Papers.

5. *New York Herald-Tribune*, Apr. 24, 1940, Scalise Trials Clipping File.

6. *Washington Post*, Apr. 28, 1940, clipping in box 82, Pegler Papers.

7. Pegler, "Fair Enough," Nov. 22, 1939; Nov. 24, 1939; Nov. 28, 1939; Dec. 18, 1939; Dec. 20, 1939; Dec. 30, 1939; Jan. 13, 1940; in boxes 119–20, Pegler Papers.

8. Pegler, "Fair Enough," Nov. 22, 1939; Jan. 19, 1940, Jan. 22, 1940, boxes 119 and 120, Pegler Papers.

9. *New York Times*, Jan. 28, 1940, 29; "A Frank Statement from George Scalise," *Building Service Employee* 1 (May 1940): 6–7.

10. *New York Times*, Feb. 21, 1940, 3.

11. *New York Times*, Jan. 28, 1940, 29; "A Frank Statement from George Scalise."

12. *New York Times*, Feb. 21, 1940, 3.

13. *New York Times*, Feb. 10, 1940, 16.

14. Pegler, "Fair Enough," Feb. 1, 1940, box 120, Pegler Papers.

15. Pegler, "Fair Enough," Aug. 15, 1939, box 119, Pegler Papers.

16. Pegler, "Fair Enough," June 9, 1937, box 118, Pegler Papers.

17. Pegler, "Fair Enough," Feb. 1, 1940, box 120, Pegler Papers.

18. Record on Appeal, People of the State of New York against George Scalise (1940) Appellant Division, First Department.

19. *New York Times*, Nov. 6, 1941, 1.

20. *New York Times*, Jan. 1, 1944, 1.

21. *Washington Post*, Apr. 23, 1940, folder Unions, American Federation of Labor, 1908–1940, box 79, Pegler Papers.

22. *Chicago Daily Times*, May 13, 1940, folder Unions, American Federation of Labor, 1908–1940, box 79, Pegler Papers.

23. Frank D. Fackethal to Westbrook Pegler, May 8, 1941, folder Pegler Awards, Pulitzer Prize, box 53, Pegler Papers.

24. *New York Times*, May 6, 1941, 1.

25. Editor, "Letters," *Time* 38 (Dec. 22, 1941): 2.

26. *New York Times*, May 6, 1941, 1; Jack Alexander, "He's Against," *Saturday Evening Post* 213 (Sept. 14, 1940): 11; Oliver Pilat, *Pegler: Angry Man of the Press* (Boston: Beacon Press, 1963), 1–2, 177; Charles Fisher, *The Columnists* (New York: Howell, Soskin, 1944), 167.

27. Edwin Emery and Michael Emery, *The Press and America: An Interpretive History of the Mass Media* (Englewood Cliffs, N.J.: Prentice-Hall, 1984), 438. Pilat, *Pegler*, 278; Diane McWhorter, "Dangerous Minds: William F. Buckley Soft-Pedals the Legacy of Journalist Westbrook Pegler in *The New Yorker*," *Slate*, Mar. 4, 2004, http://www.slatemsn.com/id/2096673/ (accessed Apr. 1, 2004); Oliver Pilat, "Westbrook Pegler: Over the Edge," *ADL Bulletin* (Jan. 1964): 4–5; "Pegler Again Man without a Publisher," *Kansas City Star*, Apr. 9, 1964, folder Communism—Opponents of, John Birch Society, 1960–1966, box 21, Pegler Papers.

28. George P. West, "The Westbrook Pegler Mind," *New Republic* 107 (Oct. 5, 1942): 407–8.

29. Christopher L. Tomlins, "AFL Unions in the 1930s: Their Performance in Historical Perspective," *Journal of American History* 65 (Mar. 1979): 1023, 1035; Robert H. Zieger, *American Workers, American Unions* (Baltimore: Johns Hopkins University Press, 1994), 26.

30. Melvyn Dubofsky, *The State and Labor in Modern America* (Chapel Hill: University of North Carolina Press, 1994), 133–35, 139; John M. Allswang, *The New Deal and American Politics* (New York: John Wiley and Sons, 1978), 19, 39–41.

31. Seymour Martin Lipset and William Schneider, *The Confidence Gap: Business, Labor, and the Government in the Public Mind* (New York: Free Press, 1983), 203.

32. Elizabeth Fones-Wolf, *Selling Free Enterprise: The Business Assault on Labor and Liberalism, 1945–1960* (Chicago: University of Illinois Press, 1994), 2; Andrew E. Kersten, *Labor's Home Front: The American Federation of Labor during World War II* (New York: New York University Press, 2006), 55–57.

33. *New York Daily News*, Nov. 8, 1941, clipping in folder Pegler, box 178; *Washing-

*ton Post*, Apr. 22, 1940, *New York Herald-Tribune*, Apr. 22, 1940, clippings in folder Unions, American Federation of Labor, 1908, 1940, box 79, Pegler Papers; "Holdup Men of Labor," *Time* 38 (Sept. 22, 1941): 14–16; "The AFL Problem," *Newsweek* 16 (Dec. 2, 1940): 36; "A.F. of L. Ditches a Racketeer," *Life* 11 (Oct. 27, 1941): 38.

34. George Gallup, "Labor Seen Losing Favor with Public," *New York Times*, Oct. 26, 1941, 32.

35. Hadley Cantril, editor, *Public Opinion, 1935–1946* (Princeton: Princeton University Press, 1951), 396.

36. R. Alton Lee, *Truman and Taft-Hartley: A Question of Mandate* (Lexington: University of Kentucky Press, 1966), 47.

37. *Chicago Tribune*, Nov. 28, 1940, 12.

38. *Chicago Tribune*, Nov. 20, 1940, 10.

39. For an overview of the historical literature on these developments, see Dubofsky, *The State and Labor*, 197–231; Ronald W. Schatz, "Into the Twilight Zone: The Law and the American Industrial Relations System since the New Deal," *International Labor and Working-Class History* 36 (Fall 1989): 51–60.

40. James B. Jacobs, *Mobsters, Unions, and Feds: The Mafia and the American Labor Movement* (New York: New York University Press, 2006), xi.

41. David M. Kennedy, *Freedom from Fear: The American People in Depression and War, 1929–1945* (New York: Oxford University Press, 1999), 341.

42. James B. Atleson, *Values and Assumptions in American Labor Law* (Amherst: University of Massachusetts Press, 1983); Gordon L. Clark, *Unions and Communities under Siege: American Communities and the Crisis of Organized Labor* (New York: Cambridge University Press, 1989); Kim Moody, *An Injury to All: The Decline of American Unionism* (New York: Verso, 1988); James A. Gross, *Broken Promise: The Subversion of U.S. Labor Relations Policy, 1947–1994* (Philadelphia: Temple University Press, 1995); Michael Goldfield, *The Decline of Organized Labor in the United States* (Chicago: University of Chicago Press, 1987); Katherine Van Wezel Stone, "The Post-War Paradigm in American Labor Law," *Yale Law Review* 90 (June 1981): 1509–80; Christopher L. Tomlins, *The State and the Unions: Labor Relations, Law, and the Organized Labor Movement in America, 1880–1960* (New York: Cambridge University Press, 1986). Useful overviews for this subject and the historiographic debates involved include Dubofsky, *The State and Labor*, 197–231; and Schatz, "Into the Twilight Zone."

43. Two works that do deal with organized labor's public image, although not specifically with corruption scandals, are Elizabeth A. Fones-Wolf, *Selling Free Enterprise: The Business Assault on Labor and Liberalism, 1945–1960* (Chicago: University of Illinois Press, 1994); and William J. Puette, *Through Jaundiced Eyes: How the Media View Organized Labor* (Ithaca, N.Y.: ILR Press, 1992).

44. Seymour Martin Lipset and William Schneider, *The Confidence Gap: Business, Labor, and Government in the Public Mind* (New York: Free Press, 1983), 202.

45. Lipset, *The Confidence Gap*, 203, 215–20.

46. Hadley Cantril and Frederic Swift, *Public Opinion and Labor Problems: Confidential Report* (Princeton: Office of Public Opinion Research, Princeton University, Nov. 11, 1941), the quote is from p. 1, document in President's Personal Files, PPF 4721, American Institute of Public Opinion, 1936–1940, Franklin D. Roosevelt Library, Hyde Park, N.Y.

47. Puette, *Through Jaundiced Eyes*, 85–86.

48. Daniel Bell, "The Racket-Ridden Longshoremen," in *The End of Ideology* (New York: Free Press, 1960), 175–209; David Witwer, *Corruption and Reform in the Teamsters Union* (Chicago: University of Illinois Press, 2003), 157–211.

49. Jacobs, *Mobsters, Unions, and Feds*, 21.

## Chapter 1. The Columnist: A Crusading Journalist

1. Westbrook Pegler, "Fair Enough," August 1, 1941; February 23, 1940, box 120; n.d. 1938, box 119, Pegler Papers. Statistics on newspaper readership show that in 1940, the ratio of circulation of newspapers to total numbers of households was 1.2:1, and that ratio climbed to a peak during WWII of 1.3:1; it has been declining ever since, falling below .7:1 in 1985 (Leo Bogart, "The State of the Industry," in Philip S. Cook, Douglas Gomery, and Lawrence W. Lichty, eds., *The Future of the News: Television—Newspapers—Wire Services—News Magazines* [Washington, D.C.: Woodrow Wilson Center Press, 1992], 8).

2. Westbrook Pegler, "Fair Enough," Nov. 1, 1937, box 118, Pegler Papers.

3. Pegler, "Fair Enough," Aug. 22, 1942, box 121, Pegler Papers.

4. Pegler, "Fair Enough," Nov. 24, 1941, box 120, Pegler Papers.

5. There are different ways of calculating popularity. In 1944, in Charles Fisher's study of newspaper columnists, he described Pegler and Raymond Clapper as first and second in popularity among a group Fisher labeled the "Think Columnists." Pegler's column was going out to 174 newspapers with 9,965,754 subscribers and Clapper to 176 newspapers but fewer subscribers, 9,898,775. In 1942, Hadley Cantril surveyed Americans and 41 percent answered yes to the question, "Do you happen to read any political writer's column which appears regularly?" Of those who answered yes, Pegler ranked second after Drew Pearson, who ranked 28 percent in this group, Pegler at 17 percent, and then Ernie Pyle, 15 percent; Walter Lippman, 12 percent; Walter Winchell, 15 percent; Paul Mallon, 6 percent; David Lawrence, 9 percent; Dorothy Thompson, 7 percent; George Sokolsky, 4 percent; and Raymond Clapper, less than 0.5 percent. Harold Ickes's study, which came out in 1939 before the Bioff and Scalise scandal broke, listed Pegler as the sixth most popular columnist in terms of newspaper circulation. Ickes cited circulation estimates that Pegler's column went out to 117 newspapers with 6.2 million readers (Charles Fisher, *The Columnists* [New York: Howell, Soskin, 1944], 152; Hadley Cantril, ed., *Public Opinion, 1935–1946* [Princeton: Princeton University Press, 1951], 518).

6. Ibid., 1–2; Harold Ickes, *America's House of Lords: An Inquiry into the Freedom of the Press* (New York: Harcourt, Brace, 1939), 96.

7. "Mr. Pegler Leads the Way Again," *Los Angeles Times*, [Sept. n.d.] 1941, box 51, folder Articles and Books About, 1915–1941, Pegler Papers.

8. "Westbrook Pegler," editorial, *Gloucester Daily*, Feb. 5, 1943, folder Articles and Books About, 1942–1943, box 51, Pegler Papers.

9. Jay N. Darling to Westbrook Pegler, Nov. 28, 1941, folder Cartoonists, 1941–1962, box 4, Pegler Papers.

10. R. R. McCormick to J. L. Maloney, Sept. 21, 1940, box I-60, Robert R. McCormick, Business Correspondence, 1927–1955, Chicago Tribune Company Archives, Colonel Robert R. McCormick Research Center, First Division Museum at Cantigny, Wheaton, Ill.

11. Westbrook Pegler, "Things I Really Like," *Cosmopolitan* 132 (Feb. 1950): 52.

12. Pegler, "Fair Enough," July 18, 1941, box 120, Pegler Papers.

13. Arthur James Pegler, "Autobiography," typescript, chapter 7, 1–4, folder Arthur James Pegler, Autobiography, chapters 1–7, box 51, Pegler Papers.

14. Untitled, undated note [probably 1951], folder Pegler, Biographical Material, 1951 and undated, box 53.

15. Ibid.; report [card] of James [Westbrook] Pegler, Loyola Academy, September and October 1912, folder Pegler, Loyola Report Card, 1912, box 58; Austin G. Schimdt to James Pegler, Jan. 9, 1912, folder Articles 1912–1929, box 112, all in Pegler Papers.

16. Westbrook Pegler, "Autobiography" typescript, page numbers irregular and incomplete, folder Books—Autobiography (1), box 114; Westbrook Pegler, "Experts," *College Humor* (Nov. 1928): 56, folder Articles, 1912–1929, box 112, all in Pegler Papers.

17. Westbrook Pegler to Helen Bisch, Dec. 9, 1915, folder 6, box 1, Collection M-247, Pegler-Bisch Collection.

18. Westbrook Pegler to Bisch, Jan. 7, 1915, folder 1, box 1, Pegler-Bisch Collection.

19. Pegler to Bisch, n.d. [from Denver], folder 11, box 1, Pegler-Bisch Collection.

20. Pegler to Bisch, n.d. [postmark May 1916], folder 16, box 1, Pegler-Bisch Collection.

21. Pegler to Bisch, n.d. [postmark May 1916], folder 17 (this is a second and slightly later letter from San Antonio), box 1, Pegler-Bisch Collection.

22. "Whaled," Pegler to Bisch, July 5, 1916, folder 19; feature stories, Pegler to Bisch, July 10, 1916, folder 20, box 1, Pegler-Bisch Collection.

23. Pegler to Bisch, July 18, 1916, folder 28, box 1, Pegler-Bisch Collection.

24. Pegler to Bisch, July 10, 1916, folder 20, box 1, Pegler-Bisch Collection; quote is from Pegler, "Fair Enough," Aug. 1, 1942, box 121, Pegler Papers.

25. Edwin Emery and Michael Emery, *The Press and America: An Interpretive History of the Mass Media* (Englewood Cliffs, N.J.: Prentice-Hall, 1984), 341–42; Pilat, *Pegler: Angry Man of the Press*, 58.

26. Pegler to Bisch, July 18, 1916, Pegler-Bisch Collection; Pilat, *Pegler: Angry Man of the Press*, 67.

27. M. L. Stein, *Under Fire: The Story of American War Correspondents* (New York: J. Messner, 1968), 61.

28. Emmet Crozier, *American Reporters on the Western Front, 1914–1918* (New York: Oxford University Press, 1959), 126–27, 131–32, 139–40.

29. Pegler to Bisch, Dec. 5, 1917, folder 31, box 1, Pegler-Bisch Collection.

30. [Westbrook] Pegler, wire dispatch, Oct. 5, 1917, folder Pegler, United Press G-2–D, Articles by Correspondents, box 6161, Record Group 120, Records of the American Expeditionary Forces (WWI), NARA.

31. Crozier, *American Reporters on the Western Front*, 128–29; Pegler explained the agreement this way: "Nothing would be concealed from us but we could not file all we knew. We would subject ourselves to censorship. We all did and I never tried to file a word outside the censorship" (Westbrook Pegler to Emmet Crozier, May 7, 1957, folder WWI Correspondents, 1917–1957, box 58, Pegler Papers).

32. Westbrook Pegler to Helen Bisch, n.d. [June-July 1917], folder 29, box 1, Pegler-Bisch Collection.

33. Crozier, *American Reporters on the Western Front*, 175–76, 180–82; Robert H. Zieger, *America's Great War: World War I and the American Experience* (Lanham, Md.: Rowman and Littlefield, 2000), 96–101, 107–8; Byron Farwell, *Over There: The United States in the Great War, 1917–1918* (New York: Norton, 1999), 92–99; Gary Mead, *The Doughboys: America and the First World War* (New York: Overlook Press, 2000), 151–69.

34. Crozier, *American Reporters on the Western Front*, 175.

35. Pegler, wire dispatch, Nov. 5 [1917], not approved by censor, Pegler AEF Correspondent File.

36. Pegler, wire dispatch, Jan. 8, [1918], Pegler AEF Correspondent File.

37. Ibid.

38. W. J. Pegler to Roy Howard, Nov. 26, 1917, copy in E. L. Keen to Roy Howard, December 8, 1917, Directorate of Special Intelligence, Press Room M.I. 9c, Dec. 8, 1917, PF File 10175–352, box 2893, Military Intelligence Division Correspondence, RG165, NARA.

39. Westbrook Pegler to Emmet Crozier, Apr. 26, 1957, folder "WWI Correspondent, 1917–1957," box 58, Pegler Papers.

40. Notation on phone call, Pershing to Major Frederick Palmer, Century Club, New York, Dec. 29, 1917, in Pegler File 7361, reel 93, microfilm series T-900, Index to the Correspondence of the Office of the Commander in Chief, American Expeditionary Force, 1917–1919, RG 120, NARA.

41. [Howard] Hawkins to [Fred] Ferguson, Feb. 11, 1918; Emmet Crozier to Westbrook Pegler, Apr. 22, 1957; both in folder WWI Correspondent, 1917–1957, box 58, Pegler Papers. In his letter, Crozier quoted a military report in the G-2–D AEF records on the correspondents, but in my search through those records I was unable to find the file he described.

42. Westbrook Pegler to Mrs. A. J. Pegler, May 12, 1918, copied by Directorate of

Military Intelligence, M.I. 9c, File PF 4147, box 56, PF Files, 1917–1919, Military Intelligence Division, War Department General Staff, RG 165, NARA (hereafter Pegler PF File, NARA).

43. Westbrook Pegler to Helen Bisch, Apr. 9, [1918], folder 24, box 1, Pegler-Bisch Collection.

44. War Service Certificate, United States Navy, No. 74467, Westbrook James Pegler, folder Pegler World War Service, box 58, Pegler Papers.

45. J. Westbrook Pegler to Arthur James Pegler, May 28, 1918, copied by M.I. 9c, June 7, 1918, Pegler PF File, NARA.

46. Arthur James Pegler, "Autobiography," typescript, chapter 7, pp. 1–4, folder Arthur James Pegler, Autobiography, chapters 1–7, box 51, Pegler Papers; Westbrook Pegler, "Autobiography," typescript, page numbers irregular and incomplete, folder Books—Autobiography (1), box 114, ibid.; Stein, *Under Fire*, 61.

47. "Pegler Joins Chicago Tribune," *Editor and Publisher* (Nov. 14, 1925), clipping in folder "Pegler, Articles and Books About, 1915–1941," box 51, Pegler Papers.

48. Pegler, "Things I Really Like," 74.

49. Interview with Arch Ward, "Welcome Travelers," 10 AM, Aug. 10, 1950, WNBC (NY) and NBC Network (radio broadcast), Radio Reports Inc., folder Pegler, Articles and Books About, 1950, box 51, Pegler Papers.

50. "Good Fights 'Fair Enough' to Pegler," *Literary Digest* (May 16, 1936): 29, clipping in folder Pegler, Articles and Books About, 1915–1941, box 51, Pegler Papers.

51. For example, see Westbrook Pegler, "Pyle Sails to Sign Susanne after His Envoys Fail," *Chicago Tribune*, July 19, 1926, 21; Westbrook Pegler, "Tis Well for Promoters, Says Peg, the Fans Aren't Skeptics," *Chicago Tribune*, Feb. 5, 1928, clipping, box 115, Pegler Papers; and "Proselyting, What of It?" n.d., clipping, ibid.

52. Westbrook Pegler, "Speaking Out on Sports," n.d. 1930, clipping, folder columns 1930–1931, box 115, Pegler Papers.

53. Westbrook Pegler, "Hollow Shell Stuff Gives Tunney a Great Big Pain," *Chicago Tribune*, Aug. 22, 1927, 23; Westbrook Pegler, "Gene's Big Words Frighten Gibson Away from Camp," *Chicago Tribune*, Sept. 11, 1926, 19.

54. Westbrook Pegler, "What's 'Loose Lip' Smith Bin Sayin' to Senators' Batters," *Pittsburgh Post*, Oct. 15, 1925, folder Columns 1925–1926, box 115, Pegler Papers.

55. "All-Star Staff to Cover Every Angle of Big Fight for the Times," *Los Angeles Times*, Sept. 23, 1926, advertisement clipping, folder Columns, 1925–1926, box 115, Pegler Papers.

56. Cover, *The Trib: Shop Talk about the Making of the World's Greatest Newspaper* 9, no. 3 (Sept. 1927), in folder Pegler, Articles and Books About, 1915–1941, box 51, Pegler Papers.

57. Westbrook Pegler, "Training Camp Is Found Where Athletes Train," Jan. 7, 1932, in Correspondents File: Pegler Westbrook, Jan. 1932, Chicago Tribune Company Archives, Colonel Robert R. McCormick Research Center, First Division Museum at Cantigny, Wheaton, Ill.

58. "Tis Well for Promoters, Says Peg, the Fans Aren't Skeptics."

59. Westbrook Pegler, "A Smashing Tap on the Wrist and Battalino Hears Birdies," *Chicago Tribune*, Jan. 29, 1932, in Correspondents File: Pegler Westbrook, Jan. 1932, Chicago Tribune Company Archives.

60. Westbrook Pegler, "Contrast to Mickey Walker Highest Praise for Flowers," *Chicago Tribune*, Nov. 28, 1927, folder Columns 1927, box 115, Pegler Papers.

61. "Fast Company," editorial reprinted in *Chicago Tribune*, Sept. 16, 1927, clipping in folder Pegler, Articles and Books About, 1915–1941, box 51, Pegler Papers.

62. Westbrook Pegler, "Fair Enough," Nov. 1, 1941, box 120, Pegler Papers.

63. See, for instance, Westbrook Pegler, "Fight's 'In the Bag': Verdict of Kilbane," United Press clipping, June 9, 1924, folder columns 1923–24; Westbrook Pegler, "Parallel Seen to Selection of Ring Champion," *Chicago Tribune*, June 11, 1928, folder Columns, 1928, both in box 115, Pegler Papers.

64. Talbot Wegg, "Pegler in Washington," letter to editor, *Chicago Tribune*, Dec. 9, 1932, clipping, folder Pegler, Articles and Books About, 1915–1941, box 51, Pegler Papers.

65. "New York We Give You Westbrook Pegler," advertisement, *New York Times*, Dec. 11, 1933, 10.

66. Emery, *The Press and America*, 342–43, 435–38; Fisher, *The Columnists*, 4–9; A. J. Liebling, "Publisher III: An Impromptu Pulitzer," *New Yorker* 17 (Aug. 16, 1941): 23–24; Leo Rosten, *The Washington Correspondents* (New York: Harcourt, Brace, 1937), 140.

67. Fisher, *The Columnists*, 7, 15.

68. In 1939, according to Harold Ickes, Pegler's column ranked sixth in terms of circulation, going out to to 117 newspapers with a total circulation of 6.2 million. Clapper ranked ninth: his column was sent to 49 newspapers that reached a total of 3.6 million readers (Ickes, *America's House of Lords*, 96). Over the next several years, both Clapper and Pegler's popularity grew, and by 1944 both ranked near the top although Pegler's popularity (in terms of circulation figures) was still greater than Clapper's. The poll of 500 newspaper editors in 1942 conducted by the Wisconsin School of Journalism listed Pegler as the best adult columnist and Clapper second (Fisher, *The Columnists*, 152, 167, 195).

69. Ibid., 151 and 154. The quote is from 151.

70. Alexander, "He's Against," 10.

71. Rosten, *Washington Correspondents*, 144.

72. Ickes, *America's House of Lords*, 102.

73. Graham J. White, *FDR and the Press* (Chicago: University of Chicago Press, 1977), 27.

74. Pilat, *Pegler: Angry Man of the Press*, pp. 95–119; Fisher, *The Columnists*, 181–84.

75. "Fair Enough," Jan. 3, 1939, box 119, Pegler Papers.

76. Milton Mackaye, "Westbrook Pegler," *Scribner's Magazine* 104 (Oct. 1938): 8.

77. *New York Times*, Oct. 11, 1936, book review sec., 4.

78. John Cameron Swayze, "Candid 'Shots' with a Typewriter," *Kansas City Journal Post*, Feb. 22, 1938, clipping in folder Pegler, Article and Books About, 1915–1941, box 51, Pegler Papers; Pilat, *Pegler: Angry Man of the Press*, 91, 152–53; "Not-So-Tough Guy," *Sir* (Mar. 1944): 30–31; Jack Alexander, "He's Against," *Saturday Evening Post* 213 (Sept. 14, 1940): 9 and 132; "Good Fights 'Fair Enough' to Pegler," 29–30.

79. Ernie Pyle, "'Pegler Personally': Answering Many Queries," *New York World-Telegram*, Apr. 7, 1942, clipping in folder Columns, 1942 Mar.-Apr., box 121, Pegler Papers.

80. "Not-So-Tough Guy," 30.

81. Pyle, "Pegler Personally."

82. Swayze, "Candid 'Shots' with a Typewriter."

83. Examples include Westbrook Pegler, "Fair Enough," Aug. 4, 1938; Aug. 11, 1938; Jan. 4, 1939, in box 119, Pegler Papers.

84. "Fair Enough," Oct. 22, 1938, box 119, Pegler Papers.

85. Westbrook Pegler to Franklin Delano Roosevelt, July 18, 1934, PPF 1403, President's Personal File, FDR Papers.

86. Westbrook Pegler, "Fair Enough," Mar. 5, 1934; and Dec. 22, 1936; boxes 116 and 117, Pegler Papers.

87. Pegler, "Fair Enough," Jan. 15, 1934, box 116, Pegler Papers.

88. Ibid.

89. Pegler, "Fair Enough," May 31, 1935, box 117, Pegler Papers.

90. Compare the column in Oct. 1935 with two from the following spring, after his return from Europe: Pegler, "Fair Enough," Oct. 28, 1935; Apr. 22, 1936; Apr. 24, 1936, box 117, Pegler Papers.

91. Pegler, "Fair Enough," Apr. 24, 1936, box 117, Pegler Papers.

92. Ibid.; Sept. 9, 1936; Sept. 19, 1936 all in box 117; Oct. 8, 1940, box 120, Pegler Papers.

93. Pegler, "Fair Enough," Feb. 26, 1937, box 117, Pegler Papers.

94. He made $46,263 in 1937, making him the fourth highest paid of the columnists ("The Press: Seals and Salaries," *Time* 33 [Apr. 17, 1939]: 69).

95. "Good Fights 'Fair Enough' to Pegler," 29; Croy, "This Man Pegler," 1944 King Features Syndicate, clipping, folder Pegler, Articles and Books About, 1944–1945, box 51; Westbrook Pegler, "Fair Enough," Aug. 1, 1942, box 121, Pegler Papers; membership card, American Newspaper Guild, issued July 1, 1934, folder Unions, American Newspaper Guild, 1933–1937, box 80, Pegler Papers; Pilat, *Pegler: Angry Man of the Press*, 136–40.

96. Pilat, *Pegler: Angry Man of the Press*, 139–41; quotes are from Robert U. Brown, "Pegler Not Satisfied with Fruits of 10 Years Racket Campaigning," *Editor and Publisher*, July 31, 1943, 7.

97. "As Pegler Sees It," Oct. 25, 1945, folder Unions, American Newspaper Guild, 1933–1937, box 80, Pegler Papers.

98. Nelson Lichtenstein, *The Most Dangerous Man in Detroit: Walter Reuther and the Fate of American Labor* (New York: Basic Books, 1995), 110; Westbrook Pegler, "Fair Enough," Jan. 18, 1937; Mar. 19, 1937; Aug. 9, 1937; Oct. 30, 1937; Jan. 20, 1938, box 118, Pegler Papers.

99. Pegler, "Fair Enough," Jan. 18, 1937, box 118, Pegler Papers.

100. Pegler, "Fair Enough," Jan. 18, 1937, box 118, Pegler Papers; July 13, 1939, box 119, Pegler Papers.

101. Pegler, "Fair Enough," Aug. 8, 1939; Apr. 1, 1938; July 27, 1939, Pegler Papers.

102. Pegler, "Fair Enough," June 18, 1937; May 29, 1937; June 9, 1937; Aug. 4, 1937; Nov. 24, 1937; Mar. 22, 1938; July 26, 1939; July 27, 1939; Sept. 22, 1939; Oct. 12, 1939; Jan. 20, 1940, boxes 118-19, Pegler Papers.

103. Pegler, "Fair Enough," Aug. 15, 1939, box 119, Pegler Papers.

## Chapter 2. The Outfit: Organized Crime and Labor Racketeering

1. Report by Thomas V. Wade, Apr. 10, 1943, p. 34, FBI Serial No. 60-2149-518, FBI Bioff File.

2. "Regency," report by Wade, Apr. 10, 1943, p. 4, FBI Bioff File; *New York Herald-Tribune*, Mar. 20.

3. Report by Wade, Apr. 10, 1943, pp. 217-19; report by John Gleason, July 30, 1941, pp. 60-61, FBI Serial No. 60-2149-166; C. A. Grill, "Memorandum to Mr. Rosen," August 8, 1941, p. 6, FBI Serial No. 60-2149-207, all in FBI Bioff File; *Chicago Daily News*, Mar. 20, 1943, 1; Mars Eghigian Jr., *After Capone: The Life and World of Chicago Mob Boss Frank 'the Enforcer' Nitti* (Nashville: Cumberland House, 2006), 3-49, 82-83, 431-32.

4. *Chicago Tribune*, Mar. 20, 1943, 1; report by Thomas V. Wade, August 26, 1943, p. 10, FBI Serial No. 60-2149-589; report by A. C. Rutzen, November 8, 1941, p. 8, FBI Serial No. 60-2149-331; report by Rutzen, December 15, 1941, pp. 5-6, FBI Serial No. 60-2149-351; report by Gleason, July 30, 1941, pp. 60-61, all in FBI Bioff File; for photos, John J. Binder, *The Chicago Outfit* (Chicago: Arcadia Publishing, 2003), 64; William F. Roemer Jr., *Accardo: The Genuine Godfather* (New York: Donald I. Fine, 1995), 68.

5. Joseph Bonanno with Sergio Lalli, *A Man of Honor: The Autobiography of Joseph Bonanno* (Cutchogue, N.Y.: Buccaneer Books, 1983), 129, 87.

6. Ibid., 160.

7. Organized Crime Intelligence and Analysis Unit, Federal Bureau of Investigation, "Chronological History of La Cosa Nostra in the United States, January 1920-August 1987," 5-6, in U.S. Senate, Permanent Subcommittee on Investigations, *Organized Crime: 25 Years after Valachi*, 100th Cong., 2nd sess., Apr. 11, 15, 21, 22, 29, 1988 (Washington, D.C.: U.S. Government Printing Office, 1988); Howard Abadinsky, *Organized Crime* (Chicago: Nelson-Hall Publishers, 1994), 43-45; Humbert S. Nelli, *The Business of Crime: Italians and Syndicate Crime in the United States* (New York:

Oxford University Press, 1976), 168; Peter A. Lupsha, "Organized Crime in the United States," in Robert J. Kelly, ed., *Organized Crime: A Global Perspective* (Totowa, N.J.: Rowman and Littlefield, 1986), 48; Ovid Demaris, *The Last Mafioso: The Treacherous World of Jimmy Fratianno* (New York: Times Books, 1981), 122; William Brashler, *The Don: The Life and Death of Sam Gianacana* (New York: Ballantine Books, 1978), 107, 182, 186–87; Roemer, *Accardo*, 62–63, 69.

8. Nelli, *Business of Crime*, 168; report by Wade, Apr. 10, 1943, pp. 4–5, 55, 58–59; report by A. C. Rutzen, February 20, 1942, p. 10, both in FBI Bioff File; Mark H. Haller, "Illegal Enterprise: A Theoretical and Historical Interpretation," *Criminology* 28, no. 2 (May 1990): 214–23; Decision, *Estate of Joseph Nitto vs. Commissioner of Internal Revenue*, United States Tax Court, November 30, 1949, 13 T.C. 858; 1949 U.S. Tax Court Lexis 29. The best evidence for this continuing formula for the division of profits can be found in the ledger sheets of the Outfit's gambling operations for July 1941, left behind in an apartment used by Jake Guzik and used by the *Chicago Tribune* for a series of news stories. "Hint Pay-off Keeps Al a Friend of New Bosses," *Chicago Tribune*, Oct. 28, 1941, clipping in the collection of Chicago Historical Society; see also an account of an FBI recording in 1960 of how Outfit profits were divided, William F. Roemer Jr., *Man against the Mob* (New York: Ivy Books, Ballantine Books, 1991), 87–88.

9. U.S. Congress, Permanent Subcommittee on Investigations, *Organized Crime in Chicago*, 98th Cong., 1st sess., Mar. 4, 1983 (Washington, D.C.: U.S. Government Printing Office, 1983), 111–13; Robert M. Lombardo and Arthur J. Lurigio, "Joining the Chicago Outfit: Speculations about the Racket Subculture and Roving Neighborhoods," in Jay Albanese, ed., *Contemporary Issues in Organized Crime* (Monsey, N.Y.: Criminal Justice Press, 1995), 96–99; Abadinsky, *Organized Crime*, 42–44; Alf Oftedal, "Memo of Interview with William Bioff," May 7, 1942, p. 3; FBI Serial No. 60–2149–410, FBI Bioff File; report by John L. Madala, May 19, 1936, FBI Serial No. 7–77–738, FBI Barker-Karpis Gang File, Freedom of Information Act; John Kobler, *Capone: The Life and World of Al Capone* (New York: Da Capo Press, 1992), 145.

10. Nelli, *The Business of Crime*, 162–67; Kobler, *Capone*, 134–46, 156–62, 184–95, 200–212; Lawrence Bergreen, *Capone: The Man and the Era* (New York: Touchstone, Simon and Schuster, 1994), 138–47, 204–10. Kobler and Nelli assert eleven cars were in the convoy at the Hawthorne Inn; Bergreen refers to seven and an earlier decoy car.

11. Kobler, *Capone*, 245.

12. Bergreen, *Capone*, 305–14; John Edgar Hoover, "Memorandum for Mr. Joseph B. Keenan, Acting Attorney General," August 27, 1936, FBI Serial No. 62–34299–19; "Memorandum Re: St. Valentine's Day Massacre," Oct. 26, 1936, FBI Serial No. 62–34299–23, both in the St. Valentine's Day Massacre File, Freedom of Information Act, Federal Bureau of Investigation, Washington, D.C.

13. Bergreen, *Capone*, 96–100, 104–8; Koebler, *Capone*, 55–57, 146.

14. Douglas Bukowski, *Big Bill Thompson, Chicago, and the Politics of Image* (Chi-

cago: University of Illinois Press, 1998), 186–87, 219; Roger Biles, *Big City Boss in Depression and War: Mayor Edward J. Kelly of Chicago* (DeKalb: Northern Illinois University Press, 1984), 103; Richard C. Lindberg, *To Serve and Collect: Chicago Politics and Police Corruption from the Lager Beer Riot to the Summerdale Scandal, 1855–1960* (Carbondale: Southern Illinois University Press, 1998), 185, 192.

15. Ted Leitzel, "Chicago, City of Corruption," *American Mercury* 49 (Feb. 1940): 143.

16. Biles, *Big City Boss*, 107.

17. Ibid., 108.

18. V. W. Peterson, "Re: The Capone Syndicate," Mar. 21, 1944, files of the Chicago Crime Commission.

19. John Bartlow Martin, "Al Capone's Successors," *American Mercury* 68 (June 1948): 733; Lindberg, *To Serve and Collect*, 238, 241; Leitzel, "Chicago, City of Corruption," 144.

20. Biles, *Big City Boss*, 106; Lindberg, *To Serve and Collect*, 246–47.

21. *Chicago Sun-Times*, Oct. 12, 1950, 4; Demaris, *Captive City*, 128, 132; report by James E. Conerty, July 7, 1943, pp. 3–4, FBI Serial No. 60-2149-554, FBI Bioff File.

22. "World's Richest Cop" tag in *New York Times*, Nov. 6, 1950, 22; nickname, *Chicago Tribune*, Nov. 10, 1950, pay-off sheet, *Chicago Tribune*, Oct. 29, 1941, both clippings, Daniel Gilbert File, Chicago Historical Society.

23. William J. Drury to John E. Babb, Sept. 13, 1950, in William Drury alphabetical name file, Records, series 29, Record Group 46, Records of the Special Committee to Investigate Organized Crime in Interstate Commerce, 1950–51, National Archives and Records Administration, Washington, D.C. (hereafter cited as Kefauver Committee files).

24. *Chicago Sun-Times*, Nov. 10, 1950, clipping in Daniel Gilbert alphabetical name file, Kefauver Committee files; *New York Times*, Oct. 18, 1950, 40; *New York Times*, Nov. 6, 1950, 22.

25. Hoover, memo for Joseph B. Keenan, Aug. 27, 1936, p. 2, St. Valentine's Day Massacre File.

26. *Chicago Tribune*, Apr. 5, 1927, 1; lawyer's quote, George Murray, *The Legacy of Al Capone: Portraits and Annals of Chicago's Public Enemies* (New York: G. P. Putnam's Sons, 1975), 70; the quote from Healy's colleague, report by John Francis Hennessey, Feb. 10, 1943, pp. 5–6, FBI Serial No. 60-2149-464, FBI Bioff File.

27. *Chicago Tribune*, Dec. 17, 1959, 1.

28. Alan Block, *East Side-West Side: Organizing Crime in New York, 1930–1950* (New Brunswick, N.J.: Transaction Books, 1983), 129–30.

29. Roemer, *Accardo*, 163–70; Permanent Subcommittee on Investigations, *Organized Crime in Chicago*, 116; Abadinsky, *Organized Crime* 43–44, 295–96.

30. Abadinsky, *Organized Crime*, 294–95; Thomas C. Schelling, "What Is the Business of Organized Crime?" *American Scholar* 40, no. 4 (Autumn 1971): 643–52.

31. "Atlantic City Calls Capone 'Undesirable,'" *New York Times*, May 16, 1929, 27;

"Capone Enters Jail to Serve One Year," *New York Times*, May 18, 1929, 1; Nelli, *Business of Crime*, 211–15; Lupsha, "Organized Crime in the United States," 45–46; Virgil W. Peterson to Sheriff Peter J. Pitchess, Apr. 22, 1959, Chicago Crime Commission Files.

32. Nelli, *Business of Crime*, 216–17; Burton B. Turkus and Sid Feder, *Murder, Inc.* (New York: Manor Books, 1974; originally published 1951), 81–89; the quote is from p. 88.

33. *U.S. v. Campagna* trial transcript.

34. R. B. Hood to [name blacked out], May 17, 1939, FBI Serial No. 60–2149–33, FBI Bioff File.

35. Haller, "Illegal Enterprise," 226–29.

36. *Chicago Tribune*, Mar. 23, 1943, 2.

37. John R. Commons, "The Teamsters in Chicago," in *Trade Unionism and Labor Problems*, ed. John R. Commons (New York: Ginn, 1905), 39–42; Jean Cowgill, "Labor's Dishonor," *Reader Magazine* 4 (June 1904): 77–78; By-laws of Teamsters Local No. 704, Pamphlets in American History, Wisconsin State Historical Society, Madison, Wisc.; "Old King Coal Has a Royal Racket," *Lightnin'* 3 (Mar. 1930): 2–4.

38. "In re: Public Enemies, Re: George 'Red' Barker," n.d., File No. 15894, pp. 1–3, the quotes are from p. 1, Chicago Crime Commission.

39. Russo, *The Outfit*, 59–63; Virgil W. Peterson, *A Report on Chicago Crime for 1965* (Chicago: Chicago Crime Commission, 1966), 53–58; *New York Times*, Nov. 24, 1965, 24; Demaris, *Captive City*, 17–22; Bergreen, *Capone*, 428; William F. Roemer Jr., *Roemer: Man against the Mob* (New York: Ballantine Books, 1989), 48–49, 51–53.

40. *Chicago Tribune*, June 7, 1932, 1; Nov. 3, 1932, 1; Jan. 25, 1934, 3; Nov. 24, 1936, 1; Mar. 26, 1943, 1; Fred D. Pasley, *Muscling In* (New York: Washburn Publishers, 1931), 1–15; John W. Tuohy, *When Capone's Mob Murdered Roger Touhy* (Fort Lee, N.J.: Barricade Books, 2001), 67–68.

41. *Chicago Daily News*, Sept. 18, 1930; *Chicago Daily News*, Oct. 15, 1930, news clippings from Chicago Crime Commission.

42. *Chicago Daily News*, Sept. 18, 1930; *Chicago Daily News*, Oct. 15, 1930; *Chicago Tribune*, Nov. 3, 1934; news clippings from Chicago Crime Commission; Henry Barrett Chamberlin to D. M. Craig, July 9, 1930, confidential reports, Chicago Crime Commission; anonymous letter [construction contractor to Chicago Crime Commission], Aug. 8, 193[0], confidential reports, Chicago Crime Commission.

43. *Chicago Tribune*, Nov. 1, 1934, 1; Chamberlin to Craig, July 9, 1930, Chicago Crime Commission; anonymous letter, Aug. 8, 193[0], Chicago Crime Commission; preexisting collusive practices, *Chicago Tribune*, Nov. 17, 1928, 2.

44. "Slay Racket Boss at Desk," *Chicago Tribune*, Nov. 17, 1928, 1; Nov. 18, 1928, 5; *Official Magazine* 26 (Jan. 1929): 11–12, 14–16.

45. *Chicago Tribune*, Aug. 9, 1938, 1; Aug. 10, 1938, 5; June 26, 1937, 1; June 27, 1937, 1; quotes are from *Chicago Tribune*, Aug. 10, 1938, 5.

46. In addition to the previously mentioned Painters Union officials, this list would

include the following Teamster Union officials: Ely H. Orr, secretary-treasurer of Local 706, Chicago Newspaper Drivers; Timothy Lynch, head of a suburban Chicago Teamsters local; Patrick Berrell, a vice president of the International Brotherhood of Teamsters; Michael J. Galvin, leader of an independent Teamster union in Chicago, Nov. 23, 1936; *Chicago Tribune*, July 26, 1931, 1; Nov. 10, 1931, 1; July 22, 1932, 1; Nov. 24, 1936.

The list in other unions would include William Rooney, a leader in the Sheetmetal Workers union and also in the Chicago Flat Janitors; Louis Alterie, leader of the Chicago Office, Theater, and Amusement Janitors' Union; Thomas Maloy, an official in the Stage Hands Union; Dennis Zeigler, leader of a local of Operating Engineers; George Sanders was a business agent in the Chicago Waiters. *Chicago Tribune*, Mar. 20, 1931, 5; Feb. 5, 1935, 1; July 19, 1935, 1; Mar. 26, 1943; George Murray, *The Legacy of Al Capone: Portraits and Annals of Chicago's Public Enemies* (New York: G. P. Putnam's Sons, 1975), 189.

47. In reference to the 1936 murder of Mike Galvin, commission investigators concluded that a review of the inquest transcript "strongly supports the previous information received that Dan Gilbert engineered his assassination" (Lou Paris to Mr. Wash, "No. 29—re Gilbert," Mar. 9, 1950, File No. 29543, p. 1, Chicago Crime Commission).

48. John B. Jentz, "Unions, Cartels, and the Political Economy of American Cities: The Chicago Flat Janitors' Union in the Progressive Era and the 1920s," *Studies in American Political Development* 14 (Spring 2000): 51–71. See also John B. Jentz, "Citizenship, Self-Respect, and Political Power: Chicago's Flat Janitors Trailblaze the Service Employees International Union, 1912–1921," *Labor's Heritage* 9 (Summer 1997): 4–23.

49. Douglas Bukowski, *Big Bill Thompson, Chicago, and the Politics of Image* (Chicago: University of Illinois Press, 1998), 186–87, 222–23; Roger Biles, *Big City Boss in Depression and War: Mayor Edward J. Kelly of Chicago* (DeKalb: Northern Illinois University Press, 1984), 103.

50. Roger Touhy with Ray Brennan, *The Stolen Years* (Cleveland: Pennington Press, 1959), 83–86.

51. *Chicago Tribune*, June 17, 1932, 1; June 18, 1932, 3; *Chicago Herald and Examiner*, July 22, 1932, 1; *Chicago Tribune*, July 22, 1932, 1; July 24, 1932, 5.

52. *Chicago Tribune*, Mar. 20, 1931, 5; Mar. 21, 1931, 2; *Chicago American*, Mar. 8, 1950, 1; Mar. 11, 1950, 1.

53. Testimony of Roger Touhy, Transcript of Proceedings, pp. 271–72, in United States of America, *ex rel, Roger Touhy vs. Joseph E. Ragen*, U.S. District Court, Northern District of Illinois, 48 C 448, box no. 1500, NARA, Great Lakes Region, Chicago, Ill.

54. Memorandum for Mr. Clegg, Mar. 22, 1934; M. H. Purvis to director, Division of Investigation, Mar. 23, 1934, section 1, FBI Files, 7–HQ-759, box 92, RG 65, NARA, College Park, Md.

55. News reports of Scalise's sentencing hearing refer to a probation report that reviewed the history of how Jerry Horan was forced by the Chicago "Syndicate" to take orders from them sometime in 1931 or 1932, which is how the group acquired control over the BSEIU. This report was not included in the official trial transcript (*New York Times*, Oct. 8, 1940, 1).

56. *U.S. v. Campagna* trial transcript; for confirmation of the Outfit's control over Horan, see "B.S.E.I.U. Background," Nov. 15, 1934, case no. 2243, People v. Scalise, box 2569, Papers of the New York County District Attorney's Office, New York City Municipal Archives, New York, N.Y.

57. *Chicago Tribune*, July 2, 1933, 1.

58. Demaris, *The Last Mafioso*, 106; Ed Reid and Ovid Demaris, *The Green Felt Jungle* (New York: Pocket Cardenil, 1964), 66–69; Director, FBI, Airtel to SAC, Los Angeles, "James Riddle Hoffa, John 'Jake the Barber' Factor, Stardust Hotel, Las Vegas, Nevada, Miscellaneous—Information Concerning (Accounting and Fraud Section)," Apr. 17, 1962, FBI Serial No. 63-7527-3, John Factor File, Freedom of Information Act Request, FBI.

59. M. H. Purvis to director, Division of Investigation, U.S. Department of Justice, Jan. 29, 1934, FBI Serial No. 7-86-282; statement of Melvin H. Purvis, special agent in charge, Chicago Office, Division of Investigation, U.S. Department of Justice, Jan. 29, 1934, FBI Serial No. 7-86-282, both in box 67, FBI Case File 7-110-86, RG 65, NARA.

60. *Chicago Tribune*, Feb. 23, 1934, 1.

61. Report by Wade, Apr. 10, 1943, p. 124, FBI Bioff File.

62. *New York Daily Mirror*, Nov. 19, 1943; *New York World-Telegram*, Nov. 19, 1943.

63. Report by Wade, Apr. 10, 1943, pp. 124–25, FBI Bioff File; Newell, *Chicago and the Labor Movement*, 84–85.

64. Report by Wade, Apr. 10, 1943, pp. 124–25, FBI Bioff File; Murray, *Legacy of Al Capone*, 185.

65. Report by Wade, Apr. 10, 1943, pp. 125–26, FBI Bioff File.

66. Murray, *Legacy of Al Capone*, 191.

67. Hutchinson, *Imperfect Union*, 372.

68. Report by Wade, Apr. 10, 1943, p. 127, FBI Bioff File.

69. Murray, *Legacy of Al Capone*, 192.

70. Report by Wade, Apr. 10, 1943, pp. 127, 131, FBI Bioff File.

71. Newell, *Chicago and the Labor Movement*, 86–87.

72. Report by Wade, Apr. 10, 1943, p. 130, FBI Bioff File.

73. Ibid., pp. 127–28; Newell, *Chicago and the Labor Movement*, 87–88.

74. Report by Wade, Apr. 10, 1943, p. 128, FBI Bioff File.

75. "Says Nitti Seized Bartenders Union," *New York Times*, Oct. 18, 1940, 44.

76. Report by Wade, Apr. 10, 1943, pp. 128–29, FBI Bioff File.

77. *New York Times*, Dec. 3, 1940, 29.

78. Report by James E. Conerty, July 7, 1943, p. 4, FBI Serial No. 60–2149–554, FBI Bioff File.

79. Roemer, *Accardo*, 83.

80. Report by John Francis Hennessey, Feb. 10, 1943, p. 2, FBI Serial No. 60–2149–464; "Chicago Presses for Labor Purge," *New York Times*, Sept. 16, 1940, 14; Demaris, *Captive City*, 25.

81. Permanent Subcommittee on Investigations, *Organized Crime in Chicago*, 82.

82. McGurn's real name was Vincenzo Gibaldi, but he had begun going by the name Jack McGurn during his days as a boxer and the name apparently stuck. Bergreen, *Capone*, 237, 251, 305–7; Sifakis, *The Mafia*, 204.

83. *U.S. v. Compagna* trial transcript, pp. 1043, 1054–55.

84. Permanent Subcommittee on Investigations, *Organized Crime in Chicago*, 207, 212.

85. U.S. Senate, Permanent Subcommittee on Investigations, *Organized Crime: Twenty-five Years after Valachi*, 100th Cong., 2nd sess., Apr. 11, 1, 21, 22, 29, 1988 (Washington, D.C.: U.S. Government Printing Office, 1988), 225.

86. New York State Organized Crime Task Force, *Corruption and Racketeering in the New York City Construction Industry: The Final Report* (New York: New York University Press, 1990); President's Commission on Organized Crime, *The Edge: Organized Crime, Business, and Labor Unions* (Washington, D.C.: U.S. Government Printing Agency, 1986); James B. Jacobs, *Mobsters, Unions, and Feds: The Mafia and the American Labor Movement* (New York: New York University Press, 2006), 34–35.

87. Permanent Subcommittee on Investigations, *Organized Crime in Chicago*, 28, 130.

## Chapter 3. Browne, Bioff, and Scalise:
## The Dynamics of Union Corruption

1. *Chicago Daily News*, Mar. 19, 1943; *New York Sun*, Oct. 18, 1943; John Hutchinson, *The Imperfect Union: A History of Corruption in Trade Unions* (New York: E. P. Dutton, 1970), 408; sense of humor, Jack Gould, "Note on the Stagehands' Meeting," *New York Times*, June 16, 1940, XI.

2. Report by W. E. Assmus, June 19, 1941, p. 5, FBI Serial No. 60–2149–140; Alf Oftedal memorandum of interview with William Bioff, Apr. 20, 1942, p. 5, FBI Serial No. 60–2149–410, both from FBI Bioff File.

3. *People v. Scalise* trial transcript, vol. 7991, p. 310.

4. Florabel Muir, "'All Right, Gentlemen, Do We Get the Money?': The Astonishing Success Story of Bad Boy Bioff in Movieland," *Saturday Evening Post* 212 (Jan. 27, 1940): 11.

5. B. E. Sacket to director, FBI, May 26, 1941, FBI Serial No. 60–2149–120, FBI Bioff File.

6. Photo No. 3207 [Chicago Police Department] Oct. 15, 1931, Exhibit 130 ID, U.S.

Dist. Court, S.D. of N.Y., Oct. 29, 1941, folder Unions, International Alliance of Theater and Stage Employees, 1941, box 87, Pegler Papers.

7. Report by John P. Gleason, Dec. 4, 1941, FBI Serial No. 60–2149–342; report by A. C. Rutzen, Oct. 10, 1941, pp. 2–3, FBI Serial No. 60–2149–270; report by W. E. Assmus, Sept. 29, 1941, pp. 2–3, "live wire" on p. 3, FBI Serial No. 60–2149–381; report by Rutzen, Oct. 10, 1941, all in FBI Bioff File.

8. *U.S. v. Campagna* trial transcript, pp. 102–3.

9. David Witwer, *Corruption and Reform in the Teamsters Union* (Chicago: University of Illinois Press, 2003), 56–57; *Chicago Tribune*, Nov. 24, 1936, 1; at his death, the *Tribune* identified Galvin as the "Republican Committeeman of the 27th or river ward." The paper indicated a switch in party identification at some point in the past: "Galvin was formerly a Democrat of the old Barney Grogan school."

10. *U.S. v. Campagna* trial transcript, pp. 105–9, quote is from p. 109; report by Thomas V. Wade, Apr. 10, 1943, pp. 25–26, FBI Serial No. 60–2149–518, FBI Bioff File.

11. Report by Gleason, Dec. 4, 1941, FBI Bioff File.

12. Report by R. E. Mayer, Sept. 3, 1941, FBI Serial No. 60–2149–231, FBI Bioff File.

13. Report by A. C. Rutzen, Oct. 17, 1941, pp. 13–14, FBI Serial No. 60–2149–305, FBI Bioff File; Dennis Lane to William Green, July 26, 1933; William Hanley to John M. Gillespie, Aug. 3, 1933, both in box 8, series 3, American Federation of Labor Correspondence, series 1, IBT Papers, 1904–1952; *U.S. v. Campagna* trial transcript, pp. 109–10, 113; "Two Public Enemies Seeking Hold in Poultry Union," *Chicago Tribune*, Feb. 3, 1933, 3.

14. Conference Transcript, July 25, 1939, p. 82, attached to R. B. Hood to director, FBI, Feb. 27, 1940, FBI Serial No. 60–2149–77, FBI Bioff File.

15. Report by Rutzen, Oct. 17, 1941, p. 13, FBI Bioff File.

16. His criminal record included the 1922 charge of pandering, a 1921 arrest for burglary and receiving stolen property that was dismissed in court, and then nothing until an arrest in 1932 on "general principles," which had to do with the complaint of the poultry merchant and was dismissed in court. The FBI worked to track down the arresting officers in these cases; if the Bureau had been able to find anything in the way of a more sinister reputation for Bioff, it would have been included in his parole report in a bid to increase the prison sentence he would receive (John P. Gleason, "Parole Report, William Bioff," Dec. 4, 1941, FBI Serial No. 60–2149–342, FBI Bioff File).

17. In 1942, Bioff told a Treasury Department agent that Chicago gang members had disliked him; they "resented his aggressiveness" and had he not been sent out to Los Angeles in 1936, he probably would have been killed eventually (Alf Oftedal, memorandum of interview with William Bioff, Apr. 20, 1942, p. 5, FBI Serial No. 60–2149–410, FBI Bioff File).

18. B. E. Sackett to director, FBI, May 26, 1941, FBI Serial No. 60–2149–119; report

by [name blacked out] May 28, 1941, FBI Serial No. 60–2149–123; J. Edgar Hoover to Thomas J. Courtney, Aug. 15, 1940, FBI Serial No. 60–2149–96, all in FBI Bioff File.

19. *U.S. v. Campagna* trial transcript, pp. 1015–16; John P. Gleason, "Parole Report: George E. Browne," Dec. 4, 1941, FBI Serial No. 60–2149–350, FBI Bioff File.

20. Quotes are from: Jack Gould, "Note on the Stagehands' Meeting," *New York Times*, June 16, 1940, XI; John P. Gleason, "Parole Report: George E. Browne," Dec. 4, 1941, FBI Serial No. 60–2149–350, FBI Bioff File; *Chicago Daily News*, Mar. 19, 1943; *U.S. v. Campagna* trial transcript, pp. 1016–18.

21. *U.S. v. Campagna* trial transcript, pp. 1018–19.

22. *U.S. v. Campagna* trial transcript, pp. 1020–22, 1144, quotes on p. 1022 and 1144.

23. Report by J. P. Gleason, Oct. 1, 1941, p. 69, FBI Serial No. 60–2149–262, FBI Bioff File; Elmer C. Williams, "The Rise of the Racketeer," *Lightnin'* 8 (May 1939): 3; *U.S. v. Campagna* trial transcript, p. 1301.

24. *U.S. v. Campagna* trial transcript, pp. 1022–23.

25. Report by Thomas V. Wade, Apr. 10, 1943, pp. 13–14, FBI Serial No. 60–2149–518, FBI Bioff File.

26. Report by Wade, Apr. 10, 1943, pp. 32, quote on p. 13, FBI Bioff File; pay cut due to be restored, stenographic minutes, U.S. v. Nitto, Tax Court of the United States, Docket Numbers 8840, 8841, 8842, Columbia Reporting Company, Washington, D.C., n.d., reprinted in George H. Dunne, "Hollywood Labor Dispute: A Study In Immorality," n.d., p. 14, in box 1, McWilliams Papers.

27. Report by Wade, Apr. 10, 1943, pp. 13–14, 31–32, "we can get," p. 13, FBI Bioff File.

28. Bioff and Circella's long acquaintance in report by Wade, Apr. 10, 1943, p. 10, FBI Bioff File; Alf Oftedal, memo on interview with Bioff, May 22, 1942, p. 1, FBI Serial No. 60–2149–418; 100 Club Encounter, *U.S. v. Campagna* trial transcript, pp. 122–24, 1028, quote is from p. 124.

29. *Chicago Tribune*, Feb. 24, 1935, 5; John Kobler, *Capone: The Life and World of Al Capone* (1971; rpt., New York: De Capo Press, 1992), 257–60; Laurence Bergreen, *Capone: The Man and the Era* (New York: Simon and Schuster, Touchstone, 1996), 329–31.

30. *U.S. v. Campagna* trial transcript, pp. 125–26, 1031–33, "you ought to know," p. 1033; report by Wade, Apr. 10, 1943, pp. 14–15, "Rio could put it how he liked," p. 15, FBI Bioff File.

31. U.S. v. Campagna trial transcript, p. 130, "We have never," p. 1033; "Rio told him," report by Wade, Apr. 10, 1943, p. 32, FBI Bioff File.

32. Report by Wade, Apr. 10, 1943, p. 15, 33, FBI Bioff File.

33. Ibid., p. 13.

34. Ibid., p. 33.

35. *U.S. v. Campagna* trial transcript, pp. 1034–36; report by Wade, Apr. 10, 1943, p. 55, FBI Bioff File.

36. *U.S. v. Campagna* trial transcript, p. 1037.

37. Report by Wade, Apr. 10, 1943, p. 15, FBI Bioff File.

38. *U.S. v. Campagna* trial transcript, p. 141.

39. *U.S. v. Campagna* trial transcript, pp. 139–40, quote is from p. 140.

40. Michael Charles Nielsen, "Motion Picture Craft Workers and Craft Unions in Hollywood: The Studio Era, 1912–1948" (PhD diss., University of Illinois, 1985), 24–38.

41. C. Lawrence Christenson, "Chicago Service Trades: Cleaning and Dyeing, Motion Picture Operators and Musicians," in Harry A. Millis, research director, *How Collective Bargaining Works: A Survey of Experience in Leading American Industries* (New York: Twentieth Century Fund, 1942), 842–43.

42. Ibid., 844–45.

43. Christenson, "Chicago Service Trades," 830–31; Nielsen, "Motion Picture Craft Workers," 129, 131.

44. Report by J. P. Gleason, Oct. 1, 1941, p. 17, FBI Serial No. 60–2149–262, FBI Bioff File.

45. Christenson, "Chicago Service Trades," 847.

46. In the course of its investigation, the FBI stumbled upon the existence of a specialist in this activity, Fred Blacker, a native of Kokomo, Indiana, who manufactured stink bombs and was brought in by locals as far away as New York City to organize stink bombings (report by Wade, Apr. 10, 1943, p. 187; Thomas V. Wade, "Summary Memorandum for the Bureau," Sept. 28, 1943, p. 43, FBI Serial No. 60–2149–610; report by J. P. Gleason, May 18, 1942, pp. 29–30, FBI Serial No. 60–2149–412; report by Charles W. Nail, Oct. 13, 1942, FBI Serial No. 60–2149–432, all in FBI Bioff File).

47. Christenson, "Chicago Service Trades," 847. In Detroit, a member estimated there were about 300 projectionists working in the city; 160 of them were members of the local union and the others worked on a union permit (report by [name blacked out], Feb. 7, 1940, p. 3, FBI Serial No. 60–2149–75, FBI Bioff File). Newark's Local 244 had about 160 members (report by H. Bruce Baumeister, Feb. 12, 1942, p. 6, FBI Serial No. 60–2149–382); in Boston Local 182, 250 members and 25 apprentices (Prescott J. Young to Westbrook Pegler, May 17, 1941, folder Unions, IATSE 1941 Jan.-Sept., box 87, Pegler Papers); St. Louis Local 143, roughly 106 members (report by [name blacked out], Aug. 2, 1939, p. 4, FBI Serial No. 60–2149–49, FBI Bioff File); Chicago Local 110, about 426 members and 200 working on permits (report by W. E. Assmus, July 17, 1941, p. 5, FBI Serial No. 60–2149–157, FBI Bioff File).

48. Christenson, "Chicago Service Trades," 833–34; unsigned to Westbrook Pegler, Oct. 23, 1940; L. A. Farris to Westbrook Pegler, May 28, 1940, both in folder Unions, IATSE 1940, box 87; Prescott J. Young to Westbrook Pegler, May 17, 1941, folder Unions, IATSE, 1941, Jan.-Sept., box 87, both in Pegler Papers; H. Bruce Baumeister, Feb. 12, 1942, pp. 8–13, 16; report by Wade, Apr. 10, 1943, pp. 146–47, FBI Bioff File.

49. Newark: report by Baumeister, Feb. 12, 1942, pp. 7–8; report by Wade, Apr. 10, 1943, pp. 146–47; report by H. Bruce Baumeister, Nov. 5, 1941, pp. 4–6, FBI Serial No. 60–2149–340. Detroit: report by [name blacked out], Feb. 7, 1940, p. 2–3. New York:

Joseph Driscoll, "Kaplan Ousted by Film Union During Trial," n.d. clipping, folder Unions, IATSE, undated, box 88, Pegler Papers; Richard Lamb, "Kaplan Is Back in Film Union Post after Prison Term," n.d. clipping in folder Unions, IATSE, undated, box 88, Pegler Papers.

50. Christenson, "Chicago Service Trades," 837–38, 840–43; report by W. E. Assmus, June 13, 1941, pp. 4–6, FBI Serial No. 60-2149-143; Lamb, "Kaplan Is Back in Film Union Post after Prison Term"; Edward F. McGrady, "Memorandum for President Green," May 26, 1933, folder Rackets, box 6, series 11, File B, American Federation of Labor Records, 1888–1955, Wisconsin Historical Society, Madison, Wisc. Newark: report by H. Bruce Baumeister, Feb. 12, 1942, pp. 2–3, FBI Serial No. 60-2149-382, FBI Bioff File.

51. St. Louis: Judge Ernest F. Oakley, Decree of Circuit Court of the City of St. Louis, State of Missouri, Feb. Term 1940, William Robinson et al., plaintiffs vs. John P. Nick et al., Defendants, Docket No. 30641, Div. No. 3, Mar. 5, 1940, in folder Unions, IATSE, 1940, box 87, Pegler Papers.

52. *Chicago Tribune*, Feb. 5, 1935, 2.

53. Barbara Warne Newell, *Chicago and the Labor Movement: Metropolitan Unionism in the 1930s* (Urbana: University of Illinois Press, 1961), 81.

54. Christenson, "Chicago Service Trades," 832.

55. Report by A. C. Rutzen, Nov. 18, 1941, FBI Serial No. 60-2149-326; report by A. C. Rutzen, Oct. 9, 1941, FBI Serial No. 60-2149-271, both in FBI Bioff File.

56. *Chicago Tribune*, Feb. 5, 1935, 2.

57. Philip Kore, Joseph Britsk, et al., to William Green, May 28, 1933, reel 141, IATSE File, American Federation of Labor Records, Office of the President, National and International Unions, Correspondence, 1890–1959, George Meany Memorial Archives, Washington, D.C.

58. Anonymous to Westbrook Pegler, Oct. 10, 1940, folder Unions, IATSE, 1940, Aug.-Jan., box 87, Pegler Papers.

59. Report by Wade, Apr. 10, 1943; report by W. E. Assumus, Aug. 22, 1941, FBI Serial No. 60-2149-191, both in FBI Bioff File; Newell, *Chicago and the Labor Movement*, 82.

60. *Chicago Tribune*, Jan. 26, 1935, 5; Economic History Services, "What Is Its Relative Value in US Dollars?" http://www.eh.net/hmit/compare/ (accessed Oct. 18, 2005).

61. Report by Wade, Apr. 10, 1943, pp. 62–63, FBI Bioff File.

62. Report by Wade, Apr. 10, 1943, p. 56, FBI Bioff File.

63. Report by Wade, Apr. 10, 1943, pp. 30–31, FBI Bioff File.

64. Joseph Driscoll, "Kaplan Ousted by Film Union During Trial," n.d. clipping, folder Unions, IATSE, undated, box 88, Pegler Papers; Lamb, "Kaplan Is Back in Film Union Post after Prison Term"; Nielsen, "Motion Picture Craft Workers," 134–36; "Sue to End Power of Union Head," *New York Times*, July 8, 1932, 22; "Kaplan Must Face Two Criminal Charges," *New York Times*, Dec. 2, 1932, 27; report by Wade, Apr. 10, 1943, p. 40, FBI Bioff File.

65. Edward F. McGrady, memorandum for President [William] Green, May 29, 1933, folder Rackets, box 6, series 11, File B, American Federation of Labor Records, 1888–1955, Wisconsin Historical Society, Madison, Wisc.; regarding Buchalter and Luciano, see Humbert S. Nelli, *The Business of Crime: Italians and Syndicate Crime in the United States* (New York: Oxford University Press, 1976), 202–12; Alan Block, *East Side-West Side: Organizing Crime in New York, 1930–1950* (New Brunswick, N.J.: Transaction Books, 1985), 168–83, 226–35.

66. Report by John P. Gleason, July 30, 1941, pp. 39–40, FBI Serial No. 60-2149-166, FBI Bioff File.

67. Report by [name blacked out], Feb. 7, 1940, pp. 2–4; report by [name blacked out], July 27, 1937, FBI Serial No. 60-2149-5, both in FBI Bioff File; "Czar Nick's Ouster from Movie Union Control Is Upheld," *St. Louis Post Dispatch*, n.d., clipping, folder Unions, IATSE, undated, box 88, Pegler Papers.

68. *U.S. v. Campagna* trial transcript, pp. 1038–39.

69. Report by Wade, Apr. 10, 1943, p. 16, FBI Bioff File.

70. *U.S. v. Campagna* trial transcript, p. 145.

71. *Chicago Daily News*, Aug. 7, 1943.

72. Report by Wade, Apr. 10, 1943, p. 16; report by Thomas V. Wade, June 28, 1943, pp. 3–29, FBI Serial No. 60-2149-552, FBI Bioff File.

73. Report by Wade, June 28, 1943, p. 29, FBI Bioff File.

74. "Racketeer Scalise," *Time* 35 (May 6, 1940): 20–21; *Chicago Tribune*, Apr. 27, 1940, Dewey Scrapbooks, vol. 3–4.

75. "Columnist Pegler Puts the Finger of the Law on a New York Union Leader," *Life* 8 (May 6, 1940): 35.

76. Memorandum to chief investigator from Thomas M. Fay Jr., May 3, 1940, box 2566, NYDA Papers; George Scalise, "A Frank Statement," *Building Service Employee* 1, no. 4 (May 1940): 6.

77. George Scalise to Jerry Horan, July 29, 1935; Scalise to Charles Hardy, Aug. 19, 1938; Paul B. David to Scalise, Aug. 22, 1938; Scalise to Hardy, Aug. 29, 1938, all in box 2567, NYDA Papers.

78. George Scalise to Paul David, Dec. 27, 1938, box 2567, NYDA Papers.

79. He first sought a pardon in 1923 and was turned down. Scalise filed a second application for a pardon in 1938, and when this one also was rejected he asked to have it reconsidered on the basis of new endorsements he had gained for his application. William Green was one of the people who had written in support of the 1939 reapplication (*New York World-Telegram*, Apr. 19, 1940, 19).

80. George Scalise, "A Frank Statement."

81. Ibid.; *New York Times*, Oct. 8, 1940, 1; *People v. Scalise* trial transcript, vol. 7991, pp. 218–20. Thomas M. Fay Jr., memorandum to chief investigator, May 3, 1940, box 2566, NYDA Papers.

82. Scalise, "A Frank Statement"; Fay, memorandum to chief investigator, May 3, 1940, NYDA Papers.

83. Thomas M. Fay Jr., memorandum to Mr. Gurfein, Subject: George Scalise, May 7, 1940, box 2566, NYDA Papers.

84. Exceptions include Andrew Wender Cohen, "The Struggle for Order: Law, Labor, and Resistance to the Corporate Ideal in Chicago, 1900–1940" (PhD diss., University of Chicago, 1999); John B. Jentz, "Unions, Cartels, and the Political Economy of the American Cities: The Chicago Flat Janitors' Union in the Progressive Era and 1920s," *Studies in American Political Development* 14 (Spring 2000): 51–71; Colin Gordon, "The Lost City of Solidarity: Metropolitan Unionism in Historical Perspective," *Politics and Society* 27 (1999): 564–68, 573; Newell, *Chicago and the Labor Movement*, 209–25.

85. *People v. Scalise* trial transcript, vol. 7991, p. 1005; *New York Times*, Oct. 8, 1940, 1; Sept. 26, 1959, 1; Sept. 27, 1959, 1; Oct. 7, 1959, 37; Peter Maas, *The Valachi Papers* (1968; rpt., New York: Pocket Books, 1986), 124 and 203.

86. *People v. Scalise* trial transcript, vol. 7991, pp. 1005, 1030.

87. *New York Times*, Oct. 8, 1940, 1; memo to Mr. Dreiband from A. Robertson, June 14, 1940, box 2566, NYDA Papers; Block, *East Side-West Side,* 225–26; James J. Bambrick, *The Building Service Story* (New York: Labor History Press, 1948), 20–21.

88. John F. O'Connell to Mr. Dreiband, June 14, 1940, box 2566, NYDA Papers.

89. Memo to Alex Dreiband from J. Barst, June 18, 1940, box 2566, NYDA Papers.

90. Memo to Dreiband from Barst, June 19, 1940, box 2566, NYDA Papers.

91. Peter Reuter, Jonathan Rubinstein, and Simon Wynn, *Racketeering in Legitimate Industries: Two Case Studies* (Washington, D.C.: National Institute of Justice, Jan. 1983), 12–14; Peter Reuter, *Disorganized Crime: The Economics of the Visible Hand* (Cambridge, Mass.: MIT Press, 1983), 150–73; Howard Abadinsky, *Organized Crime*, 4th ed. (Chicago: Nelson-Hall, 1994), 294–99; New York State Organized Crime Task Force, *Corruption and Racketeering in the New York City Construction Industry* (New York: New York University Press, 1990), 75–79.

92. Statement of Louis Marcus to Alfred J. Scotti, June 6, 1940, box 2566, NYDA Papers.

93. Thomas Hughes to J. L. Devring, Nov. 10, 1919, and J. L. Devring to Thomas L. Hughes, Nov. 14, 1919, both in box 24, series I, IBT Papers; Fred D. Pasley, *Muscling In* (New York: Washburn Publishers, 1931), 19–23; George Murray, *The Legacy of Al Capone: Portraits and Annals of Chicago's Public Enemies* (New York: G. P. Putnam's Sons, 1975), 159–61. Writing about such organizations, Pegler notes that they were "known as an ice-pick or razor blade union because it was noticed that the tires of cars which were parked in non-union garages came down of ice pick punctures in their tires and of razor slashes in their upholstery" (Pegler, "Fair Enough," Apr. 29, 1940, box 120, Pegler Papers).

94. In 1940, Dewey's staff gathered together police and prosecutor's reports made in 1932–33 on Local 272 and its activities. These reports are gathered together and annotated in the following investigative memorandum: memo to Mr. Gurfein from Mr. Mertens, Apr. 30, 1940, box 2566, NYDA Papers.

95. Ibid.

96. Signed, "8,000 Members" to President Green, A.F. of L., July 22, 1935, reel 37, American Federation of Labor Records: The William Green Era, microfilm edition.

97. Robert Zieger, *American Workers, American Unions*, 2nd ed. (Baltimore: Johns Hopkins University Press, 1994), 27–291; Melvyn Dubofsky, "Not So 'Turbulent Years': A New Look at the 1930s," in Charles Stephenson, ed., *Life and Labor: Dimensions of American Working-Class History* (Albany: State University of New York Press, 1986), 205–23; David Brody, *Workers in Industrial America: Essays on the Twentieth Century Struggle* (New York: Oxford University Press, 1980), 102–3.

98. Colin Gordon, *New Deals: Business, Labor, and Politics in America, 1920–1935* (New York: Cambridge University Press, 1994), 87–127; Newell, *Chicago and the Labor Movement*, 209–25; Donald Garnel, *The Rise of Teamster Power in the West* (Los Angeles: University of California Press, 1972), 68–73; Irving Bernstein, *Turbulent Years: A History of the American Worker, 1933–1941* (Boston: Houghton-Mifflin, 1970), 84–89.

99. Statement of Louis Marcus to Alfred J. Scotti.

100. *People v. Scalise* trial transcript, vol. 7991, p. 448.

101. Ibid., pp. 992–1001; statement by Sol Berkowitz, Sept. 20, 1935, box 2569, NYDA Papers.

102. *People v. Scalise* trial transcript, vol. 7991, p. 996.

103. Ibid., pp. 994–1005.

104. Ibid., pp. 1010–12.

105. Ibid., pp. 1013–22; *Chicago Tribune*, Apr. 28, 1940, in Dewey Scrapbooks; "Nelson Named in Inquiry on Scalise Union," *Chicago Tribune*, n.d., folder BSEIU 1935–1940, box 82, Pegler Papers.

106. Alf Oftedal, "Memo of Interview with William Bioff," May 5, 1942, pp. 1–2, FBI Serial No. 60–2149–410; report by Thomas V. Wade, Apr. 30, 1943, p. 20, FBI Serial No. 60–2149–524, both in FBI Bioff File.

## Chapter 4. The Hollywood Case: Racketeering in the 1930s from a Business Perspective

1. "Extortion Trial Nears Close," *New York Sun*, Dec. 16, 1943.

2. Ibid.

3. Robey Parks, "Felons and Film Mighty in Racket Trial Parade," *Chicago Herald and American*, Dec. 18, 1943; John Hutchinson, *The Imperfect Union: A History of Corruption in American Trade Unions* (New York: E. P. Dutton, 1970), 132; Gus Russo, *The Outfit: The Role of Chicago's Underworld in the Shaping of Modern America* (New York: Bloomsbury, 2001), 145; Malcolm Johnson, *Crime on the Labor Front* (New York: McGraw-Hill, 1950), 23.

4. Elmer L. Irey as told to William J. Slocum, *The Tax Dodgers: The Inside Story of the T-Men's War with America's Political and Underworld Hoodlums* (New York: Greenberg, 1948), 282.

5. *New York Times*, Apr. 22, 1940, 1.

6. *Chicago Tribune*, Apr. 22, 1940; *Chicago American*, Apr. 22, 1940, both in Thomas E. Dewey Scrapbooks [microfilm edition], reel 2, University of Rochester, Rochester, N.Y.

7. In a private phone conversation in Jan. 1940, Attorney General Frank Murphy told Secretary of the Treasury Henry Morgenthau Jr., "Of course, the Bioff thing is sort of a national scandal" (transcript of phone conversation, Jan. 2, 1940, p. 56, microfilm reel 62, Henry Morgenthau Jr., Morgenthau Diaries, Franklin Roosevelt Presidential Library, Hyde Park, N.Y.).

8. "Uncle Joe," *New York Times*, Apr. 17, 1941, 1; power, *New York Times*, May 10, 1943, 9.

9. [New York] *Daily News*, June 4, 1940.

10. Stipulation with Respect to the Testimony of Joseph M. Schenck, Feb. 17, 1950, p. 2, in Conference of Studio Unions et al. vs. Loew's Incorporated et al., Case No. 7306–WM, U.S. District Court, Southern District of California, Central Division, in box 1, McWilliams Papers.

11. Neil Gabler, *An Empire of Their Own: How the Jews Invented Hollywood* (New York: Crown Publishers, 1988), 112–14.

12. "General," Stipulation with Respect to the Testimony of Nicholas M. Schenck, Jan. 30, 1950, p. 1, in Conference of Studio Unions vs. Loew's Incorporated, McWilliams Papers; "cultivated power," Gabler, *An Empire of Their Own*, 113.

13. Leo C. Rosten, *Hollywood: The Movie Colony, the Movie Makers* (New York: Harcourt, Brace, 1941), 62.

14. B. E. Sackett to director, FBI, May 19, 1941, FBI Serial No. 60–2149–121; Edward A. Tamm to the director, FBI, May 19, 1941, FBI Serial No. 60–2149–117, FBI Bioff File.

15. B. E. Sackett to director, FBI, July 3, 1941, FBI Serial No. 60–2149–162, FBI Bioff File, quote is from p. 2.

16. Federal investigators had concluded by Nov. 1939 that the Hollywood studios had arranged some kind of pooled payoff in which money was collected from a number of companies and given to Bioff. But the investigators had also concluded that without the cooperation of the studios, it would be impossible to trace that money. "If such a transaction took place," reads one FBI memo, "it undoubtedly took place in the main offices of the studios involved in New York City. It appears that it would take a complete breakdown of the costs and expenses of each separate picture to trace any funds, should the $100,000 be made up from a producers' pool" (report by D. W. Magee, Nov. 14, 1939, p. 14, FBI Serial No. 60–2149–65, FBI Bioff File).

17. P. E. Foxworth to director, FBI, Nov. 27, 1941, FBI Serial No. 60–2149–338, FBI Bioff File, quote is from p. 2.

18. Indictment, United States of America vs. William Bioff, alias "Willie" Bioff, and George Browne, C110–2, May 23, 1941, U.S. District Court, Southern District of New York, pp. 1–2, copy in B. E. Sackett to director, FBI, July 3, 1941, FBI Serial No. 60–2149–162, FBI Bioff File.

19. The same language except for the fact that the 1943 indictment referred to a larger group of individuals engaged in extortion, e.g., "said defendants and said confederates" (*U.S. v. Campagna* trial transcript).

20. *U.S. v. Campagna* trial transcript, pp. 1355–56.

21. *New York Journal American*, Dec. 23, 1943, 1.

22. *Chicago Tribune*, Feb. 5, 1935, 1.

23. Ovid Demaris, *Captive City* (New York: Lyle Stuart, 1969), 34; William F. Roemer Jr., *Accardo: The Genuine Godfather* (New York: Donald I. Fine, 1995), 84–85; Gus Russo, *The Outfit: The Role of Chicago's Underworld in the Shaping of Modern America* (New York: Bloomsbury, 2001), 137; C. A. Grill, memorandum for Mr. Rosen, Aug. 8, 1941, FBI Serial No. 60-2149-207, FBI Bioff File.

24. Report by Thomas V. Wade, Feb. 15, 1943, FBI Serial No. 60-2149-469, FBI Bioff File; stenographic minutes, U.S. v. Nitto, Tax Court of the United States, Docket Numbers 8840, 8841, 8842, Columbia Reporting Company, Washington, D.C., n.d., reprinted in George H. Dunne, "Hollywood Labor Dispute—A Study in Immorality," n.d., p. 15, in box 1, McWilliams Papers.

25. Michael Charles Nielsen, "Motion Picture Craft Workers and Craft Unions in Hollywood: The Studio Era, 1912–1948" (PhD diss., University of Illinois, 1985), 128–29; C. Lawrence Christenson, "Chicago Service Trades: Cleaning and Dyeing, Motion Picture Operators and Musicians," in Harry A. Millis, research director, *How Collective Bargaining Works: A Survey of Experience in Leading American Industries* (New York: Twentieth Century Fund, 1942), 839–40.

26. Nielsen, "Motion Picture Craft Workers," 131–32; Christenson, "Chicago Service Trades," 841–42.

27. Report by W. E. Assumus, Aug. 22, 1941, pp. 4–7, FBI Serial No. 60-2149-191, FBI Bioff File; *New York Journal American*, Nov. 8, 1941, 1.

28. Report by U. J. Gerdes, Aug. 30, 1941, p. 2, FBI Serial No. 60-2149-211, FBI Bioff File.

29. Alf Oftedal, memo of interview with William Bioff, May 22, 1942, pp. 2–3, FBI Serial No. 60-2149-418, FBI Bioff File.

30. *U.S. v. Campagna* trial transcript, pp. 169–70.

31. Report by John P. Gleason, Oct. 1, 1941, pp. 20–22, FBI Serial No. 60-2149-262, FBI Bioff File; *U.S. v. Campagna* trial transcript, 169–71.

32. Report by John P. Gleason, Oct. 1, 1941, p. 21, FBI Serial No. 60-2149-262, FBI Bioff File.

33. Report by Thomas V. Wade, Apr. 10, 1943, p. 29, FBI Serial No. 60-2149-518, FBI Bioff File.

34. B&K, report by A. C. Rutzen, Oct. 17, 1941, FBI Serial No. 60-2149-305; Warner, B. E. Sackett to director, FBI, July 3, 1941, FBI Serial No. 60-2149-162; S&S, report by A. C. Rutzen, Jan. 30, 1942, FBI Serial No. 60-2149-373, all in FBI Bioff File; Economic History Services, "What Is Its Relative Value in US Dollars?" http://www.eh.net/hmit/compare/ (accessed Oct. 18, 2005).

35. Report by John P. Gleason, Oct. 1, 1941, pp. 15–20, FBI Serial No. 60–2149–262, FBI Bioff File.

36. Report by John P. Gleason, Oct. 1, 1941, pp. 15–20, FBI Serial No. 60–2149–262, quote on p. 16, FBI Bioff File.

37. Ibid., quote on p. 17.

38. Ibid., 19.

39. Ibid., 17.

40. "Union Sues on Racket Charges," *Motion Picture Herald*, Nov. 27, 1943, clipping in folder "Unions, IATSE 1943," box 87 Pegler Papers.

41. Report by U. J. Gerdes, Aug. 30, 1941, p. 30, FBI Serial No. 60–2149–211, FBI Bioff File.

42. Report by John Francis Hennessey, Feb. 10, 1943, pp. 3–4, FBI Serial No. 60–2149–464, FBI Bioff File.

43. Report by John P. Gleason, July 7, 1942, pp. 43–48, FBI Serial No. 60–2149–424, FBI Bioff File.

44. Report by U. J. Gerdes, Aug. 30, 1941, p. 1, FBI Serial No. 60–2149–211, FBI Bioff File.

45. Report by John P. Gleason, July 7, 1942, pp. 43–48, FBI Serial No. 60–2149–424; report by J. P. Gleason, Oct. 1, 1941, pp. 45–48, FBI Serial No. 60–2149–262, both in FBI Bioff File.

46. *U.S. v. Campagna* trial transcript, p. 494.

47. *New York Times*, Aug. 19, 1942, 21. The suit was settled and the companies agreed to pay $150,000 (*Gilbert et al. vs. Loew's, Inc., et al.*, Supreme Court, Special Term, New York County, 51 N.Y.S. 2d 798; 1944 N.Y., Misc. LEXIS 2615).

48. Report by John P. Gleason, July 30, 1941, pp. 42–43, FBI Serial No. 60–2149–166, FBI Bioff File.

49. Report by U. J. Gerdes, Aug. 30, 1941, p. 19, FBI Serial No. 60–2149–211, FBI Bioff File.

50. The net amount received by Bioff from these commissions would have been smaller, since over the course of those four years and four months, he paid a salary of $125 a week to the individual who officially received the commissions; that front person then passed the remainder on to Bioff. The final take would have been closer to $210,000 (C. A. Grill, memorandum to Mr. Rosen, Aug. 8, 1941, pp. 2–3, FBI Serial No. 60–2149–207).

51. Economic History Services, "What Is Its Relative Value in US Dollars?" http://www.eh.net/hmit/compare/ (accessed Oct. 18, 2005).

52. Denise Hartsough, "Crime Pays: The Studios' Labor Deals in the 1930s," in *The Studio System*, ed. Janet Staiger (New Brunswick, N.J.: Rutgers University Press, 1995), 234–35; Nielsen, "Motion Picture Craft Workers," 164; Murray Ross, *Stars and Strikes: Unionization of Hollywood* (New York: Columbia University Press, 1941), 142–48.

53. Ross, *Stars and Strikes*, 192; Nielsen, "Motion Picture Craft Workers," 11, 127–28, 176, 181–82; Christenson, "Chicago Service Trades," 846; Denise Hartsough, "Film

Union Meets Television: IA Organizing Efforts, 1947–1952," *Labor History* 33, no. 3 (Summer 1992): 360–61; regarding the studio's concern in late 1935 that Browne would resort to a projectionist's strike, see a memo enclosed in report by Thomas V. Wade, June 28, 1943, pp. 42, 48–49, FBI Serial No. 60-2149-552, FBI Bioff File.

54. *U.S. v. Campagna* trial transcript, pp. 1340–45.

55. Ibid., pp. 1809–12.

56. Ibid., p. 219.

57. Alf Oftedal, memo on interview with William Bioff, May 22, 1942, p. 4, FBI Serial No. 60-2149-418, FBI Bioff File.

58. Ibid.

59. Ibid., p. 5.

60. Report by Thomas V. Wade, Apr. 10, 1943, pp. 23–24, FBI Serial No. 60-2149-518, FBI Bioff File.

61. Report by Thomas V. Wade, Aug. 5, 1943, p. 6, FBI Serial No. 60-2149-566, FBI Bioff File.

62. Report by U. J. Gerdes, July 1, 1941, p. 41, FBI Serial No. 60-2149-133, FBI Bioff File.

63. Statement of Nicholas Schenck, president of Loew's, Inc., May 15, 1941, p. 9, in report by [name blacked out], May 31, 1941, FBI Serial No. 60-2149-123, FBI Bioff File.

64. Statement of Louis B. Mayer, May 16, 1941, pp. 2, 6, 9, in report by [name blacked out], May 31, 1941, FBI Serial No. 60-2149-123, FBI Bioff File.

65. *New York Journal American*, Oct. 21, 1943; Carey McWilliams, *The Education of Carey McWilliams* (New York: Simon and Schuster, 1979), 90.

66. Report by John P. Gleason, Dec. 4, 1941, pp. 19–20, FBI Serial No. 60-2149-346, FBI Bioff File.

67. Nielsen, "Motion Picture Craft Workers," 196–96, 217; Muir, "All Right Gentlemen Do We Get the Money?" 84; Hartsough, "Crime Pays," 238.

68. Report by James G. Findlay, Aug. 25, 1939, p. 7, FBI Serial No. 60-2149-54, FBI Bioff File.

69. Report by Thomas V. Wade, June 28, 1943, p. 43, FBI Serial No. 60-21490-552, FBI Bioff File.

70. Dunne, "Hollywood Labor Dispute," 8–9.

71. In the tax trial, the lawyers for Nitto's estate had argued that a court precedent, *Wilcox v. Commissioner*, indicated that money that was "fraudulently or illegally acquired" was nontaxable. In this case, the government and the defendants switched places: Nitto's lawyers sought to demonstrate that extortion had taken place while the government's attorney presented the money as payment for services provided (Estate of Joseph Nitto et al. v. Commissioner of Internal Revenue, U.S. Tax Court, 13 T.C. 858, 1949 U.S. Tax Court Lexis 29).

72. Report by [name blacked out], May 6, 1939, p. 12, FBI Serial No. 60-2149-33, FBI Bioff File.

73. Ibid.

74. Hartsough, "Crime Pays," 230–32; Nielsen, "Motion Picture Craft Workers," 181, 220; $1,200 annual earnings in report by [name blacked out], May 6, 1939, p. 12, FBI Serial No. 60–2149–33, FBI Bioff File.

75. Ross, *Stars and Strikes*, 105, 149–53, 161–62, 192–94.

76. Gerald Horne, *Class Struggle in Hollywood, 1930–1950: Moguls, Mobsters, Stars, Reds, and Trade Unionists* (Austin: University of Texas Press, 2001), 54–55.

77. Nielsen, "Motion Picture Craft Workers," 196–206; Ross, *Stars and Strikes*, 192–94.

78. Alf Oftedal, memorandum of interview with William Bioff, Feb. 17, 1942, pp. 8–9, FBI Serial No. 60–2149–408, FBI Bioff File.

79. Mike Nielsen and Gene Mailes, *Hollywood's Other Blacklist: Union Struggles in the Studio System* (London: British Film Institute, 1995), 27–28.

80. Ross, *Stars and Strikes*, 161–62.

81. Exhibit 29, statement of Joseph Schenck, June 21, 1938, pp. 20–21, in report by D. W. Magee, Jan. 24, 1940, FBI Serial No. 60–2149–74, FBI Bioff File.

82. Alf Oftedal, memorandum of interview with William Bioff, Feb. 17, 1942, pp. 9–10, FBI Serial No. 60–2149–408, FBI Bioff File.

83. Nielsen, "Motion Picture Craft Workers," 204–9; Ross, *Stars and Strikes*, 194–95.

84. Horne, *Class Struggle in Hollywood,* 54.

85. U.S. National Commission on Law Observance and Enforcement (Wickersham Commission), *Report on the Cost of Crime* (Washington, D.C.: Government Printing Office, 1931), 407–8; "Why Stand for Racketeers," *Saturday Evening Post* 204 (Aug. 1, 1931): 20.

86. Andrew Wender Cohen, *The Racketeer's Progress: Chicago and the Struggle for the Modern American Economy, 1900–1940* (New York: Cambridge University Press, 2004), 273–76; Alan Block, *East Side-West Side: Organizing Crime in New York, 1930–1950* (New Brunswick, N.J.: Transaction Books, 1985), 163–82.

87. Report by John P. Gleason, July 7, 1942, p. 45, FBI Serial No. 60–2149–424, FBI Bioff File.

## Chapter 5. Union Members and Corruption: Exploitation and Disillusionment

1. *Los Angeles Times*, Nov. 14, 1937, 5; Nov. 13, 1937, part 2, 1; Jeff Kibre, "Report on Motion Picture Drive," copy sent to Harry Bridges and reprinted in *Los Angeles Citizen*, June 30, 1939, 1; *Proceedings of the International Alliance of Theatrical Stage Employes and Moving Picture Machine Operators of the United States and Canada, Thirty-Fourth Convention, June 6th to 9th, 1938, inclusive, held at Cleveland, Ohio* (Cleveland: Doyle and Waltz, 1938), 52–54, 128–30.

2. *Los Angeles Times*, Nov. 14, 1937, 5.

3. Ibid.

4. *People v. Scalise* trial transcript, vols. 7991–92, pp. 177–80, 1027–29, 1031–34, 1162–64, 2373–78, 2590–91; *New York Journal-American*, Sept. 27, 1945, clipping in folder BSEIU 1945–47, box 82, Pegler Papers; *Chicago American*, May 5, 1940; *Chicago Tribune*, May 4, 1940, in Dewey Scrapbooks.

5. *People v. Scalise* trial transcript, vol. 7991, pp. 232–33,1308,1352–53; James J. Bambrick, *The Building Service Story* (New York: Labor History Press, 1948), 2–4, 7–19, 22–28, 37–40; Edward B. Bell to Westbrook Pegler, Mar. 6, 1942, folder BSEIU, 1941–43, box 82, Pegler Papers.

6. *New York Times*, Oct. 8, 1940, 1; memorandum, A. Robertson to Mr. Gurfein, May 22, 1940, box 2566, NYDA Papers; Bambrick, *Building Service Story*, 13.

7. Bambrick, *Building Service Story*, 29, 42; *New York Times*, Apr. 14, 1944, 21; Aug. 23, 1944, 20; Aug. 29, 1944, 19; *Chicago Tribune*, Apr. 27, 1940, Dewey Scrapbooks; *New York Journal American*, Sept. 27, 1945, news clipping, folder BSEIU, 1945–47, box 82, Pegler Papers; memo on Local 32B and David Sullivan, unsigned, n.d., folder BSEIU, undated, box 82, Pegler Papers.

8. Memorandum entitled "Bowling and Billiard Academy Employees Union Local 94, B.S.E.I.U.," n.d., box 2566, NYDA Papers.

9. Frank C. Neary to [received by district attorney's office, New York County], Dec. 12, 1940; memorandum entitled, "Bowling and Billiard Academy Employees Union Local 94, B.S.E.I.U.," both in box 2566, NYDA Papers.

10. An example of the way of some employers in New York's hotel industry turned to Scalise to avoid the possibility of a more militant form of labor union is described in Edward B. Bell to Westbrook Pegler, Mar. 6, 1942, folder Building Service Employees International Union, 1941–43, box 82, Pegler Papers.

11. *New York Times*, Apr. 22, 1940, 1; *Chicago Tribune*, Apr. 22, 1940; *Chicago American*, Apr. 22, 1940, both in Dewey Scrapbook.

12. *New York Times*, Apr. 27, 1940, 1; anonymous to Mr. Dewey, Mar. 17, 1940, box 2566, NYDA Papers.

13. Marie H. to Westbrook Pegler, Jan. 29, 1942, folder BSEIU 1935–1940, box 82, Pegler Papers.

14. The total in payoff money received from employers by Bioff, Browne, and the Outfit amounted to $1,310,000, while the 2 percent assessment yielded $1.5 million, report by A. C. Rutzen, Oct. 17, 1941, FBI Serial No. 60–2149–305; B. E. Sackett to director, FBI, July 3, 1941, FBI Serial No. 60–2149–162; report by A. C. Rutzen, Jan. 30, 1942, FBI Serial No. 60–2149–373; A. Grill, memorandum to Mr. Rosen, Aug. 8, 1941, pp. 2–3, FBI Serial No. 60–2149–207; report by John P. Gleason, Oct. 1, 1941, pp. 20–22, FBI Serial No. 60–2149–262, FBI Bioff File; *U.S. v. Campagna* trial transcript, 169–71.

15. Report by Thomas V. Wade, Apr. 10, 1943, p. 37, FBI Serial No. 60–2149–518, FBI Bioff File.

16. "Constitution and By-Laws of the International Alliance of Theatrical Stage

Employes and Moving Picture Machine Operators of the United States and Canada, Revised and Adopted by the Thirty-second Convention, Jefferson County Armory, Louisville, Ky., June 4, 1934," 6–15; "Constitution and By-Laws of the International Alliance of Theatrical Stage Employes and Moving Picture Machine Operators of the United States and Canada, Revised and Adopted by the Thirty-third Convention, Municipal Auditorium, Kansas City, Mo., June 10, 1936," 7–20, 25–29; both on reel 226, *American Labor Union Constitutions and Proceedings, Part 2* (Sanford, N.C.: Microfilming Corporation of America, 1978). For a sample of the convention procedures, see "Proceedings of International Alliance of Theatrical and Stage Employes and Moving Picture Machine Operators of the United States and Canada, Thirty-third Convention, Held in Municipal Auditorium, June 8th to 11th, 1936, Inclusive, at Kansas City, Mo.," 313–19, 327–28, 347–48, reel 230, *American Labor Union Constitutions and Proceedings, Part 2* (Sanford, N.C.: Microfilming Corporation of America, 1978).

17. "IATSE Constitution, 1934," 18–20, 28; "IATSE Constitution, 1936," 27–31, 74.

18. Philip Taft, *The Structure and Government of Labor Unions* (Cambridge: Harvard University Press, 1954), 65–116.

19. Report by W. F. Caldwell, June 16, 1941, p. 3, FBI Serial No. 60–2149–137, FBI Bioff File; for an example of that report, see "IATSE Proceedings, 1936," 286–87.

20. The specific amount is from the report by Wade, Apr. 10, 1943, p. 177, FBI Bioff File.

21. *Proceedings of International Alliance of Theatrical Stage Employes and Moving Picture Machine Operators of the United States and Canada, Thirty-Third Convention, Held at Municipal Auditorium, June 8th to 11th, 1936, Inclusive, at Kansas City, Mo.* (Newark, N.J.: International Musician Press, 1936), 129, 133; *Proceedings of International Alliance of Theatrical Stage Employes and Moving Picture Machine Operators of the United States and Canada, Thirty-Fourth Convention, Held in Cleveland Public Auditorium, June 6th to 9th, 1938, Inclusive, at Cleveland, Ohio* (Cleveland: Doyle and Waltz, 1938), 122, 147.

22. *Proceedings of International Alliance 1936,* 118, 128–29, 133. The variation in cites stems from the fact that over the course of research, two different editions of the proceedings were used; italicized cite refers to bound volumes at the Library of the Department of Labor, and not italicized is from the microfilm edition. The editions have different page numbers; *Proceedings of International Alliance 1938,* 131–32, 147.

23. *New York Times,* Dec. 1, 1935, 30; Dec. 9, 1935, p. 25; Dec. 10, 1935, 31; Murray Ross, *Stars and Strikes: Unionization of Hollywood* (New York: Columbia University Press, 1941), 192.

24. Alf Oftedal, memorandum of interview with William Bioff, Apr. 30, 1942, p. 2, FBI Serial No. 60–2149–410, FBI Bioff File; Thomas V. Wade, summary memorandum for the Bureau, Sept. 28, 1943, p. 42; report by Wade, Apr. 10, 1943, p. 186, all in FBI Bioff File.

25. Wade, Summary Memorandum for the Bureau, Sept. 28, 1943, pp. 41–44; report by Wade, Apr. 10, 1943, pp. 153–84, both in FBI Bioff File.

26. Report by Wade, Apr. 10, 1943, pp. 156–58, FBI Bioff File.

27. Ibid., pp. 182–83, FBI Bioff File; Economic History Services, "What Is Its Relative Value in US Dollars?" http://www.eh.net/hmit/compare/ (accessed Jan. 24, 2006).

28. Statement of General Executive Board, *Proceedings of the International Alliance of Theatrical Stage Employes and Moving Picture Machine Operators of the United States and Canada, Thirty-Eighth Convention, Held in Stevens Hotel, Chicago, Illinois, July 22 to July 26, 1946, Inclusive* (Cleveland: Lichty, 1946), pp. 182–86, quotes, p. 184 and 183; "1934: The Two Percent Assessment," http://www.iatseintl.org/about/timeline/popup.html (accessed Feb. 8, 2006).

29. Report by Wade, Apr. 10, 1943, pp. 19–20, 35–36, 155–56, 158, 195–96, FBI Bioff File; *Proceedings of the International Alliance of Theatrical Stage Employes and Moving Picture Machine Operators of the United States and Canada, Thirty-Sixth Convention, Held in Memorial Hall, June 1st to 5th, 1942, Columbus, Ohio* (Cleveland: Lichty, 1942), pp. 67–68; *Statement of the General Executive Board of the International Alliance of Theatrical Stage Employes and Moving Picture Machine Operators of the United States and Canada*, Mar. 16, 1945, in folder Unions, IATSE, 1945–1948, box 88, Pegler Papers.

30. "Proceedings of the International Alliance of Theatrical Stage Employes and Moving Picture Machine Operators of the United States and Canada, Thirty-fifth Convention, Held in Jefferson County Armory, June 3rd to 6th, 1940, Inclusive, at Louisville, Kentucky," p. 365, reel 230, *American Labor Union Constitutions and Proceedings, Part 2* (Sanford, N.C.: Microfilming Corporation of America, 1978).

31. *Proceedings of the International Alliance, 1938*, p. 121; descriptions of Circella and his role as Browne's companion in this period are in "Stipulation with Respect to Testimony of James E. Coston, Conference of Studio Unions vs. Loews Inc.," Jan. 30, 1950, p. 10, box 1, McWilliams Papers, ca. 1905–1980; report by John P. Gleason, July 30, 1941, p. 25, FBI Serial No. 60–2149–111, FBI Bioff File; Edward A. Tamm, memorandum for the director, re: Nick Circella, Sept. 2, 1941, p. 6, FBI Serial No. 60–2149–212, FBI Bioff File.

32. Report by Thomas V. Wade, June 18, 1943, pp. 9, 15, FBI Serial No. 60–2149–552, FBI Bioff File.

33. Jack Gould, "Note on the Stagehands' Meeting," *New York Times*, June 16, 1940, XI.

34. Alf Oftedal, memorandum of interview with William Bioff, May 18, 1942, p. 5, FBI Serial No. 60–2149–418, FBI Bioff File.

35. Report by I. J. Kellogg, Aug. 8, 1941, pp. 10–11, FBI Serial No. 60–2149–170, FBI Bioff File.

36. [name blacked out] to Attorney General Edgar Hoover, Nov. 26, 1937, FBI Serial No. 60–2149–12, FBI Bioff File.

37. Deposition of Helen Cumberland, Aug. 8 and 9, 1940, in the People of the

State of New York vs. George Scalise, pp. 24–25, in box 2566, NYDA Papers; *People v. Scalise* trial transcript, vol. 7991, pp. 1633–35, 2236–51, 2387–88, 2590–91; *New York Journal-American*, Sept. 27, 1945, clipping in folder BSEIU 1945–47, box 82, Pegler Papers; *Chicago American*, May 5, 1940; *Chicago Tribune*, May 4, 1940, both in Dewey Scrapbooks; *Chicago Tribune*, Sept. 18, 1940, p. 1; *San Francisco Examiner*, Feb. 15, 1940; *San Francisco Examiner*, Feb. 17, 1940, both news clippings in Envelope: labor unions—Building Service Employees, in *San Francisco Examiner* News Clipping File, San Francisco History Center, San Francisco Public Library, San Francisco, Calif.

38. Report by Wade, Apr. 10, 1943, p. 18, FBI Bioff File.

39. *Chicago Tribune*, Feb. 5, 1935, 1; report by Thomas V. Wade, Feb. 15, 1943, FBI Serial No. 60–2149–469, FBI Bioff File; stenographic minutes, U.S. v. Nitto, Tax Court of the United States, Docket Numbers 8840, 8841, 8842, Columbia Reporting Company, Washington, D.C., n.d., reprinted in George H. Dunne, "Hollywood Labor Dispute: A Study In Immorality," n.d., p. 15, in box 1, McWilliams Papers.

40. Report by Wade, Apr. 10, 1943, p. 18, FBI Bioff File.

41. Ibid.; medical information, report by James A. Conerty, Nov. 4, 1943, FBI Serial No. 60–2149–662; "acute anxiety," S. J. Drayton to the director, Oct. 26, 1943, FBI Serial No. 602149–647, FBI Bioff File.

42. *Proceedings of the International Alliance, 1942*, 67–68; Richard F. Walsh to the secretaries of all local unions, Mar. 16, 1945, with attached "Statement of the Executive Board of the International Alliance of Theatrical Stage Employes and Moving Picture Machine Operators of the United States and Canada," folder Unions, IATSE, 1945–48, box 88, Pegler Papers.

43. Report by Wade, Apr. 10, 1943, p. 69, FBI Bioff File.

44. Report by Ira J. Kellogg, Aug. 28, 1941, p. 6, FBI Serial No. 60–2149–201, FBI Bioff File.

45. Gould, "Note on the Stagehands' Meeting."

## Chapter 6. Union Members and Corruption: The Potential for Reform

1. Westbrook Pegler, "Fair Enough," Nov. 24, 1939, box 119, Pegler Papers.

2. He wrote at one point, "I am also an enthusiastic believer in Red Baiting" (Pegler, "Fair Enough," Aug. 31, 1938, box 119, Pegler Papers).

3. Alf Oftedal, memorandum of interview with William Bioff, May 19, 1942, pp. 3–4, in FBI Serial No. 60–2149–418, FBI Bioff File; and U.S. v. Campagna trial transcript.

4. Larry Ceplair, "A Communist Labor Organizer in Hollywood: Jeff Kibre Challenges IATSE, 1937–1939," *Velvet Light Trap* 23 (1989): 64–66; documents from the files of the House Un-American Activities Committee indicate that Kibre attended UCLA from 1925 to 1929, graduated with an AB, and majored in English (report entitled "Jeff Kibre, also known as Jacob Plane Kibre, Barry Wood," Sept. 16, 1947, Jeff

Kibre, Investigation Section, Un-American Activities Committee, Exhibits, Evidence, Etc., box 4, Record Group 233, Records of the House of Representatives, NARA, Washington, D.C.).

5. Ceplair, "A Communist Labor Organizer in Hollywood," 65–66; regarding his columns against ROTC, George Garrigues, "A History of the UCLA Daily Bruin, 1919–1955: Chapter 5, The Decade of the Thirties," http://www.ulwaf.com/Daily-Bruin -History/05A_Thirties.html (accessed Feb. 8, 2006); joining CPUSA, J. Edgar Hoover to Brigadier General Sherman Miles, June 18, 1941, re: North American Aviation Inc., p. 13, File No. 10104–2063, Military Intelligence Division Files, 1917–1941, Records of the War Department General and Special Staffs, Record Group 165, NARA; 1939 registration card [Jeff Kibre], Barry Wood, Jeff Kibre Investigative Name File, series 5, box 155, House Un-American Activities Committee, Record Group 233, NARA, Washington, D.C.

6. Robert H. Zieger, The CIO, 1935–1955 (Chapel Hill: University of North Carolina Press, 1995), 253 -57, quote is from 253.

7. Taft, Structure and Government of Trade Unions, 13–19; Howard Kimeldorf, Reds or Rackets? The Making of Radical and Conservative Unions on the Waterfront (Berkeley: University of California Press, 1988), 86–89, 91–92, 96–97, 120–25; David Witwer, Corruption and Reform in the Teamsters Union (Chicago: University of Illinois Press, 2003), 117–22.

8. Ceplair, "A Communist Labor Organizer in Hollywood," 66; House Un-American Activities Committee files indicate that the party listed him under the name of Barry Wood, in order to disguise his identity (1939 registration card [Jeff Kibre], Barry Wood, Jeff Kibre Investigative Name File, series 5, box 155, House Un-American Activities Committee, Record Group 233, NARA).

9. Ceplair, "A Communist Labor Organizer in Hollywood," 66.

10. Jeff Kibre, "Report on Motion Picture Drive," copy sent to Harry Bridges, Oct. 7, 1937, reprinted in Los Angeles Citizen, June 30, 1939, 1.

11. Mike Nielsen and Gene Mailes, Hollywood's Other Blacklist: Union Struggles in the Studio System (London: British Film Institute, 1995), 30–31, 74–75; House Un-American Activities Committee files put Hentschel on the membership list of the Los Angeles division of the CPUSA in 1938 and 1939; to protect his identity, the party enrolled him officially under the pseudonym John F. Meyers (report entitled "Irving Paul Hentschel," May 26, 1952, Individual Name Files, Files of the Reference Section, box 133, House Un-American Activities Committee, Record Group 233, Records of the House of Representatives, NARA, Washington, D.C.).

12. Proceedings International Alliance, 1938, 169.

13. Irving Bernstein, Turbulent Years: A History of the American Worker, 1933–1941 (New York: Houghton Mifflin, 1970), 252–98; Bruce Nelson, Workers on the Waterfront: Seamen, Longshoremen, and Unionism in the 1930s (Chicago: University of Illinois Press, 1988), 103–69, 238; Zieger, The CIO, 71–73.

14. Jeff Kibre, "Report on Motion Picture Drive"; Nielsen, *Hollywood's Other Blacklist*, 29–31; Ceplair, "A Communist Labor Organizer in Hollywood," 68–69.

15. Murray Ross, *Stars and Strikes: Unionization of Hollywood* (New York: Columbia University Press, 1941), 4; Nielsen, *Hollywood's Other Blacklist*, 33.

16. Kibre, "Report on Motion Picture Drive."

17. Michael Denning, *The Cultural Front: The Laboring of American Culture in the Twentieth Century* (New York: Verso, 1996), 4–5.

18. Kevin Starr, *Endangered Dreams: The Great Depression and California* (New York: Oxford University Press, 1996), 262–63; Daniel Geary, "Carey McWilliams and Anti-Fascism, 1934–1943," *Journal of American History* 90, no. 3 (Dec. 2003): http://www.historycooperative.org/journals/jah/90.3/geary.html (accessed Dec. 12, 2005), par. 8–9, 25–26; Carey McWilliams, *The Education of Carey McWilliams* (New York: Simon and Schuster, 1979), 86–87.

19. Carey McWilliams to Louis Adamic, Dec. 26, 1937, box 1, McWilliams Papers.

20. Geary, "Carey McWilliams and Anti-Fascism," pars. 25–26.

21. McWilliams to Adamic, Dec. 26, 1937.

22. Ceplair, "A Communist Labor Organizer in Hollywood," 68; McWilliams, *Education of Carey McWilliams*, 87.

23. "Bioff Exposed!" *IA Progressive Bulletin* 1, no. 11 (Dec. 22, 1937): 1, in folder "Unions, International Alliance of Theatrical Stage Employees, 1937–1939, box 87," Pegler Papers.

24. "Bioff Exposed!" 1.

25. McWilliams, *Education of Carey McWilliams*, 87; Howard R. Philbrick, *Legislative Investigative Report* (Sacramento, Calif.: Edwin H. Atherton and Associates, 1938), 25–27.

26. Philbrick, *Legislative Investigative Report*, 27–28.

27. Ibid., 27–30, quote appears on 29–30.

28. Ibid., 29–38; "Screen Union Quiz Launched," *Los Angeles Times*, Nov. 9, 1937, 1; "Studio Union Affairs to be Aired Today," *Los Angeles Times*, Nov. 12, 1937, part 2, 1; "Studio Union Power Told," *Los Angeles Times*, Nov. 13, 1937, part 2, 1; the allegation regarding an additional $20,000 cash payment to Neblett is from Stipulation with Respect to the Testimony of Joseph M. Schenck, Feb. 17, 1950, pp. 4–5, in Transcript of U.S. District Court for the Southern District of California, conference of Studio Unions (Plaintiffs) versus Loew's Incorporated (Defendants), box 1, McWilliams Papers.

29. Philbrick, *Legislative Investigative Report*, 36; the text of the report was inserted into *Proceedings International Alliance, 1938*, 59.

30. *Los Angeles Times*, Nov. 16, 1937, 13; Nov. 17, 1937, part 2, 1.

31. Philbrick, *Legislative Investigative Report*, 1–5, 25–39.

32. Ibid., 35–36; Report by D. W. Magee, Nov. 14, 1939, pp. 6–11, FBI Serial No. 60-2149-65, FBI Bioff File; *San Francisco Chronicle*, Aug. 5, 1938, 1.

33. *U.S. v. Campagna* trial transcript, pp. 286–87; see also report by U. J. Gerdes, July 1, 1941, FBI Serial No. 60–2149–133, FBI Bioff File.

34. *Los Angeles Times*, Sept. 8, 1938, 4.

35. Ibid., reprinted in report by [name blacked out], Apr. 21, 1939, p. 4, FBI Serial No. 60–149–29X, FBI Bioff File.

36. Alf Oftedal, memorandum of interview with William Bioff, May 19, 1942, pp. 3–4, in FBI Serial No. 60–2149–418, FBI Bioff File; *Proceedings International Alliance, 1938*, 147; *IATSE Proceedings, 1940*, 184–85.

37. *IATSE Proceedings, 1940*, 184–85; *U.S. v. Campagna* trial transcript, pp. 316–17, quote p. 317; regarding continuing role in Hollywood, report by I. J. Kellogg, July 21, 1939, pp. 8–17; FBI Serial No. 60–2149–158, FBI Bioff File.

38. Philbrick, *Legislative Investigative Report*, 35, 37; Stipulation with Respect to Testimony of Joseph M. Schenck, Feb. 17, 1950, pp. 3–4.

39. [Name blacked out] to Attorney Gen. Edgar Hoover [*sic*], Nov. 26, 1937, FBI Serial No. 60–2149–12; John Edgar Hoover, memorandum for Assistant Attorney General Dickenson, Mar. 18, 1936, FBI Serial No. 60–2149–X2; Robert H. Jackson, memorandum for the director of the Federal Bureau of Investigation, June 7, 1937, FBI Serial No. 60–2149–2; V.W. Peterson to the director, FBI, June 11, 1937, FBI Serial No. 60–2149–3; John Edgar Hoover to [name blacked out], Dec. 16, 1937, FBI Serial No. 60–2149–12, all in FBI Bioff File.

40. *Proceedings International Alliance, 1938*, 164–87.

41. Ibid., 173.

42. Murray Ross, "The C.I.O. Loses Hollywood," *Nation* (Oct. 7, 1939): 377.

43. Ross, *Stars and Strikes*, 44–47, 106, 152–53, 161; David F. Prindle, *The Politics of Glamour: Ideology and Democracy in the Screen Actors Guild* (Madison: University of Wisconsin Press, 1988), 16–29.

44. Prindle, *Politics of Glamour*, 26–31, 35–36; Ross, *Stars and Strikes*, 161–63.

45. *New York Times*, May 10, 1937, 1.

46. George Frazier, "Nobody Pushes Bob Around," *Collier's* 123 (June 4, 1949): 73.

47. Alf Oftedal, memorandum of interview with William Bioff, Feb. 17, 1942, pp. 8–9, FBI Serial No. 60–2149–408, FBI Bioff File.

48. Ross, *Stars and Strikes*, 199–200; Prindle, *Politics of Glamour*, 32–36.

49. *U.S. v. Campagna* trial transcript, pp. 326, 1124–26, quote p. 1126.

50. *New York Times*, Sept. 26, 1937, 179.

51. *Proceedings International Alliance, 1938*, 195–96.

52. Ross, "The C.I.O. Loses Hollywood," 375–76.

53. As Joseph Schenck later explained, "The Screen Actors Guild was fearful that Bioff was going to try and absorb them, particularly the junior faction of that guild. . . . They thought there was a conspiracy between the producers and that labor organization [IATSE] to take over, to force the Actors into the labor organization, and if the producers wanted to force the Actors into the labor organization they must

have some kind of an understanding with the labor organization where they could handle the Actors better through the labor organization than they could handle them independently" (Exhibit 29, deposition of Joseph Schenck, taken Nov. 22, 1938, p. 22, in report by D. W. Magee, Jan. 24, 1940, FBI Serial No. 60–2149–74, FBI Bioff File).

54. *New York Times*, Aug. 2, 1939, 24.

55. Pete Martin, "Fightin' Bob—The Hollywood Crusader," *Saturday Evening Post* 223 (Oct. 7, 1950): 41, 100; Frazier, "Nobody Pushes Bob Around," 25; *New York Times*, Sept. 28, 1981, B6.

56. Reviewing SAG's history up to 1938, one observer noted that Montgomery's achievements had "won unstinted praise from the union and the public—a public, incidentally, which not so long ago thought of him as a movie playboy" (Morton Thompson, "Hollywood Is a Union Town," *Nation* 146 [Apr. 2, 1938]: 383).

57. Prindle, *Politics of Glamour*, 32–33; Martin, "Fightin' Bob," 98; Frazier, "Nobody Pushes Bob Around," 25.

58. Martin, "Fightin' Bob," 41, 97; Frazier, "Nobody Pushes Bob Around," 72–73; *New York Times*, Sept. 28, 1981, B6.

59. *New York Times*, May 27, 1940, 9; June 30, 1940, 103; Nov. 27, 1944, 25; Mar. 17, 1943, 12; July 13, 1944, 15; James E. Wise Jr. and Anne Collier Rehill, *Stars in Blue: Movie Actors in America's Sea Services* (Annapolis, Md.: Naval Institute Press, 1997), 51–60.

60. George Murphy and Victor Lasky, *"Say . . . Didn't You Used to Be George Murphy?"* (New York: Bartholomew House, 1970), 221.

61. Ibid.; Prindle, *Politics of Glamour*, 32–33.

62. Murphy, *"Say . . .,"* 220; Elmer L. Irey, as told to William J. Slocum, *The Tax Dodgers: The Inside Story of the T-Men's War with Political and Underworld Hoodlums* (New York: Greenberg, 1948), 283.

63. FBI agents summarized the contents of SAG's file on Bioff in report by [name blacked out], Apr. 21, 1939, FBI Serial No. 60–2149–29; regarding SAG's use of the Edwin Atherton Agency, see G. N. Willis, memorandum for Mr. E. A. Tamm, Nov. 8, 1939, Serial No. 60–2149–61X, both in FBI Bioff File.

64. Transcript of meeting, July 1, 1938, p. 35, microfilm reel 36, Morgenthau Diaries.

65. L. R. Pennington, memorandum for Mr. Tamm, May 31, 1939, FBI Serial No. 60–2149–36, FBI Bioff File.

66. Ibid.; G. N. Willis, memorandum for Mr. E. A. Tamm.

67. Transcript of meeting, July 1, 1938, pp. 34–35; Henry Morgenthau Jr. to Robert Montgomery, July 2, Morgenthau Diaries.

68. James B. Jacobs, *Mobsters, Unions, and Feds: The Mafia and the American Labor Movement* (New York: New York University Press, 2006), 10–13; Claire Bond Potter, *War on Crime: Bandits, G-Men, and the Politics of Mass Culture* (New Brunswick, N.J.: Rutgers University Press, 1998), 84–106, 13–180, 188–202; Robert J. Schoenberg, *Mr. Capone* (New York: William Morrow, 1992), 241–48, 298–99; Rudolph H. Hart-

mann, *The Kansas City Investigation: Pendergast's Downfall, 1938–1939* (Columbia: University of Missouri Press, 1999), passim.

69. Prindle, *Politics of Glamour*, 33–35; Ross, *Stars and Strikes*, 199–200; Nielsen, "Motion Picture Craft Workers," 233–35.

70. Transcript of meeting, July 1, 1938, pp. 34–37, Morgenthau Diaries.

71. Ibid., 35–36.

72. Transcript of meeting, July 8, 1938, p. 288, reel 36, Morgenthau Diaries.

73. Transcript of meeting, Apr. 11, 1939, p. 223, reel 47, Morgenthau Diaries.

74. Report by [name blacked out], Apr. 21, 1939, FBI Serial No. 60–2149–29; J. Edgar Hoover to Robert Montgomery, Apr. 29, 1939, FBI Serial No. 60–2149–30, both in FBI Bioff File.

75. Report by [name blacked out] Apr. 21, 1939, FBI Serial No. 60–2149–23X; report by [name blacked out] May 6, 1939, FBI Serial No. 60–2149–33; memorandum re: George Browne, with aliases, William Bioff, with aliases, International Alliance of Theatrical Stage Employees, Antitrust, Dec. 15, 1939, FBI Serial No. 60–2149–76; Nielsen, "Motion Picture Craft Workers," 230–31.

76. [Name blacked out] to Attorney Gen. Edgar Hoover [*sic*], Nov. 26, 1937, FBI Serial No. 60–2149–12; John Edgar Hoover to [name blacked out], Dec. 16, 1937, FBI Serial No. 60–2149–12, both in FBI Bioff File.

77. Edward F. McGrady to William Green, Nov. 23, 1934; William Green to Paul David, Nov. 27, 1934, both on reel 46, American Federation of Labor Records: The Samuel Gompers Era, microfilm edition, Record Group RG-1, Records of the Office of the President: National and International Unions Correspondence, Building Service Employees, George Meany Memorial Archives, Silver Spring, Md.

78. *New York Times*, Aug. 2, 1939, 24.

79. Westbrook Pegler, "Fair Enough," Feb. 28, 1938, box 119, Pegler Papers.

80. Pegler, "Fair Enough," Mar. 1, 1938, box 119, Pegler Papers.

81. Carey McWilliams, "Racketeers and Movie Magnates," *New Republic* 105, no. 17 (Oct. 17, 1941): 534; Westbrook Pegler to Roy Howard, Mar. 19, 1938, folder Executive Correspondence, City File, New York City, Westbrook Pegler, box 142, Howard Papers; "Bioff Exposed!" *IA Progressive Bulletin* 1, no. 11 (Dec. 22, 1937): 1, in folder Unions, International Alliance of Theatrical Stage Employees, 1937–1939, box 87, Pegler Papers.

82. Pegler, "Fair Enough," May 19, 1938, box 119, Pegler Papers.

83. Pegler, "Fair Enough," Aug. 31, 1939, box 119, Pegler Papers.

84. IA Progressives told FBI agents this history firsthand; those accounts, including descriptions of the harassment dissidents encountered, can be found in report by [name blacked out], May 6, 1939, pp. 5–10, FBI Serial No. 60–2149–33; and [n.a.], memorandum for the director, Oct. 6, 1939, FBI Serial No. 60–2149–57X; another firsthand account of a participant in the IA Progressives is Nielsen, *Hollywood's Other Blacklist*, 53–56.

85. Ross, "The C.I.O. Loses Hollywood," 374–75; Nielsen, *Hollywood's Other Black-list*, 57–58; Ceplair, "A Communist Labor Organizer in Hollywood," 66, 72.

86. "AFL Unions Join in Opposition to CIO-Communist Move to Control Stu-dios," *Los Angeles Citizen*, Sept. 15, 1939, 1; Ross, "The C.I.O. Loses Hollywood," 375; Nielsen, *Hollywood's Other Blacklist*, 58–60.

87. Nielsen, "Motion Picture Craft Workers," 235–36; Ross, *Stars and Strikes*, 200–201; Denise Hartsough, "Studio Labor Relations in 1939: Historical and Social Analy-sis" (PhD diss., University of Wisconsin, 1987), 65–77.

88. Ross, "The C.I.O. Loses Hollywood," 377.

89. Nielsen, *Hollywood's Other Blacklist*, 62–63; Nancy Lynn Schwartz, *The Holly-wood Writers Wars* (New York: Knopf, 1982), 221–22; report by [name blacked out], Sept. 2, 1940, pp. 4–9, FBI Serial No. 60–2149–101, FBI Bioff File.

90. Report by [name blacked out], Sept. 2, 1940, p. 8, FBI Serial No. 60–2149–101, FBI Bioff File.

91. Nielsen, *Hollywood's Other Blacklist*, 62.

92. Report by [name blacked out], Sept. 2, 1940, p. 4, FBI Serial No. 60–2149–101, FBI Bioff File.

93. *New York Times*, Sept. 4, 1939, 18.

94. Minutes of a special meeting of the board of directors of the Screen Actors Guild, Inc., Sept. 2, 1939, p. 1274; minutes of a special meeting of the board of di-rectors of the Screen Actors Guild, Inc., Sept. 3, 1939, p. 1276; Kenneth Thomson to William Bioff, Sept. 3, 1939, printed on p. 1277 of the minutes, Screen Actors Guild, Los Angeles, Calif.

95. Prindle, *Politics of Glamour*, 35–36; the full text of the statement appears in "AFL Unions Join in Opposition to CIO-Communist Move to Control Studios," *Los Angeles Citizen*, Sept. 15, 1939, 1.

96. E. A. Tamm, memorandum re: George E. Browne, Oct. 6, 1939, p. 6, FBI Serial No. 60–2149–57X1, FBI Bioff File.

97. *New York Times*, Sept. 10, 1939, X1.

98. [N.a.], memorandum for the director, re: George E. Browne, with aliases, Wil-liam Bioff, with aliases, International Alliance of Theatrical Stage Employees, Oct. 6, 1939, FBI Serial No. 60–2149–57X1, FBI Bioff File; Elmer Irey, memorandum for the secretary, Apr. 8, 1939, folder Confidential Reports about People, Jan.-June 1939, box 36, Morgenthau Papers; J.W. Buzzell, "Offer to Aid Him in Every Way," *Los Angeles Citizen*, Aug. 18, 1939, 1; *New York Times*, Aug. 15, 1939, 23.

99. "Nothing to indicate," J. G. Findlay, memorandum for the SAC re: International Alliance of Theatrical Stage Employees, Oct. 13, 1939, FBI Serial No. 60–21490–57X3; "fishing expedition," J. P. Wenschel to Samuel O. Clark Jr., in re: Joseph M. Schenck et al., Oct. 12, 1939, pp. 274–75, microfilm reel 58, Morgenthau Diaries.

100. D. W. Magee, memorandum for special agent in charge, personal and confi-dential, Oct. 13, 1939, p. 1, FBI Serial No. 60–2149–57X2, FBI Bioff File.

101. Findlay, memorandum for the SAC.

102. Wenschel to Clark, in re: Joseph M. Schenck et al., Morgenthau Diaries.

103. D. W. Magee, memorandum for SAC, FBI Bioff File.

104. Memorandum from Mr. Hanes to the secretary, re: "Chronological order of events in the so-called 'movie cases,'" Oct. 7, 1939, pp. 262–62, reel 58, Morgenthau Diaries.

105. Report by [name blacked out], Sept. 2, 1940, pp. 2–3, FBI Serial No. 60–2149–101; "Chaplin, 6 Others Indicted for Plotting against Girl," *New York Times*, Feb. 11, 1944, 1; "Carr, Charles Hardy," Biographies of Federal Judges since 1789, Federal Judicial Center, http://www.fjc.gov/servlet/tGetInfo?jid=381 (accessed Feb. 16, 2005).

106. Transcript of phone conversation, Henry Morgenthau Jr. and Attorney General Frank Murphy, Nov. 15, 1939, pp. 311–13, quote on p. 312, reel 61, Morgenthau Diaries.

107. J. P. Wenschel to Samuel O. Clark, Oct. 12, 1939, pp. 274–75; Wenschel to Clark, Oct. 27, 1939, pp. 277–79, both in reel 58, Morgenthau Diaries.

108. E. H. Foley to Secretary Morgenthau, re. Willie Bioff, Nov. 29, 1939, pp. 144–45, reel 60, Morgenthau Diaries.

109. Transcript of meeting in the office of the Secretary of the Treasury, Saturday, Dec. 30, 1939, p. 460, reel 62, Morgenthau Diaries.

110. Transcript of phone conversation, Henry Morgenthau Jr. and Frank Murphy, attorney general, Jan. 2, 1940, 3:44 p.m., p. 56, reel 62, Morgenthau Diaries.

111. *New York Times*, Jan. 11, 1940, p. 27; DOJ transfers Schenck's case reported in E. H. Foley to Secretary Morgenthau, Apr. 10, 1940, p. 35, reel 68, Morgenthau Diaries; Schenck decides to cooperate, B. E. Sackett to director, FBI, May 19, 1941, FBI Serial No. 60–2149–121; Edward A. Tamm to the director, FBI, May 19, 1941, FBI Serial No. 60–2149–117, FBI Bioff File.

## Chapter 7. The Newsmen: "Molders of Public Opinion"

1. Jay "Ding" Darling, "Russia's Not the Only One That Fights Alone," *New York Herald-Tribune*, Nov. 24, 1941, 26.

2. Westbrook Pegler, "Fair Enough," Apr. 23, 1942, box 121, Pegler Papers.

3. Pegler, "Fair Enough," Oct. 17, 1940, box 120, Pegler Papers.

4. Roy W. Howard to George B. Parker, June 4, 1937, Executive Correspondence, City File, Washington, D.C., box 133, Howard Papers.

5. Pegler, "Fair Enough," Apr. 23, 1942, box 121, Pegler Papers.

6. Graham J. White, *FDR and the Press* (Chicago: University of Chicago Press, 1979), 1, 689–90.

7. Forrest Davis, "Press Lord," *Saturday Evening Press* 210 (Mar. 12, 1938): 6.

8. *New York Times*, Mar. 4, 1938, 23.

9. Gerald J. Baldasty, "The Economics of Working-Class Journalism: The E. W. Scripps Newspaper Chain 1878–1908," *Journalism History* 25 (Spring 1999): 3–12.

10. Baldasty, "The Economics of Working-Class Journalism," 3–12; Vance H. Trimble, *The Astonishing Mr. Scripps: The Turbulent Life of America's Penny Press Lord* (Ames: Iowa State University Press, 1992), 21–48, 54–55; Edwin Emery and Michael Emery, *The Press and America: An Interpretive History of the Mass Media* (Englewood Cliffs, N.J.: Prentice-Hall, 1984), 316–18; the quote, "always opposing the rich . . ." is from Emery and Emery, *The Press and America*, 317.

11. Emery and Emery, *The Press and America*, 318, 432–33; Robert Bendiner and James Wechsler, "From Scripps to Howard," *Nation* 148 (May 13, 1939): 533–34; George Seldes, "Roy Howard," *New Republic* 95 (July 27, 1938): 322; *New York Times*, Mar. 5, 1938, 21; Davis, "Press Lord," 30, 32; A. J. Liebling, "Publisher: Part 2, The Pax Howardiensis," *New Yorker* 17 (Aug. 9, 1941): 27– 29.

12. A. J. Liebling, "Publisher: Part 1, The Boy in the Pistachio Shirt," *New Yorker* 17 (Aug. 2, 1941): 19–20.

13. Davis, "Press Lord," 32.

14. Liebling, "Publisher: Part 2," 22–27; A. J. Liebling, "Publisher: Part 4, Once Again She Lorst 'Er Name," *New Yorker* 17 (Aug. 23, 1941): 26, 28; Davis, "Press Lord," 5–7, 30, 32, 34.

15. White, *FDR and the Press*, 55–60, the quote is on 57.

16. Roy W. Howard to George B. Parker, June 4, 1937, Executive Correspondence, City File: Washington, D.C., box 133, Howard Papers; regarding Corcoran and Cohen: David M. Kennedy, *Freedom from Fear: The American People in Depression and War, 1929–1945* (New York: Oxford University Press, 1999), 353; William Lasser, *Benjamin V. Cohen: Architect of the New Deal* (New Haven: Yale University Press, 2002); Joseph P. Lash, *Dealers and Dreamers: A New Look at the New Deal* (New York: Doubleday, 1988).

17. Roy W. Howard to George B. Parker, Feb. 15, 1937, Executive Correspondence, City File: Washington, D.C., box 133, Burton K. Wheeler to Roy W. Howard, Apr. 9, 1938, Executive Correspondence, City File: Washington, D.C., box 145; Roy W. Howard to John H. Sorrells and W. W. Hawkins, July 21, 1939, Executive Correspondence, City File: Washington, D.C., box 157; Roy Howard to Arthur H. Sulzberger, *New York Times*, Sept. 27, 1940, Executive Correspondence, City File: New York City, Wendell Willkie folder, box 167, all in Howard Papers. The shift to anti-New Deal status was widely remarked upon at the time by liberal voices in the media: see Bendiner, "From Scripps to Howard," 554–55; Seldes, "Roy Howard," 322–25; Liebling, "Publisher: Part 4," 26, 28.

18. White, *FDR and the Press*, 58; Bendiner, "From Scripps to Howard," 554–55; Liebling, "Publisher: Part 4," 24–26.

19. Irving Bernstein, *Turbulent Years: A History of the American Worker, 1933–1941* (Boston: Houghton Mifflin, 1970), 127–37.

20. Roy W. Howard to G. B. Parker, Apr. 10, 1941, Executive Correspondence, City File: Washington, D.C., box 180, Howard Papers.

21. George Seldes, *Lords of the Press* (New York: Julian Messner, 1938), 3–19; Harold Ickes, *America's House of Lords: An Inquiry into the Freedom of the Press* (New York: Harcourt, Brace, 1939), x.

22. Seldes, *Lords of the Press*, 206; Frank Freidel, *Franklin D. Roosevelt: Rendezvous with Destiny* (Boston: Little, Brown, 1990), 276.

23. James T. Patterson, *Congressional Conservatism and the New Deal: The Growth of the Conservative Coalition in Congress, 1933–1939* (Lexington: University of Kentucky Press, 1967), 87–88.

24. *Chicago Tribune*, Apr. 2, 1940, clipping in folder 35, box 2, Frank Ernest Gannett Papers [ca. 1859]-1958, Kroch Library, Cornell University, Ithaca, N.Y.

25. Seldes, *Lords of the Press*, 227; Kennedy, *Freedom from Fear*, 404.

26. Emery, *The Press and America*, 430–31; Richard Norton Smith, *The Colonel: The Life and Legend of Robert R. McCormick, 1880–1955* (New York: Houghton Mifflin, 1997), 330–31, 342, 346–48; David Nasaw, *The Chief: The Life of William Randolph Hearst* (New York: Houghton Mifflin, 2000), 492–94, 513–16, 522–24.

27. White, *FDR and the Press*, 94.

28. Patterson, *Congressional Conservatism and the New Deal*, 191.

29. Leo Calvin Rosten, *The Washington Correspondents* (New York: Harcourt, Brace, 1937), 221–26. The quotes are from 221 and 225.

30. Rosten, *Washington Correspondents*, 221, 225.

31. Robert Bendiner and James Wechsler, "From Scripps to Howard: Part 2, Columns Right!" *Nation* 148 (May 20, 1939): 580–81; Ickes, *America's House of Lords*, 45–47; "Attention Roy Howard," *Nation* 146 (May 14, 1938): 548–49.

32. Roy Howard to John Sorrells, May 23, 1938, Executive Correspondence, City File: New York City, box 142, Howard Papers; Roy Howard to G. B. Parker, Sept. 16, 1940, Executive Correspondence, City File: Washington, D.C., box 169, Howard Papers.

33. Roy Howard to G. B. Parker, Jan. 17, 1941, Executive Correspondence, City File: Washington, D.C., box 180, Howard Papers.

34. Examples include Roy Howard to Raymond Clapper, June 8, 1937, box 8, Raymond Clapper Papers, Library of Congress, Washington, D.C.; Roy Howard to G. B. Parker, Mar. 13, 1938, Executive Correspondence, City File: Washington, D.C., box 145; Roy Howard to G. B. Parker, Feb. 15, 1937, Executive Correspondence, City File: Washington, D.C., box 133, both in Howard Papers.

35. Clapper, *Watching the World*, 23.

36. William H. Hawkins to Howard, July 29, 1936, box 4, Walker Stone Papers (Wisconsin State Historical Society, Madison). Howard to Sorrells, May 23, 1938, City File: New York, box 142, Executive Correspondence; Howard to Westbrook Pegler, Jan. 19, 1934, City File: New York, box 94; Howard to Westbrook Pegler, July 7, Aug. 26, 1938, City File: New York, box 142; Julie Pegler to Howard, Apr. 14, 1942, City File: New York, box 186; Julie Pegler to Howard, May 10, 1943, City File: New York, box 195; Julie Pegler to Peg, Jane, and Roy Howard, Jan. 18, 1936, City File: New York, box 117, all in Howard Papers; Pilat, *Pegler*, 105–9, 138–39; Forest Davis, "Press

Lord," *Saturday Evening Post*, Mar. 12, 1938, 6, 30; Liebling, "Publisher: Part 3," *New Yorker* 17 (Aug. 16, 1941): 24.

37. Howard to Hugh Johnson, Feb. 9, 1937, City File: Washington, D.C., box 133, Executive Correspondence; Howard to Parker, June 10, 1938, City File: Washington, D.C., box 145, Howard Papers.

38. Roy W. Howard to G. B. Parker, Apr. 2, 1940, Executive Correspondence, City File: Washington, D.C., box 169, Howard Papers.

39. John H. Sorrells to Walker Stone, Aug. 25, 1939, Executive Correspondence, City File: New York City, box 155, Howard Papers.

40. Westbrook Pegler, "Fair Enough," Feb. 28, 1938; Mar. 1, 1938; May 19, 1938, box 119, Pegler Papers.

41. Pegler, "Fair Enough," Mar. 2, 1938, box 119, Pegler Papers.

42. Pegler, "Fair Enough," Nov. 28, 1939, box 119, Pegler Papers.

43. Pegler, "Fair Enough," Nov. 24, 1939; Nov. 28, 1939; Nov. 22, 1939; Dec. 18, 1939; Dec. 20, 1939; Dec. 30, 1939; Jan. 13, 1940; boxes 119–120, Pegler Papers.

44. Pegler, "Fair Enough," Dec. 20, 1939, box 119, Pegler Papers.

45. Ibid.

46. Pegler, "Fair Enough," Jan. 6, 1940, box 120, Pegler Papers.

47. Pegler, "Fair Enough," Jan. 13, 1939, box 119, Pegler Papers.

48. Ibid.

49. Pegler, "Fair Enough," Nov. 12, 1941, box 120, Pegler Papers.

50. "Poetic Pegler," *Newsweek* 22 (Oct. 11, 1943): 92.

51. Pegler, "Fair Enough," Nov. 4, 1941, box 120, Pegler Papers.

52. Pegler, "Fair Enough," Jan. 4, 1944, box 122, Pegler Papers.

53. Ibid.; the third reference to this subject was on May 21, 1943, box 122, Pegler Papers.

54. For an example of a specific reference to this source of background information, Pegler, "Fair Enough," Nov. 28, 1939, box 119, Pegler Papers.

55. Diary entries for Oct. 25, 1941, pp. 5973–74 and Nov. 30, 1941, pp. 6070–71, in Harold L. Ickes Diaries, reel 4, microfilm, Library of Congress Manuscript Division, Washington, D.C.; "Initials and Code Words Used on Corruption Roll," *Chicago Tribune*, Oct. 29, 1941, clipping in Daniel Gilbert File, Chicago Historical Society, Chicago, Ill.

56. Pegler, "Fair Enough," Apr. 3, 1940; June 8, 1940, both in box 120, Pegler Papers.

57. Pegler, "Fair Enough," Aug. 6, 1942, box 121, Pegler Papers.

58. Pegler, "Fair Enough," May 13, 1940, box 120, Pegler Papers.

59. Pegler, "Fair Enough," Oct. 15, 1941, box 120, Pegler Papers. In terms of blurring the distinction, in Oct. 1941, Pegler wrote, "Now I suppose everyone knows that George Browne, the Chicago gangster, is a vice president of the A.F.L." "Fair Enough," Oct. 7, 1941, box 120, Pegler Papers.

60. Pegler, "Fair Enough," Jan. 19, 1940, box 120, Pegler Papers.

61. Ibid.

62. Pegler, "Fair Enough," Feb. 1, 1940, box 120, Pegler Papers.

63. Pegler, "Fair Enough," June 7, 1940, box 120, Pegler Papers.

64. Canavarro v. Theatre, etc., Union (1940), 15C2nd 495, California Supreme Court, May 3, 1940, http://online.ceb.com/calcases/C2/15C2d495.htm (accessed Jan. 12, 2006); the quote is from A. T. Baum, "Court Gets Union Fight," *San Francisco Examiner*, Dec. 28, 1939, in Hardy, Charles, Labor, *San Francisco Examiner* News Clipping File, San Francisco History Center, San Francisco Public Library, San Francisco, Calif. (hereafter *SFE* Clipping File); Order to Show Cause and Temporary Restraining Order, Superior Court of State of California, County of San Francisco, Case of Theodore Canavarro et al. vs. Theatre and Amusement Janitors Union, Local 9, et al., Dec. 27, 1939, in box 2566, NYDA Papers.

65. George Scalise to Charles Hardy Jr., Dec. 22, 1939, folder 1/7, George Hardy Papers, Accession # 1991/055, Labor Archives and Research Center, San Francisco, Calif. (hereafter Hardy Papers).

66. Anonymous, undated pamphlet, included in Jack Foley to Dear Members of Organized Labor, Jan. 11, 1940, box 2566, NYDA Papers.

67. Ibid.

68. *San Francisco Chronicle*, May 25, 1948, 3; "Proceedings [of] Special Convention, Building Service Employees' International Union, May 11 to May 14, 1942, Radisson Hotel, Minneapolis, Minn.," 130, in reel 191, *Labor Union Constitutions and Proceedings* (Glen Rock, N.J.: Microfilm Corporation of America, 1978); David Ransom, *"So Much to Be Done": George Hardy's Life in Organized Labor* (Service Employees International Union, 1980), 1–2.

69. *San Francisco Chronicle*, May 25, 1948, 3; Ransom, *"So much to be done,"* 3–5, 7–8, quotes are from 3 and 8; *New York Times*, Sept. 18, 1990, B10; he was named to a VP post in Feb. 1937 (*Chicago Tribune*, Mar. 6, 1940, 12).

70. *San Francisco Examiner*, Dec. 28, 1939, in Hardy, Charles, Labor, *SFE* Clipping File; quote is from *San Francisco Chronicle*, Feb. 27, 1940, 9.

71. *San Francisco Chronicle*, Feb. 27, 1940, 9.

72. Ibid.

73. *San Francisco Examiner*, Feb. 29, 1940, in "labor unions, Building Service," *SFE* Clipping File.

74. Canavarro v. Theatre, etc., Union (1940).

75. *San Francisco Chronicle*, July 25, 1941, 6.

76. "BSEIU Proceedings, 1942," 56–57, 130–31; "Proceedings of the Tenth General Convention of the Building Service Employees' International Union, May 1–5, 1950, Olympic Hotel, Seattle, Washington," in reel 191, *Labor Union Constitutions and Proceedings*; *New York Times*, Sept. 18, 1990, B10.

77. Ransom, *"So much to be done,"* 8.

78. "Proceedings [of the] Eighth General Convention, Building Service Employees' International Union, May 6, 1940 [to May 8, 1940], Ritz-Carlton Hotel, Atlantic City, New Jersey," 25, 27, in reel 191, *Labor Union Constitutions and Proceedings*.

79. S. J. Duffy to Mr. Pine, Nov. 10, 1939, folder 1/5 SEIU Correspondence General, 1939–1981, Hardy Papers.

80. Jack Alexander, "He's Against," *Saturday Evening Post* 213 ( Sept. 14, 1940): 132.

81. *San Francisco Examiner*, Jan. 11, 1940, in "Hardy, Charles, Labor," *SFE* Clipping Files; Jack Foley to Dear Members of Organized Labor, Jan. 11, 1940, box 2566, NYDA Papers.

82. Westbrook Pegler to Jack Foley, Mar. 7, 1940, folder 1/7, Hardy Papers.

83. Pegler, "Fair Enough," Jan. 31, 1940; Feb. 17, 1940, box 119, Pegler Papers, quote is from Jan. 31, 1940.

84. Alexander, "He's Against," 132.

85. Pegler, "Fair Enough," Jan. 13, 1940, box 120, Pegler Papers.

86. Pegler, "Fair Enough," *New York World-Telegram,* Apr. 16, 1940, 17.

87. Pegler, "Fair Enough," *New York World-Telegram*, Apr. 18, 1940, 19.

88. Andrei S. Markovits and Mark Silverstein, "Introduction: Power and Process in Liberal Democracies," in Markovits and Silverstein, eds., *The Politics of Scandal: Power and Politics in Liberal Democracies* (New York: Holmes and Meier, 1988), 1–4; John B. Thompson, *Political Scandal: Power and Visibility in the Media Age* (Cambridge: Polity Press, 2000), 13–30, 61–77, 86–89; Robert Williams, *Political Scandals in the USA* (Edinburgh: Keele University Press, 1998), 6–7, 122–23, 129–30.

89. *Washington Post*, Apr. 28, 1940, clipping in box 82, Pegler Papers.

90. "Racketeer Scalise," *Time* 35 (May 6, 1940): 20–21, the picture and both quotes on 21.

91. Both quotes are from *New York Herald-Tribune*, Apr. 22, 1940, Scalise Trials Clipping File; for other stories that illustrate these points, see *New York Sun*, Apr. 22, 1940; *New York World-Telegram*, Apr. 22, 1940; *New York Herald Tribune*, Apr. 23, 1940; all in Scalise Trials Clipping File; also "Columnist Pegler Puts the Finger of the Law on a New York Union Leader," *Life* 8 (May 6, 1940): 34–35.

92. "Olive complexioned" in *New York Herald Tribune*, Apr. 22, 1940; "swarthy" and "Italian born parents," *New York Sun*, Oct. 8, 1940; "Italian born defendant," *New York Herald Tribune*, Oct. 8, 1940, all in Scalise Trials Clipping File.

93. *New York Herald-Tribune*, Oct. 8, 1940, Scalise Trials Clipping File.

94. David E. Ruth, *Inventing the Public Enemy: The Gangster in American Culture, 1918–1934* (Chicago: University of Chicago, 1996), 66–73, 82–85.

95. Marilyn Yaquito, *Pump 'Em Full of Lead: A Look at Gangsters on Film* (New York: Twayne Publishers, 1998), 26–47.

96. *New York Sun*, Oct. 7, 1940, Scalise Trials Clipping File.

97. *New York Herald-Tribune*, Sept. 16, 1940, Scalise Trials Clipping File.

98. *New York Herald Tribune*, Apr. 22, 1940, Scalise Trials Clipping File.

99. Carey McWilliams, "Racketeers and Movie Magnates," *New Republic* 105 (Oct. 17, 1941): 533–35, quote is from 533.

100. McWilliams, "Racketeers and Movie Magnates," quotes on 534, 535.

101. *Newark Evening News*, Dec. 23, 1943.

102. *New York Daily News*, Nov. 8, 1941, clipping in folder Pegler, box 178, Pegler Papers.

103. *Washington Post*, Apr. 22, 1940; *New York Herald-Tribune*, Apr. 22, 1940, clippings in folder Unions, American Federation of Labor, 1908, 1940, box 79, Pegler Papers.

104. "Holdup Men of Labor," *Time* 38 (Sept. 22, 1941): 14–16, the quote is from 14.

105. "The AFL Problem," *Newsweek* 16 (Dec. 2, 1940): 36; the quote is from "A.F. of L. Ditches a Racketeer," *Life* 11 (Oct. 27, 1941): 38.

106. Robert M. Entman, *Democracy without Citizens: Media and the Decay of American Politics* (New York: Oxford University Press, 1989), 50–52.

107. Walker Stone to George B. Parker, n.d., Dick Lamb Correspondence File, box 6, Walker Stone Papers, Wisconsin State Historical Society, Madison, Wisc.

108. Richard Lamb, "How 'Fifth Column of Criminals' Penetrates High Places of American Labor Movement," *New York World-Telegram*, July 15, 1940, 1.

109. Richard L. McCormick, "The Discovery that Business Corrupts Politics: A Reappraisal of the Origins of Progressivism," *American Historical Review* 86 (Apr. 1981): 264–65, esp. 265.

110. Alexander L. Crosby, "Survival of Unions at Stake in National Showdown," Nov. 14, 1941, clipping in file newspapers, suppression and distortion, microfilm reel 9098, Federated Press Records [ca. 1915]-1955, Rare Book and Manuscript Library, Columbia University, New York, N.Y.

111. Roy Howard to Westbrook Pegler, Oct. 22, 1941, Executive Correspondence, City File New York City, Westbrook Pegler folder, box 169, Howard Papers.

112. Roy Howard to G. B. Parker, Oct. 26, 1941, Executive Correspondence, City File Washington, D.C., G. B. Parker folder, box 180, Howard Papers.

## Chapter 8. The Scandal's Political Impact: Pegler and Antiunionism

1. "Democrats: Campaign's Beginning," *Time* 36 (Sept. 23, 1940): 11.

2. "Address of the President, Delivered at Constitution Hall to the International Brotherhood of Teamsters, Chauffeurs, Stablemen and Helpers, Wednesday, Sept. 11, 1940, 9:30 P.M., E.S.T.," President's Personal Files, PPF 792, FDR Papers.

3. *Christian Science Monitor*, Sept. 12, 1940, 1.

4. "Address of the President, Sept. 11, 1940."

5. Mrs. Hammond Miller to Franklin Roosevelt, Sept. 14, 1940, President's Personal Files, PPF 200, box 66, FDR Papers.

6. John M. Allswang, *The New Deal and American Politics* (New York: John Wiley and Sons, 1978), 39–41; James MacGregor Burns, *Roosevelt: The Lion and the Fox* (New York: Harcourt, Brace, 1956), 454; J. David Greenstone, *Labor in American Politics* (New York: Alfred A. Knopf, 1969), 40–41.

7. *New York Times*, Dec. 1, 1940, sec. 4, 8.

8. W. L. Rifenbrick to the president, Oct. 24, 1940, President's Personal File, PPF 200, box 68, FDR Papers.

9. Milton Derber, "Growth and Expansion," in Milton Derber and Edwin Young, eds., *Labor and the New Deal* (Madison: University of Wisconsin Press, 1957), 3–4, 17, 22–23.

10. Irving Bernstein, *Turbulent Years: A History of the American Worker, 1933–1941* (Boston: Houghton Mifflin, 1970), 642, 647, 671–72, 677–78; Melvyn Dubofsky, *The State and Labor in Modern America* (Chapel Hill: University of North Carolina Press, 1994), 142–46, 149–51.

11. Bernstein, *Turbulent Years*, 727–29, 734–45; Joel Seidman, *American Labor from Defense to Reconversion* (Chicago: University of Chicago Press, 1953), 53.

12. Andrew E. Kersten, *Labor's Home Front: The American Federation of Labor during World War II* (New York: New York University Press, 2006), 49–57; Jerold S. Auerbach, *Labor and Liberty: The La Follette Committee and the New Deal* (Indianapolis: Bobbs-Merrill, 1966); Walter Goodman, *The Committee: The Extraordinary Career of the House Committee on Un-American Activities* (New York: Farrar, Straus and Giroux, 1968), 3–58; Seidman, *American Labor from Defense to Reconversion*, 69–70; Howell John Harris, *The Right to Manage: Industrial Relations Policies of American Business in the 1940s* (Madison: University of Wisconsin Press, 1982), 37–38; Richard Polenberg, *War and Society: The United States, 1941–45* (New York: J. B. Lippincott, 1972), 167; Bernstein, *Turbulent Years*, 450–51, 668, 670; James T. Patterson, *Congressional Conservatism and the New Deal: The Growth of the Conservative Coalition in Congress, 1933–1939* (Lexington: University of Kentucky Press, 1967), 377–79.

13. Allswang, *The New Deal and American Politics*, 59.

14. Raymond Clapper, *Watching the World* (New York: McGraw-Hill, 1944), 147.

15. Patterson, *Congressional Conservatism and the New Deal*, 1–136, 211–324; Alan Brinkley, *The End of Reform: New Deal Liberalism in Recession and War* (New York: Alfred A. Knopf, 1995; reprint, New York: Vintage Books, 1996), 15–30, 137–43.

16. The column appeared on Nov. 11, 1939, reprinted in Raymond Clapper, *Watching the World*, 130.

17. Patterson, *Congressional Conservatism and the New Deal*, 198–210, 233–42, 322–29; David L. Porter, *Congress and the Waning of the New Deal* (Port Washington, N.Y.: National University Publications, Kennikat Press, 1980), 137–38.

18. Patterson, *Congressional Conservatism and the New Deal*, 85–127, 215–29, the quote is from 229.

19. Arthur H. Vandenberg, "The New Deal Must Be Salvaged," *American Mercury* 49 (Jan. 1940): 7; Patterson, *Congressional Conservatism and the New Deal*, 316.

20. Clare Hoffman to Leo C. Lillie, Apr. 26, 1939, folder 1939 Wagner Act Correspondence, box 1, Clare E. Hoffman Papers, Bentley Historical Library, University of Michigan, Ann Arbor.

21. Quoted in Dubofsky, *The State and Labor in America*, 155.

22. Bernstein, *Turbulent Years*, 718–19.

23. Clare Hoffman to A. L. Jones, Nov. 21, 1939, folder 1939, Wagner Act Correspondence, box 1; Clare Hoffman to W. T. Walsh, Jan. 2, 1940, folder Wagner Act, 1940, both in Hoffman Papers.

24. Clare Hoffman to Francis J. Bussone, Nov. 12, 1945, folder Adverse Outside of District, box 5, Hoffman Papers.

25. *Philadelphia Record*, June 18, 1944, in folder Newspapers Outside of District, 1944, box 5, Hoffman Papers.

26. Clare Hoffman to Joseph W. Martin Jr., May 27, 1946, folder M, box 8; Frank O. Horton to William J. Ditter, Oct. 18, 1940, folder Political 1940, box 55, both documents in Hoffman Papers.

27. List of Conferees, May 14, 1947, folder Labor Committee, box 30, Hoffman Papers; Clare Hoffman to J. P. Dixon, Mar. 25, 1949, folder Taft-Hartley, box 34, Hoffman Papers.

28. *Congressional Record* (May 3, 1940), 86, pt. 15: 2679.

29. *Congressional Record* (Nov. 20, 1940), 86, pt. 12: 13703–4.

30. *Congressional Record* (Aug. 5, 1940), 86, pt. 16: 4767–68.

31. Frank D. Fackethal to Westbrook Pegler, May 8, 1941, folder Pegler Awards, Pulitzer Prize, box 53, Pegler Papers; "Effective Journalism," *Newark Evening News*, Apr. 24, 1940, in folder Unions, American Federation of Labor, 1908–1940, box 79, Pegler Papers.

32. Westbrook Pegler, "Fair Enough," Jan. 22, 1942, box 121, Pegler Papers.

33. Ibid.

34. Pegler, "Fair Enough," July 25, 1940, box 120, Pegler Papers.

35. See, for example, Pegler, "Fair Enough," July 31, 1940, box 120; Dec. 20, 1941; July 10, 1942; July 23, 1942; May 26, 1943, box 121, Pegler Papers.

36. Pegler, "Fair Enough," Jan. 26, 1943, box 121, Pegler Papers.

37. Pegler, "Fair Enough," June 21, 1941, box 120, Pegler Papers.

38. Pegler, "Fair Enough," Sept. 5, 1941, box 120, Pegler Papers.

39. Pegler, "Fair Enough," Dec. 5, 1941, box 120, Pegler Papers.

40. Pegler, "Fair Enough," Aug. 12, 1941, box 120, Pegler Papers.

41. Pegler, "Fair Enough," May 23, 1940, box 120, Pegler Papers.

42. Pegler, "Fair Eough," Oct. 4, 1941, box 120, Pegler Papers.

43. Pegler, "Fair Enough," Feb. 17, 1940, box 120, Pegler Papers.

44. Pegler, "Fair Enough," Apr. 27, 1942, box 121, Pegler Papers.

45. Pegler, "Fair Enough," Oct. 20, 1941, box 120, Pegler Papers.

46. David Witwer, *Corruption and Reform in the Teamsters Union* (Chicago: University of Illinois Press, 2003), 20–21.

47. Andrew Wender Cohen, *The Racketeer's Progress: Chicago and the Struggle for the Modern American Economy, 1900–1940* (New York: Cambridge University Press, 2004), 260.

48. Ibid., 233, 261.

49. Selig Perlman and Philip Taft, *History of Labor in the United States*, vol. 4, *Labor Movements* (New York: MacMillan, 1935), 129–38; Sidney Fine, *"Without Blare of Trumpets": Walter Drew, the National Erectors' Association, and the Open Shop Movement, 1903–57* (Ann Arbor: University of Michigan Press, 1995), 1–11, 34–38, 50–54, 201–21; Witwer, *Corruption and Reform in the Teamsters Union*, 20–37; Cohen, *Racketeer's Progress*, 140; Finley Peter Dunne, "Mr. Dooley on the Open Shop," 1920, in *Unions, Management, and the Public*, ed. E. Wight Bakke and Clark Kerr (New York: Harcourt, Brace and World, 1948), 120–21.

50. "Referred to the People," *Printers' Ink*, Dec. 5, 1941, 88.

51. James A. Gross, *The Reshaping of the National Labor Relations Board: National Labor Policy in Transition, 1937–1947* (Albany: State University of New York Press, 1981), 5, 24–28, 34–35, 42, 48–52, 85, 100–108; Gilbert J. Gall, "CIO Leaders and the Democratic Alliance: The Case of the Smith Committee and the NLRB," *Labor Studies Journal* 14 (Summer 1989): 4–5, 11, 14–16.

52. "No man," Patterson, *Congressional Conservatism and the New Deal*, 180; Gross, *Reshaping of the National Labor Relations Board*, 151–213, 224–40; Gall, "CIO Leaders and the Democratic Alliance," 4–5, 14–16.

53. Howard W. Smith to William Green, Apr. 13, 1942, and "Green Assailed for Defending 'Bad' in the AFL," *Chicago Daily Tribune*, Apr. 15, 1942, p. 10, both in box 3, Howard Worth Smith Papers, [1883–1976], MSS 8731, Alderman Library, University of Virginia, Charlottesville.

54. Kenneth O'Reilly, *Hoover and the Un-Americans: The FBI, HUAC, and the Red Menace* (Philadelphia: Temple University Press, 1983), 37–38, 48–49; speech enclosed in memo from Robert E. Stripling to Westbrook Pegler, Dec. 3, 1941, folder Communism, Opponents of, House Un-American Activities Committee 1941, box 21, Pegler Papers.

55. David M. Kennedy, *Freedom from Fear: The American People in Depression and War 1929–1945* (New York: Oxford University Press, 1999), 474–77; Dubofsky, *The State and Labor*, 171–73; Seidman, *American Labor from Defense to Reconversion*, 30, 41–46, 52–53.

56. Dubofsky, *The State and Labor*, 184–85; Richard Polenberg, *War and Society: The United States, 1941–1945* (New York: J. B. Lippincott, 1972), 158–59.

57. Polenberg, *War and Society*, 159–65; Robert H. Zieger, *American Workers, American Unions* (Baltimore: Johns Hopkins University Press, 1994), 86–87.

58. Westbrook Pegler, "Fair Enough," Feb. 28, 1942, box 121, Pegler Papers.

59. Pegler, "Fair Enough," Oct. 4, 1941, box 120, Pegler Papers.

60. Pegler, "Fair Enough," Oct. 3, 1941, box 120, Pegler Papers.

61. Pegler, "Fair Enough," June 8, 1942, box 121, Pegler Papers.

62. Pegler, "Fair Enough," Apr. 4, 1942, box 121, Pegler Papers.

63. Pegler, "Fair Enough," Aug. 14, 1941, box 120, Pegler Papers.

64. Pegler, "Fair Enough," May 26, 1941, box 120, Pegler Papers.

65. Elizabeth Fones-Wolf, "Creating a Favorable Business Climate: Corporations and Radio Broadcasting, 1934–1954," *Business History Review* 73 (1999): 238–39.

66. Giraud Chester, "The Radio Commentaries of H. V. Kaltenborn: A Case Study in Persuasion" (PhD diss., University of Wisconsin, 1947), 455–59.

67. Ibid.; "tribute" on 394, "union funds" and "union racketeers" on 395.

68. Fones-Wolf, "Creating a Favorable Business Climate," 239.

69. Chester, "Radio Commentaries of H. V. Kaltenborn," 402.

70. Ibid., 406.

71. Ibid., 402.

72. Max Lerner, "Meeting the Blitz on Labor," *New Republic* 104 (Apr. 28, 1941): 598–99.

73. Congress of Industrial Organizations, Proceedings of International Executive Board Meeting, Washington, D.C., Hotel Lafayette, Mar. 24, 1942, p. 139–40, CIO executive board minutes, in box 1, CIO Executive Board Minutes/Proceedings, Walter P. Reuther Library, Wayne State University, Detroit, Mich.

74. Robert M. Entman, *Democracy without Citizens: Media and the Decay of American Politics* (New York: Oxford University Press, 1989), 75–88.

75. *New York Times*, June 13, 1941, 12.

76. Hadley Cantril and Frederic Swift, *Public Opinion and Labor Problems: Confidential Report* (Princeton: Office of Public Opinion Research, Princeton University, Nov. 11, 1941), 9; this report was found in President's Personal Files, PPF 4721, American Institute of Public Opinion, FDR Papers.

77. George H. Gallup, *The Gallup Poll: Public Opinion, 1935–1971*, vol. 1, *1935–1948* (New York: Random House, 1972), 277–78.

78. Cantril, *Public Opinion and Labor Problems*, 8.

79. Ibid., 15.

80. Marcus Goin to Clare Hoffman, Dec. 16, 1940, folder Unions, etc., 1940, box 2, Hoffman Papers.

81. Robert E. Price to Clare Hoffman, Feb. 14, 1943, folder Labor—Outside of District, box 26, Hoffman Papers.

82. Mrs. Henry A. Tredwell to Clare Hoffman, May 26, 1943, folder Labor—Outside of District, box 26, Hoffman Papers.

83. *New York Times*, Sept. 8, 1941, 14.

84. Louis Schaeffer to Howard Smith, Nov. 22, 1941, folder HR 6066 Labor Bill, box 2, Smith Papers.

85. In one example, Pegler wrote to denounce the CIO's president John L. Lewis: "Mr. Lewis's racket is political. He is a man of vanity and great ambition, and his pet scheme is the closed shop plus the check-off" (Westbrook Pegler, "Fair Enough," May 23, 1940, box 120, Pegler Papers).

86. A. G. Dobbins to Clare Hoffman, May 23, 1943, folder Labor—Outside of District, box 26, Hoffman Papers.

87. Public opinion poll results attached to Hadley Cantril to Anna Rosenberg, Nov. 17, 1941, Public Opinion Polls, President's Secretary's File, PSF box 157, FDR Papers.

88. Pegler, "Fair Enough," June 22, 1937; Feb. 26, 1937; June 8, 1937; Aug. 20, 1937; Nov. 11, 1937; Apr. 28, 1938; n.d. 1938; June 8, 1939; June 24, 1939; Aug. 8, 1939; boxes 117–19, Pegler Papers.

89. Pegler, "Fair Enough," Aug. 8, 1939, box 119, Pegler Papers.

90. Pegler, "Fair Enough," Oct. 15, 1940, box 120, Pegler Papers.

91. Ibid.

92. Pegler, "Fair Enough," Sept. 26, 1940, box 120, Pegler Papers.

93. Pegler, "Fair Enough," Oct. 8, 1941, box 120, Pegler Papers.

94. *New York Times*, Dec. 4, 1941, 1; Dec. 7, 1941, sec. 4, 8.

95. *Congressional Record* (Dec. 2, 1941), 87, pt. 9: 9356–57.

96. E. Eugene Cox Dies, Representative, 72," *New York Times*, Dec. 25, 1952, 29; Gall, "CIO Leaders and the Democratic Alliance," 12–13; Patterson, *Congressional Conservatism and the New Deal*, 181.

97. *New York Times*, Dec. 3, 1941, 20; *Congressional Record* (Dec. 2, 1941), 87, pt. 9: 9338–39, the quotes are from the *Congressional Record*.

98. Ibid.

99. *Congressional Record* (Dec. 2, 1941), 87, pt. 9: 9352.

100. *Congressional Record* (Dec. 1, 1941), 87, pt. 9: 9305.

101. *Congressional Record* (Dec. 2, 1941), 87, pt. 9: 9358; "Jerry Voorhis, '46 Nixon Foe," *New York Times*, Sept. 12, 1984, B6; Stephen E. Ambrose, *Nixon: The Education of a Politician, 1913–1962* (New York: Simon and Schuster, 1987), 128–40.

102. Seidman, *American Labor from Defense to Reconversion*, 72–73; *New York Times*, Dec. 4, 1941, 1 and 23.

103. Ibid.

104. Seidman, *American Labor from Defense to Reconversion*, 72–73.

105. *New York Times*, Dec. 7, 1941, 52.

106. Dubofsky, *The State and Labor in America*, 174–75.

107. Ibid., 174–75, 182–88.

108. Polenberg, *War and Society*, 166.

109. Dubofsky, *The State and Labor in America*, 188–90.

110. Polenberg, *War and Society*, 170–75.

111. James B. Atleson, *Labor and the Wartime State: Labor Relations and Law during World War II* (Chicago: University of Illinois Press, 1998), 196–97; Seidman, *American Labor from Defense to Reconversion*, 279; John Caldwell Foster, *The Union Politic: The CIO Political Action Committee* (Columbia: University of Missouri Press, 1975), 5–15; Roland Young, *Congressional Politics in the Second World War* (New York: Columbia University Press, 1956), 63–66, 83.

112. Foster, *The Union Politic*, 11; Seidman, *American Labor from Defense to Reconversion*, 70, the quote is from 73.

113. Newsclipping, Henry R. Lieberman, "Industry Has Two Preoccupations: Labor and 6 Per Cent (Plus)," *PM,* Dec. 5, 1941, 18, box 6, Smith Papers.

114. Richard W. Steele, "The Pulse of the People: Franklin D. Roosevelt and the Gauging of American Public Opinion," *Journal of Contemporary History* 9 (Oct. 1974): 195–216.

115. Edwin M. Watson, memorandum to president, Nov. 28, 1941, President's Secretary's File, PSF, box 157, FDR Papers.

116. Cantril, *Public Opinion and Labor Problems,* 1.

117. George Gallup, "Labor Seen Losing Favor with Public," *New York Times,* Oct. 26, 1941, 32.

118. Richard Norton Smith, *Thomas E. Dewey and His Times* (New York: Simon and Schuster, 1982), 347.

119. Opinion Research Corporation, *Dewey vs. Roosevelt: An Analysis of the Presidential Campaign* (Princeton, N.J., Aug. 21, 1944), 6, in box 57, Bruce Barton Papers, Wisconsin State Historical Society, Madison, Wisc.

120. Ray Rubicam to Bruce Barton, July 29, 1944, Republican folder, 1944, box 57, Barton Papers.

121. Memo from Stanley High, July 28, 1944, Republican folder, 1944, box 57, Barton Papers.

122. Dubofsky, *The State and Labor,* 206.

123. Pegler, "Fair Enough," Nov. 19, 1940, box 120, Pegler Papers.

## Chapter 9. "Labor Must Clean House": The Challenge of Responding to Pegler

1. Transcript of two phone conversations, Aug. 16, 1943, included in E. E. Conroy to director, FBI, Aug. 24, 1943, FBI Serial No. 62–36434–132, Westbrook Pegler Federal Bureau of Investigation Files, Raynor Memorial Library, Marquette University, Milwaukee, Wisc.

2. Ibid. In the end, they went with the following phrasing: "We sharply protest the vile, Nazi-like statements of your columnist, Westbrook Pegler, against the valiant men of the merchant marine" (text of letter submitted by National Maritime Union Protest Committee to Lee B. Wood, executive editor, *New York World-Telegram,* press release, PM Papers, Aug. 19, 1943, in folder NMU v. Westbrook Pegler, box 2, NMU Files).

3. "Labor Must Clean House," *New Republic* 102 (Feb. 5, 1940): 168.

4. Ibid., 169.

5. Ibid.

6. Nelson Lichtenstein, *State of the Union: A Century of American Labor* (Princeton: Princeton University Press, 2002), 141.

7. Craig Phelan, *William Green: Biography of a Labor Leader* (Albany: State University of New York Press, 1989), 107.

8. Benjamin Stolberg, "Sitting Bill," *Saturday Evening Post* 214 (Oct. 18, 1941), 27.

9. Phelan, *William Green*, 1–22, 25–28; Stolberg, "Sitting Bill," 27.

10. Stolberg, "Sitting Bill," 92; Walter Galenson, *The CIO Challenge to the AFL: A History of the American Labor Movement, 1935–1941* (Cambridge, Mass.: Harvard University Press, 1960), 8.

11. David Brody, *Workers in Industrial America: Essays on the Twentieth Century Struggle* (New York: Oxford University Press, 1993), 31–32.

12. Phelan, "William Green," ix, 80–85, 102–3, quote is from 30.

13. Robert H. Zieger, *American Workers, American Unions* (Baltimore: Johns Hopkins University Press, 1994, second edition), 41–55.

14. Phelan, *William Green*, 137–42, 146–50, 152; Andrew E. Kersten, *Labor's Home Front: The American Federation of Labor during World War II* (New York: New York University Press, 2006), 139–65.

15. James A. Gross, *The Reshaping of the National Labor Relations Board: National Labor Policy in Transition, 1937–1947* (Albany: State University of New York Press), 66–68, 75–77, 191.

16. George L. Meany, "AFL at Greatest Strength," *The Carpenter* 60 (Sept. 1940): 4.

17. Stolberg, "Sitting Bill," 97; Christopher L. Tomlins, "AFL Unions in the 1930s: Their Performance in Historical Perspective," *Journal of American History* 65 (Mar. 1979): 1023, 1035.

18. Daniel J. Tobin, "Editorial," *Official Magazine I.B.T., C., S. and H. of A.* 37 (Mar. 1940): 10.

19. "Daily Newspapers Hostile to Labor," *Federation News*, Mar. 2, 1940, 9.

20. Bill Ainsworth, "Trade Unionists Know Propaganda," *Federation News*, Apr. 27, 1940, 1.

21. Allen Lee Appelbaum, "George E. Sokolsky: A Political Journalist in Retrospect" (master's thesis, Ohio University, 1963), 35–38; Charles Fisher, *The Columnists* (New York: Howell, Soskin Publishers), 278–90.

22. "Daily Newspapers Hostile to Labor," *Federation News*, Mar. 2, 1940, 9.

23. *New York Times*, Nov. 25, 1939, 1.

24. *New York Times*, Feb. 21, 1940, 3.

25. Ibid.

26. True Copy, Telegram Meyer L. Lewis to William Bioff, Feb. 22, 1940, Office of the President Files, President's Files, William Green, 1869–1955, folder 12, box 7, RG 019, George Meany Memorial Archives, Silver Spring, Md.

27. *New York Times*, Jan. 28, 1940, 29; "A Frank Statement from George Scalise," *Building Service Employee* 1 (May 1940): 6–7.

28. *New York Times*, Jan. 28, 1940, 29; "A Frank Statement from George Scalise."

29. Minutes of the Meeting of the Executive Council, American Federation of Labor, Hotel Everglades, Miami, Fla., Jan. 29–Feb. 9, 1940, 67–73, George Meany Memorial Archives, AFL-CIO, Silver Spring, Md.

30. Joseph A. Padway to George Scalise, Jan. 21, 1940, enclosed with Beth Pitt to Westbrook Pegler, June 18, 1944, box 82, folder : Building Service Employees International Union, 1944, box 82, Pegler Papers.

31. *New York Times*, Feb. 10, 1940, 16.

32. Ibid.

33. "President Green in Retort Courteous to Labor Smearing Attacks of Hessian," *Federation News*, Jan. 27, 1940, 1.

34. *New York Times*, Feb. 10, 1940, 16.

35. *Washington Post*, Apr. 23, 1940, 10.

36. "On Trial with Scalise," *New York Herald-Tribune*, Apr. 22, 1940, clipping in "The Trials of George Scalise, President of the Building Service Employees' International Union, and James J. Bambrick, president of Local 32–B of that union, who were charged with federal tax evasion, forgery and grand larceny," Newspaper Clipping File, 1940–1941, Scalise Trials Clipping File.

37. John P. Frey to Victor A. Olander, May 16, 1940, box 13, John P. Frey Papers, Library of Congress, Washington, D.C.

38. Daniel J. Tobin, "Editorial," *Official Magazine I.B.T., C., S. and H. of A.* 37 (Mar. 1940): 11.

39. William Green to Andrew Schmitzer, Mar. 31 1941, series 3A, box 14, IBT Papers.

40. Criminal Record, Police Department, City of New York, George Scalise, May 24, 1940, box 2566, NYDA Papers.

41. Westbrook Pegler, "Fair Enough," Feb. 1, 1940, box 120, Pegler Papers.

42. Pegler, "Fair Enough," Feb. 6, 1940, box 120, Pegler Papers.

43. William Green to Ed Phelan, Feb. 1, 1940, Building Service Employees Correspondence, microfilm reel 18, RG1–003. Office of the President, National and International Unions, Correspondence, 1890–1959, George Meany Memorial Archives, Silver Spring, Md.

44. *People v. Scalise* trial transcript, vol. 7991, 232–33.

45. David Scott Witwer, "The Scandal of George Scalise: A Case Study in the Rise of Labor Racketeering in the 1930s," *Journal of Social History* 36 (Summer 2003): 917–40.

46. Harry Rose to William Green, Dec. 9, 1938; William Green to George Scalise, Nov. 3, 1938, both in reel 10, William Green Papers, Ohio Historical Society, Columbus, Ohio.

47. George Scalise to Paul David, Dec. 27, 1938, box 2567, NYDA Papers.

48. Tobin, "Editorial," 11.

49. Ibid.

50. Ibid.

51. William Green, "A.F.L. President Replies to the Criticisms by Pegler," *New York World-Telegram*, Mar. 28, 1940, 18.

52. William Green, "Green Replies to Pegler in Bioff and Scalise Cases," *New York World-Telegram*, Mar. 29, 1940, 11.

53. William Green, "Green Denies A.F.L. Condones, Protects Dishonest Unionism," *New York World-Telegram*, Mar. 30, 1940, 32.

54. Ibid.

55. Westbrook Pegler, "Fair Enough," Apr. 1, 1940, box 120, Pegler Papers.

56. Pegler, "Fair Enough," Apr. 5, 1940, box 120, Pegler Papers.

57. Pegler, "Fair Enough," Apr. 1, 1940, box 120, Pegler Papers.

58. Pegler, "Fair Enough," Apr. 6, 1940, box 120, Pegler Papers.

59. John P. Frey to Victor A. Olander, May 16, 1940, box 13, Frey Papers.

60. "Gangsterized Unionism," folder : Rackets, box 6, series 2, File B, American Federation of Labor Records, 1888–1955, Wisconsin Historical Society, Madison, Wisc.

61. See, for example, Phillip J. Kore et al. to William Green, Sept. 16, 1933; William Green to Phillip J. Kore Nov. 22, 1933; William Green to William C. Elliot, Nov. 22, 1933, all in reel 41, International Alliance of Theatrical Stage Employes, microfilm edition, American Federation of Labor Records: Gompers Era.

62. Minutes of the Meeting of the Executive Council of the American Federation of Labor, May 21, 1940, 121–22, George Meany Memorial Archives, Silver Spring, Md.

63. Minutes of the Meeting of the Executive Council of the American Federation of Labor, Oct. 10, 1940, 133–45, George Meany Memorial Archives, Silver Spring, Md.

64. Ibid., 137–38, 145–46.

65. Mrs. Henry A. Tredwell to Clare Hoffman, May 26, 1943, folder Labor Outside of District, box 26, Clare Hoffman Papers, Bentley Historical Library, University of Michigan, Ann Arbor.

66. David Dubinsky and A. H. Raskin, *David Dubinsky: A Life with Labor* (New York: Simon and Schuster, 1977), 8–11, "blurred Yiddish accent," 11; Irving Bernstein, *Turbulent Years: A History of the American Worker, 1933–1941* (Boston: Houghton-Mifflin, 1970), 80–81; "ILGWU published," Galenson, *CIO Challenge to the AFL*, 311.

67. Robert D. Parmet, *The Master of Seventh Avenue: David Dubinsky and the American Labor Movement* (New York: New York University Press, 2005), 4–188; Galenson, *CIO Challenge to the AFL*, 311–12; Zieger, *American Workers, American Unions*, 29–30.

68. Parmet, *Master of Seventh Avenue*, 121–28, 132–37, 146–53, 162–79; Raskin, *David Dubinsky*, 235–38; "Labor: The Big Split," *Time* (Dec. 4, 1939), 14; *New York Times*, May 31, 1940, 37.

69. Raskin, *David Dubinsky*, 145–55, quote is from 155; Parmet, *Master of Seventh Avenue*, 69, 116–18.

70. Raskin, *David Dubinsky*, quotes from 156–57, 155, respectively.

71. David Dubinsky, "Opening Session Speech," May 27, 1940, Madison Square Garden, 24th Convention of the ILGWU, folder 1A, box 32, ILGWU Papers.

72. Frederick F. Umhey to George Meany, Oct. 18, 1940, File 4B, box 2, ILGWU Papers.

73. In reviewing the particular choice of language for the resolution, Dubinsky's attorney explained at one point, "Nevertheless, I think it is important that the words, 'moral turpitude' be continued in the resolution so that a situation like the one presented in the Bioff case may properly come within the summary jurisdiction of the A.F. of L." (Emil Schlesinger to David Dubinsky, Nov. 20, 1940, folder 4A, box 2, ILGWU Papers).

74. Frederick F. Umhey to George Meany, Oct. 18, 1940, File 4B, box 2, ILGWU Papers.

75. "They agreed," *New York Times*, Nov. 17, 1940, 1; *New York Times*, June 7, 1940, 18; Raskin, *David Dubinsky*, 158–59.

76. Ibid., 159; *New York Times*, Nov. 28, 1941, 13; July 21, 1942, 10; Mar. 15, 1945, 1; Apr. 6, 1945, 1; Jan. 14, 1947, 1; Oct. 25, 1953, E10.

77. Raskin, *David Dubinsky*, 159–60; *New York Times*, Nov. 21, 1940, 1; *Chicago Tribune*, Nov. 22, 1940, 1.

78. *New York Times*, Nov. 21, 1940, 1; *Washington Post*, Nov. 24, 1940, 1; Raskin, *David Dubinsky*, 162–64.

79. *Report of Proceedings of the Sixteenth Annual Convention of the American Federation of Labor, Held at New Orleans, Louisiana, Nov. 18 to 29, Inclusive, 1940* (Washington, D.C.: Ransdell, 1940), 504–6.

80. Stolberg, "Sitting Bill," 95; Raskin, *David Dubinsky*, 164; *New York Times*, Nov. 29, 1940, 15.

81. *New York Times*, Nov. 28, 1940, 22.

82. "Convention Condemns Racketeering," *Federation News*, Dec. 4, 1940, 3.

83. Raskin, *David Dubinsky*, 164.

84. Dubinsky quoted in ibid.; *New York Times*, Oct. 5, 1941, 43.

85. Raskin, *David Dubinsky*, 169.

86. "Crime News from the AFL," *UE News* 2 (Feb. 3, 1940): 8.

87. "AFL Crime News: Scalise Convicted, Faces Long Term; Bioff Released," *CIO News* (Baltimore edition), Sept. 23, 1940, 6.

88. "A Contrast" (unsigned editorial), *CIO News* (Milwaukee edition), Mar. 25, 1940, 4.

89. "Bridges Reply: 'Clean Up Yourself,'" *San Francisco Chronicle*, Jan. 26, 1940, 5.

90. Ray Librizzi, "Punctures Pegler Scandal Balloon," *UE News* 3 (Nov. 29, 1941): 8.

91. "Anti-Union Legislation—Labor," *UE News* 3 (Dec. 13, 1941): 4.

92. Memorandum to Westbrook Pegler, Aug. 16, 1941; Robert E. Stripling to Westbrook Pegler, Sept. 6, 1941, both in folder Communism, Opponents of, House Un-American Activities Committee, 1941, box 21, Pegler Papers; Pegler, "Fair Enough," Sept. 5, 1941; May 7, 1942, boxes 121–22, Pegler Papers.

93. Conference of Representative of Congress of Industrial Organizations, National Press Club Auditorium, Washington, D.C., Mar. 23, 1942, pp. 4–5, in box 1, CIO Executive Board Minutes/Proceedings, Walter P. Reuther Library, Wayne State University, Detroit, Mich.

94. CIO Press Release, Apr. 13, 1942, folder PR Editors' Conferences, 1942–46, De Caux Papers; "Labor Haters on the March—The Union Times," *UE News* 3 (Dec. 6, 1941): 6.

95. James B. Carey, "Is Pegler Fair to Labor? No, Says James B. Carey, CIO Secretary-Treasurer," *Ladies' Home Journal* 60 (Oct. 1943): 128.

96. Untitled, typewritten notes, July 19, 1943, file Westbrook Pegler Debate, box 2, James B. Carey Papers, Walter P. Reuther Library.

97. "Hireling": p. 12, report of the National Officers of the National Council, National Maritime Union of America, CIO, July 10, 1944, submitted by Joseph Curran, president, in folder NMU #20, National and International Union series, box 7, Congress of Industrial Organizations Records, Catholic University, Washington, D.C.; "press lies," National Maritime Union, "The Enemy at Home" (pamphlet), p. 2, in folder Journalism: Articles, Pamphlets, Releases on, 1937–1956, box 15, Carl Haessler Papers, Walter P. Reuther Library.

98. Pegler, "Fair Enough," May 10, 1943, copy in folder NMU v. Westbrook Pegler, box 2, NMU Files.

99. Ferdinand C. Smith to all agents, Aug. 20, 1943, folder NMU v. Westbrook Pegler, box 2, Standard, NMU Files.

100. The columns concerned the case of a member of the CIO's International Longshoremen's and Warehousemen's Union who claimed to have been stripped of his union membership and his job because said he intended to vote for Thomas Dewey. The columns also insinuated that members of the ILWU were forced to make contributions that went to the Communist Party and that the union's internal judicial process was controlled by criminals and Communists (Westbrook Pegler, "A Union Member Tells Why He's Voting for Dewey," Sept. 26, 1944, box 123, Pegler Papers; see also notes titled, "Bridges," undated, in folder Libel, Bridges, box 56, Pegler Papers).

101. *New York Times*, Dec. 10, 1944, 45.

102. James B. Carey to Walter Fuller, folder Ladies Home Journal, box 24, CIO Secretary-Treasurer Collection.

103. Pilat, *Pegler: Angry Man of the Press*, 204.

104. Ward Greene to Westbrook Pegler, May 7, 1945; Clarence R. Lindner to Westbrook Pegler, May 8, 1945; Westbrook Pegler to care [of] W. R. Hearst, draft column, May 8, 1945, all in folder Libel, Bridges, box 56, Pegler Papers.

105. Grove J. Fink to John P. Gortatowsky, Feb. 26, 1947; undated notes, titled "Bridges," both in folder Libel, Bridges, box 56, Pegler Papers.

106. William L. Standard to Joseph Curran, June 1, 1945, folder NMU v. Westbrook Pegler, box 2, NMU Files.

107. *New York Times*, Aug. 20, 1943, 16.

108. "Pegler Picketed," *Collier's* (Oct. 2, 1943), 74, clipping in Pegler folder, box 195, Howard Papers.

109. Leo Huberman to the editor, *Collier's Weekly* (Sept. 26, 1943), folder NMU v. Westbrook Pegler, box 2, NMU Files.

110. L. J. Callinan to William Green, Dec. 1, 1941, folder 3, box 2, ILGWU Papers.

111. James P. Casey to William Green, Apr. 4, 1942, series 3A, box 15, IBT Papers.

112. Philip Pearl, "Warning to Racketeers," *Federation News*, Nov. 22, 1941, 1.

113. "A Bold Stroke for Labor," editorial, *New Republic* 105 (Nov. 10, 1941): 607.

114. Other calls for union regulation include R. S. Binkerd, "Will Congress Rescue the Unions?" *Atlantic* 168 (Nov. 1941): 549–56; John P. Troxell, "Protecting Members' Rights within the Union," *American Economic Review* 32 (Mar. 1942): 460–75; "Labor Can't Afford Obtuse Leadership," editorial, *Saturday Evening Post* 215 (Aug. 15, 1942): 104; William Hard, "Regulating Unions for the Common Good," *Readers' Digest* 41 (Sept. 1942): 43–47; see also "Proposed Federal Regulation of American Labor Unions," *Congressional Digest* 20 (Nov. 1941): 258–88.

115. Oswald Garrison Villard, "Why Unions Must Be Regulated," *Readers' Digest* 45 (Aug. 1944): 29; reprint from *American Mercury* 58 (June 1944): 667–74.

## Conclusion: Opportunities Lost and Opportunities Taken

1. Pegler, "Fair Enough," June 11, 1940; July 10, 1942, boxes 120 and 121, Pegler Papers.

2. Pegler, "Fair Enough," June 19, 1944, copy in folder 4, box 450, ILGWU Papers.

3. David Dubinsky to Westbrook Pegler, Nov. 28, 1942, folder 2, box 440, ILGWU Papers; David Dubinsky to Roy W. Howard, June 23, 1944, folder 4, box 450, ILGWU Papers.

4. Howard to Dubinsky, July 10, 1944, folder 4, box 450, ILGWU Papers.

5. Dubinsky to Howard, July 20, 1944, folder 4, box 450, ILGWU Papers.

6. Roy W. Howard to Westbrook Pegler, July 13, 1942, folder 1942, City File, New York, box 186, Howard Papers.

7. Howard to Pegler, Feb. 10, 1943, folder Executive Correspondence, New York, Westbrook Pegler, box 195, Howard Papers.

8. Roy W. Howard to Westbrook Pegler, May 23, 1944, Executive Correspondence, City File New York City, Westbrook Pegler folder, box 202, Howard Papers.

9. Pegler to Howard, Apr. 29, 1944, Executive Correspondence, City File New York City, Westbrook Pegler folder, box 202, Howard Papers.

10. Ibid.

11. Jimmy Mills, untitled, undated memo, enclosed in Howard to Pegler, May 23, 1944, Executive Correspondence, City File New York City, Westbrook Pegler folder, box 202, Howard Papers.

12. Charles Fisher, *The Columnists* (New York: Howell, Soskin, 1944), 167, 188–90.

13. Robert U. Brown, "Pegler Not Satisfied with Fruits of Ten Years Racket Campaigning," *Editor and Publisher* (July 31, 1943), 34.

14. Pegler, "Fair Enough," July 11, 1940, box 120, Pegler Papers.

15. Ibid.

16. Steven Fraser, "Is Democracy Good for Unions?" *Dissent* 45 (Summer 1998): 33–39; Joseph A. McCartin, "Democratizing the Demand for Workers' Rights," *Dissent* 52 (Winter 2005): 61–66; David Witwer, *Corruption and Reform in the Teamsters Union* (Chicago: University of Illinois Press, 2003), 207–8; Gilbert J. Gall, *The Politics of Right to Work: The Labor Federations as Special Interests, 1943–1979* (New York: Greenwood Press, 1988), 1–8, 17–19, 33–43.

17. American Civil Liberties Union, *Democracy in Trade Unions: A Survey, with a Program of Action* (New York: American Civil Liberties Union, 1943); Clyde W. Summers, *Democracy in Labor Unions: A Report and Statement of Policy* (New York: American Civil Liberties Union, 1952); for an example of a claim that union democracy will reenergize the labor movement, see Herman Benson, *Rebels, Reformers, and Racketeers: How Insurgents Transformed the Labor Movement* (Brooklyn: Association for Union Democracy, 2005), ix–xv.

18. Willard Shelton, "Labor," *New Republic* 116 (Mar. 3, 1947): 31.

19. David Witwer, "The Landrum-Griffin Act: A Case Study in the Possibilities and Problems in Anti-Union Corruption Law," *Criminal Justice Review* 27 (Autumn 2002): 301–20; Michael Goldberg, "Cleaning Labor's House: Institutional Reform Litigation in the Labor Movement," *Duke Law Journal*, no. 4 (September 1989): 965–83; Clyde Summers, "Democracy in a One Party State: Perspectives from Landrum-Griffin," *Maryland Law Review* 43, no. 1 (1984): 93–117; James B. Jacobs, *Mobsters, Unions, and Feds: The Mafia and the American Labor Movement* (New York: New York University Press, 2006).

20. Westbrook Pegler, "As Pegler Sees It: New Pross Estate Recalls Scalise Case," June 18, 1946, box 124; example of such an invocation in "Punitive Labor Laws and the Racketeers," Jan. 11, 1947, box 125, Pegler Papers.

21. Westbrook Pegler to William J. Clothier, Sept. 14, 1948, folder Unions, Correspondence, 1922–1963 and undated, box 76, Pegler Papers.

22. Oliver Pilat and John Grover, "Pegler Pits Pen against Anything," *Los Angeles Mirror*, Aug. 16, 1954, 1.

23. Lawrence Van Gelder, "Victor Riesel, 81, Columnist Blinded by Acid Attack, Dies," *New York Times*, Jan. 5, 1995, B11; Pete Hamill, "In Defense of Honest Labor," *New York Times Magazine*, Dec. 31, 1995, 18; "Riesel's Labor," *Newsweek* 37 (Jan. 15, 1951): 60.

24. U.S. National Labor Relations Board, *Legislative History of the Labor Management Relations Act, 1947* (Washington, D.C.: U.S. Government Printing Office, 1948), 2: 1470.

25. *Congressional Record* (Jan. 29, 1937), 81, pt. 1: 586.

26. *Congressional Record* (Jan. 23, 1938), 83, pt. 1: 1020; *Congressional Record* (Mar. 30, 1937), 81, pt. 2: 2915; *Congressional Record* (Feb. 25, 1937), 81, pt. 2: 24–25.

27. "Unbridled Union Power Threat to Security," editorial, *Saturday Evening Post* 129 (May 24, 1947): 176.

28. NLRB, *Legislative History of LMRA, 1947*, 2: 1325.

29. *New York Times*, July 14, 1938, 2; May 12, 1969, 57; Andrew E. Kersten, *Labor's Home Front: The American Federation of Labor during World War II* (New York: New York University Press, 2006), 59; NLRB, *Legislative History of LMRA, 1947*, 2: 1325.

30. *New York Times*, May 18, 1947, E1; Beverly Smith, "What Joe Martin Wants to Do," *Saturday Evening Post* 219 (Jan. 18, 1947): 13; Clare Hoffman to Harry H. Whiteley, Feb. 18, 1946, folder Newspapers-District, box 8, Clare E. Hoffman Papers, Bentley Historical Library, University of Michigan, Ann Arbor.

31. About Ball: James T. Patterson, *Mr. Republican: A Biography of Robert A. Taft* (Boston: Houghton Mifflin, 1972), 354. Ball's quote: NLRB, *Legislative History of LMRA, 1947*, 2: 1198; Hoffman, NLRB, *Legislative History of the LMRA, 1947*, 1: 622; Fred A. Hartley Jr., *Our New National Labor Policy: The Taft-Hartley Act and the Next Steps* (New York: Funk and Wagnalls, in association with Modern Industry Magazine, 1948), 48.

32. NLRB, *Legislative History of LMRA, 1947*, 1: 630.

33. R. Alton Lee, *Truman and Taft-Hartley: A Question of Mandate* (Lexington: University of Kentucky Press, 1966), 47.

34. *Chicago Tribune*, Dec. 6, 1946, 43; secondary boycott, NLRB, *Legislative History of LMRA, 1947*, 2: 1371.

35. Lee, *Truman and Taft-Hartley*, 61–63, 66.

36. William S. White, "Conferees Approve Bill to Curb Labor in Victory for Taft," *New York Times*, May 30, 1947, 1; NLRB, *Legislative History of LMRA, 1947*, 2: 1542; Patterson, *Mr. Republican*, 363; Westbrook Pegler, "As Pegler Sees It: Chance to End Wagner Act Appears to Stun G.O.P.," Dec. 31, 1946, box 125, Pegler Papers.

37. Lee, *Truman and Taft-Hartley*, 1–79, 96–105; James Boylan, *The New Deal Coalition and the Election of 1946* (New York: Garland, 1981), 32–54.

38. NLRB, *Legislative History of LMRA, 1947*. Twyman's quote is on p. 1: 802, O'Toole on p. 1: 684.

39. Willard Shelton, "Unions and Racketeering," *New Republic* 116 (Apr. 21, 1947): 34.

40. *New York Times*, Aug. 10, 1954, 1; Gerald Meyer, *Vito Marcantonio: Radical Politician, 1902–1954* (Albany: State University of New York Press, 1989), 62–65, 80–86; Allan Schaffer, *Vito Marcantonio: Radical in Congress* (Syracuse: Syracuse University Press, 1966), 149–59.

41. NLRB, *Legislative History, LMRA, 1947*, 1: 606; postwar inflation issue, Boylan, *New Deal Coalition and the Election of 1946*, 55–70; Meg Jacobs, "'How about Some Meat?': The Office of Price Administration, Consumption Politics, and State Build-

ing from the Bottom Up, 1941–1946," *Journal of American History* 84 (Dec. 1997): 935–41.

42. Leo Egan, "Accord with Taft Detailed by Ives," *New York Times*, May 25, 1947, 38.

43. Christopher L. Tomlins, *The State and the Unions: Labor Relations, Law, and the Organized Labor Movement in America, 1880–1960* (Cambridge: Cambridge University Press, 1985), 247–51, 284–97, quote is on p. 288.

44. Harry A. Millis and Emily Clark Brown, *From the Wagner Act to Taft-Hartley: A Study of National Labor Policy and Labor Relations* (Chicago: University of Chicago Press, 1950), 537–44 ; Pegler, "'Punitive' Labor Laws and the Racketeers," Jan. 11, 1947, box 125, Pegler Papers; Robert F. Kennedy, *The Enemy Within* (New York: Popular Library, 1960), 30–31.

45. Southern states: William H. Miernyk, *Trade Unions in the Age of Affluence* (New York: Random House, 1962), 25, 135–36; Millis, *From the Wagner Act to Taft-Hartley*, 399–400, 428–40, 455–81, 489–96; quote is from Timothy J. Minchin, *Fighting against the Odds: A History of Southern Labor Since WWII* (Gainesville: University Press of Florida, 2005), 45.

46. Lichtenstein, *State of the Union*, 118–19.

47. Zieger, *American Workers: American Unions*, 110–11.

48. *New York Times*, June 24, 1947, 1.

49. Quote is from Lichtenstein, *State of the Union*, 120. Discussions of Taft-Hartley's limited immediate impact include Tomlins, *The State and the Unions*, 247–51, 286–316; and Melvyn Dubofsky, *The State and Labor in Modern America* (Chapel Hill: University of North Carolina Press, 1994), 201–12.

50. Robert H. Zieger, *American Workers: American Unions*, 2nd ed. (Baltimore: Johns Hopkins University Press, 1994), 130–34; Lichtenstein, *State of the Union*, 115–17.

51. U.S. Congress, House Committee on Education and Labor, "The Dock Street Case, Philadelphia, Pa.," *Hearings*, 80th Cong., 1st sess., Feb. 7, 1947 (Washington, D.C.: U.S. Government Printing Office, 1947); *Chicago Tribune*, Feb. 27, 1947, 1.

52. Pegler, "Fair Enough," Oct. 12, 1940, box 120, Pegler Papers.

53. *New York Times*, Apr. 7, 1947, 1.

54. Examples of Hoffman's prominent role in these investigations can be found in Willard Shelton, "Unions and Rackets," *New Republic* 116 (Apr. 21, 1947): 34; and *New York Times*, Nov. 28, 1953, 32. The role of Goldwater and conservative Republicans in the McClellan Committee is described in Anthony V. Baltakis, "Agendas of Investigation: The McClellan Committee, 1957–1958" (PhD diss., University of Akron, 1997), 37–67, 118–22, 223–43, 275–76. The New York State hearings are documented in New York State Crime Commission, *Public Hearings (No. 5) Conducted by the New York State Crime Commission Pursuant to the Governor's Executive Orders of March 29, 1951 and Nov. 13, 1952* (Albany: New York State, 1952). A search of the *Readers' Guide* for the term "labor racketeering" in the time period from 1945 to 1960 comes up with

278 articles, most of which are on the congressional or New York State investigations. *On the Waterfront*, dir. Elia Kazan, Columbia Pictures, 1954.

55. David Witwer, *Corruption and Reform in the Teamsters Union* (Chicago: University of Illinois Press, 2003), 183–204, 210–11.

56. *Wall Street Journal*, July 22, 1959, 12; "bulldozer," Alan K. McAdams, *Power and Politics in Labor Legislation* (New York: Columbia University Press, 1964), 69–70; Witwer, *Corruption and Reform*, 204–11.

57. President's Commission on Organized Crime, *The Edge: Organized Crime, Business, and Labor Unions* (Washington, D.C.: U.S. Government Printing Office, Mar. 1986), 1–7, 241–51; James B. Jacobs, *Mobsters, Unions, and Feds: The Mafia and the American Labor Movement* (New York: New York University Press, 2006), 23–39, 122–28; Witwer, *Corruption and Reform*, 157–82.

58. E. H. Foley, Inter-Office Communication to Secretary Morgenthau, Apr. 10, 1940, p. 35, microfilm reel 68, Henry Morgenthau Jr., Morgenthau Diaries, Franklin Roosevelt Presidential Library, Hyde Park, N.Y.

59. *Chicago Daily News*, Mar. 1, 1943; *Motion Picture Herald*, June 26, 1943, descriptive quote is from *New York World-Telegram*, Nov. 5, 1943; *New York Times*, Apr. 15, 1985, D1; Kostelanetz quote is from author's interview with Boris Kostelanetz, Oct. 6, 2001; regarding his previous prosecutions at U.S. Attorneys Office, *New York Times*, May 17, 1939, 12; Jan. 30, 1940, 7; Dec. 17, 1940, 29.

60. Fourteen filing cabinets: "Personal," *True Detective* (Dec. 1944), clipping from Kostelanetz; Kostelanetz's role in leading the investigation and prosecution: Kostelanetz interview with author; C. A. Grill, memorandum for Mr. Rosen, Feb. 3, 1942, FBI Serial No. 60–2149–376; James Rower Jr., assistant to the attorney general to Mathias F. Correa and J. Albert Woll, Apr. 5, 1942, FBI Serial No. 60–2149–427; P. E. Foxworth to director, Aug. 8, 1942, FBI Serial No. 60–2149–428; E. E. Conroy to director, June 29, 1943, FBI serial no. 60–2149–549, all in FBI Bioff File; regarding Browne and Bioff's cooperation, Conroy teletype to director, Aug. 2, 1943, FBI Serial No. 60–2149–569; P. E. Foxworth to director, Apr. 27, 1942, FBI Serial No. 60–2149–408; Alf Oftedal, memorandums of interviews with William Bioff, Apr. 20, 1942, Apr. 30, 1942, May 7, 1942, all in FBI Serial No. 60–2149–410; Boris Kostelanetz, memorandum to Robert J. Lynch, Jan. 8, 1943, FBI Serial No. 60–2149–443, all in FBI Bioff File; description of Bioff taking part in meeting with grand jury witness, *Chicago Tribune*, Mar. 20, 1943, 7.

61. *New York Herald-Tribune*, Mar. 20, 1943, 1; *Chicago Daily News*, Mar. 20, 1943, 1; *New York Sun*, Dec. 31, 1943, 1.

62. *New York Herald-Tribune*, Mar. 20, 1943, 1; *Chicago Sun*, Jan. 1, 1944, 1; *Chicago Tribune*, Mar. 20, 1943, 1.

63. C. A. Grill, memorandum for Mr. Rosen, Feb. 3, 1942, FBI Serial No. 60–2149–376; P. E. Foxworth to director, Oct. 23, 1941, FBI Serial No. 60–2149–295, both in FBI Bioff File.

64. *Chicago Daily News*, Mar. 19, 1943; Kostelanetz quote in *Newark Star-Ledger*,

Dec. 31, 1943; predictions of further indictments, *Chicago Herald-American*, Feb. 14, 1944; *Chicago Sun*, Jan. 1, 1944.

65. *Philadelphia Record*, Apr. 5, 1944; *Scranton Times*, Apr. 6, 1944; postponements of mail fraud case, E. E. Conroy to director, Mar. 10, 1944, FBI Serial No. 60–2149–702; report by Thomas V. Wade, Feb. 3, 1945, FBI Serial No. 60–2149–738; R. D. Scott to Mr. Rosen, Apr. 3, 1945, FBI Serial No. 60–2149–741, all in FBI Bioff File; parole decision: report by [name blacked out], Mar. 13, 1953, especially pp. 1–3, FBI Serial No. 58–2000–2450, FBI Bioff File; Mars Eghigian Jr., *After Capone: The Life and World of Chicago Mob Boss Frank 'the Enforcer' Nitti* (Nashville: Cumberland House, 2006), 407–11; *New York Times*, June 17, 1948, 26.

Although the board approved early parole for six of the defendants (Campagna, Gioe, D'Andrea, De Lucia, Roselli, and Maritote—the Outfit leaders), only five of them were released immediately; a technicality regarding how Maritote had chosen to serve his time meant that he officially had served less of his sentence than the other defendants (House of Representatives, Subcommittee of the Committee on Expenditures in the Executive Departments, "Investigation as to the Manner in Which the United States Board of Parole Is Operating and as to Whether There Is a Necessity for a Change in Either the Procedure or the Basic Law," *Hearings*, 80th Cong., 2nd sess. [Washington, D.C.: U.S. Government Printing Office, 1948], 550–51).

66. "Investigation as to the Manner in Which the United States Board of Parole Is Operating"; Mr. Ladd to Mr. Rosen, Nov. 14, 1952, FBI Serial No. 158–2000–2127, FBI Bioff File; Eghigian, *After Capone*, 407–11.

67. Lester Velie, "A Man Is Waiting to Be Murdered," *Reader's Digest* 68 (Mar. 1956): 46–47.

68. Quote is from *Washington Daily News*, Nov. 5, 1955, 2; wife looking out window, *Chicago Tribune*, Nov. 5, 1955, 1; allegations regarding activity in Las Vegas, SAC Phoenix to director, FBI, Mar. 16, 1956, FBI Serial No. 95–61386–18; H. L. Edwards to Mr. Mohr, Mar. 29, 1956, FBI Serial No. 95–61386–20, in FBI Bioff File; the sheriff's report on the bomb, L. C. Boies to John Edgar Hoover, re: Willie Bioff, aka William Nelson, Nov. 9, 1955, FBI Serial No. 95–61386–1, FBI Bioff File.

69. Warren Olney III, assistant attorney general, Criminal Division, to director, Federal Bureau of Investigation, Nov. 14, 1955, FBI Serial No. 95–61386–5, FBI Bioff File.

70. Teletype, SAC Phoenix to Director, FBI, Nov. 19, 1955, FBI Serial No. 95–61386–6, FBI Bioff File.

71. In 1956, after another federal grand jury witness in this case, Louis Greenberg, had been killed, Lester Velie, a journalist who wrote frequently on union corruption, did an article claiming that George Browne was an obvious target for an Outfit assassination. One of the article's readers was moved to write Senator John F. Kennedy who passed the letter along to the FBI, apparently with the intent that the FBI would protect Browne. The Bureau's internal memoranda repeats the same formula they had invoked to avoid involvement in investigating Bioff's death. "No specific informa-

tion has been received indicating Browne is the intended victim of any conspiracy to obstruct justice," the memo reads, "or that either Bioff or Greenberg were killed as a result of their testimony." According to a Bureau informant, Browne saw things differently and expected to be killed at any time. He was living in Burlington, Iowa, at the time and that was the last any Bureau memoranda ever referred to him. After that he disappears from the federal record (C. A. Evans to Mr. Rosen, May 22, 1956, FBI Serial No. 60–2149–767, FBI Bioff File).

72. Quote is from report by James E. Conerty, Aug. 6, 1943, p. 9, FBI Serial No. 60–2149–565, FBI Bioff File; long-term corruption, Ovid Demaris, *Captive City* (New York: Lyle Stuart, 1969), 33–36.

73. "Slaying Is Linked to Union Rackets," *New York Times*, Mar. 3, 1960, 59.

# Index

American Federation of Actors (AFA), 132–33, 142

American Federation of Labor (AFL): break from Committee on Industrial Organization, 210–11; response to Pegler, 211, 213–26. *See also* William Green

Baer, John M., 206

Balaban, Barney, 65, 82

Balaban and Katz Theater Chain, 64–65, 89–92, 95

Barker, George ("Red"), 47

Bioff, William: corrupt union activities of, 64–67, 89–97; criminal conviction of, 5; investigation of in California, 126–28; loan from Joseph Schenck, 128–29; murder of, 252–53; news coverage of 170–71; Pegler's exposé of, 2, 155–61; personal history, 59–64; photograph of, 58; resigns from IATSE, 129; response to Pegler, 3, 212

Bonanno, Joseph, 38–39

Boyle, Michael, 183

Bridges, Harry, 122–23, 198, 226–29, 246

Browne, George: corrupt union activities of, 64–65, 93–96; criminal conviction of, 5, 60, 182; Pegler's description of, 159; personal history, 63–64; relationship with Outfit, 66–67, 114–15

Buchalter, Louis, 72, 76

Building Service Employees International Union: early union history, 49–50; Local 32B, 106; Local 32J, 108; Local 94, 106–7; Local 117, 166; Outfit co-opts leadership of, 50, 67, 79; Scalise's early history in, 79–80

Burke, Thomas, 80, 163

California State Assembly, Interim Committee on Capital and Labor (aborted investigation of William Bioff), 126–28

Capone, Alphonse, 36–37, 39, 44

Capone, Ralph, 39

Carey, James, 227–28

Carfano, Anthony (also known as Little Augie Pisano), 75–76, 79–80, 105

Carrazzo, Michael, 67

Chicago Exhibitors' Association, 90–91

Circella, Nicholas, 65, 88, 90–92

Clay, John, 48

Chicago Teamsters, 46–47

Columbia Pictures, 94, 112

columnists, syndicated newspaper, 27–28

Communist Party of the United States (CPUSA), 121–22

congressional investigations of labor racketeering, 247–49

Congress of Industrial Organizations (CIO), 121, 125, 141, 210–11, 183, 226–30

Courtney, Thomas, 42–43

Cox, Eugene, 197–98
Curran, Joseph, 205, 228. *See also* National Maritime Union

Darling, Jay "Ding," 16, 146
Dewey, Thomas, 2, 203–2, 248
Dies, Martin, 187–88. *See also* House Un-American Activities Committee
Dubinsky, David, 221–26, 234–35
Drucci, Vincent, 43
Dungan, John, 48–49

Employers' Association of Chicago, 185

Fay, Joseph, 183, 224
Federated Motion Picture Crafts (FMPC), 100–103, 123, 131
Flore, Edward, 53. *See also* Hotel and Restaurant Employees International Union

Gannett, Frank, 151
Gilbert, Daniel, 42–43, 51, 54–55, 159
Goldberg, Rube, 232
Goldwater, Barry, 248
Green, William, 5, 157–60, 209–10, 213–20. *See also* American Federation of Labor

Hardy, Charles Jr., 162
Hardy, Charles Sr., 161–66
Hardy, George, 163–65
Hartley, Fred, 247
Hearst, William Randolph, 151–52
Hentschel, Irving, 122, 127
Hoffa, James R., 248–49
Hoffman, Clare, 180–81
Horan, Jerry, 50, 67, 79. *See also* Building Service Employees' International Union.
Hostetter, Gordon L., 185
Hotel and Restaurant Employees' International Union: Local 278, 51–55. *See also* Edward Flore; George McLane
House Un-American Activities Committee, 178, 187–88. *See also* Martin Dies
Howard, Roy W.: background of, 150; Dubinsky correspondence, 234–35; managing columnists, 152–54; New Deal, attitude towards, 150–51; news media's role, view of, 147–48; Pegler's campaign, assessment of, 173, 235–36; Wagner Act,

view of, 154. *See also* Scripps-Howard Newspaper Chain
Humphreys, Murray, 47, 51–52, 54

International Alliance of Theatrical Stage Employes: early history, 68; governance structure of, 109–10; Local 2, 64; Local 37, 97–99, 103–4, 119–20; 123; Local 110, 70–72, 89–91, 94, 114, 253; Local 144, 73; Local 306, 72–73, 92–93; projectionists' locals, 68–73; Studio Basic Agreement, participant in, 94–95; two percent assessment, 108–17. *See also* William Bioff; George Browne; IA Progressives
International Alliance (IA) Progressives: exposé of Bioff, 118, 125–26; formation of, 123–24; reform efforts, 126–27, 128–29, 140–42; source for Pegler's exposé, 139–40
International Brotherhood of Teamsters, 76–79, 81, 175–76, 183–84. *See also* Chicago Teamsters
International Longshoremen's and Warehousemen's Union (ILWU), 122–23. *See also* Harry Bridges

Jones, William Mosley, 126–27
Justice Department (United States), 86–87, 143–45

Kaltenborn, Hans von (H.V.), 191, 227
Kaplan, Samuel, 72
Kelly-Nash Machine (Chicago), 41–42
Kent, Sidney, 82, 95–96
Kibre, Jeff, 121–23, 140
Kostelanetz, Boris, 249–51

Landrum-Griffin Act (1959), 239–40
Leonard, Morris, 90–91
Lewis, John L., 189, 194–95, 197, 244
licensing, 44, 55
Loews Theater Chain, 93–94, 96
Luciano, Charles ("Lucky"), 45

Mafia, 38–39. *See also* Outfit
Maloney, William, 183
Maloy, Thomas, 70–72, 88, 89, 114. *See also* International Alliance of Theatrical Stage Employes, Local 110

Marcontonio, Vito, 244–45
Mayer, Louis B., 96–97, 100, 126, 131
McCormick, Richard L., 172
McCormick, Robert R., 151–52
McLane, George, 51–55. *See also* Hotel and
    Restaurant Employees' International
    Union
McWilliams, Carey, 119–20, 124–27, 170–71
Montgomery, Robert: background of,
    133–34; leadership of Screen Actors
    Guild, 130, opposition to William Bioff,
    131–32, 134–35; refers leads to law en-
    forcement, 135–37, 142; source for Pegler's
    exposé, 139
Moran, George ("Bugs"), 40–43
Morgenthau, Robert, 136–37, 143–45
Murray, Phillip, 227

National Association of Manufacturers,
    186–87, 201–2
National Labor Relations Act (1935),
    (Wagner Act), 4
National Maritime Union (NMU), 205, 207,
    228–30. *See also* Joseph Curran
Neblett, William, 126–27
New Deal, 175–81
Newspaper Guild, 32, 151
Nitti, Frank: criminal career, 37–39, 45, 56,
    67; involvement in IATSE corruption, 67,
    88; meets with George McLane, 51–52;
    Pegler writes about, 159; suicide of, 250;
    tax case against, 97–98

Outfit (Chicago Mafia), 38–56, 86–87, 158

Padway, Joseph, 74, 220–21
Paramount Pictures, 94–95, 110
Parrish, Joseph, 174, 176
Pegler, James (Westbrook): anti-union cor-
    ruption crusade, 147–48, 155–61, 182,
    184–85; attacks war-time union abuses,
    189–91; CIO, criticism of, 183; decline
    in later career, 236–37, 240–41; early bi-
    ography of, 17–19; exposés of Bioff and
    Scalise, 1–6, 119–20, 138–40, 155–61; fame,
    6–7, 16–17; Federal Bureau of Investiga-
    tion file on, 2–5; George Spelvin charac-
    ter, 15; New Deal, attitude toward, 30–32,
    195–97; organized labor, views on, 32–35;

response to criticism, 236; sports writ-
    ing, 23–26; union reform, goal of, 237–38;
    writing style, 15–17, 28–30, 184–85; World
    War I correspondent, 19–23
public opinion polls, 192–93, 202–3

racketeering, 185–86, 193–94, 240–45
Republican Party, 203–4
Reynolds, Robert, 181
Ricca, Paul, 45
Rio, Frank, 43, 65–66
RKO (Radio-Keith-Orpheum) Pictures,
    93–95
Romano, Louis, 52
Roosevelt, Franklin Delano, 17, 175–77,
    202
Rosenblatt, Sol, 95–96

S and S Theaters, 89–90, 92
Scalise, George: arrest of, 1, 84; biography
    of, 74–79; career in BSEIU, 79–80; cor-
    rupt activities, 105–8; description of, 59;
    news coverage of, 3–4, 168–71; opponents
    within union, 161–66; Pegler campaign
    against, 1–3, 166–67; responds to Pegler,
    3, 212–13
Schenck, Joseph, 85–86, 97, 100–101, 128,
    145, 157
Schenck, Nicholas, 82, 83, 86–87, 95–97
Schwartz, Isadore, 79
Screen Actors Guild (SAG), 99–101, 119–20,
    130–37, 142–45. *See also* Robert Mont-
    gomery
Scripps, Edward Wyllis, 149–50
Scripps-Howard Newspaper Chain, 149–52,
    154, 172
Smith, Howard W., 187, 201
Smith-Connally War Labor Disputes Act,
    12, 200–201
Spitz, Leo, 82, 95
St. Valentine's Day Massacre (1929), 40–41,
    43

Taft, Robert, 204, 243
Taft-Hartley Act (1947), 12, 242–47
Taylor, Matthew, 46
Teamsters. *See* International Brotherhood of
    Teamsters; Chicago Teamsters
Thompson, William (Big Bill), 41, 49

Touhy, Roger, 43, 51
Twentieth Century-Fox, 85–86, 94–95

union democracy, 237–39
United Studio Technicians Guild (USTG),
    140–42. *See also* IA Progressives

Voorhis, Jeremiah (Jerry), 199

Warner Brothers, 89–90, 94, 104
Whitehead, Ralph, 132, 142
Willkie, Wendell, 173, 180
World War II, 188–95

Zuta, Jack, 62, 125
Zwillman, Abner (Longie), 72–73

**DAVID WITWER** is an associate professor of history at Penn State–Harrisburg. He is the author of *Corruption and Reform in the Teamsters Union*, which won the Wentworth Prize and was named a *Choice Magazine* outstanding academic book of 2003.

## THE WORKING CLASS IN AMERICAN HISTORY

Worker City, Company Town: Iron and Cotton-Worker Protest in Troy and Cohoes, New York, 1855–84 *Daniel J. Walkowitz*

Life, Work, and Rebellion in the Coal Fields: The Southern West Virginia Miners, 1880–1922 *David Alan Corbin*

Women and American Socialism, 1870–1920 *Mari Jo Buhle*

Lives of Their Own: Blacks, Italians, and Poles in Pittsburgh, 1900–1960 *John Bodnar, Roger Simon, and Michael P. Weber*

Working-Class America: Essays on Labor, Community, and American Society *Edited by Michael H. Frisch and Daniel J. Walkowitz*

Eugene V. Debs: Citizen and Socialist *Nick Salvatore*

American Labor and Immigration History, 1877–1920s: Recent European Research *Edited by Dirk Hoerder*

Workingmen's Democracy: The Knights of Labor and American Politics *Leon Fink*

The Electrical Workers: A History of Labor at General Electric and Westinghouse, 1923–60 *Ronald W. Schatz*

The Mechanics of Baltimore: Workers and Politics in the Age of Revolution, 1763–1812 *Charles G. Steffen*

The Practice of Solidarity: American Hat Finishers in the Nineteenth Century *David Bensman*

The Labor History Reader *Edited by Daniel J. Leab*

Solidarity and Fragmentation: Working People and Class Consciousness in Detroit, 1875–1900 *Richard Oestreicher*

Counter Cultures: Saleswomen, Managers, and Customers in American Department Stores, 1890–1940 *Susan Porter Benson*

The New England Working Class and the New Labor History *Edited by Herbert G. Gutman and Donald H. Bell*

Labor Leaders in America *Edited by Melvyn Dubofsky and Warren Van Tine*

Barons of Labor: The San Francisco Building Trades and Union Power in the Progressive Era *Michael Kazin*

Gender at Work: The Dynamics of Job Segregation by Sex during World War II *Ruth Milkman*

Once a Cigar Maker: Men, Women, and Work Culture in American Cigar Factories, 1900–1919 *Patricia A. Cooper*

A Generation of Boomers: The Pattern of Railroad Labor Conflict in Nineteenth-Century America *Shelton Stromquist*

Work and Community in the Jungle: Chicago's Packinghouse Workers, 1894–1922 *James R. Barrett*

Workers, Managers, and Welfare Capitalism: The Shoeworkers and Tanners of Endicott Johnson, 1890–1950 *Gerald Zahavi*

Men, Women, and Work: Class, Gender, and Protest in the New England Shoe Industry, 1780–1910 *Mary Blewett*

Workers on the Waterfront: Seamen, Longshoremen, and Unionism in the 1930s
    *Bruce Nelson*
German Workers in Chicago: A Documentary History of Working-Class Culture from
    1850 to World War I    *Edited by Hartmut Keil and John B. Jentz*
On the Line: Essays in the History of Auto Work    *Edited by Nelson Lichtenstein and
    Stephen Meyer III*
Labor's Flaming Youth: Telephone Operators and Worker Militancy, 1878–1923
    *Stephen H. Norwood*
Another Civil War: Labor, Capital, and the State in the Anthracite Regions of
    Pennsylvania, 1840–68    *Grace Palladino*
Coal, Class, and Color: Blacks in Southern West Virginia, 1915–32
    *Joe William Trotter, Jr.*
For Democracy, Workers, and God: Labor Song-Poems and Labor Protest, 1865–95
    *Clark D. Halker*
Dishing It Out: Waitresses and Their Unions in the Twentieth Century
    *Dorothy Sue Cobble*
The Spirit of 1848: German Immigrants, Labor Conflict, and the Coming of the Civil
    War    *Bruce Levine*
Working Women of Collar City: Gender, Class, and Community in Troy, New York,
    1864–86    *Carole Turbin*
Southern Labor and Black Civil Rights: Organizing Memphis Workers
    *Michael K. Honey*
Radicals of the Worst Sort: Laboring Women in Lawrence, Massachusetts, 1860–1912
    *Ardis Cameron*
Producers, Proletarians, and Politicians: Workers and Party Politics in Evansville and
    New Albany, Indiana, 1850–87    *Lawrence M. Lipin*
The New Left and Labor in the 1960s    *Peter B. Levy*
The Making of Western Labor Radicalism: Denver's Organized Workers, 1878–1905
    *David Brundage*
In Search of the Working Class: Essays in American Labor History and Political
    Culture    *Leon Fink*
Lawyers against Labor: From Individual Rights to Corporate Liberalism
    *Daniel R. Ernst*
"We Are All Leaders": The Alternative Unionism of the Early 1930s    *Edited by
    Staughton Lynd*
The Female Economy: The Millinery and Dressmaking Trades, 1860–1930
    *Wendy Gamber*
"Negro and White, Unite and Fight!": A Social History of Industrial Unionism in
    Meatpacking, 1930–90    *Roger Horowitz*
Power at Odds: The 1922 National Railroad Shopmen's Strike    *Colin J. Davis*
The Common Ground of Womanhood: Class, Gender, and Working Girls' Clubs,
    1884–1928    *Priscilla Murolo*
Marching Together: Women of the Brotherhood of Sleeping Car Porters
    *Melinda Chateauvert*

Down on the Killing Floor: Black and White Workers in Chicago's Packinghouses,
  1904–54   *Rick Halpern*
Labor and Urban Politics: Class Conflict and the Origins of Modern Liberalism in
  Chicago, 1864–97   *Richard Schneirov*
All That Glitters: Class, Conflict, and Community in Cripple Creek
  *Elizabeth Jameson*
Waterfront Workers: New Perspectives on Race and Class   *Edited by Calvin Winslow*
Labor Histories: Class, Politics, and the Working-Class Experience   *Edited by*
  *Eric Arnesen, Julie Greene, and Bruce Laurie*
The Pullman Strike and the Crisis of the 1890s: Essays on Labor and Politics   *Edited*
  *by Richard Schneirov, Shelton Stromquist, and Nick Salvatore*
AlabamaNorth: African-American Migrants, Community, and Working-Class
  Activism in Cleveland, 1914–45   *Kimberley L. Phillips*
Imagining Internationalism in American and British Labor, 1939–49   *Victor Silverman*
William Z. Foster and the Tragedy of American Radicalism   *James R. Barrett*
Colliers across the Sea: A Comparative Study of Class Formation in Scotland and the
  American Midwest, 1830–1924   *John H. M. Laslett*
"Rights, Not Roses": Unions and the Rise of Working-Class Feminism, 1945–80
  *Dennis A. Deslippe*
Testing the New Deal: The General Textile Strike of 1934 in the American South
  *Janet Irons*
Hard Work: The Making of Labor History   *Melvyn Dubofsky*
Southern Workers and the Search for Community: Spartanburg County, South
  Carolina   *G. C. Waldrep III*
We Shall Be All: A History of the Industrial Workers of the World (abridged edition)
  *Melvyn Dubofsky, ed. Joseph A. McCartin*
Race, Class, and Power in the Alabama Coalfields, 1908–21   *Brian Kelly*
Duquesne and the Rise of Steel Unionism   *James D. Rose*
Anaconda: Labor, Community, and Culture in Montana's Smelter City   *Laurie Mercier*
Bridgeport's Socialist New Deal, 1915–36   *Cecelia Bucki*
Indispensable Outcasts: Hobo Workers and Community in the American Midwest,
  1880–1930   *Frank Tobias Higbie*
After the Strike: A Century of Labor Struggle at Pullman   *Susan Eleanor Hirsch*
Corruption and Reform in the Teamsters Union   *David Witwer*
Waterfront Revolts: New York and London Dockworkers, 1946–61   *Colin J. Davis*
Black Workers' Struggle for Equality in Birmingham   *Horace Huntley and*
  *David Montgomery*
The Tribe of Black Ulysses: African American Men in the Industrial South
  *William P. Jones*
City of Clerks: Office and Sales Workers in Philadelphia, 1870–1920
  *Jerome P. Bjelopera*
Reinventing "The People": The Progressive Movement, the Class Problem, and the
  Origins of Modern Liberalism   *Shelton Stromquist*
Radical Unionism in the Midwest, 1900–1950   *Rosemary Feurer*

Gendering Labor History   *Alice Kessler-Harris*

James P. Cannon and the Origins of the American Revolutionary Left, 1890–1928
   *Bryan D. Palmer*

Glass Towns: Industry, Labor, and Political Economy in Appalachia, 1890–1930s
   *Ken Fones-Wolf*

Workers and the Wild: Conservation, Consumerism, and Labor in Oregon, 1910–30
   *Lawrence M. Lipin*

Wobblies on the Waterfront: Interracial Unionism in Progressive-Era Philadelphia
   *Peter Cole*

Red Chicago: American Communism at Its Grassroots, 1928–35   *Randi Storch*

Labor's Cold War: Local Politics in a Global Context   *Edited by Shelton Stromquist*

Bessie Abromowitz Hillman and the Making of the Amalgamated Clothing Workers
   of America   *Karen Pastorello*

The Great Strikes of 1877   *Edited by David O. Stowell*

Union-Free America: Workers and Antiunion Culture   *Lawrence Richards*

Race against Liberalism: Black Workers and the UAW in Detroit
   *David M. Lewis-Colman*

Teachers and Reform: Chicago Public Education, 1929–70   *John F. Lyons*

Upheaval in the Quiet Zone: 1199/SEIU and the Politics of Healthcare Unionism
   *Leon Fink and Brian Greenberg*

Shadow of the Racketeer: Scandal in Organized Labor   *David Witwer*

The University of Illinois Press
is a founding member of the
Association of American University Presses.

_____

Composed in 10.5/13 Adobe Minion Pro
with FF Meta display
at the University of Illinois Press
Manufactured by Sheridan Books, Inc.

University of Illinois Press
1325 South Oak Street
Champaign, IL 61820-6903
www.press.uillinois.edu